General Sir Peter de la Billière was born in 1934 and educated at Harrow School. He joined the King's Shropshire Light Infantry in 1952, and after commissioning into the Durham Light Infantry he saw active service in Korea and Egypt. He saw further active service throughout the Middle and Far East over the next thirty years, much of it with the Special Air Service, which he commanded from 1979 to 1982.

After further senior appointments he assumed command of the British Forces in the Middle East in October 1990, a position he held until the liberation of Kuwait from the invading Iraqi forces in 1991.

During his service he was Mentioned in Despatches, won two MCs and was appointed DSO and CBE. In 1988 he was appointed KCB and after the Gulf War he was promoted to General and appointed KBE.

He is married and has three children and eight grandchildren.

Storm Command, his account of the Gulf War, and *Looking for Trouble*, his autobiography, were both bestsellers.

SUPREME COURAGE

Heroic Stories from 150 Years of the Victoria Cross

GENERAL SIR
PETER DE LA BILLIÈRE

ABACUS

ABACUS

First published in Great Britain in September 2004 by Little, Brown
This paperback edition published in September 2005 by Abacus
Reprinted 2005

A CIP catalogue record for this book
is available from the British Library.

ISBN-13: 978-0-349-11898-7
ISBN-10: 0-349-11898-1

Printed and bound in Great Britain by
Clays Ltd, St Ives plc

Abacus
An imprint of
Time Warner Book Group UK
Brettenham House
Lancaster Place
London WC2E 7EN

www.twbg.co.uk

Contents

Acknowledgements

I am extremely grateful to all the people who have helped me collect material for this book, and in particular to Mrs Didy Grahame, Secretary of the Victoria Cross & George Cross Association, whose encyclopedic knowledge of the subject is matched by her boundless enthusiasm.

I should also like to single out Virginia and Forbes Mackenzie, daughter and son-in-law of Charles Upham, who gave me unstinting hospitality and assistance in New Zealand.

I am grateful to John Chavasse for permission to quote extensively from the letters of his uncle Noel, and from other family papers, and to Countess Bente Bernstorff-Gyldensteen, Anders Lassen's sister, for permission to print passages from their mother's biography *Anders Lassen, VC*. I should like to thank the following authors for permission to quote or use material from their books: Jim Allaway (*Hero of the Upholder*), Ann Clayton (*Chavasse Double VC*), Ian Grant (*Jacka VC*), Mike Langley (*Anders Lassen, VC, MC, of the SAS*), Harry Moses (several books, principally *The Fighting Bradfords*), Wayne Ralph (*Barker VC*), Kenneth Sandford (*Mark of the Lion*) Major-General Mathew Thomas (*Lt. Gen. P. S. Bhagat, PVSM, VC*). Thanks also to David Higham Associates for permission to quote from Guy Gibson's *Enemy Coast Ahead*.

I am especially indebted to the late David Harvey, who spent much of his life researching his two-volume history of the VC, *Monuments to Courage*, and shared his immense knowledge with unfailing generosity.

I am also grateful to the following for help of various kinds:

Michael Atkinson (Army Medal Office), Admiral of the Fleet Sir Benjamin Bathurst, Wyn and Alice Beasley, Michael Beinke, Captain Christopher Belton, RN, Brigadier Christopher Bullock, Lieutenant General Sir Adrian Clunies-Ross, Major Michael Cole, Diana Condell (Head of the Medals Department, the Imperial War Museum), Captain M. L. C. Crawford, Mrs Arthur Denaro, Lizzie Everall, Geoffrey Fouquet (St Peter's College, Oxford), Richard Frame, Major-General Ken Gordon (New Zealand Army, Rtd), Billy and Alice Griffiths, Ian Haig, Ian Hywel-Jones, Jack Hurran (batman to Charles Upham), Earl Jellicoe, WO 1 Daryl Kelly (Australian Army), Alan Martin, Geeta Mohite, Colonel 'Mini' Mohite (Indian Army, Rtd), Colonel Rupert Nicholas, Bill Nott-Bower, the staff of the Nottingham Public Archives, Major George O'Kane, Reggie Perrin, Dr Cameron Pulsifer (Canadian War Museum), Geoffrey Stevens, Brigadier Bill Strong, Roderick Suddaby (Imperial War Museum), Colonel David Sutherland, Jeff Tall (Director of the Submarine Museum), Staff Sergeant Julian Thompson (821 EOD Squadron), S. R. Tomlinson (Assistant Librarian, Bodleian Library, Oxford), Ian Wanklyn (son of David Wanklyn), Sir John White.

Many others contributed stories and ideas that helped shape the book.

I owe much to the encouragement given by my literary agent, Anthea Morton-Saner, and by Richard Beswick and Stephen Guise, my publisher and editor respectively at Little, Brown.

My thanks above all to my wife Bridget for invaluable support, both literary and domestic.

1

The Medal

The Victoria Cross was instituted in 1856, when Queen Victoria endorsed the proposition that bravery should be recognised in every rank of the armed forces. The original suggestion had been made two years earlier by the Duke of Newcastle, Secretary of State for War, and after extensive debate, in which senior commanders, the House of Commons, Prince Albert and Victoria all took part, the Monarch signed the royal warrant for creating the medal at Buckingham Palace on 29 January 1856. She herself held the first investiture at a review in Hyde Park on 26 June 1857, when she appeared riding a horse in public for the first time.

The Queen had already reigned for twenty years, yet she saw this as a momentous occasion, which she described at length in her journal:

> A thick, heavy morning. – Full of agitation for the coming great event of the day, viz: the distribution of 'Victoria Cross'. Breakfast early, & ½p.9 we went down & mounted our horses,

> I, in my full uniform, riding 'Sunset'. The whole was conducted in full state. Several interesting circumstances combined to make this day an important one. It was, in the 1st place, the solemn inauguration of the new and honourable order of valour, – also the day of Albert's new title becoming known & the first time *I* had ever ridden on horseback at a great Review in London . . .
>
> The road all along was kept clear, & there was no pushing or squeezing. Constant cheering, & noises of every kind, but the horses went beautifully . . . The sight in Hyde Park was very fine – the tribunes & stands, full of spectators, the Royal one being in the centre. After riding down the Line the ceremony of giving medals, began. There were 47 in number, with blue ribbons for the Navy, & red, for the Army. I remained on horseback, fastening the medals, or rather crosses, on recipient [*sic*] . . . This over, the march past began. I never saw finer troops, nor better marching, excepting the Life Guards, who did not come by well, in quick time. The heat very great, but I felt it less than I had expected.[1]

As the recipients dispersed, each was surrounded by spectators eager to get a glimpse of the new medal. Most of the crowd were disappointed to find that the cross was so small and plain. 'In the centre is a small crown and lion,' reported *The Times* irritably, 'with which latter's natural proportions of mane and tail the cutting of the cross much interferes . . . the whole cross is, after all, poor looking and mean in the extreme.'[2] It went on to say, 'The merit of the design, we believe, is due to the same illustrious individual who once invented a hat.'[3]

Until that day, in recognition of gallantry, officers above a certain rank had been able to receive the Order of the Bath, or be promoted, or mentioned in despatches; and during the Crimean War of 1854–6 the Distinguished Conduct Medal and the Conspicuous Gallantry Medal were instituted for other ranks in the Army and Navy respectively. At a time when rank and privilege were so dominant in society, the inception of an award open to all ranks proclaimed Victoria's far-sightedness.

The Queen specifically required that the medal should be awarded 'only to those Officers or Men who have served Us in the presence of the Enemy and shall then have performed some signal act of valour or devotion to their Country'.[4] In other words, at first the medal could be won only in battle; but a new warrant signed by Victoria in August 1858 extended eligibility beyond the battlefield to members of the armed forces who showed 'conspicuous courage and bravery . . . under circumstances of extreme danger, such as the occurrence of fire on board Ship, or of the foundering of a vessel at Sea, or under any other circumstances in which through the courage and devotion displayed, life or public property may be saved'.

Four months later, in December 1858, yet another warrant extended the boundaries again, this time to include civilians who fought alongside troops in the field – a response to the fact that volunteers had 'performed deeds of gallantry' against the 'insurgent mutineers' at Lucknow and elsewhere in India.

Each winner was granted an annual tax-free pension of £10, and £5 for a second award, or Bar, the aim being not to set financial incentives, but to create a medal which would, in the words of the original warrant, be 'highly prized and eagerly sought after' for its rarity and its connotations.[5] One question which worried the Queen was that of how winners should be styled. Three days after the ceremony in Hyde Park she wrote to Lord Panmure, who had succeeded the Duke of Newcastle as Secretary for War, pointing out that the medal was not an order, but merely 'a Naval and Military decoration':

> The Queen thinks the persons decorated with the Victoria Cross might very properly be allowed to bear some distinctive mark after their name . . . VC would not do. KG means a Knight of the Garter; CB a Companion of the Bath; MP a Member of Parliament; MD a Doctor of Medicine, etc., etc. – in all cases denoting a person. No one could be called a Victoria Cross. VC, moreover, means Vice-Chancellor at present. DVC, Decorated with the Victoria Cross, or BVC, Bearer of the Victoria Cross, might do. The Queen thinks the last the best.[6]

Notwithstanding the Queen's reservations, senior officers and members of the public accepted the straightforward 'VC', which soon caught on, and seemed entirely natural.

The design, in the form of a Maltese cross, is generally attributed to H. H. Armstead, a young employee of Hancocks, the London jewellers who have made the crosses ever since; and Queen Victoria herself chose the simple inscription 'For Valour', which she preferred to the first suggestion, 'For the Brave'. The ribbon was originally red for Army winners and blue for the Navy, but later a dark-red ribbon was used for all the services. A second award is shown by a small bar across the ribbon.

The metal from which all the crosses have been made was cut from two cannons captured from the Russians at Sevastopol, in the Crimea, in 1854. The bronze was taken from the cascabels – the large knobs at the rear of the cannon, used for securing ropes – and scientific analysis has confirmed that it came from the two artillery pieces which stand outside the Rotunda of the Royal Arsenal at Woolwich, in London. The remaining metal is kept in the Small Arms building of the Royal Logistic Corps' Defence Stores Distribution Centre at Donnington, in Worcestershire, and even now contains enough for another eighty-five medals.

Intrinsically they are worth almost nothing, but the associations they carry mean that when one is sold, it commands an enormous price: at a recent auction the medal won in 1918 by Temporary Commander Daniel Beak (who later transferred from the Royal Naval Volunteer Reserve to the Army and became a major-general) fetched the colossal sum of £178,000. More recently still, the VC won by Sergeant Norman Jackson, RAF (see page 14), fetched £235,000.

The earliest awards were backdated to include the Crimean War, but the first winner was Lieutenant Charles Lucas, Royal Navy, who received his medal for gallantry in the Baltic Sea in 1854, during the first Russian War, when, instead of taking cover, he ran forward to pounce on a live shell and throw it overboard, saving the crew of his ship HMS *Hecla* from death or serious injury.

Victoria herself took a close interest in recommendations, and asked to have one potential recipient disqualified. This was Private

P. M'Gwire of the 33rd (Duke of Wellington's) Regiment, who was taken prisoner by two Russians near Sevastopol but managed to dispatch both of them. An officer's report recorded:

> The Englishman kept wary watch and, when he fancied his captors off their guard, sprang on the one who carried his musket, seized it and shot dead the other of his foes . . . Meanwhile the Russian from whom our fellow had taken his own musket and who had then fallen to the ground, when rising from his recumbent position fired, missed, and finally had his brains knocked out by the butt-end of the Englishman's musket; after which the man coolly proceeded to take off the Russian accoutrements, etc, with which he returned laden to the post where he had been surprised, fired at by the Russian sentries and received with loud cheers by our own pickets.[7]

Lord Panmure reported that the Queen wished M'Gwire's name to be omitted from the list:

> His deed, although publicly praised and rewarded by Lord Raglan, was one of very doubtful morality, and if pointed out by the Sovereign as praiseworthy, may lead to the cruel and inhumane practice of never taking prisoners, but always putting to death those who may be overpowered, for fear of their rising on their captors.[8]

The VC set new standards in the annals of British military gallantry. The emphasis of the award was to be on courage and sacrifice, and it is no coincidence that of the 1354 recipients to date, sixteen served in the Royal Army Medical Corps. Stretcher-bearers from infantry regiments have also been conspicuous winners. Among these, the most astonishing performance was that of Thomas Young, a 'hewer' from a mining family in County Durham who served with the 9th Battalion, Durham Light Infantry. In 1915, at the age of nineteen, he was thrown into the battle of Ypres, where he was wounded, and he returned to England for treatment. He rejoined his unit in 1917, and in March

1918 his battalion was engaged in stemming the bloody German offensive at Bucquoy, near Arras.

Many soldiers wounded in the initial attacks lay in no man's land for five days without water, food or treatment. On nine separate occasions Young went out under intense enemy fire, and managed to rescue nine wounded men, several times himself treating injuries in the forward battle area. One of his officers wrote of him, 'He had in fact no lethal weapon, just his quiet determination to bring in the wounded . . . and nine times he went calmly out, unarmed to what ought to have been certain death.'[9]

The formal, rather stilted language of citations hardly ever conveys the violence, danger and sheer excitement of the actions which win awards; but occasionally a contemporary account brings the circumstances to life. The official dispatch about Corporal John Prettyjohns of the Royal Marines, who won his VC in the fog at the Battle of Inkerman on 5 November 1854, recorded merely that he 'placed himself in an advanced position' and 'shot four Russians'. But a report by his colleague Sergeant Turner was far more vivid:

> The bugle sounded the 'Fall-in' at the double, and officers were flying about giving orders, saying vast columns of the enemy were moving up to our rear. The roll of musketry was terrific; we were advanced cautiously until bullets began to fall in amongst us, the Sergeant Major was the first man killed; order given to lay down; it was as well we did so; a rush of bullets passed over us; then we gave them three rounds, kneeling, into their close column . . .
>
> A division under Sergeant Richards and Corporal Prettyjohns was then thrown out to clear the caves [which had been occupied by enemy sharpshooters] . . . We, under Richards and Prettyjohns, soon cleared the caves but found our ammunition nearly all expended, and a new batch of the foe were creeping up the hillside in single file, at the back.
>
> Prettyjohns, a muscular West Countryman, said, 'Well lads, we are just in for a warming, and it will be every man for himself in a few minutes. Look alive, my hearties, and collect all the stones handy and pile them on the ridge in front of you.

> When I grip the front man, you let go the biggest stones upon those fellows behind.'
>
> As soon as the first man stood on the level, Prettyjohns gripped him and gave him a Westcountry buttock, threw him over upon the men following, and a shower of stones from the others knocked the leaders over. Away they went, tumbling one over the other, down the incline; we gave them a parting volley, and retired out of sight to load; they made off and left us, although there was sufficient to have eaten us up.[10]

It so happened that the inauguration of the medal coincided almost exactly with the Indian Mutiny, which broke out in 1857; and, since India was one of the Empire's most important military theatres, the Victorian authorities were much exercised by the question of whether or not the VC could be awarded to native soldiers. At first the only award for gallantry they might receive was the Indian Order of Merit, of which there were three grades, each bringing an increase in pay; and only the European officers commanding them might win VCs. Years of discussion and argument took place between the India Office and the War Office. General Sir Garnet Wolseley, the Commander-in-Chief, supported the idea of extending the award to native troops during his tenure, but it was not until 1911, years after he had left office, that a new warrant, signed by King George V, at last extended the possibility of winning a VC to native officers, non-commissioned officers and men of the Indian Army.

At the beginning, awards were sometimes determined by a form of ballot. A certain number of medals were allocated to each unit that had played a gallant role in some action; officers and men who had taken part put up their candidates, and the ones who received most votes got medals. This happened first during the Indian Mutiny, when no fewer than twenty-nine VCs were awarded to men who had fought in the siege of Delhi, the charge of the 8th Hussars at Gwalior, and the siege and relief of Lucknow. Surviving anecdotes suggest that recommendations for medals, made from the field, were often fairly casual and haphazard – as in the story of two private soldiers discussing tactics:

'Well,' said one, 'who are you going to vote for?'
'So and so. What about you?'
'I think I shall vote for our doctor.'
'Why so?'
'Because he's the most likely man among us to live to wear it.'
'What makes you think that?'
'Because he takes such ******* good care of 'isself!'[11]

The last engagement after which a ballot was held was the naval raid on Zeebrugge, which took place on the night of 22–3 April 1918 (see chapter 10). Later, in a radio interview, Sergeant N. A. Finch of the Royal Marine Artillery, who won a VC at Zeebrugge, made a memorable remark: 'This isn't really mine. I'm only selected to wear it on behalf of the regiment, and when I die it will have to be returned to the regiment.' Many later winners have expressed the same sentiment – not because they got their award after a ballot, but out of genuine modesty, because they felt that they had been part of a team effort, and that they had been singled out merely as representatives of the general excellence of their colleagues.

Today the process is more elaborate: witnesses' reports and supporting evidence are carefully evaluated at various levels in the chain of command, passing eventually through the commander-in-chief of the forces involved to the Ministry of Defence, before the monarch gives or withholds final approval.

At first only survivors could win VCs, which were officially described as 'an order for the living': to gain the medal, the soldier had to be still alive when recommended. This was something of an anomaly, for the regulations allowed the Distinguished Conduct Medal to be awarded posthumously – and if one medal could go to a man who had been killed in action, why not the highest award also? After intense debate among senior officers and government officials, the change was sanctioned in an official announcement issued on 8 August 1902, which gave news of the first six posthumous awards, two of them to soldiers killed at Isandhlwana in actions against the Zulus during the Zulu War:

> The King [Edward VII] has been graciously pleased to approve of the decoration of the VC being delivered to the relatives of the undermentioned officers, NCO and men who fell during the recent operations in South Africa in the performance of Acts of Valour which would, in the opinion of the C-in-C of the forces in the field, have entitled them to be recommended for the distinction had they survived.[12]

Lieutenant Coghill, of the 24th Regiment (now the Royal Regiment of Wales), died on 22 January 1879 after the battle of Isandhlwana, when he, together with Lieutenant Melvill (who also had his Victoria Cross backdated), rode with the regimental Queen's Colour with the Zulus in fast pursuit. Crossing the Buffalo river, Melvill lost his horse, and Coghill turned to assist him just as the enemy arrived. Both were killed in ensuing struggle, and both were finally buried in an isolated grave at Fugitives' Drift.

Another keenly debated question was whether or not a man might win the VC when simply doing his duty. Some senior officers maintained that the carrying out of duty positively precluded a soldier from gaining the award, no matter how bravely he might act, but others held another view – that every soldier was bound to do his duty, whatever might be happening. The arguments were brought to a head by the exploits of Surgeon-Captain Arthur Martin-Leake, who served in the Boer War. When he was recommended for a VC by the Inspector-General of the South African Constabulary, the authorities sought confirmation. Had Martin-Leake merely done his duty as a doctor, or had he done more?

He was, by any standards, an unusual character. Born in March 1874 at Thorpe Hall in Essex, he once in India stalked and killed a rogue elephant, cut out its brain and sent it to his surgeon, Sir Victor Horsley, writing to a relative:

> The object I was in pursuit of was a rogue elephant. A few days before I arrived at the place he had killed a man and the damage he used to do to the crops was enormous. However, he has now gone to the place of perpetual sugar cane and buns.

Martin-Leake came from a family of five brothers, all of whom achieved distinction: one became a famous balloonist, and another a vice admiral who was appointed Companion of the Bath and a member of the Distinguished Service Order. From his early days Arthur sought adventure, and found it on his family estate, which offered a wide range of sporting opportunities for a young lad keen on gun and rifle. After Westminster School and University College, London, he studied to become a doctor, and the outbreak of the South African War gave him the chance to see action with the Hertfordshire Company of the Imperial Yeomanry, which he joined as a trooper. Later he served in the South African Constabulary under General Baden-Powell, and it was in this force, as a surgeon-captain, that

> he went out into the firing-line to dress a wounded man under very heavy fire from about forty Boers only 100 yards off. When he had done all he could for him, he went over to a badly wounded officer, and while trying to place him in a comfortable position he was shot about three times. He only gave up when thoroughly exhausted, and then he refused water until other wounded men had been served.[13]

This was surely beyond the call of normal duty, and in due course it was recognised as such by the Principal Medical Officer in South Africa, who, in answer to the question 'Had Martin-Leake merely done his duty?', produced a masterly riposte. Such a question, he said, 'would exclude every one from the VC for it is every one's duty to do his very best'. Even after that burst of common sense, arguments continued at high level, with some officers maintaining that the doctor should get only a DSO; but in the end he received his first VC, which was gazetted – announced in the *London Gazette* – on 13 May 1902.[14]

Very few holders have themselves recorded the action in which they won the medal, but one who did was Sir Percival Marling, whose autobiography included a vivid description of events at Tamai, in the Eastern Sudan, during 1883. He was then a lieutenant in the 3rd King's Royal Rifle Corps, and his account of an attempt to rescue a wounded comrade, couched in characteristic Victorian argot, gives a lively idea of the chaos that reigned in the campaign against followers of the Mahdi:

> I thought there were some 6,000 Fuzzie-wuzzies [in a ravine], but the bush was so thick one could only guess. I went to look again over the edge . . . An Arab about twenty feet below shoved up his long gun and shot Private Morley, M.I., who was about three feet from me, in the stomach, and about 2,000 niggers scrambled up the side of the ravine. I emptied my revolver into the brown of them.
>
> My orderly brought up my horse and put Morley up in front of me, but after going with him a short way he fell off, I couldn't hold him on. I then got off and put him across my saddle, and held him on with another fellow . . . We got him back about 200 yards to a place not quite so dangerous, and I went into the square to get a stretcher . . . I remember seeing Colville who was wounded by a bullet in the thigh, shouting to some men, saying, 'D—n it, men, don't run away from a lot of bare-backed savages.' His boot was full of blood, and the next moment he collapsed fainting off his horse. I stood over him with my revolver until I could get a couple of Tommies to look after him.[15]

Private Morley died next day, but for his gallant attempt to rescue him Marling received a VC, which was gazetted a year later.

In 1918 the question of whether or not women should become eligible to win the VC was extensively debated in the higher echelons of all three services. The only serious opposition came from Rear Admiral Sir A. M. Everett, Naval Secretary at the Admiralty, who voiced several worries, among them that standards might be lowered because men, undermined by 'their ordinary gallantry', might have their judgement warped by the involvement of the 'so-called frail sex', and grant awards that were hardly justified. His long letter of objection included some stirring rhetoric:

> Let us hypothecate a retreat where some bloody-minded virago WAAC is overtaken by a Hun. Might she not be the more

> induced to take up a bundook and battle with a Hun; might she not be all the more tempted to take some very unladylike action or conduct herself in such an unseemly manner from the universal standard expected of the fair sex that the enemy would proclaim all women combatants and shoot them at sight?
>
> To my mind . . . it would be a dangerous move to include females into the VC area. There are enough bickerings in the masculine line as to whether this man or that should or should not have been awarded a VC, but if the hysterical female world is to be allowed in, God help the poor devils who have to make decisions.[16]

The admiral found an ally in the form of the King, who was against the inclusion of women, but nevertheless in 1919 signed a new warrant which extended the possibility of winning the VC to the female nursing staff of the armed services, 'and civilians of either sex serving regularly or temporarily under the orders, direction or supervision of any of the above mentioned forces'.

There is no doubt that in earlier days the medal was awarded more freely than later. During the Indian Mutiny of 1857–8 no fewer than 182 men won VCs – almost exactly the same number as in the whole of the Second World War. At Rorke's Drift, in the Zulu War, eleven men – out of a force barely more than a hundred strong – won VCs in the single action, and the First World War yielded 628 VCs, 188 (30 per cent) of them posthumous. The Second World War witnessed 181 awards, of which 87 (48 per cent) were posthumous. Since the end of the conflict in 1945 only eleven VCs have been awarded – four in Korea, four in Vietnam (all to Australians), one to a Gurkha, Rambahadur Limbu (see chapter 13) in Sarawak, and two in the Falkands – to Lieutenant Colonel 'H' Jones and Sergeant Ian McKay, both of the Parachute Regiment. Both these last awards were posthumous.

The declining numbers reflect in part the changes that have taken place in the nature of fighting over the past 150 years. The trench warfare of 1914–18 was a deadly and terribly wasteful form of conflict, but it provided the most opportunities for individual acts of heroism. The Second World War also saw much hand-to-hand combat. Twenty-first-century warfare, in contrast, is so highly mechanised, so predominantly electronic, that it offers fewer opportunities to act with the level of gallantry which becomes possible in close fighting on the ground. Nevertheless, Trooper Christopher Finney, who won a George Cross during the Iraq war of 2003, demonstrated that acts of extreme individual courage can still be performed (the GC is the highest civilian award, and this one, although won during battle, was granted because of the exceptional circumstances prevailing).

The winning of a VC has never guaranteed a man's character, and recipients, though indisputably courageous in the heat of action, have sometimes turned out to be thoroughly disreputable, or have found the pressure of the publicity that follows the announcement of the award too much to handle. This was particularly so in the early days, when the names of several winners were struck from the record as a punishment for some misdemeanour such as drunkenness, theft or desertion. The question of whether such defaulters should forfeit their actual medals was fiercely debated, until King George V made his own view on the subject clear. In a letter dated 26 July 1920 his private secretary, Lord Stamfordham, wrote:

> The King feels so strongly that, no matter the crime committed by anyone on whom the VC has been conferred, the decoration should not be forfeited. Even were a VC to be hanged for murder, he should be allowed to wear the VC on the scaffold.[17]

Late in the 1920s an Interdepartmental Committee recommended that all gallantry awards should be regarded as irrevocable, but in 1931 a new warrant, signed by the King, reserved the right to 'cancel and annul the award of the Victoria Cross' in certain cases. In all, the VC has been forfeited by eight recipients – for desertion in order to avoid investigation of a disgraceful offence, theft of a cow, theft of a comrade's medals, theft of ten bushels of oats, desertion on active service, theft and embezzlement from an officer, bigamy, and theft of iron.[18]

Without exception, winners have shown a complete disregard for themselves and indeed for their own lives – and nobody more so than Private Harry Brown, a runner serving with 10 Quebec Battalion of the Canadian Division in Flanders during the summer of 1917. As part of the diversionary operations supporting the British offensive near Loos, the Canadians were tasked to capture Hill 70. The Fighting Tenth took vital ground at Chalk Quarry, but were so under strength that they had difficulty holding it. On 16 September the Germans counter-attacked, and the battalion desperately required fire-support to retain their position.

Brown and another soldier set off over the bullet- and shell-swept ground to carry a message urgently requesting artillery support. Brown's companion was killed, and he himself severely wounded, but he pressed on, one arm shattered and hanging loose, to arrive at his headquarters. There he collapsed, but before losing consciousness he gave his crumpled, blood-soaked note to an officer, who called down the requested fire, which broke up the German attack. Next day Brown died of his wounds in a field dressing station, but his selfless deed had won him a posthumous Victoria Cross.

His commanding officer wrote of him: 'His devotion to duty was of the highest possible degree imaginable, his action undoubtedly saved the loss of the position . . . and saved many casualties to our own troops.'

Of all the heroic feats performed by VC holders, perhaps the most astonishing ever was that of Sergeant Norman Jackson, RAF, who, on the night of 26–7 April 1944, climbed out along the wing of a Lancaster bomber after a raid on Nuremberg in an attempt to put out an engine fire. It is difficult to imagine any more daunting circumstances, or any greater courage. The aircraft was flying at 22,000 feet, at 200 mph, in the dark, over enemy territory, and it was under attack from a German fighter. The air temperature was many degrees below zero.

With one engine on fire, and threatening to detonate the fuel tank in the wing, Jackson volunteered to try to extinguish the blaze. Inside the fuselage, he unpacked his parachute, and then, with other crew members paying out the rigging lines, he crawled out, down over the side of the body and along the wing with a fire-extinguisher stowed inside his tunic, clinging to an air intake to hold himself against the ferocious slipstream.

Operating the extinguisher with one hand, he had almost put the fire out when the Luftwaffe fighter pilot came in for another cannon attack. The Lancaster banked steeply to the left: Jackson was wounded in the back and legs by shrapnel and swept backwards off the wing. For a few seconds he remained tethered to the doomed bomber by his parachute: as the rest of the crew baled out, he was dragged along, whirling in its slipstream. At last his chute came free – although not before holes had been burnt in the canopy. This made his descent far faster than it should have been, but by a miracle he landed in some thick bushes and survived.

No rank or person has the prerogative over courage: it is rankless. Officers have a greater motivation to act bravely, and greater opportunities to demonstrate courage, by virtue of their position and their responsibilities as leaders. A non-commissioned rank has less opportunity to attract attention or to have an impact on the overall battle than an officer who is in charge of a unit or ship. This in no way diminishes the gallantry of lower ranks, but it does go some way towards explaining why officers receive proportionally more gallantry awards than non-commissioned ranks – there are 645 officer holders of the VC, to 705 non-commissioned ranks.

In war every increase of rank above lieutenant colonel brings with it a reduction of the physical risks, but also of the opportunity to win medals for courage, as opposed to leadership. This is reflected in the small number of senior officers awarded the Victoria Cross. In the Army only five VCs have been awarded to officers holding the rank of colonel or above, in contrast to the 493 won by commissioned ranks of lieutenant colonel and below. Corresponding with the reduction in physical risks is the increase in moral responsibility.

The records show that commissioned winners have always given exceptional priority to the care of men under their command. This is not to say they treat them softly, nor do they expect them to avoid risks. Rather the reverse – but officers are prepared to fight as ferociously for the rights and meagre comforts that come to a ranker in war as they are to take on the enemy.

It is a sad fact that many holders of the VC, particularly those without commissions, have found it difficult if not impossible to handle the consequences of the fame that inevitably settles on a winner of the medal. Of the 111 men who gained the VC during the Crimean War, seven took their own lives, at a time when the national suicide rate was about eight per hundred thousand. Among them was Private John Byrne, who won his VC at the Battle of Inkerman in 1855, and committed suicide in 1872 after he had left the army. Two holders were murdered, and eleven spent their final years in workhouses, overcome by poverty.[19] In the words of Ian Fraser, who won a VC as a naval lieutenant in 1945, 'A man is trained for the task that might win him the VC. He is not trained to cope with what follows.'[20] The society of the day should have examined its conscience: it is they who neglected men who put their nation first.

The history of the medal includes some curious statistics. The oldest recipient is thought to have been Lieutenant W. Raynor of the Bengal Veteran Establishment, Indian Army, who won a VC at Delhi in May 1857, during the Mutiny, at the age of almost sixty-two. The youngest winners to date are Hospital Apprentice A. FitzGibbon of the Indian Medical Establishment, who earned his decoration at Taku Forts in China in August 1860, when he was fifteen years and three months, and Drummer T. Flinn, who was exactly the same age when he won his VC at Cawnpore, during the Mutiny, in November 1857. (He died in the Athlone Workhouse at the age of fifty.)

Two crosses have been won by men who saved the lives of their brothers – Major C. J. S. Gough, who rescued his brother, Lieutenant H. H. Gough (who already had a VC) during the Mutiny, and Trooper H. E. Ramsden, who saved his brother's life during the Boer War in 1899. The remarkable Gough family further distinguished itself when Major J. E. Gough, son of Major C. J. S. and nephew of Lt H. H., won yet another VC in Somaliland in 1903.

Because courage cannot be weighed or measured, assessments of any valiant action are bound to be subjective: everything depends on who witnessed what in the heat of battle. The result is that debate inevitably rages about the justice or injustice of awards. Scarcely ever does one hear that a VC winner was not worthy of the medal; but often people do maintain that a soldier who won a DSO should have had a VC, and was prevented from doing so only by the circumstances, or by lack of witnesses.

One instance of this occurred in July 1972 at the battle of Mirbat, on the southern coast of Oman, where the Special Air Service had been clandestinely deployed to counter a Communist-inspired insurrection aimed at subverting the Arabian peninsula. Over the preceding weeks the *adoo* (enemy) had surreptitiously collected together a force of some three hundred rebel tribesmen, assembling men so skilfully that we had got no wind of their intentions as they advanced eastwards from the Yemen. Then, at first light on the morning of 19 July, they attacked the fort at Mirbat which was manned by a tiny garrison of eight SAS, supported by about thirty policemen. In command was Captain Mike Kealy, a short, fair-haired man of twenty-three, who showed quite astonishing courage and leadership in the action that followed.

His own base was a mud-walled house, with machine guns mounted on the roof, just outside the town; but the main defensive position was in the old fort – a tall, square building also made of mud, manned by local gendarmerie and loyal tribesmen, some half a mile away. Inside the compound of a fort was a 25-pounder artillery piece, dug into the ground and manned by a Fijian member of the SAS, Corporal Labalaba, and one Omani soldier, Walid Khalfan.

The rebels launched their assault at 0530, in the first light of dawn, and fierce fighting raged as wave after wave of them stormed in on foot, firing rifles and machine-guns until they were sometimes within 30 yards of the fort's walls. Together with one SAS man, Trooper Tobin, Kealy was trapped in his house by the intense battle; but when the 25-pounder in the fort fell silent, the two men raced across nearly half a mile of open ground to go to the aid of the crew.

They found that Labalaba had had his jaw shot off, but was still trying to fire the 25-pounder over open sights at point-blank range. Other men were seriously wounded. Moments after they reached the gun pit, Labalaba was shot dead and Tobin was mortally wounded, but continued to fight.

Kealy did the same, and over the next four hours he showed positively superhuman courage. He sent out an urgent call for support from the Sultan of Oman's air force, but because monsoon mist was hanging low over the coast, the Strikemaster jets could not fly at once. Partly through sheer force of character, and partly as a result of his own rigorous training, he somehow kept up the morale of his little force and fought off the enemy until the aircraft could fly. When they did come in, to strafe the *adoo* with bombs and machine-gun fire, the pilots flew so low that several jets were holed by bullets fired from above them. Eventually, helicopter-borne reinforcements arrived, and the day was saved. The action went down as one of the greatest victories in the SAS's history: for the loss of only two members of the regiment, the garrison killed some eighty of the enemy and effectively brought to an end the insurrection which threatened the stability of the entire region.

Four years after the event, Kealy was awarded a DSO, the announcement having been delayed for security reasons. Many people felt that his extreme bravery should have been rewarded with a VC – and indeed it probably would have been, had not the SAS presence in Oman been a closely guarded secret. It was felt that the award of a VC would have attracted too much publicity, and drawn attention to the presence of special forces in a part of the world where they had not been reported. Trooper Tobin received a posthumous Military Medal, and Corporal Labalaba – who had been a great character in the SAS – a posthumous Mention in Despatches.

Thirty years on, during the second Gulf War, there occurred another act of outstanding bravery which, in different circumstances, would also surely have qualified for a VC. On 28 March 2003 Trooper Christopher Finney, an eighteen-year-old member of D Squadron, the Household Cavalry Regiment, was driving a Scimitar armoured vehicle in the Iraqi desert when his troop was attacked by two American aircraft, whose pilots mistook the British for Iraqis.

Both vehicles were set on fire by cannon shells. Ammunition began exploding inside the turrets. Finney scrambled out and started to run for cover, only to realise that his gunner had been wounded and was trapped inside the burning Scimitar. At once he went back, climbed aboard, dragged the injured man out, moved him to a safer position and bandaged his wounds. Then, knowing that his headquarters must be told what had happened, he returned for a second time to his blazing vehicle and sent a lucid situation report by radio, before helping the casualty towards a Royal Engineers vehicle which had come to help.

Had this not been a 'blue-on-blue' – service jargon for an accidental attack by friendly forces – Finney would surely have been awarded a Victoria Cross for his courage and coolness, outstanding in anyone, but altogether exceptional in somebody so young and inexperienced. As it was, he won a George Cross, and the citation accorded him glowing praise:

> During these attacks and their horrifying aftermath, Finney displayed clear-headed courage and devotion to his comrades which was out of all proportion to his age and experience. Acting with complete disregard for his own safety, even when wounded, his bravery was of the highest order throughout.

Among non-combatants, priests feature in the roll of honour far more rarely than medical staff, and only three VCs have been won by members of the Royal Army Chaplains' Department. That, however, is not to diminish the performance of padres in battle, or their importance to ship and unit welfare and morale.

When I commanded the Special Air Service in the early 1970s, our unit was blessed with an outstanding cleric, Walter Evans, commonly known as 'Evans Above'. This small, unobtrusive Welshman was endowed with a quiet wit, wisdom and humanity which enriched all our lives. He was frequently seen in remote parts of the globe, visiting units on operations, even though his age and physique were not suited to the demanding terrain and conditions.

With no weapon other than his dog collar, he shared the risks faced by his parishioners with selfless courage. That courage extended to his relationship with his various commanding officers, to whom he freely brought unbiased and rank-free criticism of morale and personal welfare in the unit.

The finest of all non-combatant holders, in my view, is the Royal Army Medical Corps doctor Captain Noel Chavasse (chapter 3); but another star was the Reverend Theodore Hardy, who showed such exceptional bravery during the First World War that he won the DSO, MC and VC – in that order – all in eighteen months.

Chavasse had at least had some military training, in the RAMC and the Liverpool Scottish Regiment. Hardy had none. Having been a modest schoolteacher, he was vicar of Hutton Roof, a tiny parish in Westmorland, when he volunteered for service as an army chaplain and was posted to France in 1916. There he was attached to the 8th Battalion of the Lincolnshire Regiment, and later served also as chaplain to the 8th Battalion of the Somerset Regiment – an insignificant-looking man, only 5′ 4″ tall and already, at the age of fifty-three, old enough to have been the father of most of the fighting soldiers.

At first he was disappointed that so few men attended his services, and he thought he was doing no good; but his life changed when he took the advice of another remarkable padre, Geoffrey Studdert-Kennedy. 'Live with the men,' his friend urged him:

> Go everywhere they go . . . You can take it that the best place for a padre (provided he does not interfere with military operations) is where there is most danger of death. Our first job is to go beyond the men in self-sacrifice and reckless devotion. Don't be bamboozled into believing that your proper place is behind the line; it isn't . . . Your place is in the front. The line is the key to the whole business. Work in the front, and they will listen to you when they come out to rest, but if you only preach and teach behind, you are wasting time, the men won't pay the slightest attention to you.[21]

Spurred on by these challenging words, Hardy arrived at the

front near Lens in the bitter winter of 1916, and at once put his colleague's advice into practice, constantly going out into no man's land to comfort the dying or rescue the wounded. Details of the dreadful battles in which his battalions were involved – especially at Arras and Passchendaele – are scarcely relevant here. Suffice it to say that, wherever he was, Hardy again and again took terrible risks and worked himself into a state of exhaustion, his fear kept at bay by his absolute trust in God.

On nights when there had been no fighting, he would act as a humble porter, carrying rations up to the trenches, chatting to the men and bringing back their letters for the post. Whenever he came upon someone in the dark, he would announce himself with a quietly spoken, self-effacing introduction, 'It's only me' – and that became a kind of catchphrase, often quoted by the soldiers. 'It's only me,' one would say to another, in fond reference to the padre. Such was his courage, devotion and humility that many men felt they were in the presence of a saint.

He received his DSO for his heroic attempt to rescue a wounded man who had been left stuck in the mud between the lines. Handicapped though he was by a broken wrist, and with his left arm in a splint, Hardy crawled out to within seventy yards of the German trenches and remained with the casualty all one day and half the night, talking to him and feeding him, pinned down by sniper and machine-gun fire. 'Conspicuous gallantry and devotion to duty', his citation called it – and colleagues felt that he would have been awarded a VC had enough eyewitnesses been found to record what he had done.

His next award was an MC, gained when he was helping bring in wounded, and what his colleague Geoffrey Vallings called 'an appalling bombardment' came down on the party. Vallings could not understand how anyone lived through it, as 'the whole surface of the ground seemed to be shot away', yet Hardy remained calm and confident, and brought the people out, consolidating his reputation for being 'unkillable'.

His VC, which he won in April 1918, came as the cumulative result of four separate recommendations. The first was the most striking. After a prolonged and bitter battle for Rossignol Wood, the Somersets were forced to withdraw, and as the remnants of the battalion regrouped, Hardy was missing. Then, at dusk, his diminutive figure appeared out of the wood, and it was found that he had spent the whole day lying within ten yards of a German machine-gun post, comforting a man too seriously wounded to stand. As if that were not enough, he asked for a volunteer to help him recover the casualty, and a sergeant agreed to go with him: the two crawled silently forward and somehow managed to extricate the victim.

In this, and in the three similar incidents that led to the award of his VC, Hardy displayed superhuman fortitude, and by his example fired countless soldiers to persevere in their ghastly task. 'What is courage but the inspiration of the Spirit?' he himself asked – and it seems cruelly unjust that a man of such uplifting faith should have died of a bullet wound six months after winning the supreme award.

2

On Courage

Who would true valour see,
Let him come hither.

JOHN BUNYAN,
THE PILGRIM'S PROGRESS

Britain's highest military decoration bears the simple legend 'For Valour'. That word has a pleasantly old-fashioned ring, but it means the same as 'courage', and is defined in dictionaries as such: 'Intrepidity, courage, bravery'. 'Courage' is similarly defined, as a quality that enables men to meet danger without giving way to fear: 'Bravery, spirit'. The Victoria Cross is awarded for supreme courage in battle, and there can be few who do not admire the quality in others. It brings out the best in everyone: it is an inspiration.

War, by its nature, offers opportunities for courage and the making of heroes that seldom present themselves to the person in the street. At the same time, outstanding courage in battle, where risking life and limb is part of one's duty, is bravery of the very highest order. In most cases it is accompanied by an exceptional display of leadership unrelated to rank or position.

Sir Winston Churchill once remarked, 'Courage is rightly esteemed the first of human qualities . . . because it is the quality which guarantees all others', and after the Second World War that great commander Field Marshal Lord Slim echoed him in a radio broadcast: 'I don't believe there's any man who, in his heart of hearts, wouldn't rather be called brave than have any other virtue attributed to him.'

Slim discerned two fundamental types of courage, which he called 'physical' and 'moral'. Physical courage, he thought, is 'an emotional state, which urges a man to risk injury or death', the second 'a more reasoning attitude, which enables [a man] coolly to stake career, happiness, his whole future, on his judgment of what he thinks either right or worthwhile'.

He went on:

> Now these two types of courage, physical and moral, are very distinct. I have known many men who had marked physical courage, but lacked moral courage. Some of them were in high places, but they failed to be great in themselves because they lacked it. On the other hand I have seen men who undoubtedly possessed moral courage very cautious about taking physical risks. But I have never met a man with moral courage who would not, when it was really necessary, face bodily danger. Moral courage is a higher and a rarer virtue than physical courage.[1]

The physical type can be divided into two categories: hot courage and cold courage. An infantryman in a charge or a pilot in a dog-fight, when the adrenalin is running and there is no time to think or worry – both are fired by hot courage. A good example is Private Bill Speakman,[2] who in 1951 won his VC in Korea with the King's Own Scottish Borderers, defending a hill against hordes of attacking Chinese. As the enemy pressed home wave after wave of attacks against his position, he led hand-to-hand fighting, and when his ammunition ran out resorted to the use of his bayonet and anything else that came to hand. He led countercharge after countercharge to recover the battalion's wounded, and although he himself was injured by mortar fragments, thanks to his inspiration and leadership the position was held. Yet he dismisses his heroic action in a few words: 'There were so many of them you just had to get on with it.' His was an outstanding display, inspiring others and saving the day in that particular battle.

The cold form of courage is the calculated sort exemplified by the bomber crews in the Second World War, who flew sorties over Germany again and again, well knowing that every time they took off a percentage of aircraft and crewmen would not return. At sea, an outstanding example was that of Leading Seaman Mick Magennis who, in July 1945, serving as a diver in HMS midget submarine *XE3*, attached limpet mines to the Japanese heavy cruiser *Takao* in the Johore Strait near Singapore Island.

The 10,000-ton target was lying in such shallow water that *XE3* became jammed beneath her, and Magennis found that the outside hatch, through which he had to emerge to place the mines, would open no more than a few inches. As he forced himself through the gap, he damaged his breathing equipment, which began to release a stream of telltale bubbles – and when he tried to place the first of his limpet charges, he found that the hull of the *Takao* was so thickly encrusted with barnacles that the magnets would not hold. For half an hour he scraped patches clear, ripping his hands to shreds, and in the end managed to fix six pairs of timed charges, before scrambling back into the submarine and collapsing with exhaustion.

Then, to his dismay, *XE3*'s captain, Lieutenant Ian Fraser, found that his craft would not move, even with the engine at full-ahead or full-astern. Somehow she had become hooked up on the cruiser, and, with the minutes ticking away towards detonation, it seemed certain that she and her crew would be annihilated by their own charges. Suddenly the submarine came free and shot to the surface – and miraculously she was not spotted by the Japanese before she dived again; but Fraser realised that his port limpet-container, which protruded from the hull, had failed to release itself – and only if they jettisoned it could they make their escape.

Exhausted as he was, Magennis volunteered to go out again. Away he went, armed with a large spanner, and after a seven-minute struggle he freed the retaining bolts and crawled back through the hatch into the control room – whereupon Fraser cautiously and with consummate skill navigated his way out through the Japanese defences of mines and nets. At nightfall *XE3*'s mines exploded, blowing a gaping hole in the *Takao*'s hull and putting her out of action. Magennis and Fraser were both awarded the VC for their extraordinary bravery and self-control in exceptionally frightening circumstances.

Cool, calculated courage is also the hallmark of men who risk their lives to rescue others. In this field, no one will ever surpass the example set by Captain Noel Chavasse, the Royal Army Medical Corps doctor who won two Victoria Crosses during the First World War, and whose career is described in chapter 3. But perhaps in this context I may mention my own father, a naval surgeon who died when German bombers sank his ship, the cruiser HMS *Fiji*, off the south coast of Crete in May 1941. I have only their word for it, but survivors told my family he was on deck and could have left the ship when the crew took to the lifeboats. He chose to go back below decks into the sickbay – not to treat anyone, because he knew the vessel was sinking, but presumably to die with his patients, or perhaps in a final and vain attempt to rescue some of them. He was never seen again, and went down with his ship with the wounded in his care. His courage was typical of that of the majority of ordinary servicemen on the battlefield, in the air or at sea: routine and taken for granted. No medal, still less a Victoria Cross, for most people; they are just doing their duty.

In his book *The Anatomy of Courage*, Sir Winston Churchill's personal physician Lord Moran wrote: 'The thing in the world I am most afraid of is fear', and he worked out his theory of the 'bank balance' of courage from his experience of the dreadful casualties suffered in the First World War:

> Even prodigal youth had to husband its resources. Likewise in the trenches a man's willpower was his capital, and he was always spending, so that wise and thrifty company officers watched the expenditure of every penny lest their men went bankrupt. When their capital was done they were finished.[3]

Each of us has a bank of courage. Some have a significant credit balance, others little or nothing; but in war we are all able to make the balance last longer if we have training, discipline, patriotism and faith. We can enhance these through managing our fear, while always remembering that on the battlefield unfairness rules.

During my first experience of war, as a nineteen-year-old second lieutenant in the Durham Light Infantry, fighting in Korea, I joined a platoon of men who had already spent eight months in the theatre and had been continually exposed to shellfire and the pressure of raids and patrolling. They had suffered many casualties and seen some of their best mates killed or wounded. No respite was in sight, so it was not surprising that for some their bank balance of courage was running low.

A lance corporal, a brilliant Bren-gunner in my platoon, was typical of these battle-weary veterans. One night he went out on yet one more patrol, to set up an ambush in front of our position on Hill 355 – an honourable, brave man who had survived months of continuous warfare and patrolling without complaint. During the night we heard a single burst of machine-gun fire from the patrol's location in no man's land, and in due course the survivors returned with two casualties. The lance corporal had heard a noise and nervously overreacted, shooting his own companions by mistake.

Such errors are regrettably commonplace in war. But in the case of this man, who had given gallant service, the credit in his bank of courage had run out, and his nerves and fears got the better of him. Through my lack of experience, I had failed to identify his condition. In the event, he was sent home suffering from extreme battle stress and fatigue, but I should have dispatched him to the rear echelons for a rest much earlier, before he had reached this stage of nervous breakdown. Had I done so, he might have recovered and returned to give further valuable front-line service. I should have appreciated that his bank balance had moved into the red – but this was my first experience of the truth that courage is an expendable reserve.

Such a rest for a battle-weary man benefits not only the individual, but also his commander, for if the victim is not treated with consideration, he may well break down completely from shell shock, battle fatigue, or whatever doctors choose to call it, and never recover. This is one way in which an experienced officer can minimise casualties. He will probably have to witness at least one breakdown to recognise the symptoms, but once he has seen them, and if he knows his men well, he should spot someone who is developing battle fatigue, and so save him from collapse before it is too late. However, in the chaos of battle and with death all around, it is not easy to judge such matters.

In war much depends on a man's ability to manage his fear. I do not accept that any human being is truly 'fearless'. Lord Moran once inquired of Lord Gort, a Victoria Cross holder, whether he ever felt fear. 'Of course,' he answered, 'all animals feel fear. When I used to go back to the trenches after some time out of the line I had to adjust myself.'[4] Moran himself concluded that 'sooner or later all men feel fear'. Intelligent people are more prone to fear because in a battle they have a vivid appreciation of what is happening all round them and the danger which the immediate threat poses. They have to make a positive effort to control themselves, and an intelligent person may well break down because of his temperament and imagination. On the other hand, really stupid people, who do not see that there is anything to be fearful of, may do deeds that appear to be brave but are really not so, because they lack imagination. Courage is an individual's exercise of mind over fear – the complete and disciplined subjugation of fear, coupled with personal sacrifice, in situations where one places more importance on the needs of others than on one's own, even to the point of giving one's life for them.

Nobody can predict how a serviceman will behave under fire until he is tested in action, for it is impossible to replicate the conditions of battle in a civilian or peacetime context. Soldiers may train on ranges and experience live rounds fired close over their heads, creating what is known as 'crack and thump', but you cannot imitate the real thing: the fear that you may die from those bullets, or the mental stress that comes from knowing that those to whom you give orders may die as a result of your instructions. I found at all levels of command that ordering other people to risk their lives, when I was to remain in relative safety, was one of the most stressful aspects of battlefield leadership.

Before troops joined their units in Korea, they were put through tough, realistic training at the battle school at Hura Mura, in Japan. The motto 'Train Hard, Fight Easy' was plastered up in the corridors, and 5 per cent training casualties were permitted. Some men died, but more were saved when they faced the real thing, by the insight the experience gave them. And yet, however harsh this preparation, it could never replace the pressures of combat, where the other side is out to get you by any means possible, be it bullet, bayonet or bomb.

I was immensely keen to fight in the war, partly because that was what I had been trained for, and partly because, at that age, I could not make any mature assessment of the risks. But after a few days in the forward positions, when several of the twenty-eight men in our platoon had become casualties, I began to ask myself, 'What the hell am I doing this for? It could be the finish of my life – and if I get killed tonight, I shall never achieve anything.' Yet it never crossed my mind that I should find a reason to duck out and desert my mates: rather the reverse. It was this sense of personal peer loyalty that motivated VC winners like Albert Ball, Albert Jacka and Charles Upham (all described in later chapters) to keep returning to the fight when demonstrably they had more than paid their way already.

In the course of my career I have asked many people if they were frightened while on operations in war: each one replied in the affirmative. I myself was exceedingly scared in Korea when I went out at night on my first patrol in the no man's land between the British and Chinese front lines. We had to thread our way through our own minefields, and hope that the enemy's harassing artillery fire would not land on us; there was also a very good chance that the Chinese, who were skilled and tenacious fighters, would be lying in wait far closer to our lines than we expected, and ambush us.

We did bump a Chinese patrol: spurts of flame flashed out of the darkness ahead of us, and small-arms fire crackled over our heads, competing with the screech and roar of incoming shells to create a terrifying noise. I thought we were lost, in all senses of the phrase, until I realised that our patrol commander, Lieutenant Bill Nott-Bower, was yelling out orders in a loud, clear voice. It was his calmness and leadership that brought the patrol home, albeit with several members wounded. His example taught me a lesson I have never forgotten – namely, that at one time or another all military leaders are frightened, but that they become good leaders because they have learnt to control their fear, and above all not to let it show.

Discipline is an important prop to courage. Soldiers do what they are told, even if it seems dangerous or foolhardy, because peacetime training has inculcated discipline and conditioned them to carry out orders. The fact that a section or platoon of men is obeying orders plays a significant role in bolstering group courage. In a battalion or a fighting ship, training and discipline are the cement that keeps a unit together when the pressure comes on; and if either of those two fundamentals breaks down or is weak, the unit will fall apart. There is nothing more terrifying than to see a unit breaking down in battle.

Many people in the services never have their courage recognised by gallantry awards. One humbling example is that of 'Reggie' Perrin, who showed great promise in the Royal Marines and had been promoted at an early age to the rank of staff sergeant. As he supervised a training exercise, a live grenade failed to explode. Having waited for the appropriate time in case there was a delayed fuse-burn, he moved forward on his own to place an explosive charge to destroy the faulty weapon. The grenade blew up in his face, leaving him blind and paraplegic.

The prognosis showed that he was unlikely to live long, had suffered severe brain damage and would never again move out of a wheelchair. But here was a man who would not accept the doctors' verdict. As a trained mountaineer, he was determined to return to the heights – and over a period of years, with the devoted help of friends and relatives, he gradually dominated his disability. He remained 90 per cent blind, paralysed down one side – and yet, with astonishing courage and determination, he planned not only to rid himself of his wheelchair but to work towards the objective of climbing Mount McKinley in Alaska, reputedly the coldest mountain in the world, on which an average of three to five climbers die annually.

In 1995 he began his assault on the mountain. His brain told him that his left side was incapable of helping him, but through sheer guts he overruled these cerebral instructions and forced his left side to help, albeit in a limited way. He had to rely on other people to make up for his lack of sight, but by using his old skills as a mountaineer, reinforced by dogged determination, he stretched himself to the limits of his physical ability and defied medical science.

During his ascent of the mountain he fell into a crevasse, and it was only his accompanying friend, roped to him while he swung blind and incapacitated over an abyss, who prevented him falling to his death and enabled the team to recover him. He refused to turn back, struggling on upwards until he reached nearly 17,000 feet, just 3000 feet below the summit. At this point the doctor ordered him either to rest for a week or to turn back. With the weather about to break and endanger the lives of the whole party, he was left with no alternative but to return reluctantly to base – a decision which in itself required courage, as it meant sacrificing his own hopes and plans for the sake of other people's safety.

There were no medals for Reggie Perrin; there was no great battle with the enemy. Yet here was a serviceman demonstrating an outstanding example of cool, calculated and selfless courage.

Some of the bravest people in the Second World War never wore uniform but served in Special Operations Executive (SOE), working with the Resistance in German-occupied Europe. Ordinary men and women showed immense courage, holding out for years under extreme stress and constant, threatening danger. One of them, described by M. R. D. Foot in his book *Six Faces of Courage*, was Jeannie Rousseau, who wrote: 'It is not easy to depict the lonesomeness, the chilling fear, the unending waiting, the frustration of not knowing whether the dangerously-obtained information will be passed on – or passed on in time – or recognised as vital in the maze of couriers.'[5]

Foot's book brings out the lone courage of the resistance workers, and the readiness with which they would sacrifice themselves for others. The head of Jeannie Rousseau's network, *Les Druides*, was Georges Lamarque, a former university friend in his early twenties. Ultimately traced by the Germans to a particular village through his radio transmissions, he gave himself up to save the local people from retribution and savagery, and was summarily executed.

Jeannie herself was captured with two companions, after D-Day in 1944, as they were about to board a boat for England from Brittany. She had left her colleagues in a car when the Gestapo caught her and made her walk back to the vehicle with them. One can guess at the fears running through her mind during those minutes: at best a concentration camp, at worst a lonely, unwitnessed death after torture. Despite her dire predicament, she talked to her captors loudly in German, to give her companions a chance to escape. One got away; the other, Yves le Bitoux, appreciating that he was in his home town and the Germans might wreak vengeance on it if he were to escape, also allowed himself to be taken. He died in a concentration camp. Jeannie was also sent to a concentration camp, but survived.

Many people – and I am sure that includes holders of the Victoria Cross – accept that such silent and unrecognised bravery falls into a class of its own. These people fought not under the umbrella of group discipline but through steely self-control.

Patriotism and a belief in one's cause, be it religious, righteous or plain fanatical, are powerful suppressors of fear. When the battleship *Tirpitz* was sunk in 1944, many German sailors were trapped below decks. As they went down to an inevitable death, they could be heard singing their national anthem with a gusto more appropriate to the conclusion of a successful concert than to their certain extermination. Theirs was indeed a patriotic end.

For two years my family and I lived in Sudan on the edge of the site of the Battle of Omdurman, where Winston Churchill, as a young officer, had some of his earliest experiences of war, fighting the followers of the Mahdi in 1898. Egypt was then a British protectorate, and the Mahdists were religious and nationalist fanatics, driven as an army to pit themselves against the modern weapons of the foreigners, who were serving with the Egyptians under the overall command of Lord Kitchener. The native troops suffered enormous and futile casualties, and after Omdurman Churchill wrote, 'Yet these were as brave men as ever walked the earth . . . destroyed not conquered by machinery.'

Peer pressure and faith also play their part in sustaining a person in war. People place high value on the regard in which their peers hold them, worrying about their comrades' reaction if they let them down. They find that their localised public image is of great importance, and it motivates them to overcome fear on the battlefield – in schoolboy terms 'peer pressure'.

Japanese captured during the Second World War would ask to be executed, or given the opportunity to commit suicide, for in Japan a soldier who had been captured was no longer acceptable in society: he became an outcast, a reject, a failure who was better off dead.

In the West, pride in one's ship, regiment or squadron is an extension of peer pressure in corporate form. When a man joins a unit with a fine reputation in war, its renown sets its own standards for contemporary members, who will not wish to diminish that reputation and lose the respect of their peers, to become condemned in the history of the unit.

Faith is also important – and no less so today than it has always been. It is surprising how in war and in prison camps, when the future is grim and people are dying, even the toughest serviceman has a reawakening of faith. When men of the SAS return from operations to their base in Herefordshire, the garrison church, which on an average Sunday might have one or two in the congregation, becomes full to overflowing with people commemorating the casualties of the recent tour. In his address at the inauguration of the Victoria Cross and the George Cross Memorial at Westminster Abbey in May 2003, the Archbishop of Canterbury told the congregation: 'Courage as a true virtue is the kind of courage that reflects the bravery of Christ, courage that does not deny the reality of fear but is moved and energised by vision.'

In the words spoken by Jesus to the disciples during the Last Supper, 'Greater love hath no man than this, that a man lay down his life for his friends.'[6]

The battlefield is governed by three influences: luck, opportunity and unfairness. It is not possible to quantify the part that luck plays, but it is vital to the survival of individuals. The bravest of the brave may be unlucky enough to be killed by a stray bullet, or be in the wrong place at the wrong second when an incoming shell explodes – and no one will ever know what achievements that man might have been capable of. It is almost a condition of winning a Victoria Cross that luck is on your side. In Korea two new officers arrived in my battalion and were being shown round the company's position by a battle-experienced subaltern when a stray mortar winged in from the Chinese lines as they were peering over the parapet. Because they did not react fast enough, one of them was killed and the other became a Blighty casualty. But who knows what they might have achieved had luck not been against them?

Wing Commander Guy Gibson was amazingly fortunate in surviving the Dambuster raid of 1943, when he repeatedly flew over the Möhne dam at low level, into an intense barrage of fire. With clear intention and great personal courage, he escorted his Lancaster bombers down the correct approach path, while himself drawing the flak of the defenders' guns. Several of his aircraft were destroyed, and his colleagues who died flew with exceptional gallantry; yet he himself survived and came home, to be awarded a VC.

An important prerequisite of demonstrating courage is opportunity, over which an individual can exercise a considerable amount of personal control. When Lieutenant Colonel H. Jones, commanding 2nd Parachute Battalion at Goose Green in the Falkland Islands, realised that the lack of artillery support had allowed the Argentine forces to pin down his forward company, he saw a chance of regaining the initiative. Grasping the opportunity, he led an assault against the enemy positions occupied by superior numbers and dominating the ground. He so inspired his men that they attacked against overwhelming odds, and despite the lack of artillery support won the battle which proved the turning point in the war, leading to victory and recovery of the Islands into British hands. Jones won the Victoria Cross but lost his life; a courageous and selfless act indeed.

Charlie Upham, VC and Bar (chapter 9), never missed an opportunity to come to grips with the Germans. He arranged his posting to ensure he reached the war zone at the earliest occasion, and when wounded and captured, he took every opportunity to try to escape, despite his severe injuries and the immense risks involved. He could have accepted captivity, allowed his wounds to heal and awaited the end of the war, secure in the knowledge that he had already achieved more than most on the battlefield – but such passivity was not in his nature.

Unfairness – closely akin to bad luck – is prevalent throughout military operations. No bullets, shells or torpedoes are discriminate in selecting their target: they have no regard for rank or position.

It has been my privilege to meet many of that exceptional and brave group who belong to St Dunstan's, the training centre and home for blinded ex-servicemen. They are remarkable people, and they are some of the bravest men in war who never have their courage formally recognised and who have suffered grievously from the random unfairness of the battlefield.

In this sphere I know of no finer example than Billy Griffiths, who was captured by the Japanese when they overran Singapore and Java in 1942. Surrounded by twenty guards, he was forced at bayonet point to strip the camouflage netting from what he and they knew to be a booby-trapped area. Inevitably the device exploded in his face and he was hideously wounded, losing the sight of both eyes, both his hands, and sustaining severe injuries to his right leg.

His wounds would have killed many people, but despite his pain and fear he survived the most appalling conditions as a prisoner of war of the Japanese for the next three years. His captors frequently threatened to bayonet him because they considered him useless, and it was only the dedication of Sir Edward Dunlop, a remarkable Australian surgeon, that saved him. In his foreword to Billy's book *Blind to Misfortune*, Dunlop wrote:

> In Java in 1942, as commanding officer of a hastily improvised Allied general hospital, as the victorious Japanese closed in, I was required both to establish priorities for treatment and to lead an operating team in dealing with the rush of casualties. A bomb-shattered body of a young man, Leading Aircraftman

> Griffiths, posed special problems. His eyes were shattered in the wreck of his face, his hands blown away, one leg with severe compound fracture; he was peppered everywhere with embedded fragments and was exsanguinated and shocked. Surprised that he should have reached hospital at all, I took the rather illogical decision to allot him top priority, and to treat him myself. His torn bloodstained clothing removed, it seemed less than a kindness to try to prolong his life.[7]

For years Billy suffered excruciating pain in his arms twenty-four hours a day, with no prospect of drugs or treatment to ease it. He not only lived in continual fear of death from his wounds, or on the bayonets of the Japanese guards, but also suffered the torment they inflicted on him when they would creep up and tickle his feet or other parts of his body just to annoy him, knowing he could not scratch himself. Over agonising months and years he gradually came to terms with his disability. Thanks to brilliant surgery in primitive conditions his leg was preserved, and his indomitable spirit started to show through. As the co-author of his book, Hugh Popham, described it: 'The future, when he thought about it, held little enough promise, but the present had ceased to be beyond bearing, and something of his old buoyant spirit began to revive. This is what is commonly known as courage.'[8]

For three Christmases he suffered as a POW. Then came the days in 1945 when the atom bombs dropped on Hiroshima and Nagasaki brought the war against Japan to an abrupt end, thereby saving tens of thousands of Allied lives. Billy and his fellow captives found themselves freed from their tormentors with such speed that the Japanese had no time to carry out the massacre of prisoners which they had planned, should they face defeat.

Returning home, he discovered to his huge disillusionment that life was still full of disappointment and pain – mental pain now, as some of his family rejected the emaciated, blind and crippled skeleton that came back after four years of war. His wife had left him, and his ailing mother had difficulty coping with a son who could neither feed nor wash himself, or see where he was going. His family transport business had been dissolved and he seemed to have no prospects. Once again fear played its part – this time anxiety for what the future might hold, and apprehension that he had no role in it.

Yet again Billy overcame fear with long-term, cold courage, and for the next twenty years rehabilitated himself in society, learning to live with and manage his disabilities. Amazingly, with the help of St Dunstan's and two of his brothers, he re-established his own transport business, but by 1949 the firm had become financially unviable, and yet again Billy had to search for a future. His indomitable courage came to the rescue once more, and he developed a career in singing. In 1969 he was also voted Disabled Sportsman of the Year. All this he achieved with the help and love of Alice Jolly, a girlfriend from his pre-war days, whom he married on 26 May 1962.

Thanks to her devotion and the teamwork of the two of them, Billy Griffiths not only came to terms with his disabilities and injuries, but also trained himself to make the best of his remaining physical attributes. He is now a full member of society, at peace with himself. There is no self-pity, no 'Why me?' in his life. Leading Aircraftman Billy Griffiths sacrificed himself for his country, and received no form of public recognition. He is a supreme example of courage overwhelming injustice and the unfairness of war.

In a democratic society moral courage is an essential ingredient of leadership; it is far more important than popularity, which so many erroneously consider a requirement for managing other people. Popularity is irrelevant to the gaining of respect, but respect demands moral courage.

Of course it is easy to lead through fear and repression, and there are plenty of examples of this in the modern world among criminal classes and national leaders of countries where the state system is used to suppress dissent and disagreement. Under such conditions people follow because they fear the alternative of torture or death, not because they support or respect their leader.

Major-General Hugh Beech, Commandant at the Army Staff College when I was a student, told us always to stand up for what is right, and reminded us that it is remarkable how much you can achieve as a leader if you are prepared to give the credit for your own work to others under your command. This is something easily said but not so easily achieved, for it requires a high level of moral courage.

In Korea, I learnt that moral courage is an indispensable part of leadership, and that a commander needs it to enforce unpopular decisions. One day Colonel Peter Jeffreys, my commanding officer, sent a man from the rear echelon to be attached to my platoon for battle experience. He already had a high reputation as a soldier in peacetime, but this was to be his battlefield inauguration. I decided to initiate him gradually to the risks of no man's land by sending him on a standing patrol in front of our platoon position.

Standing patrols were essentially a form of guard duty, designed to deny the Chinese the opportunity of creeping in through the minefield gaps that gave us access routes into no man's land: the patrols amounted to a routine task which all forward platoons had to fulfil every night, all night.

On this night the patrol was about to leave when my platoon sergeant came to my 'hutchie', or dugout, to tell me this soldier was refusing to go out with the others. He had given no reason: he just flatly declined to leave, despite direct orders from the sergeant.

I went out to talk to him and found he was adamant: he was not taking the risk of committing himself to no man's land. Until then he had had a quiet war, with little or no exposure to danger, but now, faced with battlefield risks, he had succumbed to what one can only describe as a demonstration of self-preservation and cowardliness which threatened to undermine the discipline of other members of the platoon. There had been no depletion of his courage bank – rather a capitulation to his own fear.

I ordered him to go. He still refused. Here was a man disobeying my orders in war. At once I was in a leadership crisis: the rest of the patrol were watching to see what I, a young, untried officer, would do. Even if I invoked the support of a senior officer, I would lose much of my authority, for not having dealt with the problem on my own. I had to settle the matter myself.

I pulled out my revolver, cocked it and pointed it at the soldier. 'Go,' I told him, 'or I shoot you.' To my intense relief, he went – but ever since I have wondered what would have happened if he had held out. In those few seconds I saw that a leader often has to take difficult and risky decisions without concern for the consequences to himself. This is what moral courage is about.

Immediately afterwards, I realised I had made an appalling threat. But at the time, under the intense stress of the moment, I saw no alternative. I had created a situation in which the man's fear of going on patrol was less than his fear that I might shoot him. But the rule of military law prevails even on the battlefield, and I know that, had he called my bluff, I would have been the loser, whether I fired that pistol or whether I dodged the issue and lost my credibility among the rest of my men. A certain level of fear can be overcome by a greater threat from elsewhere, and can give a man courage when he may be lacking it.

An officer in senior command finds it increasingly difficult to share the risks faced by his subordinates, although he must visit forward areas to familiarise himself with the battle conditions and the morale of his men. General Slim managed to achieve this balance of physical exposure and sound management when he led the 14th Army in the Far East in 1942–5. He took risks by flying into the most forward positions, and at least once nearly failed to return. His combat experience told him he had to familiarise himself with the battlefield and conditions in forward areas, as well as to demonstrate to his men that he could share the physical risks he was asking them to take – but it was not his business to interfere in the day-to-day command of minor units.

The balance between exercising leadership and interfering with junior commanders is not always easy to strike. However, it is certain that the commander who fails to get out on the ground from time to time will lose touch with the battle and forfeit the respect of his men. He will have little idea of the problems they face in terms of living conditions, or of the going – and his ignorance will show in decisions based on poor comprehension of the topography. In short, he will already have conceded a vital facet of the battle to the enemy.

Courage is a quality we all admire, a goal to which we all aspire, and an essential ingredient at all rank levels in war. All of us possess it in some measure, but our personal bank balance varies between individuals, and none of us knows our credit limit until tested. War offers people opportunities to test themselves to their limits. The award of medals recognises a person's courage in battle, but gallantry is not restricted to those who are decorated, still less to holders of the Victoria Cross. Indeed, a man awarded several Distinguished Service Orders or a couple of Distinguished Conduct Medals may well have shown gallantry beyond that of the holder of a single VC.

Most winners of the highest military distinction are ordinary men who do not wish to stand out in society. I have had the privilege of knowing a few holders from the Second World War. Stanley Hollis, as Company Sergeant Major of 6th Battalion, the Green Howards, gained his VC for outstanding courage during the Normandy landings in 1944. When he came under machine-gun fire from two pillboxes only twenty yards away, he rushed at one with his Sten gun and threw a grenade, taking all five Germans inside prisoner. He then captured the second box, and with it twenty-six prisoners, saving his company from coming under fire. Later he put a field gun and its crew out of action before going out under heavy fire to rescue two of his men, among many he saved by his actions that day. Yet away from exploding shells, the threat of anti-personnel mines and the stammer of German machine guns, Hollis was a quiet, likeable Englishman – just the sort with whom to enjoy a pint in the local.

Dick Annand, the first soldier in the Second World War to be awarded the VC, won his with the Durham Light Infantry as a Second Lieutenant, while his platoon was holding a bridge astride the River Dyle before the evacuation from Dunkirk in 1940. 'Oblivious of mortars and machine gun fire, he repeatedly dispersed the Germans with grenades, which he carried in a sandbag. Thrice he personally repulsed the Germans – he just went mad.'[9] Yet in peacetime Dick Annand is a delightful gentleman – modest, kind and absolutely lacking in aggression.

Unexceptional in normal life, these two Englishmen typify holders of the Victoria Cross who in battle stood out from their peers and displayed unique courage and selfless disregard for their own lives. They would be the first to join me in saluting those many sailors, soldiers and airmen who never received recognition but put their lives on the line or died, and without whom no commander is able to fight his battle or win his war. Each one is a hero.

3

Captain Noel Chavasse VC and Bar, MC

1884–1917

Most winners of the Victoria Cross are, of necessity, killers, for it is in the heat of battle that they display extreme courage. Noel Chavasse never killed anyone, nor did he even fire a shot in anger. He was never aggressive or vindictive; never for a moment did he lose his essential decency and restraint. Yet he is one of only three men who have won the VC twice, and in some ways he is the most remarkable of all.

A photograph taken in 1914, when he was thirty, gives a clear pointer to the mainspring of his heroism: his eyes show a glint of humour, but they also suggest that he harboured a boundless store of compassion – and it was this feeling for his soldiers, allied to an exceptionally powerful sense of duty and an unshakeable faith in God, that made him a legend, in his lifetime and after.

He was born in Oxford on 9 November 1884, twenty minutes later than his brother Christopher. The twins were so alike, then and throughout their development, that people had the greatest difficulty telling them apart. Their mutual affinity was amazing: at school their teachers sometimes became suspicious because in their work they independently made the same mistakes, as if they had been collaborating. Moreover, twins ran in the family, for two years later their mother Edith gave birth to Marjorie and May (these two, however, were not identical). In all Edith produced seven children, from Dorothea, the eldest, through the two sets of twins, to Francis and Aidan.

Their father, Frank Chavasse, was the descendant of a Frenchman who had settled in England early in the eighteenth century. Medicine and the Church were the family's chosen fields. Frank's father and grandfather were both surgeons, and in 1884 he himself was Rector of St Peter-le-Bailey, in Oxford – a small man, only 5′ 3″ tall, and hunchbacked as the result of a childhood illness, but extremely active as parish priest and teacher of young men aspiring to enter the Church. Edith, the daughter of a vicar, also had powerful religious beliefs, so that the boys grew up in a close-knit family strongly imbued with Christian principles. Marjorie later remembered the 'atmosphere of calm and integrity in the house' – a background which gave them enormous emotional strength in later life.

In 1889, when Noel and Christopher were five, their father was promoted to become Principal of Wycliffe Hall, the college which prepared students for ordination in the Church of England, and the family moved to live in part of its premises, numbers 52 and 54 Banbury Road. There the twins were taught by a governess and a tutor.

At twelve they went as day-boys to Magdalen College School, pedalling there and back on their bicycles. Noel's report for 1897 described him as 'rather an imp of mischief', and said that he was 'far too much interested in other boys' mischief', but conceded that he had real ability. By the time he was fifteen he knew every inch of Oxford and its environs, and he expected to remain in the place he loved not just for the rest of his schooldays, but throughout his university career as well.

Then came an upheaval: in 1900 his father was appointed Bishop of Liverpool, and the family moved north, to take up residence in the Bishop's Palace at 19 Abercromby Square, on the high ground north-east of the Mersey. Noel and Christopher both wanted to stay at school in Oxford, as boarders, but their father overruled them, on the grounds that it would be better for their moral and mental development if they all remained together during their formative years. The importance of family and home was one of Frank Chavasse's central beliefs: he once said in a sermon that 'if the home be weakened or corrupt, the life of the nation is poisoned at its very springs, for it is the greatest factor in the formation of the character of its people'.

So the twins were enrolled at Liverpool College, a fee-paying school (with reductions for the sons of clergy) which prepared boys for university. There – only a short walk from their new home – both performed adequately on the academic front, but it was in athletics that they proved outstanding. Although as a boy Noel had often been sickly, by the time he was nineteen he had grown into a fast, powerful runner, and in his final year he set new school records in the 100 yards, the 440 yards and the mile. Chris, meanwhile, came third in the 100 yards and second in the 440.

Noel's most valuable extramural activity was his involvement with the Holy Trinity Certified Industrial School for Boys in Grafton Street, Toxteth Park, one of the institutions whose aim was to rescue deprived slum children 'from present wretchedness and vice, and from future criminality'. As a volunteer, he led sing-songs and Bible readings, organised games and went with the boys on their annual summer camps, showing the same concern for his young charges as he later displayed for the soldiers in his care.

Already his aim was to become a missionary doctor, so he applied to Trinity College, Oxford, to read Natural Sciences, which would put him on the first rung of the ladder leading to medical employment. Christopher, wanting to follow his father into the Church, opted for History as his main subject, and Trinity accepted them both. They went up to the university in the autumn of 1904, and soon felt at home, not least because they already had many friends in the town.

Noel's interest in medicine grew rapidly, especially when, in his second year, he began to dissect bodies. 'I enjoy it very much,' he reported to his parents; and to increase his experience, during his vacations he arranged to go the rounds with Dr Charles Macalister, the Chavasses' family doctor, who was Consultant Physician at the Royal Southern Hospital in Liverpool. By June 1907, with his Oxford finals approaching, his ambition (he told his mother) was to dissect a head, 'and they are not so plentiful as legs and arms'.

An enemy – if he had one – might have sought to portray Noel as a goody-goody. Like his father, he did not drink alcohol, and tended to be censorious about those undergraduates who indulged. In his letters home he constantly upbraided himself for not working hard enough: at first his target was six hours' study a day, then eight, then ten. A regular and devout churchgoer, he deplored merry-making on Sunday, and was closely interested in religious thought.

His serious intentions, however, were lightened by his intelligence, his energy, his ebullient sense of humour and his humility, all of which enhanced the lives of those he met. When his father offered to give him a volume of Robert Browning's poems, he sent a letter of thanks, remarking that he already had a Shakespeare and a Tennyson, and that Browning 'would give a finished look to my shelf and make people imagine the owner cultivated'.

There was also his athletic prowess. In 1906, when he won a 440-yard race by fourteen yards, he remarked to his mother, 'I was awfully lucky yesterday'; but in fact he and Christopher were highly talented. In 1907 they both won Blues for running against Cambridge: Chris won the 440 yards, with Noel second, and Noel dead-heated first in the 100 yards. In Oxford's own university sports Noel won the 100 yards, with Chris second, and Chris again won the 440.

With characteristic self-deprecation, Noel claimed that he had wasted his time at school, and he consistently played down his chances of getting a good university degree. He and his parents were therefore thrilled when he was awarded a First – but his triumph was marred by a minor disaster, when Chris failed in History. How he managed this never became clear, but he immediately settled down to work all out so that he could take the exam again.

Noel, rather than move to Liverpool University for further studies, as he had planned, lived at home for a while, but chose to stay with his brother, and so returned to Oxford to pursue his education in medicine. The twins took lodgings in Museum Road, and in the winter both turned out as wing three-quarters for the Trinity rugby XV. The first time Noel played on the wing, he scored four tries – and typically played down his success:

> I hang outside on the wing, and when the other ¾ get the ball they burst along until they have drawn men on to them. Then they pass out to me, and everybody yells 'NOW RUN'. So I just run. That is all my job.[1]

Strenuous team games proved something of a revelation. 'I must say you do get to know people well when you are both battling and sweating to win a match for your College,' he wrote home. 'Altogether a much decenter thing than winning pots for oneself.'

He must have been working hard, as well, for when exams came round again in June, he once more got a First. He claimed that nobody had thought he had a chance, and that when the results were published, everyone greeted him 'with incredulous smiles'. To the relief of the family, Christopher also achieved a pass.

With a degree of sorts under his belt, Chris went down from Oxford and began studying for ordination; but Noel continued learning about anatomy by every means he could – staying on at Oxford to do research, attend lectures and check patients at the Radcliffe Hospital.

His sense of duty was growing fast. 'When one enjoys life so much, one is rather afraid of not being so strenuous as duty demands,' he told his father – and one manifestation of this was his sudden interest in the university's Officer Training Corps, which he joined in the winter of 1908–9, along with his younger brother Bernard, who by then was an undergraduate at Balliol.

He did not much care for the drill-parades, which started at 7.30 in the morning, but soon he was telling his mother, 'I feel very virtuous being a Territorial, as I feel that at last I am really doing my duty and am not a mere "flannelled fool" or "muddied oaf".' His first taste of military life was brief, but the experience appealed to him, and had a lasting effect.

In June 1909 he finally left Oxford and returned to Liverpool, where, in the autumn, he joined the Medical School of the University as a full-time student. Even though one of his teachers was the outstanding Robert Jones – already well known as an orthopaedic surgeon – he failed in his first attempt to become a member of the Royal College of Surgeons in London, partly because he was ill when he went to take the exam. But at his second attempt, in May 1910, he passed – an achievement which elicited an ebullient telegram from his sister Marjorie:

> Your wire has sent us all into transports of delight. Father is telephoning, Mother is laughing foolishly, and I am jumping . . . In case you are feeling too uplifted, let me remind you that you had a tremendous pull over everyone else who went in, possessing as you do such a particularly righteous Father, Mother and SISTER, indeed my firm conviction is that it is entirely owing to these that you have passed.[2]

Based now in Liverpool, and living at home, Noel found time to visit old friends in Oxford, and during one of his trips to the south he called on his Uncle Tom (his father's brother, Sir Thomas Chavasse) and Aunt Frances at their home at Barnt Green, in Worcestershire. Sir Thomas was a distinguished surgeon, knighted in 1905 for services to medicine, so that he and his nephew shared many interests; but for Noel the main attraction at Barnt Green was the family's second daughter, his cousin Gladys. Born in 1893, she was only seventeen in 1910 – nine years younger than him – and at that stage their relationship seems to have been platonic. But when Noel reported, 'I am haymaking here and having a right royal time,' it alarmed Gladys's father, who privately told her mother that there could be no question of a marriage between first cousins.

In Liverpool Noel extended his studies into several new fields – pathology, vaccination, bacteriology, infectious diseases. Then in the summer of 1911 he took the placement which all medical students were obliged to go through, and spent three months at the Rotunda Hospital in Dublin. In January 1912 he passed his final medical examination; in March he was awarded the Derby

Exhibition at the Medical Faculty of Liverpool University, and in the summer he at last qualified as a doctor.

His first post was as house-surgeon at the Royal Southern Hospital, the establishment in the Toxteth area of the city which provided medical care for the poor. He enjoyed his first year there very much, but was delighted when, in October 1913, he was appointed house-surgeon to the leading orthopaedic specialist Robert Jones – for orthopaedics was the area of medicine that fascinated him most.

Busy as he was in the hospital, he again felt drawn to the Army, and as a junior medical officer with the rank of surgeon-lieutenant he joined the Royal Army Medical Corps, and through them, the 10th Battalion of the King's (Liverpool) Regiment, known as the Liverpool Scottish. As he put it, he was only attached to the Liverpool unit: 'I am really RAMC. I am in it but not of it.' Nevertheless, he developed a fierce loyalty to the regiment, whose members were required to have a Scottish parent or grandparent, to be at least 5′ 6″ tall, and able to boast at least a 35-inch chest. Two immediately distinguishing features were their uniform of kilts and sporrans, and the bagpipes played by the bandsmen – something that had made a deep impression on Noel the first time he saw them, years earlier, when a detachment skirled and marched at the annual sports day of his school in Liverpool.

Drill parades at the regiment's headquarters in Fraser Street, weapon training, rugby and athletics, tented summer camps – all these suited Noel admirably, and he was pleased to find that many of the part-time soldiers were intelligent young men, who had white-collar jobs with banks or insurance firms, rather than working-class lads with little education. Even so, he was nervous before going to his first camp: he 'felt very raw at first', but soon was 'getting knocked into shape', and he was relieved to find that 'most of the fellows seem to be teetotal', and that he heard very little bad language.

He was so busy, both in the hospital and with his Territorial training, that the grim political developments in the summer of 1914 apparently passed him by – and indeed the entire Liverpool Scottish Regiment seems to have been taken by surprise when war broke out. On 2 August some 900 officers and other ranks set off for their annual camp at Hornby, in Lancashire, but they had hardly arrived when, at 2 a.m. next morning, a telegram ordered them back to Liverpool. One day later, at 11 p.m. on 4 August, England declared war on Germany.

For the time being Noel returned home to the Bishop's Palace in Abercromby Square, where his three brothers had already gathered. Having signed off from the hospital for the fortnight's camp, he never went there again; instead, he took the train to London to volunteer for active service as a doctor, and Chris went with him, determined to become an army chaplain.

When Colonel W. Nicholl, commanding officer of the Liverpool Scottish, offered his battalion for service at the front, Noel was sent to Chester to examine and vaccinate recruits, and he was 'terribly afraid' that he was going to be left behind. In a revealing letter home he reported that he was doing all he could to learn about the hygiene of a fighting army, and went on:

> I have a great longing to take care of a regiment. When I go out with the Scottish boys I feel quite paternal, and love keeping them fit and dressing their minor injuries. I think it is the pastoral spirit, for the care and cure of bodies instead of souls, although I do care for their souls too – only it is not my business to cater for them. If ever I get sent to the Front with a regiment I shall almost shed tears of joy.

He joined the Liverpool Scottish under canvas in the King's Park, in Edinburgh, and there he set out to vaccinate the entire battalion – 1000 men – against typhoid. Many of the soldiers went down with colds or influenza – which he attributed to 'their being clerks, unused to roughing it and unused to kilts' – and his early-morning sick-parades were crowded. Hard physical training soon brought about an improvement, and Noel much enjoyed joining in the men's drills, as he found it 'a good opportunity of seeing their point of view and getting to know them without lowering one's rank'. He himself was training a squad of eighteen stretcher-bearers, and 'getting very fond of them'. He also had five men to look after the water-carts, and nine sanitary policemen 'who see that the camp is kept sweet and clean'. Then, and for the rest of his life, hygiene was one of his main preoccupations.

Early in October the regiment was ordered south to Tunbridge Wells, in Kent. Its members still fully believed that, if they went to France or Belgium, they would be used only in support roles, for nobody had yet conceived the idea of sending a Territorial unit to fight in the front line. Noel supposed that they would go first 'to the lines of communication and I expect will remain there for some time. But it is a great honour to be sent out so soon.'

By then, he claimed, the Liverpool Scottish was 'one of the best-inoculated regiments in the country', and he was determined to prevent men who had refused inoculation from going abroad, as he thought it wrong that 'after all the rest had submitted, they should have any risk from ignorant and superstitious shirkers'.

After three weeks of suspense, the regiment received the 'unexpected but very excellent news' that it was to go abroad. At the last moment the battalion was issued with new weapons and kit: their obsolete rifles were replaced with new models, their sporrans with khaki aprons, their leather equipment with webbing. Noel had wired his sister Dot (Dorothea) with a request for 'woolly comforts', and he told his father:

> I feel in loco parentis towards my little lot and don't intend that they shall die of cold. You feel very warm towards people who are going to rough it with you (even the rotters), and when they are only lads and they are after the same job that you are you feel more soft towards them still . . .
>
> I feel glad I am going with the Scottish . . . A great many of the Scottish, who did not volunteer for foreign service because of home ties, are now rushing up to be examined, and to offer themselves now the real call has come . . . I think the fighting stuff is still in England, but I am very sorry for the wife and kids.
>
> Goodbye, my dear Father. I am going to do my best to be a faithful soldier of Jesus Christ and King George.
>
> Ever your loving son, Noel.

On 1 November 1914 the battalion embarked on the 8000-ton *Maidan* at Southampton, and that night the ship steamed across the Channel to Le Havre as part of a small convoy. Because the captain missed the tide, he had to put to sea again, and the men did not go ashore in France until dawn on 3 November. They then marched through the town, spent a night in tents at a camp outside, and in the morning entrained for Rouen, Amiens and finally St Omer, whence they marched in drenching rain three miles to billets near the village of Blendecques.

Already, after only two months of the war, the Allied and German armies were locked together in the murderous stalemate of trench warfare which claimed hundreds of thousands of lives in Flanders. For the next two weeks the Scottish trained within earshot of the artillery blasting away at the front, a few miles to the east. For the time being conditions were deceptively comfortable. Noel was quartered in an empty house, where he slept in a large bed, and the local French inhabitants proved outstandingly hospitable, bringing him bowls of pears and giving his orderlies hot soup in the middle of the day. Already he was getting tough with malingerers, sorting them out at his 6 a.m. sick parades and sending away anyone he did not think was going to be able to 'stick it'.

Yet in a few days the battalion's expectations changed entirely, and it looked as though they would be sent to the front at any moment. 'The men (apparently) will be in the trenches alternate twenty-four hours, changing with a fresh lot of men during the night,' Noel told his parents, looking ahead with his usual optimism:

> I am behind at headquarters, probably a dug out, where I sit and wait for the wounded to be brought to me. I believe that doctors are not allowed in the trenches, so really I shall run very little risk during the war, and I do not intend to run any risk at all, unnecessarily; my blood is not heroic.

In trying to look after his men, he was not helped by their uniform. When they set off for Bailleul on a two-day march over roads coated with ice and snow, the pleats of their kilts froze into long spikes of ice, which lacerated their thighs. Their brand-new boots, which had just been issued to replace their civilian shoes and spats, chewed up their feet. On the morning of 25 November the regiment was inspected by General Sir H. Smith-Dorrien, Commander of II Corps, who was accompanied by Edward, the young Prince of Wales. In his address the General said that all the British and French had to do was to keep the Germans pinned down until the spring of 1915, whereupon the Russians would drive through to Berlin from the east, and the war would be over by the summer – an opinion which shocked the men, who had assumed that hostilities would cease long before that.

At Westoutre, where they spent a night, the soldiers learnt that they were to relieve the Highland Light Infantry, providing 150 riflemen for the front line, and another 100 in support, with two platoons in reserve. They were told to remove all means of identification, including cap badges and shoulder flashes, and warned about the dangers of the front: shelling was liable to start up at any hour of the day or night, and snipers were active.

Noel already knew, in theory, the procedure for dealing with wounded men: stretcher-bearers were supposed to collect casualties and bring them in to the doctor, who would be waiting at the regimental aid post, the most forward position for medical care. After initial treatment there, the wounded would be sent back to the advanced dressing station, then to the main dressing station, and if necessary to the casualty clearing station or to one of the base hospitals.

No doubt on paper everything sounded precise and orderly; but when the regiment's Y Company was ordered into the front line, brutal reality took over. Within twenty-four hours the Liverpool Scottish suffered its first casualty, when a company commander, Captain Arthur Twentyman, was shot dead by a bullet through the heart. Noel was badly upset by his death, for Twentyman had been a close friend; but when the Colonel told him to go out with his stretcher-bearers and bring the body back, he did not hesitate:

> At first the zip, zip of bullets hitting the sandbags close to one's head was rather disconcerting, then it became just part of the

general environment. At one place we had to get out and double past a gate where a sniper lay in wait. I went by doing the 100 well within 10 sec. We got to the poor Captain lying in the mud at the back of the trench.

We fitted up a temporary stretcher with two poles and a greatcoat. Then we climbed out of the trench and two of us carried him back . . . This was the most risky part, because the moon was full and bright . . . He was dreadfully heavy . . . We had to cross a ploughed field for about 400 yards, but now the moon had gone in and we were safer. But we had to rest five times during this bit. During one of these halts we stopped where about ten dead Frenchmen lay. When we reached safety, two of the men were sick and another had to sit down for quite a while.

Such was his first experience under fire, and such the first of his innumerable forays into no man's land, the lethally dangerous area between the front lines, where snipers' bullets were constantly flying, shells exploding, and (at night) enemy might be on the move. Other medical officers might have sent their stretcher-bearers out while they themselves remained in the relative safety of the regimental aid post: not Noel. His sense of duty, reinforced by love of his men, whom he came to see as his children, sent him over the top again and again to rescue the dead or wounded.

Ever since he was at school he had made a habit of writing home on Sundays, and now his letters from the front – long, articulate and full of vivid descriptions – became immensely important to his parents. So good were his dispatches that his father had many of them typed out, and some were printed for private circulation. His handwriting – always small and neat – became positively microscopic whenever he was confined to a trench or a dugout and resorted to pink Budget Letter Cards, which folded in three for posting, and on to which he crammed hundreds of words, tiny yet still perfectly legible.[3]

Although he was careful never to give away potentially sensitive information, and played down the risks that he himself was taking, he sent searing accounts of how mere rumours of trench warfare had all too suddenly turned into the real thing. Mostly he wrote to his father, but even in letters to 'My Dear Old Mother' he did not spare details of grisly deaths and maimings, and occasional poetic flashes served only to heighten the realities of trench warfare: 'It was now clear moonlight, and we lined the grave with yew.'

The wounds he had to deal with – out in the bullet- and shrapnel-ridden darkness of no man's land, or in makeshift, candle-lit dressing stations – were often horrifying: once out in the open he found a man's arm dangling by a few shreds, and had to cut it off there and then with a pair of scissors. Far from the clean puncture which he had imagined a gunshot injury would be, a rifle bullet through the fleshy part of the thigh left only a small entrance hole, 'but the exit was a gaping burst, a big hole that I could put my fist into, with broken muscles hanging out'. When one of his soldiers was shot in the head, he described how he had 'lost the whole side of his head and a large part of his brain, yet he lived and was semi-conscious for two days'.

Occasional touches of humour showed how well he preserved his own sanity:

> I had a grim job the other day. There was a very wet trench being drained when the diggers came upon a dead leg – so I volunteered to take up the sanitary policemen and dig up our unknown friend, and dispose of him in a grave where he would not impede the traffic.
>
> I gave my men hot cocoa, took them up, and we dug him out. They stuck at it very well and rather enjoyed the horror of it all. The obstructor turned out to be an Englishman and a corporal, dead I should say about three months and rather horrible.

Even without enemy bombardments and small-arms fire, Noel had plenty of problems. One was lice, which infested everybody in the front line and caused untold irritation: scratching could lead to skin infections, poisoning, boils and impetigo. A more serious hazard was the disease known as trench foot, which was brought on by standing in cold water and mud. In this early stage of the war the trenches were in an appalling state, often two feet deep in glutinous mud, so that even to move along them was an exhausting struggle. When men took off their boots after hours or days of immersion, their feet were dead and white, and their legs had often swollen as high as the knee; sometimes gangrene would set in, or blisters became infected. So severe was the incidence of this ailment, akin to frostbite, that in five weeks from the end of November to January the battalion's effective strength was reduced from a total of 850 to a mere 370. Thirty-two officers and men had been killed or wounded in battle, but most of the rest had gone down with trench foot.

Noel's remedy was an all-out attempt to keep feet clean, warm and dry. In his letters home he constantly asked for more socks, his aim being that every man should have at least two pairs, including one dry one. As for treatment, he gave tablets of soda salicylate, a form of aspirin, long before its efficacy was officially recognised, and he tried to revive dead feet by rubbing them with spirit. Better hygiene was also his main weapon in the fight against lice, which he called 'the plague of vermin'. Whenever he could, he arranged for batches of men to have hot baths and clean underclothes. Writing to Dot from a ruined village, he told her:

> Often there are only two pumps for the whole battalion . . . I have collected tubs, and by making friends with the cooks have managed to give hot baths to about 100 men in the last two days. At the same time I overhauled their underclothes, and whenever I spotted one [a louse] (I am getting a very practised eye) I had the garment soaked in petrol. It was dry by the time the wearer was.

Christmas brought a brief respite, for the regiment was not in the front line, and a special parade was held in a field, at which the battalion's pipes (brought out of store for the occasion) were played, presents sent from home were handed round, a carol was sung, and a great deal of food distributed – green turtle soup and turkey for the officers, fresh meat, bread and rum for the men. Noel managed to attend a service conducted by the padre, and this came as a relief, since he had had no chance of receiving Holy Communion since his departure from Liverpool in August.

As the winter wore on, he refined the organisation of his dressing stations, wherever they were, getting lightly wounded men to help with the routine tasks of collecting firewood, cleaning the room or dugout and trying to make sure that when men came back exhausted from the trenches, they would get a hot drink and a chance of warming up. His own resilience was already remarkable:

> They say that after three months an officer loses his nerve, from sheer nervous drain, but so far I have, please God, a good hold on myself, and am doing my best to cheer up the poor officers as they come back wearied from the strain of trench work. I have won several good friends up here, and am perfectly happy and in good health . . . My great fault is irritation, when a bit over-pressed with work (which scrimshanks have found to their cost). I ask God daily to give me courage and patience, for naturally I am not overburdened with either.

On 10 March 1915 came a major change, when the Liverpool Scottish were ordered to march half a dozen miles north-east to Ypres, the medieval town which the Allies had decided they must defend at all costs. In bitter fighting the previous autumn Sir Douglas Haig's I Corps had advanced beyond the town, to the east, and then, after a ferocious battle, had established a salient, or defended buffer zone, to protect the town against counter-attacks. Into the trenches of the salient, at Hill 60, went two companies of the Scottish, with the rest of the regiment billeted as reserves at the barracks in the town itself.

Later in the war most of the town's buildings were reduced to shattered stumps by repeated shelling; but in the spring of 1915, the place was still inhabited by a few hardy citizens, who had stayed on in order to make money from the occupying forces, and British officers happily patronised the restaurants, bars and tea shops that had remained open. Somehow Noel was finding time to read: he was delighted by *David Copperfield*, 'every page of which is a joy', but struggled with Shakespeare's *Richard II*, which he could take 'only in minimum doses'. In the barracks he established a new front in his battle against lice:

> I found a washhouse and a copper. I also found four big tubs . . . I can wash a company (about 120 men) a day, so they all get a hot tub during their rest period. They appreciate this very much – all they have to do is to bring a pail of cold water from the town moat . . .
>
> Every time we are resting (ten days' trenches, four days' rest) one day the men march to some baths rigged up in some schools. There, each man is given soap and a clean towel, and they have a hot tub [*sic*] in a tub. They give in all their dirty underclothing and are given new or clean underclothing. If necessary they get a complete refit. Also their kilts are ironed. Meanwhile, all their blankets are given in, and exchanged for blankets which have been stoved [baked] for an hour . . . This seems to me to be the only real attempt to rid men of vermin.

Noel's high morale seems all the more extraordinary in view of the fact that every loss of a good man distressed him profoundly – as he showed when one of his stretcher-bearers was hit by a stray bullet:

> He had gone out full of life and spirits, shouting goodnight to everybody . . . Then just at the corner of the road he was hit and was carried in to us again, sick and cold and clammy. He had been shot through the stomach, and there was never any hope for him, and he died in about ¾ hour. He was a fine, upstanding, broad-shouldered lad of twenty, the cheeriest and the coolest of the party, strong, willing and wonderfully deft and tender with the wounded. I feel his death very much.

As for taking risks himself – earlier he had promised his parents that he would do nothing rash, but in emergencies he lost all inhibition. Once, when a man had been severely wounded in the head, he ignored the communication trench, along which he could have made his way forward slowly but in safety, and sprinted up the road in full view of the enemy.

The battalion's next post was at St Eloi, due south of Ypres, and the area was what Noel described as 'lively', because it lay beneath the trajectory of the heavy, high-explosive shells with which the Germans were bombarding the town. 'Every now and then there passes overhead a thunderous shriek, like an express train tearing through a small station,' Noel told his parents:

> This is followed by a dull roar, these are the real Jack Johnsons, on their way to level an ancient city to the ground.[4] I don't know what thunderbolts of wrath were hurled on the cities of the plains, but they could not have been more terrible than those forged by the Hun. We hear them pass all day and we hear them crash, and looking over tangled and shell-pocked fields we can see great pillars of smoke and dust rising from the tortured city.

One day he was agreeably surprised by a telegram telling him that his brother Chris had been posted to Ypres, and was only a mile away. The twins met for lunch, to their great delight, and afterwards Chris came to the Scottish dugout, where he held a short service and gave what Noel called 'a rattling good address'. Although the service was voluntary, all the men turned out. By then both the other Chavasse brothers were also in the army, Bernard with the RAMC, and Aidan with the 11th (Pioneer) Battalion of the King's. Meanwhile the women in the family were contributing to the war effort in various ways, and none more actively than May, who travelled out to Étaples in March to work as a ward maid in a mobile prefabricated hospital, financed by the people of Liverpool and built there in wooden sections before being shipped across the Channel.

One problem which exercised Noel more and more was that of men who collapsed under the cumulative strain. Some deserted, others put a bullet through hand, arm or leg, hoping to be invalided back to England; but doctors could generally tell from the nature of a wound if it was self-inflicted, and anyone convicted of cowardice was liable to be shot. Moreover such executions, though not reported in Britain, were deliberately publicised on the Western

Front, to set an example, and it infuriated Noel to know that 'poor jaded and terrified boys of eighteen years of age' were being shot 'for shirking the cruel hardships of winter trenches', while at home 'boozy and cushy' munitions workers were going on strike without retribution.

Self-inflicted wounds distressed him – as when a man was brought in with most of his calf shot away:

> He had dropped out on the way to the trenches . . . and crawled into a dug out, where I am afraid he shot himself (he said he was cleaning his rifle – they all say that). When he gets well the poor chap will be court-martialled and either shot or given penal servitude, I fear.

At that date very few doctors recognised the existence of shell shock, and condemned anyone who broke down as a coward. Noel, more sensitive and humane than most, saw that men often became completely exhausted, and that their courage simply ran out for the time being. Whenever he could, he quietly moved such people out of the front line and put them on light duties for a spell until they recovered.

His own resilience remained astonishing, as he showed in a letter of 19 April:

> I am now in the proud position of being the only regimental doctor who has not broken down – and as for me, I am like 'Johnnie Walker' (if you know who he is) and still going strong.[5] I am very glad I am so fit, because I have a tremendous attachment to the regiment and could not bear to leave it. As for the war itself, it is beginning to bore me a bit – and I shall not be sorry when it is over.

The battle of Hooge, which began on 16 June 1915, rapidly turned into a nightmare. The Allied aim was to push the Germans back out of a salient they had occupied some two miles east of Ypres by storming their trenches with a three-stage attack, in which various battalions were to leapfrog each other. The Liverpool Scottish were paired with the Lincolns to make the second assault: once the first line of trenches had been captured, they were to go through and take the next.

Special training, in barbed-wire-cutting and bomb-throwing, began a week before the deadline – and the fact that the attack went disastrously wrong was in large part due, paradoxically, to the verve with which it was carried out. The operation began with a heavy artillery bombardment, which started at 0200 on the 16th and continued for two hours. Then, at 0400, the first infantry attack went in, and, as Noel described the action later, the Scottish 'made such a splendid rush that they carried all three trenches in fifteen minutes, and even penetrated the fourth line'. Disaster ensued because the artillery gunners, far to the rear, continued to shell their preordained targets, which were obscured by smoke, not realising that the ground had already been captured. The result was that a great many men were killed or wounded by their own artillery. At the same time, the wings of the assault collapsed, so that the Scottish began to be encircled and had to withdraw, allowing many wounded to fall into German hands.

The carnage was so appalling that by the time the battalion was relieved the next night, the Liverpool Scottish had been almost annihilated. Of the twenty-three officers who went into the battle, four had been killed, six were missing and eleven were wounded, leaving only two intact. Of 519 other ranks, seventy-five had been killed and 103 were missing, with 201 wounded.

None of the survivors can have had a more exhausting or harrowing time than Noel, who struggled to save the wounded for forty-eight hours on end, repeatedly exposing himself to enemy fire; and the letter he sent home four days later, although playing down his own courage and stamina, gave a horribly vivid idea of how chaotic the battle became.

He was already so tired before it began that he slept through the initial bombardment. Then at 5 a.m. the wounded began straggling back to his dressing station.

> They came down a long communication trench in a steady stream. Meanwhile the Huns began to put crumps [shell-bursts]

and shrapnel down the road. Our CO arrived with an artery bleeding in his head, which was troublesome to stop, and we had to lie him down at the back, as a crump landed too near the dressing-station for safety.

Then news came that a Captain Cunningham was lying exhausted at the top end of the communication trench. So he had to be fetched down. I then found the trench blocked with men who had dropped exhausted trying to drag themselves along. The Huns were putting big shells into the trench and making direct hits, so that in places the trench was blown in, yet not a single wounded man was hit all day.

It was a weary job helping poor Cunningham down the trench. He was hit in the leg and arm, and was very brave. We got some more men back at the same time, but arrived back to find that another crump had burst just outside our dressing-station, had killed four men next door and wrecked the place.

So we took all our men a quarter of a mile down the road to an industrial school, where the RAMC had an advanced dressing-station. I left three dressers with them . . . while I slipped up to the trenches to see how our boys were getting on there. I took with me besides more dressings two bottles of lime juice and a sack full of water bottles left by wounded men.

We found the top end of the communication trench blocked by the wounded. I dressed thirty of them and sent them on to the ambulance. I found the little path behind the dug-outs a shambles. Our stretcher-bearers, who had carried very well all the morning, were now lying exhausted. The wounded men of my battalion were lying out in a road in front of a mud wall – no protection at all against crumps or the sun, and one poor chap, half naked, was blistered already, so I set about and dressed them, and then tried to get shelter for them with sandbags. You should have seen them lap down my lime juice. None of them were in great pain.

Then stories began to pour in about chaps lying out [in no man's land]. A message came to say that the Adjutant was hit, so I went out with two stretcher-bearers and his servant. We found him along a trench where another battalion crouched in support, and his servant saved us the trouble by carrying him on his broad back. But we had to wait a bit, for during the next hour the trench was heavily crumped, and men were getting hit, so I had to run up and down the trench with my dressings, dressing people, most were only slight.

When I got out it was getting dusk, so I went off with a trusty man and searched for the wounded (I knew where the charge had taken place). We found most of them in a little coppice. They lay behind trees, in dug-outs, and at the bottom of trenches. They were so weak they could not call out. Their joy and relief on being found was pitiful, and fairly spurred me on to look for more. It was awful work getting some out of their trenches and dug-outs. It was hard to find men enough to carry them away. I had to appeal for volunteers – but they were dead beat. Finally, at dawn, we got our last men away from a very advanced point, at four in the morning. Altogether, we had collected fifteen men behind the trenches, and were certain (pretty well) that none were left.

On getting back to the dump, we found that the RAMC had failed us, and had not carried any of our wounded back. I had about twenty-five on my hands, but fatigue parties took pity on the poor chaps, and carried all away one by one – except eleven. Then I set to work to dress those we had carried in, got them arranged along the mud wall, and then fell asleep sitting on a petrol tin.

All that day Noel had to look after his eleven wounded, trying to shelter them from the sun under the mud wall. But his sense of duty drove him to make another tour of the trenches, and then, as soon as dark fell, he wriggled out with another officer from the regiment to the Jack Johnson hole in no man's land where a wounded man was known to be lying:

When we crawled into the hole I found that it was an officer, such a nice chap, with a broken thigh, you bet he was glad to see us. The other officer went back to get the stretcher, and the poor wounded chap put his hands in mine, and we sat in the JJ

> hole, holding hands like kids. Then we got him onto the stretcher, and ran him back to the trench, where many willing hands helped to lift him in.
>
> And then I went to see another bit in front of another part of our trenches. The Engineers were out already, putting up barbed wire, and they had searched the ground thoroughly, but we carried back a poor chap from another regiment.
>
> I was beat then for a bit, but a dash of brandy made me feel fine. So I did one more little crawl to search some dug-outs in front of another part of our line, but only found dead Germans . . . Arrived at the camp at 5 am, and slept for twelve hours. And after a meal felt as fit as ever I did in my life, but dreadfully saddened. I am missing jolly faces everywhere, and it was dreadful to see great big fellows strewn on the ground as cannon fodder.

For that epic display of courage and endurance Noel was awarded the Military Cross – but when the award was announced at a church parade on 27 June, he kept away, and according to Private Finlay of the Liverpool Scottish, he was 'later found in a little wood, weeping'.[6] The regiment's commanding officer had recommended several men for decorations, but by some awful mischance his list was lost, with the result that announcement of the awards was delayed for months. In the end four members of the battalion received the Distinguished Conduct Medal and ten the Military Medal for their heroism in an action which, in spite of its cost, won high praise from the Major-General Commanding. Noel's MC was promulgated on 14 January 1916, but because of the lost recommendations, no citation for it was issued.

A few days' leave gave him a severely needed respite at home, and he returned to Belgium on 9 July, full of plans for increasing his men's health and comfort. Using money contributed by well-wishers, he asked his parents to send out magazines, twenty-four copies of the *Liverpool Evening Echo* every day, sixpenny books, a Primus stove and a prayer book he had left behind in the pocket of his suit during his last visit: 'I value it very much as I have buried so many men with it'. Locally, he bought potatoes, which the men loved making into chips with their home-made cookers in the dug-outs, and he established 'a recreation room with magazines, three stoves, tea and buns'.

The strain of war had made him value religion more highly than ever, and he drew particular strength from properly structured services, once writing, 'The Holy Communion is the best steady and comfort to the nerves that I know.' Bad preachers annoyed him intensely – he described one visiting padre as 'socially poisonous as ever, and his voice a disease' – but whenever he could, he laid on a service for his men.

In July the battalion again spent many days in the front line, and Noel had many wounded to succour. In August one of his men was hit in the mouth by a shell splinter, and he described how he sat in a trench 'very happily stitching him up':

> His lip was very badly cut in several places, right through, but after pulling out two teeth and bits of broken bone I began putting in stitches here and there, and was surprised as well as pleased when slowly a mouth reappeared from the ragged mess.

When he was elevated to captain, he dismissed the promotion as routine, and signifying no special merit ('there is no glory attached to it. Existence is the only qualification'). Nevertheless, he was glad of the extra pay, which was backdated six months. As he was the only doctor who had been with a battalion since November 1914, he became senior medical officer of the brigade.

During the autumn fresh drafts of men sent from England gradually restored the Liverpool Scottish to full strength, and at the end of September the battalion was detailed to take part in an attack at Sanctuary Wood, just south of Hooge. Once more a massacre ensued, and Noel again pitched into rescue work with superhuman devotion, made all the more remarkable by the fact that for much of the time he was risking his life to save men from units other than his own. His account of the attack had a rare immediacy:

> The trench first led through a dreadful wood. The trees, stark and blasted, dripped with rain. Straggling briars were the only

vegetation. The ground was pocked with shell holes, through which poured muddy water. A smell of death hung on the damp air. Bullets snapped among the splintered and blasted trees, and every now and then a shell fell and burst somewhere.

We hurried on, picking our way by spasms of light, and suddenly found the trench ended in a large shell hole, in which floated the body of a Highlander. A Highlander limping back from the trenches – the only thing near us – pointed out our direction, and we emerged from the wood, and saw before us a muddy, shell-stricken rise of clay, on the ridge of which were our trenches.

I have described the place in detail, because by many it is supposed to be the dreariest and most dreadful spot in the whole of that desolation of abomination called the firing line. It is indeed the Valley of the Shadow of Death. Bunyan alone could describe its weird horror. It fairly grips the heart.

All that night Noel crept and crawled about, searching the shattered trenches for wounded, some of whom were 'pitiful beyond words', treating them as best he could and sending them back 'down the stricken slope, through the dismal wood to the dug-out dressing-station'. At 0400 he went up to the most advanced trenches of all, still in search of casualties, and it was there that he saw his first live German – 'a wild Hun in his lair' – so close in front that he thought it must be one of his own men. He was soon disabused of this idea when a sniper sent three bullets cracking past his head – but this did not stop him organising a party of men to carry boxes of grenades up to the front line. This was the nearest he came to acting as an infantry soldier, and he did it, he reported, because he feared that if the supply of grenades was interrupted for a moment, the line would be overrun.

His conduct that night brought him a Mention in Despatches. Once again his luck had matched his fortitude and devotion, and once again he emerged from hell with his nerve intact.

In February 1916 he managed to get a few days' leave in England, and he spent some of them at Barnt Green. Now that his Uncle Tom had died – from complications after a hunting accident –

there was nobody to inhibit his courtship of his cousin Gladys, for whom his affection had been steadily growing. Indeed, her mother Frances and sister Esme positively encouraged the couple's relationship by leaving them unchaperoned for some of the time – and when Noel returned to the war, his emotions were thoroughly stirred up. He had fallen deeply in love, and yet, crippled by the strict confines of Edwardian morality, he had not told Gladys as much.

Now, writing to Marjorie, he shot off a volley of questions. 'Can you please tell me where I stand [*vis-à-vis* Gladys] and what I ought to do to make things square and happy? . . . Do the parents object much? . . . What are G's feelings, for I don't want to hurt them?' As always, he was a model of restraint and self-effacement, and on 12 March he rehearsed his problems to his parents:

> I wonder if Marjorie told you that I wrote to Gladys and told her that I would not propose to her but that I loved her, and that if
> (1) I got home sound
> (2) I got a home (having now no prospects) and
> (3) If she had not by then married a better man,
>
> 'Barkis was willing.'[7]
>
> I did this for two reasons.
>
> (1) So that if I died Gladys might know that I did love her, in case she might marry just anybody because she thought I did not care for her.
>
> If a good man is going to come along, perhaps that will be best . . . But I don't want to see her go off with a rotter and I certainly don't want her to be unhappy. I have said nothing so far, for things are so uncertain –
>
> 1. I might not get back, and if I do I may not be a whole man.
> 2. If I do get back whole I shall have to settle down and get a living and perhaps I may think I ought to be a missionary or a clergyman.
>
> So you see it is very hard. I would like to tell the girl all this,

> but I don't want to make her unsettled, and if she only likes me in a cousinly sort of way, I would let well alone. If there is more, then I think I ought to do something. So if you have got anything to tell me I would very much like to know.

Marjorie soon unravelled the knot, writing to Gladys and to Noel, who then felt able to declare his love more fully. Even though he did not make a formal proposal, Gladys responded enthusiastically, promising that she would wait for him whatever happened, and his parents readily gave him their blessing. Writing back to them, he said that he was trying 'in a blundering sort of way' to make himself 'a proper husband and I hope some day a father'.

> The danger is in making Gladys my religion, but I seem to love my poor men, and to feel for them more than ever. But at last I have a great longing to get through with the war, before I never thought about it. I hope it will not tempt me to neglect my duty. I expect from this letter you will see that I am in love, but then I have been for years, but might not say so.

His happiness would have been unbounded – 'I feel quite in the air with delight,' he told Chris – had not a family tragedy occurred at that very moment. Gladys's brother Arthur had also qualified as a doctor, and had joined the RAMC. Early in February 1915 he was working at the General Hospital in Abbeville, but then he fell ill with a chest infection and went into hospital at Le Havre, where he died of pneumonia on 12 March. His mother and Gladys, who had arrived in France the day before, were with him at the end. Noel felt his death as 'a terrible blow', which left a gap in his own life.

In April, getting unexpected leave to go to London for the presentation of his medal, he sent agitated instructions to his parents:

> I want Gladys to come to meet me in London . . . Now could Marjorie chaperone Gladys to London . . .? It is very hard to know what to do, so please tell me what you advise, but don't give too much cold, dispassionate judgement. Please remember

> what I am feeling like. I want to see my maid for as long as I possibly can.

For various reasons, his April leave was deferred, but he did get some in May, and then, back in the war zone, he had time to look ahead:

> I sometimes feel very worried about what will happen after the war . . . I feel certain I ought to have been a doctor, and was meant to fight in this battalion. I know that Gladys and I were meant for each other, but I cannot see forward at all clearly. Of course it is silly to think of these things – but is it silly really? It is planning and trying to prepare for after the war that keeps one cheerful and calm out here.

Even if he now had a long-term goal, and a new determination to survive the war, he continued to act exactly as before, with the same disregard of his own safety – and never more so than in the Liverpool Scottish's next major engagement, the attack on Guillemont, which began at dawn on 8 August 1916 as part of the terrible battle of the Somme. After being held in reserve until that night, the battalion followed up earlier assaults with four successive charges, but everything went disastrously wrong, and casualties were devastating. Of twenty officers, five were killed, five went missing and seven were wounded. Of nearly 600 other ranks, sixty-nine were dead, twenty-seven missing and 167 wounded. Almost half the regiment had been cut down.

As always during and after a battle, Noel was out with his stretcher-bearers all night and all day, his task made even more disagreeable than usual by the prevalence of flies, and the fact that many wounds were full of maggots. Afterwards, he described how they had collected a lot of identification discs, 'and so cut down the tragic missing list', how they found three badly wounded men lying within 25 yards of the German line, and how grenades had been thrown at them from close range; but his own account of his actions was extremely modest, and it was left to others to relate what he had done. Private Frederick Jackson remembered how

> That night, Dr Chavasse went out into no-man's land with his devoted stretcher-bearers, looking for wounded men and bringing them in. The amazing thing about this rescue exploit was that he carried and used his electric torch as he walked about between the trenches, whistling and calling out to wounded men to indicate their whereabouts, and so be brought in. Ignoring the snipers' bullets and any sporadic fusillade, he carried on with his work of succour throughout the hours of darkness.[8]

Others saw him creeping from one shell hole to the next in broad daylight, and one of his stretcher-bearers, Private Edmund Herd, spoke for them all when he recorded that he was 'completely exhausted after the severe and ghastly work'. Another stretcher-bearer remembered that 'at times it was almost impossible to stand up without being hit'.

> The Captain took no more notice of the enemy's fire than he would of a few raindrops, and even when bullets were whistling all round he didn't get in the least bit flustered in his work.

Miraculously, the only casualty among the stretcher party was Noel himself, who was hit by two shell splinters in the flank. The wounds were slight, and he did not even realise he had sustained them until he at last undressed; but when he went to the dressing-station to have the punctures cleaned, he was so filthy that he was given an anti-tetanus injection, and he was seriously annoyed at being ordered not to go back to work. 'It is absolutely nothing,' he assured his parents. 'The merest particle of shell just pricked me' – but for once a marked deterioration in his handwriting betrayed the stress he was suffering.

Forbidden to leave the dressing-station, he spent the next night treating casualties brought in by his stretcher-bearers, but felt that 'dispatching parties seems a disaster instead of leading them'. He did slip out once in search of a wounded officer, but was 'found out and admonished. I feel just as if I had been gated.'

A spell of sick-leave enabled him to see Gladys again, but nearly two months passed before he heard the momentous news that he had been recommended for the Victoria Cross. Typically, he told his father that 'recommending is not getting', and that he would adopt the attitude of a Doubting Thomas until he saw the award in print. But the VC was his. For their gallantry during the action at Guillemont, two of his sixteen stretcher-bearers had won the Distinguished Conduct Medal and two the Military Medal, and on 26 October 1916 his own award was announced in the *London Gazette*, 'for the most conspicuous bravery and devotion to duty'. The citation read as follows:

> During an attack he tended the wounded in the open all day, under heavy fire, frequently in view of the enemy. During the ensuing night he searched for wounded on the ground in front of the enemy's lines for four hours. Next day he took one stretcher-bearer to the advanced trenches and, under heavy fire, carried an urgent case for 500 yards into safety, being wounded in the side by a shell-splinter during the journey.
>
> The same night he took a party of trusty volunteers, rescued three wounded men from a shell-hole twenty-five yards from the enemy's trench, buried the bodies of two officers, and collected many identity discs, although fired on by bombs and machine-guns. Altogether he saved the lives of some twenty badly-wounded men, besides the ordinary cases which passed through his hands. His courage and self-sacrifice were beyond praise.

Letters of congratulation poured in at such a rate that, even trying to answer ten a day, he could not keep up with the flood – and another deluge landed on his parents at the Bishop's Palace in Liverpool. Well-wishers arrived at the house in droves. In a glowing tribute the *Liverpool Daily Post & Mercury* reported:

> Few have inspired such wonderful affection for themselves amongst the ranks of their colleagues. Letters from the front have constantly told how eager he was, how ready to expose

himself to dangers beyond those called for in the discharge of his duties, and how many a wounded soldier has brightened under the radiance of his cheery disposition . . . His battalion regard him almost as their mascot.[9]

On 28 October his fellow officers threw a grand celebration dinner in the château at Elverdinghe, where they were billeted behind the lines. The menu included turtle soup, curried prawns, fillets of beef with asparagus, fruit salad and 'Macarrons au Gratin', besides sherry, champagne, port and liqueurs. The menu survives, decorated with pencil-and-ink drawings depicting highlights of Noel's service.

It seems ironic that, at the height of his fame and popularity, he fell out with senior officers of the RAMC, first by complaining about the poor performance of the Field Ambulance Service, which had often let him down, and second by his stance on the growing problem of venereal disease, which he thought should be brought under control by moral instruction rather than by physical countermeasures or the provision of sanctioned brothels. The result was that he incurred the wrath of senior officers, and as a form of rebuke he was sent for a spell to a field ambulance, and then on a basic course in sanitation – a subject in which he had had infinitely more practical experience than his instructors. Both attachments took him away from his beloved battalion, and he missed it badly.

That Christmas he could not get leave, but even as he organised a special dinner for his stretcher-bearers in the little town of Poperinghe, his mind was ranging ahead, and to his sister Dot, who was already married with two children, he wrote:

> I wonder if next Christmas my wife and I will come and spend the day with you, or shall I have to go to my wife's home? Anyway, what bedroom shall you give us? When Chris has a wife too there will be a lot of jealousy as to who gets the best spare room.

With 5 February 1917 fixed as the day for the presentation of his VC by King George V, he at last got leave, and spent some days in

Liverpool, some with Gladys and her mother at Barnt Green. At his behest Marjorie had bought a ring set with three diamonds, which he happily presented, and when he went to Buckingham Palace for his investiture, he was accompanied by no fewer than four women: Gladys, her younger sister Esme, their mother and Marjorie. They, however, had to wait outside the palace gates for two hours in freezing weather while the ceremony took place, and Noel's own description of the event was rather cool: he told his parents that it 'passed off all right', and that 'the King seemed to be quite sincere and was certainly very kind'. Typically he added, 'There were seven of us up there, four being NCOs and men, and these had really performed marvels.' Later he gave the monarch a better rating, saying, 'What a man! I could readily die for him.'

In the early months of 1917 the Liverpool Scottish had a relatively quiet time, which Noel used to make still further improvements in his arrangements for maintaining hygiene. The return of spring refreshed his spirits, and he delighted in the song of blackbirds, thrushes and larks:

> I cannot tell you how very much the singing of birds affects me out here. It is quite uplifting, in the rather mournful surroundings it gives a feeling of hope. I suppose we must be nearing the end of the war now. I hope so, even if it will be a bloody business, it cannot be any worse than what, in God's mercy, we have already been through.

Then in June he received a letter which unsettled him. It came from a doctor at the base hospital, where the surgeon Douglas Crawford, whose houseman he had been at the Royal Southern Hospital in Liverpool before the war, was working. It invited him to apply for the post of surgeon, which was vacant. 'It is a great temptation,' he told his parents.

> I could use all I have learnt at orthopaedic surgery, and rub up my surgery again under Mr Crawford, so that at the end of the war I shall be a skilled surgeon instead of having to learn it all again, and of course it would look well on future testimonials.

> But it is too comfortable. Such jobs are for the elder men, young fellows like myself ought to be with the fighting men. And I am by no means done yet, in fact I am settling down to this mode of living as my life work, and don't look now for the end. And I don't think I could leave the young lads here to fight it out while I luxuriated in a coast town. The infantry lad does not want to get hurt or killed any more than I do . . . yet he has to stick it out. So why should not I, who as it is have a softer time than they? And although, actually, medicine is nil, yet one has boundless chances of helping men, if one wants to. And really the wounded, the sick, and weary, slogging, anxious infantry soldier do make a tremendous appeal to all the best in a man.

For a few days he struggled with his conscience, then decided that he had 'better stay with the lads', and did not apply for the job, after which he felt rather depressed 'for about ¼ hour'. Thus he remained with the battalion as spring turned into summer, and he was still with them at the beginning of July, when training began for a monumental new offensive – the attack on the ridge above the village of Passchendaele.

Inevitably, he was thinking more and more of his own future, and decided that if the war did not 'get over any quicker', he would 'take time by the forelock and get married somewhere about Xmas'. He seems to have had a great wish to father a child, for in the same letter home he remarked, 'It's a bit pathetic to have to leave a bronze cross to a nephew or a cousin twice removed. I don't think I really earned it, as many have had to do, but deep in me I prize it more than I can say.' Gladys, if anything, was even keener on a quick marriage: she and Esme decided to give up nursing at their mother's hospital so that they could both go to Paris and do voluntary work at the Gare du Nord, and without telling Noel she applied for a special licence that would enable her to be married in France.

In July, as preparations for the Passchendaele offensive went forward, the family received good and bad news. The good tidings were that Chris had been recommended for a DSO, for his outstanding courage in rescuing wounded men at Bullecourt in France (in the event he received not a DSO, but an MC); the bad news was that their youngest brother Aidan was missing, wounded in fighting at Observatory Ridge, close to Hooge. His brother Bernard (also a doctor) had made heroic efforts to find him in no man's land, and his parents clung to the hope that he was alive and had been taken in by the Germans: only in February 1918 did they accept that he must be dead. (Such was Bernard's conduct at Passchendaele that he, too, was recommended for a VC; but in the end he received an MC.)

Meanwhile Noel had been swept into the Liverpool Scottish's latest action, and one of its most desperate. Even before the battalion reached its allotted position for the assault on the Passchendaele ridge, it suffered numerous casualties from gas and shell attacks. Then, on the night of 29 July, as twenty-five officers and 475 other ranks moved up to their assembly positions in a five-hour march, a torrential thunderstorm broke over them, drenching everybody and turning the tracks to liquid mud.

Battalion headquarters was set up in the Wieltje dugout, a deep and extensive subterranean complex. By Zero Hour – 0350 on 31 July – the Scottish were already out in the open, and they advanced north-eastwards behind a creeping artillery barrage, first downhill to the Steenbeke stream, then up the gentle slope opposite, with the enemy withdrawing in full view ahead of them. In spite of heavy machine-gun fire, they made rapid progress, quickly reaching their first objective, the Blue Line, and then their second, the Black Line, by 0900. Battalion headquarters moved forward from the big dugout to Bossaert Farm, and Noel established his regimental aid post at Setques Farm, a collection of ruined buildings a couple of hundred yards to the south. The area proved so hot that the headquarters moved yet again, but Noel remained where he was, in a small captured German dugout with room for only six or seven men.

The place offered relatively poor protection, for it had been designed to face the Allied lines, and now the front had leapfrogged it, so that German fire was coming in from its undefended side. Early in the attack, as Noel stood up to wave men in to the aid post, he was hit in the head by a shell splinter. Whether or not his skull was fractured – as his brother Chris believed it was – he managed to walk back to the dressing-station in the Wieltje dugout and have the wound dressed. Told to stay there until he could be taken back to the casualty clearing station for further treatment, he refused, and returned to his own little station closer to the action.

There, throughout the day, he treated the wounded brought in by stretcher-bearers. There was so little space that, as soon as a man had been patched up, he had to be sent out to take cover in one of the nearby trenches, or in shell craters among the shattered farm buildings, and wait there for the relative safety of darkness before being evacuated. When dark fell, Noel took his torch and went out to search for wounded on the torn-up ground ahead – not, strictly speaking, no man's land, for the Germans had been pushed back, but an exceedingly dangerous area, continuously pounded by enemy artillery and by Allied shells that fell short.

At about 2000 hours heavy rain set in, and the downpour continued through the night. Trenches became ditches, filled halfway to the brim with mud and water, in which men simply had to stand and shiver. Outside the aid post a queue of injured men stood wretchedly in the rain, awaiting their turn for treatment, while the doctor and his helpers (one of them a captured German) worked frantically to clean and dress wounds. Noel had one last miraculous escape when an incoming shell missed him by inches, hurtled down the stairs of the dugout and killed a man waiting to be evacuated.

Such was the noise and confusion that different people later gave different accounts of what happened during that awful day. But it seems clear that Noel was again hit in the head by shrapnel, at least once, and that from then on he was in severe pain. Even so, he refused to go back, insisting that he carry on treating other wounded men. A stretcher-bearer sent to fetch him found him sitting at a table, with his feet and ankles in six inches of water, and a bandage round his head. Still refusing to desert his post, he told his would-be rescuers to take someone else.

Then at about 0300 in the morning of 2 August another shell penetrated the dugout, killing or incapacitating everyone inside. Noel received four or five splinter wounds, the worst a big gash in his abdomen, which bled profusely. Somehow he dragged himself up the steps, into the ruined trench, and along it to the lane leading back to Wieltje. On the way he stumbled into another aid post, where he examined his own wound, having insisted that the medical personnel be sent to bring down his men.

He was then quickly taken down to No. 32 Casualty Clearing Station. Next morning, 3 August, a surgeon operated to remove shell splinters, and for a while he seemed to be doing well, sedated with morphia, not in pain, and much comforted by the fact that he knew Sister Ida Leedam, the nurse who looked after him.

Before the war Ida had been on the staff of the Royal Southern Hospital in Liverpool, while Noel was the registrar there, and now they at once recognised each other. In a simple, heartfelt letter, written in pencil, which so moved his father that he had it printed and sent to members of the family, she told of his final night.

> I asked him how he felt and what kind of a day he had, he answered, very good, I feel very fit, when you have a little time write a letter for me to my girl, I will tell you what to say. So after I had fixed the other officers up I went and sat down by his bed. He changed his mind and said, 'Wait, later, Sister.'
>
> At 11 pm he became restless, pulse poor and asked me not to leave him . . . At 3 am [4 August] pulse much worse, still more restless but cheerful. At 4 am became worse. The MO coming in every hour.
>
> These are the last words he ever spoke to me. 'Sister, write that letter for me,' which I did and sent to Miss G. Chavasse. 'Give her my love, tell her duty called and called me to obey. Take care of Aidan, Sister, if ever he comes to you, try and find him and let Father know all about him.'
>
> What about your father, I said. The Colonel will write to him [he said], but when you get leave go round and see him. Give him my love and tell him about everything. It will be better than writing and you live in the same town. Poor dear Father, he loves his boys, and we are causing him a great deal of pain, with all his hard work, but cheer him, Sister, tell him I am quite happy . . .

At 4.30 am the Chaplain came in and your son asked me what he was doing. I told him, bringing Communion to a sick officer who had asked him. 'Sister, it is up with me. I would like to have the same.'

So I went up and brought Padre Hill to him and at 5 am he made his last Communion on earth, and when it was all over he said, 'Do not forget what I have told you.' He became very quiet until 10.00 am and then wandering and restless, his men always in his thoughts, and passed away 1 pm the same day . . .

He was much loved by his men, and he is mourned by the medical officer and the nursing staff as one of the finest comrades we have ever known.[10]

He was buried next day in a large field, alongside some of the men he had loved. His horse was led to the graveside, pipers played, Colonel Davidson, the commanding officer, stood by the grave and saluted, and (according to his brother Bernard, who himself had been wounded in the knee, and had come looking for him) almost all the survivors of the battalion turned out. Exhausted as they were, they were not to be denied, and Bernard wondered whether 'any such tribute was paid to any man before'. Everyone who had seen him working at Passchendaele agreed that he had been magnificent, and men were saying that on his last day he had won the Victoria Cross four times over.

The family, already tortured by uncertainty about Aidan's fate, was plunged into mourning, and an eloquent letter from Bernard, about Noel's final hours, repeatedly reduced his parents to tears. The Bishop, drawing strength from his religious conviction, replied:

Ah, my dearest boy, he was indeed a hero, and as you say justly, he was a man of valour because he was a man of God. Continually your dear Mother and I thank and glorify God for such a son and for his wonderful and beautiful life spent in helping others, and crowned at last by his noble death, for the sure and certain hope that he is with Christ.[11]

A sympathetic letter came from Lord Stamfordham, private

secretary to King George V, who wrote from Windsor Castle on behalf of the monarch:

> His Majesty sympathises truly with you in your sorrow and feels that the whole Army will mourn the loss of so brave and distinguished a brother.[12]

Senior army officers sent warm tributes, none more heartfelt than that from Brigadier General Louis Green Wilkinson, who had commanded 166 Infantry Brigade until April that year:

> I constantly met your son and appreciated his work. He was quite the most gallant and modest man I have ever met, and I should think the best liked. What he did for his battalion of Liverpool Scottish was wonderful, and his loss to them is irreparable. I do not believe a man of more noble character exists.[13]

Deluged by messages of condolence, Noel's parents could not answer them all personally; instead, they sent out a printed letter which gave an account of his last hours, and included the statement:

> In the assurance that our most dear boy is with Christ, that he laid down his life for others, and that God cannot make a mistake, lie our strength and hope . . . We know that He has our son, and that one day He will place us again at his side.[14]

The family's grief was partially assuaged by the announcement, on 14 September, that Noel had been posthumously awarded a bar to his Victoria Cross. The citation described him as 'a devoted and gallant officer', and recalled how, though severely injured early in the action at Passchendaele, he had refused to leave his post. It concluded that 'by his extraordinary energy and inspiring example he was instrumental in rescuing many wounded who would have otherwise undoubtedly succumbed under the bad weather conditions'.

Two VCs and three MCs amounted to an astonishing statement of the Chavasses' courage, humanity and patriotism. Yet Mrs Chavasse never recovered from the shocks that the war had dealt her: every year, on the anniversary of Aidan's death, she dreamt that he was calling to her from no man's land – and on the eve of the tenth anniversary, she died. Gladys, with typical Chavasse fortitude, continued her voluntary work with the Church Army both during and after the war; in 1919 she married a padre, the Reverend James Ferguson Colquhoun, but the couple had no children.

Today Noel's name is honoured in all the establishments with which he was associated, and memorials to him abound. A painting of him commissioned by his brother hangs in St Peter's College, Oxford. A house at Magdalen College School, Oxford, was named after him, and there is a Chavasse House at Liverpool College. In Liverpool the family's name is everywhere. His medals, presented by his family, are on permanent loan at the Imperial War Museum in London.

Inevitably, the person who felt his death most keenly was his twin. Chris was eighty miles from Passchendaele at the moment his brother died, but somehow he knew what had happened – and nearly half a century later he wrote to a friend:

> My loss of my twin was like amputation – I felt half of me had gone, for we were extremely close . . . I still mourn my Noel every day of my life, and have done so for forty-four years . . . I still seem to think over things with Noel, and to feel he might walk into the room any minute. And sometimes I wake in the morning, feeling I have been with him in my sleep – and I believe that our spirits have been together.[15]

Having survived the war, Chris devoted his life to the Church of England. In 1928, in memory of his father, he established St Peter's Hall in Oxford, and in 1942 he became Bishop of Rochester. Before that, in June 1935, at Birmingham Parish Church, he preached a memorable sermon which distilled his thoughts about Noel. The occasion was an annual parade, held in memory of soldiers who had fallen on the Somme.

'Would you forgive me,' he asked, 'if I were to say a few words about my brother?' He then described Noel's final hours, and quoted his last message to Gladys:

> 'Tell her,' he said, 'that duty called, and duty must be obeyed.'
>
> How does that sound to you? Heroic enough, and yet rather terrible and inhuman? But it was not. What he termed duty was simply the call of humanity, which, even from a boy, had sounded very insistently at his heart. He once said to my father, 'The fact is, I can't bear to think of my boys lying out there needing me.'
>
> What do you think duty is? Duty is simply idealism put into practice. It is stern stuff, I grant you, because it is compounded of service and sacrifice, of blood and tears, but yet it is that divine alchemy that makes our dreams come true and builds the castles of our visions, not in the air, but on England's green and pleasant land.

4

Colour Sergeant John Byrne VC, DCM

1832–79

The award of a Victoria Cross by no means guarantees a recipient's happiness. On the contrary, many winners have been discomfited by the fame and publicity which the medal attracts; all too many have descended into poverty, and others have been left so disturbed by their battle experiences that they became depressed or unbalanced and were driven to suicide. Of the 1354 winners, nineteen are known to have taken their own lives, and of the 111 Crimean winners, seven did so – a percentage one hundred times greater than the national average. Looking back, it is easy to see that too much was demanded of them, and that they were given little or no support by the community.

One typical Crimean casualty was John Johnstone, a naval stoker who won a VC in August 1854 for his audacious feat of ambushing and capturing messengers from the Tsar and seizing vital dispatches. Three years later he was serving as a cook aboard HMS *Brunswick* in the West Indies when he was overcome by what the ship's log called 'a fit of temporary insanity': first he attacked one of the stokers with a razor, slashing him across the face, hands and back, and then he cut his own throat.

That was a grisly end. But to me the saga of John Byrne, another Crimean VC, is even more disturbing.

It was in the summer of 1985, when I was General Officer Commanding the British troops serving in Wales, that my regiment, the Durham Light Infantry, contacted me to say that they had recently identified the grave of Colour Sergeant John Byrne. At the battle of Inkerman on 5 November 1854 he had won the first Victoria Cross awarded to the regiment, but he had died a pauper in wretched circumstances. I was asked to head a small group, including Lieutenant Colonel John Arnott, the Regimental Secretary, to refurbish his grave in St Woolos cemetery in Newport, and then pay homage to it.

Black Forty-Seven, more commonly referred to as the Potato Famine, struck Ireland in 1847, causing death and migration on a terrible scale. Until then the Irish had lived largely on potatoes, which were cheap and nourishing and grew prolifically on their small farms. Then in 1846 and 1847 a fungal disease, imported from North America, caused the crops to rot in the ground: starvation set in, aggravated by numerous diseases, among them scurvy, dysentery, typhus and 'relapsing fever' – the last two being collectively known as 'famine fever'. The British Government was desperately slow to recognise the plight of the Irish, and mismanaged the crisis when it did – and as a result, out of a population of eight million over one million people died.

Thousands tried to escape to America in overloaded 'coffin ships', while others migrated to various parts of the United Kingdom, many of them joining the army. One of these was John Byrne.

The 68th Regiment of Foot (which in 1873 became the Durham Light Infantry) had a recruiting office in Ireland, and at one stage over 40 per cent of this great county regiment were recruited from the ranks of the Irish. They were fine fighting soldiers, and when it came to battle John Byrne was one of the finest.

No picture is known to exist of this brave soldier, and little is known of his early life, except that he was born on 27 September 1832 in Castlecomber, Kilkenny. He seems to have come from a poor family, and it is probable that he joined the army to escape the poverty at home. He is described as 5′ 7″ tall, with grey eyes, brown hair and a fresh complexion. He never married. It would appear he had little or no education, and his signature was almost illiterate when, at the age of 17 years and ten months, on 27 July 1850, he enlisted in the 68th Light Infantry at Coventry, with the service number 2832.

His career started inauspiciously, and it was not long before he found himself in trouble with the authorities for some unknown offence. This set a trend in his early military life, and in November 1853, after a court martial, he served six months in prison. He was imprisoned again from July to August 1854, but he was released early to rejoin the 68th as they embarked for garrison duties in Malta during the Crimean War.

In that conflict he fought in the battles of Alma, Balaclava, Inkerman and Sevastopol. Operations clearly suited him and satisfied his relish for adventure, challenge and the chance of a fight. The fluctuations of his early military career epitomised the combination of distinguished conduct and petty crime which persisted throughout his twenty-one years of service.

In 1854 the Russians' overwhelming aggression against the Turkish Empire provided a convenient justification for the United Kingdom and France to challenge Tsarist expansion in the Balkans and Turkey with a combined military operation. During the first six months of the year forces were assembled in the Turkish province of Bulgaria to form four infantry divisions into cavalry brigades. However, they were under-strength, and eventually it was agreed to release the 68th Light Infantry, among other units, from their duties in Malta to join the Fourth Division for the forthcoming campaign.

A huge Franco-British army numbering in all more than sixty thousand men was landed without incident in Kalamita Bay, about 25 miles north of Sevastopol. After pursuing the Russian army south towards the town and naval base, the Allied forces eventually established themselves in siege positions and settled down for what proved to be a year-long, debilitating campaign. As the two armies faced each other, neither the Russians nor the Franco-British conceded any suggestion of defeat.

The battle positions and tactics adopted were not dissimilar to those developed in the trenches during the First World War, with stalemate prevailing and each side mounting irregular patrols and sorties against the enemy. It was in these conditions that Byrne won his Victoria Cross.

The Russians made six major attempts to break up the Franco-British positions, including a full-scale attack in early November 1854, when they launched a massive, two-corps assault, deploying over fifty thousand men. A major battle raged near Inkerman Ridge, including a day of vicious close-quarters fighting. The 68th were sent to reinforce other British troops threatened with being overrun, and in their enthusiasm they overstretched themselves and were ordered to withdraw, while French reinforcements moved forward to cover them.

In swirling fog, with winter setting in, the Durhams fought a gallant if somewhat chaotic withdrawal. Not only was the weather icy and damp: their logistic support was gravely deficient, and having initially held the Russian assault, they suffered such severe casualties that they had to begin withdrawing from their positions before the French arrived.

After the issue of further ammunition they attempted to recover as many casualties as possible, and it was at this juncture that Private John Byrne, lately released from detention, excelled himself. When his company was finally ordered to retreat, he, together with Sergeant Daniel Dwyer, returned on his own initiative towards the Russian lines under heavy small-arms and artillery fire and recovered one Private Harmon who had been left behind wounded. Byrne did this at great personal risk and the possible sacrifice of his own life, and in contradiction to his orders to pull back to relative safety. The sergeant and two other privates vouched for his action, and although no award was available to him at the time, his name, together with Dwyer's, was later put forward for the award of a Victoria Cross. (It should be remembered that the medal was not promulgated by Queen Victoria until 1856, but was then back-dated to include the Crimean campaign.)

Byrne's fighting spirit was in no way spent as a result of his Inkerman experience. On 13 January 1855, in a minor skirmish, he was slightly wounded in the foot, although little is known of this action, and he stood out once more towards the end of the siege of Sevastopol on 11 May 1855.

That day he was again involved in a savage fight. During the night, in the middle of a storm, a large Russian force had attacked the British trenches near Woronzoff Road, which were held by just two companies of the 68th. The assault was eventually driven off, but only after fierce hand-to-hand fighting. In one contest, Byrne struggled in the dark and driving rain with a Russian soldier on the parapet of a trench, before bayoneting him and capturing his musket – 'an example of bravery the consequence of which was the speedy repulse of the sortie'.[1]

It was recognised that his action made a positive contribution to the outcome of the engagement, and there is no doubt that his consistent gallantry throughout the campaign influenced the decision that, despite his poor disciplinary record, he should receive the first Victoria Cross awarded to a soldier of the DLI.

This, however, was by no means the end of his courageous service. He continued to serve with the 68th, and in 1861 he was raised to the rank of corporal – a promotion which undoubtedly reflected his distinguished operational performance and presumably rather more disciplined behaviour.

For the ten years after Inkerman the 68th led a quiet and uneventful existence, much of it in Burma. The Crimean War had initiated many changes within the army, and modern young officers, although admiring the warriors who had fought at Inkerman and Sevastopol, felt that many of them had been left in the past. A newly commissioned subaltern of the 68th, joining at Fermoy, was quoted as saying:

> Nearly all the older officers had seen service in the Crimean War, which was then only a recent event. The majority of them were splendid fellows: that long siege had been a wonderful school for the forming of manly characters. They had a type and manner of their own. Their hair was not cut short, as in the present day, but was worn long over the ears: and they had large fuzzy whiskers with moustaches that went straight into

them. They smoked much and some of them drank a good deal but they carried their liquor well'.[2]

The other ranks were of the same robust stamp.

It is reasonable to assume that in peacetime Corporal Byrne managed to contain his aggression. No doubt to his delight, he faced further action when, towards the end of 1863, the battalion unexpectedly sailed from Rangoon to New Zealand and arrived in Auckland during January 1864 to reinforce the overstretched British forces engaged in the Maori Wars.

Barely two decades had passed since the British had occupied New Zealand, where they had adopted a policy of purchasing Maori tribal land, often at absurdly low prices. Disputes led to inevitable confrontations, from which the Maori Wars developed and ran for a quarter of a century until 1871. Calumny by the British, combined with tribal dissension among the warlike natives, proved a recipe for fierce engagements; but despite their superiority of weapons and organisation, the British did not have it all their own way.

Intelligent and always ready for a scrap, the Maoris could be depended upon to defend their possessions with courage and without fear of death. Having suffered immense duplicity at the hands of the British settlers and the army, they were ready to fight like demons when they found that the agreements they had made, for retaining their land and selling it if they wished to, were consistently abused.

In 1863 there had been a series of critical confrontations south of Auckland – at that time a town of wooden houses with a population of about 14,000. General Cameron, the General Officer Commanding, had urgently requested reinforcements, and hence the 68th, among others, were dispatched from Burma.

The Maoris were redoubtable combatants, who offered all the fighting skill and aggression that the Russians had been able to throw at Byrne and his companions during the Crimean War. Despite their lack of the sophisticated weapons and artillery available to the British, in terms of courage and individual fighting qualities they wanted nothing. They were experts at guerrilla and bush warfare, and Light Infantry units such as the 68th found their flexible tactics hard to combat (the British in turn had to modernise their tactics in this war). On one occasion, as General Cameron followed up his elusive opponents and cornered a group in a *pa* (a fort or fieldwork), the Maori chief sent him a message: 'The word of the Maori is, we will fight for ever and ever and ever.' He was told, 'Send away the women', to which the response came, 'The women will fight too.'[3]

The 68th were deployed to an important forward base at Tauranga Harbour in the Bay of Plenty, south-east of Auckland, where the battalion received a new commanding officer, one Lieutenant Colonel Greer, aged forty and already with twenty-one years of military service behind him. He had the added distinction of being an Irishman, with, it is reported, a hot temper and an independent mind. He was described by some as a despot and typical of many senior officers of his day. However in battle he proved a redoubtable and decisive commander, leading the 68th to several victories. Byrne will have taken part in them all, and once again distinguished himself.

Their initial deployment was to Te Pa Pa Mission, the forward base for British troops operating out of Auckland, on a spit of land in Tauranga Harbour. This promontory joined the mainland at a narrow neck where the Maoris had established themselves at the Gate Pa, or Pukehinahinia. Being skilled engineers, they constructed their bases in key tactical positions, generally forming an intricate network of trenches surrounding the centre, where their flag flew. They defended these redoubts with determination and courage, evacuating them and disappearing into the bush only if they were overwhelmed.

The Gate Pa was just such a position, sealing the peninsula from the mainland and the Te Ranga mountains. On 29 April, while other troops created a diversion, the 68th surrounded the position during the night, and surprise was achieved. After a lengthy exchange of fire and an artillery bombardment, the British, supported by a mixed force of seamen from HMS *Curacao*, attempted to assault the strongpoint during the day. However, the Maoris beat off the attack before filtering away into the Te Ranga range, carrying many of their dead and wounded. They lost about twenty-five men killed, but the 68th also suffered over twenty casualties.

Encouraged by their relative success, the Maoris regrouped in the mountains and posed a threat to Colonel Greer and his men during the South Pacific winter months of May and June. Over six hundred native warriors formed up, and Greer decided to move out of Gate Pa, which he had occupied after the bloody April battle, to attack them in the foothills. The Maoris put up a spirited resistance from temporary defences, and the 68th lost several officers and men in the initial assault, which developed into bloody hand-to-hand fighting.

Corporal Byrne was one of the first over the top, no doubt fired up by memories of his Crimean battles as he dived into the midst of the Maori weapon pits. Relying on his bayonet as a primary weapon, he managed to 'spit' his first opponent, but the Maori grabbed his rifle, despite the bayonet sticking in his body. A mortal struggle ensued, with Byrne facing imminent death when Sergeant John Murray came to his rescue.

Murray, also relying on his bayonet, had launched himself into the trenches, and in ferocious fighting had already killed over eight of the enemy when he saw Byrne in trouble. He rushed across to his rescue, stalling the tomahawk assault and saving his colleague's life. The gallantry and prowess he displayed in this battle were so distinguished that he too was later awarded the Victoria Cross, the third member of the 68th to gain this distinction.

Byrne's leadership and inspiration at the heart of the assault made a significant contribution to the success of the day: he again proved himself an outstanding fighting soldier, and was awarded the second-highest honour for bravery, the Distinguished Conduct Medal, making him one of the most decorated soldiers of his time. His achievement was all the more remarkable in that it came in an era when other-ranks rarely gained recognition in battle.

Greer's troops finally carried the day: the Maoris were driven into the hinterland, and tranquillity settled on Tauranga, although the war continued elsewhere. Thanks to Byrne and Murray, the 68th of Foot enjoyed the unique distinction of having its first holder of the Victoria Cross, gained at Inkerman, rescued by a sergeant in his own regiment at a battle 11 years later, for which the sergeant also won the Victoria Cross.

Byrne continued to serve, and was eventually promoted to sergeant in 1866, when he transferred to Queen's County Militia in Ireland. Later he returned to the 68th, but once again peacetime soldiering did not suit his temperament and in 1872, shortly after his promotion to colour sergeant, he was court-martialled and discharged with ignominy for an unrecorded offence. Such setbacks notwithstanding, he suited the army, and the army suited him, and the happiest days of his relatively short but full life were undoubtedly those when he served with the 68th.

Despite his court martial he was permitted to retain his Victoria Cross, although there is no record of the medal's whereabouts today. (It is possible that it was buried with him. The Durham Light Infantry Museum holds his New Zealand Campaign Medal.) There is no doubt that the VC brought him great pride and pleasure – and indeed he eventually gave his life in defence of its honour.

On his discharge in 1872 he went home to Ireland, but then returned to England, and in 1878 appeared in Bristol, destitute, and claiming to have lost all his possessions in a fire. At forty-six he was already regarded as too old to get a job, but in view of his distinguished service he was taken on by the Ordnance Survey, working as a labourer at Newport in Monmouthshire. It was there in 1879 that he met his fate.

He was drinking in a pub when a lad of nineteen called John Watts insulted him, and in particular made disparaging remarks about the Victoria Cross. Byrne took this as an insult to the Queen and to the award, and turned on Watts, calling him a 'cur puppy'. There the row might have ended – but later in the day the two met again, and this time Byrne pulled a Bulldog revolver from his pocket and shot Watts in the right shoulder. He then held the revolver to his own ear, but without firing it put it back into his pocket, smiled at his companions and walked away to his lodgings at 7 Crown Street, Maindy, where he was living in a room of a house owned by Mrs Eliza Morgan, a widow. He told Mrs Morgan that he would not be coming out of the house any more that day.

Later the police arrived. When Sergeant Thomas McGrath, together with Police Constable Conway, sought to interview him over the shooting of Watts, he initially refused to come out of his room, telling them through the door that he would do so at three o'clock. When the hour came round he failed to appear, and a minor siege developed. Eventually the police, by now led by Inspector Shepperd, broke into his room, telling him that his time had come, and at that moment he put his revolver to his mouth and pulled the trigger. His death certificate recorded that he had 'shot himself when in an unsound state of mind'.

John Byrne, VC, DCM, was buried in St Woolos cemetery, outside Newport, in a pauper's grave. A hero who had given so much for his country and his regiment, he lay forgotten for over a century – but at least he had been interred in a place with strong historical connotations.

Legend handed down by monks has it that Earl Harold (later King of England) burst into the church of St Woolos, hell-bent on destroying it, only to see a huge cheese resting on the altar. When he slashed at it with his sword, to his horror blood spurted out, and he fled: the church was saved, but the omen presaged Harold's death at the Battle of Hastings, where his defeat by the Normans determined the future history of England.

For centuries Newport flourished, but by the 1850s the graveyard of the church could accommodate no more burials, and so the first municipal cemetery in Britain was opened to the west of the city, away from any supply of drinking water which it might pollute, the very year in which Byrne had won his VC. There he was buried in 1878, but by the 1980s his grave had fallen into disrepair, his headstone had vanished, and the DLI, commendably enough, decided that it should be replaced.

So it was that a short ceremony was held on 4 November 1985, when Councillor T. C. Warren, the mayor of Newport, with Bugler Roberts of 7th Light Infantry and a small group of DLI representatives in attendance, gathered round St Woolos's Block 14 E 15. After a short address and prayers given by Father Fenwick, a former Territorial officer, I saluted the grave and had the privilege of laying a wreath below the new headstone. As I stood back, I hoped that in death Byrne might have found the peace and comfort denied him in life.

He was typical of many outstanding soldiers who are at their best in the close-knit society of the army and under the tight code of discipline that governs service existence. Without these props, he lacked the self-discipline and control to run his life effectively. He was certainly a wild Irishman, but he was also an extremely brave soldier who risked his life on many occasions for Queen and Country, and stood out among his contemporaries on the battlefield.

In his day the Victoria Cross was not held in the regard and respect that it is accorded today, but his story emphasises the ease with which sacrifices made in battle are forgotten once the priorities of conflict are overtaken by those of the ensuing peace.

5

Captain Albert Ball VC, DSO and two Bars, MC

1896–1917

As an example of sustained courage, displayed over many months in the face of acute danger, the record of Captain Albert Ball, Royal Flying Corps, will surely never be surpassed. By the time he was killed at the age of only twenty on 7 May 1917, he had destroyed or forced down nearly seventy German aircraft, often taking on four or six opponents at a time; yet mere figures give no idea of the superhuman determination with which he fought for Britain.

In character and behaviour he was anything but flamboyant, yet in the dark days of 1916 and 1917 he fired the whole of the Royal Flying Corps with new hope. 'Ball was a quiet, simple little man,' wrote his fellow pilot Cecil Lewis. 'He never boasted or criticised, but his example was tremendous.'[1] Another colleague, Roderic Hill, reckoned that he was 'evidently the offspring of a vixen and a lion', and that he 'did the work of a whole squadron by himself'.[2] He had no blood-lust, and hated sending hostile pilots to their death; but a sense of duty far beyond the normal made him take to the skies again and again, ferociously determined to shoot down his country's enemies.

He was born at Lenton, near Nottingham, on 14 August 1896, the elder son of Albert and Harriet Ball. His father had started life as a plumber, but by the end of the century he had risen to become an estate agent, with an office in Nottingham, and a councillor for the Castle ward of the city. Later he became a Justice of the Peace, was four times Mayor of Nottingham, and in the New Year Honours list of 1924 was knighted in recognition of his long public service.

Young Albert grew up with an elder sister, Lois (Lol, to him, and his lifelong confidante), and a younger brother, Cyril, in a warm, close-knit family at their home, Sedgely House, set in a good-sized garden in the Park district of Nottingham. He had a room of his own at the top of the building, but his favourite retreat was a wooden shed round the back, where he indulged his strong mechanical bent by stripping and rebuilding petrol engines and fiddling with electrical gadgets like dynamos, wirelesses and Morse transmitters.

Always good-looking, with thick dark hair, he was friendly and even-tempered; but in a photograph taken when he was eight years old, steely determination is already apparent in his eyes and the set of his mouth. From an early age he was fizzing with nervous energy, eager to press ahead and get things done, and his father encouraged him in precocious new pursuits, whether it was flying kites, shooting with a revolver or driving cars and motorcycles.

After various earlier schools, in 1911, when he was fifteen, he and Cyril were both sent to Trent College, a minor public school at Long Eaton, near Nottingham, whose Spartan regime came as a shock: reveille with a bugle-call at 6.25 a.m., compulsory cold baths every morning, cross-country runs, scanty food, beatings for misbehaviour. Quickly adjusting, Albert soon mastered his new surroundings, and regular chapel-going strengthened his religious belief – something which found an echo in a letter to his mother:

> Dear Mother,
> I wish you one of the happiest birthdays and hope that it will be God's pleasure to shield and protect you and give you good health for many more years.[3]

He never showed any great interest in academic work, or had much time for team games like soccer: rather, he went in for individual pursuits that enabled him to exploit his exceptional coordination of hand, eye and brain – woodwork, metalwork, playing the violin. He built himself a boat, which he sailed home via river and canal to Nottingham, and on holiday at Skegness he put together a raft which got away from him and drifted out to sea. On the whole he enjoyed school, especially the activities of the Officer Training Corps; but one curious episode suggests that he may have felt less settled than he seemed: one day he vanished, and he was eventually found stowed away in the engine room of a steamer about to depart from the port of Liverpool.

By the time he was sixteen he had begun looking ahead beyond school. 'I am anxious to know what I shall be when I leave,' he wrote to his mother. He wanted to make money, he told her, but also to 'bring out the best' in himself, and he said he would like to find a job 'in a large electrical engineering factory where they make all kinds of machinery'.

In a further year at school he took extra maths, technical drawing and practical engineering, spurred on by his belief that there was an enormous future in the electrical business, especially in the construction of small electric light generators for country houses. He left at the end of the summer term in 1913, just past his seventeenth birthday, and found the kind of employment he had hoped for in the Universal Engineering Works, a company that made electrical equipment and did some brass-founding. As he increased his skills, he looked forward to making a career in business – but scarcely a year later hostilities broke out in Europe, and he, with his burning sense of duty, was one of the first to answer the call for volunteers.

On 1 September 1914 he enlisted as a private in the 2/7th Battalion, the Nottinghamshire and Derby Regiment, better known as the Sherwood Foresters or, colloquially, as the Robin Hoods, which was billeted in Nottingham. Because he had been a member of the OTC at school, he was promoted within days to the rank of sergeant, and at the end of October he received his commission as second lieutenant. A sturdy fellow, only 5′ 6″ tall but powerfully built, he took part in weapon-training, route-marches, field days and so on enthusiastically enough; but, along with most of his contemporaries, he yearned to be posted to the front in France.

On 1 January 1915, goaded by fear that the war might be over before he had a chance to prove himself, he obtained a secondment to the North Midlands Divisional Cyclist Company, hoping that this would accelerate his progress towards action, and he was posted to Bishop's Stortford in Hertfordshire. His letters home betrayed his impatience, but absolutely no sign of apprehension. 'It is surprising what a lot of brave fellows are killed every day,' he wrote on 24 February. 'I notice that it is mostly the best men who are killed.'

In March he received orders to join the Reserve, but still no posting came for him, and it was only in June that there was any major change in his routines. Then, it seems, pure coincidence set him on the path to fame and early death.

Posted to a platoon commanders' training course, which took place in a tented camp at Perivale, north-west of London, he found that Hendon aerodrome lay only four miles away. Its proximity turned his thoughts to flying: he was attracted partly because he thought it would be exciting, and partly because he hoped that, if he became a pilot in the Royal Flying Corps, he might reach the front in France that much quicker.

At Hendon he could take a course at one of several civilian flying schools for £75 – a large sum, and the equivalent of more than £2000 today; but if he reached a high enough standard, £60 of the fee would be returned, and he would earn a Royal Aero Club Pilot Certificate – an essential prerequisite for anyone who wanted to apply for training in the Royal Flying Corps or the Royal Naval Air Service. So, without telling his family, he paid a £10 deposit and enrolled as a trainee at the Ruffy-Baumann School at Hendon; but because this was a private initiative, he had to pursue it out of service hours, and so began a punishing schedule, getting up at 3 a.m., riding to Hendon on his motorbike, and squeezing in as much training as the weather allowed before scooting back to Perivale for the first parade at 6.45.

'I go in for a little flying now and find it great sport,' he told his family casually in a letter of 4 July – the first they had heard of his latest venture. 'Please do not be very cross with me for flying, for it means that if the country is very short of pilots, I shall be able to go.'

His main instructor was Edouard Baumann, proprietor of the school, whose flying uniform appears from contemporary photographs to have been a smartly cut tweed jacket and chequered cap. The aircraft used were very light, single-engined biplanes, in which instructor and pupil sat one behind the other in open cockpits, and they were so low-powered that they were not allowed to take off if the wind exceeded 8 mph. This meant that a frustrating number of potential sorties had to be cancelled, and Ball's training dragged on well beyond the 'few weeks' which he had optimistically predicted would be all he needed to obtain his certificate.

In August, when he finished his army course and rejoined his own platoon near St Albans, he had much farther to travel to Hendon (20 miles each way, as opposed to 4). Undaunted, he kept up his flying, sometimes riding to the airfield twice in the same day. He seems to have remained unmoved when fellow pupils were injured or killed in crashes: he recorded various accidents in his letters home, but his descriptions were almost brutal in their lack of feeling:

> Yesterday a ripping boy had a smash, and when we got up to him he was nearly dead, he had a two-inch piece of wood right through his head and died this morning. If you would like a flight I should be pleased to take you any time you wish.

At last, in October, he obtained his longed-for certificate. In a photograph taken as he finished his course at Hendon, which shows him standing proudly in front of an aircraft, kitted out in uniform and Sam Browne belt, he looks dashingly handsome; but once again, the expression in his eyes and the set of his mouth suggest controlled aggression. After further training at the Central Flying School at Upavon, in Wiltshire, and a short spell acting as an instructor at Gosport, near Southampton, he finally achieved his ambition and was posted to No. 13 Squadron in France on 17 February 1916.

The first aircraft he flew over the Continent was the slow and heavy BE2 biplane, at that date the main workhorse of the Royal Flying Corps, which had a cruising speed of 70 mph and took nearly an hour to reach its service ceiling of 10,000 feet. By the middle of 1916 there were about 185 BE2s scattered round the RFC's fields in France – nearly half the total of British aircraft deployed. Two-seaters, they carried an observer in front of the pilot, and were being used mainly for bombing, artillery observation and intelligence gathering: the pilots would fly out over the front lines to bomb or spot enemy positions, and, although they could not receive messages on their primitive radios, they could sometimes transmit to the ground. More often they had to resort to physical signals – flares, lamps, smoke grenades – and if they needed to impart precise information, their only option was to land.

The BE2s had been given makeshift armament in the form of a .303 Lewis machine gun mounted in front of the observer, which fired detachable canisters of ammunition known as 'drums'; but they were not fighter aircraft, and no match for the slender, speedy Fokker E1, a monoplane capable of 110 mph, which the Germans had just brought into service. This was the first aircraft on either side armed with a machine gun synchronised to fire through the propeller arc, and for a few months it seized the air initiative.[4]

Nevertheless, Ball continued to fly aggressively whenever he got the chance. Tactics were rudimentary. BE2s took off in small formations of three or four aircraft on reconnaissance or bombing sorties over the enemy lines, escorted by one or two faster, single-seat machines known as scouts. These were, in effect, fighters, but in 1916 there was no such expression as 'fighter pilot': the single-seat specialists were known as 'scout pilots'. Much of each mission would be spent cruising in search of chance targets, but Ball developed a habit of going down low to shoot up the German trenches on his way back to base.[5]

Even without plane-to-plane combat, his life was dangerous enough. On 20 March his engine failed on take-off, the aircraft ploughed into the ground nose-first, and he and his observer were trapped in the wreckage – from which they emerged unhurt. On 27

March his engine was smashed by anti-aircraft fire, and he had to nurse the aircraft down on to rough ground. (During the First World War the British fighter pilots had no parachutes: the only Allied personnel equipped with means of escape were the aerial observers who went aloft in balloons. The Germans did introduce parachutes in 1918, when mounting losses reduced their pilot strength to a critical level.)

Ball's first real combat came on 29 March, when, with his friend Lieutenant S. A. Villiers acting as his observer, he dived to attack a German aircraft below him, only to find himself being strafed by another enemy pilot from behind. Although one round cut a wire securing his engine, he survived otherwise unscathed; but that evening, at the end of a letter to his father, he betrayed some of the strain he was already feeling: 'I like this job, but nerves do not last long, and you soon want a rest.'

For an infantryman like myself, it is difficult to comprehend the wild variations that occur in the lives of aircrew. One moment they are living in safety and relative comfort, with no immediate threat to their lives; the next they are on their nerves' edge for hours on end, with a high chance of death. I think this contrast must be harder to cope with than the long-term, permanent discomfort of living in a foxhole.

Ball's career as an active fighter pilot took a great leap forward on 7 May when he was posted to No 11. Squadron RFC and test-flew what he called the 'new French machine': a Nieuport Scout, an agile biplane which had originally been designed for racing. In the past eleven weeks he had flown more than forty operational sorties, besides many hours in the air on test and practice missions, and he was overdue for leave. But on the ground the Allied armies were massing for one of the greatest infantry attacks ever mounted – the battle of the Somme – and every pilot was needed to support the coming offensive.

Perhaps it was exhaustion that made him behave in a slightly eccentric fashion when he arrived at No. 11 Squadron. At first his adjutant found him a bit brash, 'with more self assurance than his experience justified', but soon he was impressed with the way Ball took things steadily for the first few days, wandering round on his own, watching the mechanics at work. As for his living quarters – he turned his back on the billet assigned him in the village of Aubigny, and set up home in a bell tent on the airfield, surrounded by a wire fence, inside which he began to cultivate a vegetable garden. Later he replaced the tent with a home-made wooden hut, and soon had crops growing from seeds sent out from home. Clearly it suited his introspective nature to be on his own, and digging his patch brought relief from the stresses of war: he was friendly enough with fellow airmen, and never stand-offish, but generally preferred his own company. He also spent much time and effort making small modifications to whatever aircraft he had been allocated, to increase its performance and efficiency.

After a few days flying fast, single-seat Bristol Scouts, in which he forced several German aircraft to land, without positively destroying them, he took charge of a Nieuport Scout, which had a Lewis machine gun mounted on a swivel above the upper wing, aligned to fire ahead, outside the propeller arc. A sergeant of 11 Squadron, R. G. Foster, quickly devised a curved rail which allowed the pilot to tilt the weapon back and fire it at a steep angle upwards – an improvement which led Ball to develop his favourite tactic of dropping down behind an enemy, coming up from below, out of the pilot's sight, and easing in to amazingly close quarters (often no more than fifteen yards) before raking the fugitive's belly with machine-gun bursts.

His terse letters home did not conceal the fact that he was in mortal danger every day he flew, and his parents were naturally in a state of constant apprehension. When his father wrote to him early in June expressing some of their fears, he replied:

> Re – you saying that if anything happens to me . . . If anything did happen, as it quite easily may, I expect you and wish you to take it well, for men tons better than I go in hundreds every day. However, I will be careful, as you wish, but I do like my job, and this is a great help.

In June a twelve-day spell of leave, long overdue, did much to restore him, but he had scarcely returned to duty on the 23rd when, as part of the preparations for the assault on the Somme, all available fighters were detailed to attack the observation balloons flying behind the German trenches. On the 25th Ball flew two sorties against the balloons: on the second he destroyed his target, but then was hit by anti-aircraft fire which damaged his engine, so that he had to limp home at half speed. Two days later his aircraft was hit again: this time the engine was put out of action, but he managed to glide back into friendly territory.

On the last day of the month he learned with amazement and delight that he had been awarded a Military Cross. The citation, published in the *London Gazette* of 27 July, recorded that the award was

> For conspicuous skill and gallantry on many occasions, notably when, after failing to destroy an enemy kite balloon with bombs, he returned for a fresh supply, went back and brought it down in flames. He has done great execution among enemy aeroplanes. On one occasion he attacked six in one flight, forced down two and drove the others off. This occurred several miles over the enemy's lines.

The 'great execution' was only a beginning. On 1 July – a cloudless day – 66,000 British troops were launched and became bogged down in the biggest infantry assault ever known. That day it was safer to be in the air than on the ground, for the infantry suffered appalling casualties, and none worse than Ball's former regiment, the Sherwood Foresters, who went into action with 627 men and came out with ninety. A collier from Mansfield later told how, after going over the top, his company was pinned down by cross-fire in no man's land, and a young officer shouted, 'Remember Captain Ball, Sherwoods!' as he led them in a charge.

Airborne above the battle was Cecil Lewis, a former public-school boy who had joined the RFC at the age of seventeen by lying about his age. Above the Somme he won a Military Cross for many courageous actions, but his lasting contribution to history was his book *Sagittarius Rising*,[6] the most vivid and lyrical description of early aerial combat ever written. Lewis brought to life – as

Ball never could have – the horror below as the mighty assault was launched:

> We climbed away on that cloudless summer morning towards the lines . . . and the devastating effect of the week's bombardment could be seen. Square miles of country were ripped and blasted to a pock-marked desolation. Trenches had been obliterated, flattened out, and still, as we watched, the gun fire continued, in a crescendo of intensity. Even in the air, at 4,000 feet, above the roar of the engine the drumming of firing and bursting shells throbbed in our ears.
>
> Now the hurricane bombardment started. Half an hour to go . . . The clock hands crept on, the thrumming of the shells took on a higher note. It was now a continuous vibration, as if Wotan, in some paroxysm of rage, were using the hollow world as a drum, and under his beat the crust of it was shaking. Nothing could live under that rain of splintering steel.[7]

Ball saw all this, and he did what he could to help. Although he did not secure any victim, he flew almost continuously from 2.30 p.m. to 9.30 p.m., and in clear moments his thoughts must surely have been with the Robin Hoods below. On the evening of the 2nd he scored a double success, first shooting down a German Roland two-seater bomber, then closing under the tail of a lumbering two-seater Aviatik, to riddle its belly and send it falling sideways. On the 6th he flew twelve separate sorties.

His letters home were so stilted that it is difficult to determine how distressed he was by the constant loss of friends and colleagues. Perhaps he stuck to his rather wooden language as a means of keeping his emotion under control. 'I am having a very poo-poo time,' he told Lois on 10 July. 'On the 6th three topping chaps went off and never returned. Yesterday four of my best pals went off, and today one of our new chaps has gone over.' To his father he wrote on the same day:

> You ask me to 'let the devils have it' when I fight. Yes, I always let them have all I can but really I don't think them devils. I

> only scrap because it is my duty, but I do not think anything bad about the Hun. He is just a good chap with very little guts, trying to do his best. Nothing makes me feel more rotten than to see them go down, but you see it is either them or me, so I must do my best to make it a case of them.

What happened to him next is not quite clear. It seems unlikely that he would have boasted about his success, for that was not his nature. More likely, cumulative exhaustion led him to criticise the aircraft or equipment the RFC was using. Whatever the problem, when he asked his squadron commander for a few days' leave, he was unpleasantly surprised to be told that he was being sent to No. 8 Squadron, back on to the lumbering BE2s which were being used for bombing and reconnaissance operations.

The transfer may have been made for purely humane reasons by a senior officer who realised that Ball must have a rest. Word went round that he had become 'difficult to handle', and although the change of station depressed him at first, it did have a beneficial effect. During the next three weeks he flew plenty of sorties – including one extraordinary mission on which he took a secret agent deep into enemy territory at night, only to find that his passenger repeatedly refused to leave the aircraft – but at a lower tempo than those of his frantic previous existence. A photograph of him off duty shows him smiling and relaxed: again he lived in a tent, and on fine evenings he would play records on his gramophone to entertain fellow pilots.

One of them, Lieutenant William Fry, left a vivid snapshot of him in his memoirs, *Air of Battle:*

> No one could say he was welcoming or forthcoming; he was briefly polite, and then carried on with what he was doing. All the same he was bound to make an immediate impression on anyone. He was short and slight, beautifully proportioned, with black hair, dark eyes and a rosy complexion almost of the kind one would associate with a girl . . .
>
> Ball was utterly fearless and uncommunicative. Though he was considered somewhat unfriendly, he was never unpopular

> and did not make unkind remarks to or about anyone. Unexpectedly sensitive, he was nonetheless a self-effacing, skilled and dedicated killer, with no other motive than to use his machine and armament to shoot down enemy aeroplanes.[8]

On 14 August, his twentieth birthday, he received a splendid present in the form of a telephone call ordering him to rejoin his former unit. Back he went, full of delight, to find a brand-new Nieuport Scout 16 awaiting him, and his garden, which had been looked after by a civilian while he was away, in good order. Two days later he was in action, attacking a formation of five German aircraft and driving two of them down.

On 21 August he flew eight sorties: the first seven were inconclusive, but the last – even by his own standards – was a triumph. He took off at 7 p.m. as escort to a formation of bombers, which met opposition soon after they had crossed the front line at 5000 feet. Seeing a posse of seven Rolands approaching, Ball immediately went for them, scattered the formation, and after repeated attacks shot one of them down. As he climbed back towards his charges, he spotted five more Rolands, came up under the rearmost from behind and riddled its belly from a range of only ten yards until it turned on its side and fell away on fire. As three of the German's fellow aircraft attacked him from above, he climbed at them and poured a whole drum of ammunition into the nearest from a distance of no more than twenty feet. That Roland, also, fell away, and smashed through the roof of a house 6000 feet below.

With his ammunition gone, Ball had no option but to dive away from the remaining two Rolands – but his sortie was far from over. Having landed at Bellevue to replenish his drums, he took off again in pursuit of his own bombers, but on the way met another trio of Rolands and attacked all three, pressing them so hard that they broke and fled. Shortage of fuel then forced him to turn for home: he just cleared the front line before he ran out, then had to put down in a field near Senlis, with four bullet-holes in the windscreen and seven more hits elsewhere, including one on the car mirror which he had fixed in the middle of the upper wing above his head, so that he could see behind him – a vital innovation, soon widely copied. A message to 11 Squadron brought out a maintenance party, who worked on the plane during the night while he, exhausted, slept on the ground beside it.

It is difficult to imagine how even a young man could survive the physical strain of so many sorties a day, let alone the mental demands of fighting as well as flying his aircraft. Another transfer, this time to 60 Squadron, barely interrupted his aggressive sorties. On 23 August he flew his own aircraft to join his new unit at Izel le Hameau, between Arras and St Pol, and the next day he was airborne again, searching alone for enemy to destroy. By now he was treated like the star he had become, being assigned his own groundcrew and given free rein to fly as he liked by his new commanding officer, Major Robert Smith-Barry. He also had a visit from Brigadier General Higgins, Commander of III Brigade, RFC, who told him, 'I'm putting your name on a big board in the trenches in order to frighten the Huns!' A much more potent generator of fear in the enemy was the red spinner, or nose-cone, which had been fitted to the propeller boss of his Nieuport by one of the air mechanics: this struck such terror into some German pilots that they turned and fled if they so much as saw him approaching. In the opinion of one of his colleagues, he effectively did the work of a whole squadron himself.

On 30 August, when heavy rain made flying impossible, Ball found time to write to Lois and tot up his score to date:

> You will be pleased to hear that I have now got more Huns to my credit than any English or French pilot. The Major asked for a list today, and it worked out:
> 84 combats.
> 11 Hun machines and one balloon brought down and seen to crash.
> 5 Hun machines brought down but not seen to crash.
> 12 forced down and damaged.
> So it is not bad, and I have done my best.

It was the record confirmed by this list that led the authorities to award Ball his second decoration, the DSO, not for any particular sortie or combat, but 'for conspicuous gallantry and skill'. The award, gazetted on 26 September, briefly described several of his actions during July; but before Ball even knew he had won it, he had engaged in still more reckless encounters.

On the evening of 31 August he flew out over the lines and high above German territory at Cambrai; when he saw twelve Rolands forming up below him, he dived straight at them, scattering them in all directions, then pulled up under one of them, closed to fifteen yards, raked it with a fifty-round burst and sent it spinning down, only to find himself under fierce attack from the rest of the formation. Firing sporadically, he wove his way between the enemy aircraft until a burst from one of them severed his ignition leads and cut his engine. Bereft of power, and out of ammunition, he drew his pistol and fired at his nearest opponent as he set the Nieuport in a glide towards the lines, which he just cleared, skimming through volleys of small-arms fire to land safely at Colincamp. Once again he was so exhausted that he slept on the ground beside the aircraft.

This was the action which, along with others, brought him the award of a second DSO within days of the first – a uniquely swift double, both gazetted on the same day. Back with 60 Squadron on the morning of 1 September, he learnt of his first DSO, and heard – almost better news – that the unit was about to move back to his former base at Savy Aubigny. Hardly had he returned to his beloved hut and garden when someone brought him a warrant for ten days' home leave, effective from next day – and so, on 2 September, he set off for England.

If he hoped to spend his leave quietly with his family, he was disappointed, for his fame had run ahead of him: articles had appeared in the local newspapers, and he could not even go for a walk in Nottingham without constantly being stopped by strangers wishing to congratulate him. Praise disconcerted him, especially when it came from older men, and he declined as many invitations as he decently could, preferring to stay at home. Although thoroughly modest in public, in private he was thrilled with his medals, which he looked upon as rewards for good work, and which he thought reflected credit on his family.

When he returned to 60 Squadron on 11 September, he was

appointed commander of A Flight, which meant that he was often required to lead other pilots on patrols, but whenever he could he continued his lone sorties, sometimes taking off with such a rush in the early morning that he had no time to dress, but going up in his pyjamas. By then the opposition had been considerably strengthened, not only by an increase in the number of German fighter squadrons, but also by the arrival of a powerful new aircraft, the sleek-looking Albatros DI, which, with its 160 hp Mercedes engine, was faster and better armed than the Nieuport Scout.

None of this worried Ball. Ferocious as ever in pursuit of the enemy, he carried on as before, flying numerous missions on most days, and sending one victim after another down in flames; but on 19 September his own combat report carried a faintly sinister new element. Having sent a Roland spinning towards the ground, he dived down low to confirm what had happened to it, and when he saw its wreckage scattered along a hedge, he sprayed two whole drums of ammunition into the remains 'to make certain of the passengers'. Never before had he shown such a lust for killing Germans, and perhaps it was this change in outlook that persuaded his squadron commander, Major Smith-Barry, to accede to his request – made on grounds of exhaustion – and have him posted back to England – undoubtedly a wise decision. In short, the war and the killing had brutalised Ball, and transformed the benign and Christian attitude he had emphasised previously in a letter to his father – 'Nothing makes me feel more rotten than to see them go down, but then you see it is either them or me.'

Already he had done enough to earn his third DSO, 'for conspicuous gallantry in action'. The citation (not published until 25 November) recorded that he had 'displayed great courage and skill, and had brought down eight hostile aircraft in a short period, forcing many others to land'.

When he left Savy Aubigny on 4 October, after embarrassingly fulsome tributes from senior officers, and a send-off in the squadron mess, he was easily the most celebrated pilot in the Royal Flying Corps. To colleagues in the squadron he was a slightly odd fish: because he lived alone in the hut, playing his violin, they called him 'Lonely Testicle' or 'Pill' (schoolboy slang for 'Ball'); but to the

RFC as a whole he was a hero, who had carried the fight to the enemy and given his own side new heart by his shining example. Nobody had taught him how to fight air battles: with military aviation in its infancy, he had had to work out tactics for himself – and he had succeeded brilliantly. It must also be said that he was amazingly fortunate: in an era when the average survival of a pilot in the front line was three weeks, he returned to base time and again with the flimsy wings and fuselage of his aircraft shot through by machine-gun fire; yet he himself, sitting in open cockpits, with head and shoulders sticking up above the sides, had never suffered so much as a scratch.

In Nottingham he was mobbed by newspaper reporters, photographers and members of the public, and invited by the mayor and aldermen to a formal lunch, at which, as the guest of honour, he had to reply to his host's speech of praise – no light ordeal for a twenty-year-old who tended to be shy. Between his numerous engagements he found time to call on the families of men he had served with in France, to assure them that their loved ones were safe. This must have required a high degree of moral courage, especially as he knew that some were almost bound to die later in the war – but he will have brought comfort to the families at the time.[9]

All too soon, on 18 October, his leave ran out, but this time, on orders from the highest authorities, who considered him too valuable to be exposed to danger unnecessarily, he did not return to France. Instead, he remained in England for over six months, working mainly as a flying and fighting instructor at Orfordness, on the east coast, and King's Lynn, in Norfolk. His presence in England at least enabled him to attend the investiture at Buckingham Palace on 18 November, when King George V presented him with his DSO and bar, and his MC. There was also a grand ceremony in the Albert Hall in Nottingham in December, when he was made an Honorary Freeman of the city; but soon he became bored – especially when sent on a routine gunnery course – and he began to agitate for a return to France, appealing to senior officers and even seeking the support of the press magnate Lord Northcliffe.

At last, in February 1917, he was posted to a new unit being put together for operations in France, and on the 25th he joined No. 56

(Training) Squadron, which was then being brought up to full operational readiness at London Colney airfield, in Hertfordshire. Major-General Hugh Trenchard, Commander of the RFC, popularly known as 'Boom', had agreed to let him go, but on the understanding that he would serve in France only for the first month of the squadron's stay there, so that he could help train young pilots – after which he would come home.[10]

The prospect of returning to the fray cheered him immensely – but from the start, for various technical reasons, he took against the brand-new fighter, the SE5, with which the squadron was being equipped, and when his personal aircraft, No. A4850, arrived in crates, he set about having it extensively modified, removing the windscreen that enclosed much of the cockpit, installing a smaller one, and fitting a second Lewis gun to the floor of the cockpit so that he could fire downwards. He surprised his new colleagues on the squadron by going cheerfully to work with the mechanics, and was often to be seen in dungarees, covered from head to foot in oil.

One day towards the end of March he was hit by a kind of fire he had never known before. A friend with whom he had once shared a billet heard he was in the area, and asked an attractive eighteen-year-old girl called Flora Young, known as 'Bobs', to drive him to the airfield, so that he could renew acquaintance. She drew up wearing a pale yellow dress and hat, with her thick hair piled up. Ball, taking an instant fancy to her, asked if she would like a flip in an aeroplane, and when she said 'Yes', he borrowed a leather flying-coat and gave her a joyride in an Avro 504. That night he wrote to her in – for him – exceptionally outspoken terms: 'Just cannot sleep without first sending you a line to thank you for the topping day I have had with you. I am simply full of joy to have met you.' Next day he wrote again, saying that the other pilots on the squadron realised that he had been smitten, and had been ribbing him, but he was suddenly so much in love that he did not care.

Flora was obviously quite a catch. At the time she was working on a farm as a land-girl, but she had a fine voice, and had been trained as an opera singer. Yet Ball's time for courtship was pitifully short: he met her on 26 March, and on 7 April – Easter Saturday – his squadron left for France. During those hectic days of preparation for departure, he saw her at every opportunity: in the evenings, once he was off duty, she would drive out to the airfield to pick him up, and when the pilots held a farewell dinner at a hotel on Good Friday, he slid away early to be with her. Having had no chance to buy her an engagement ring, he gave her the gold identity bracelet he had been wearing, promising that they would be married as soon as he came back from France, and in return she presented him with a small volume of poems by Robert Louis Stevenson.

Did Ball have a premonition that he would never see England again? Some writers have suggested this – mainly on the grounds that at home he tidied his room, putting all his papers and effects into order, and asked that nothing should be moved until he came back. Yet anybody going abroad on a dangerous mission might well have done the same. Other factors suggest that he had every hope of returning. His devotion to his family was unchanged, as was his faith in God – and now he was in love as well.

Stronger than any of these, however, was his sense of patriotic duty. 'I cannot leave dear old England without a word of thanks to you,' he wrote to his parents just before he departed:

> It is hard to leave such dear people, but you are brave as well as dear, and it makes it less hard. It is an honour to be able to fight and do one's best for such a country and for such dear people. I shall fight for you, and God always looks after me and makes me strong; may He look after you also.

Take-off from London Colney was scheduled for 11 a.m. on 7 April 1917. Ball had forbidden Flora to come and see him off, so her father and brother were there instead, and at the last moment he passed her brother a note which read, 'God bless you dear.' Moments later the thirteen SE5s of 56 Squadron began to line up, and away they went, led by Cecil Lewis.

Their destination was the military airfield at Vert Galand, eleven miles north of Amiens, where they joined 9th (Headquarters) Wing of the RFC. The squadron had been allotted a patrol area around Cambrai, but because the SE5s were a new design, and most of the pilots lacked experience, they were ordered not to cross the front lines on patrol for their first two weeks in France. The enforced delay gave time for the aircraft to be extensively modified on the lines Ball had already pioneered, principally by the removal and replacement of the wrap-round windscreens, which everyone agreed were a menace. Ball once again set about building himself a hut and establishing a garden, and Lewis never forgot his habit of lighting a red magnesium flare outside the hut after dinner and walking round it in his pyjamas, playing the violin.

On the flying front Ball was less happy. Still considering the SE5 not much of an aircraft, he schemed by every means at his command to acquire another Nieuport, provoking his father to write to General Trenchard on his behalf. Such manoeuvres could well have blown back on someone with a less distinguished record, but Ball's persistence was rewarded: in the middle of April Trenchard made a tour of the RFC squadrons in France, and on 13 April invited the star pilot to join him for tea with the squadron commander.

'The General is delighted with Ball,' reported the author Maurice Baring, who was travelling with Trenchard, 'and is giving him two machines: the SE 5 for his ordinary work and a Nieuport for his individual enterprises.'[11] To Ball, the key advantage of the Nieuport was its manoeuvrability: the SE5 was definitely less agile, but it provided a steady platform for gunnery, and it had two weapons instead of one – a Lewis machine gun mounted on the upper wing, and a Vickers recessed into the fuselage ahead of the pilot, firing through the propeller.

When the squadron began active operations on 22 April, the honour of leading the unit's first hostile patrol fell to Ball, who set out with five other SE5s to patrol on the Allied side of the front lines. From that moment – except on days when bad weather prevented flying – he was seldom out of action, and his tally of kills mounted quickly until he passed that of the French ace Georges Guynemer. His worst frustration, shared by most of his colleagues, was that both the Lewis and the Vickers guns kept jamming, so that the pilots repeatedly had to pull out of dogfights, and lost numerous chances.

By then the whole tenor of the air war had changed, for the Germans had far more aircraft flying, and had taken to sending them up in *Jagdstaffeln*, or fighter formations of up to half a dozen, and when there was a clash, a large-scale dogfight would develop, often with twenty or thirty machines involved. Opposing 56 Squadron were many of Germany's finest pilots, among them Rittmeister Manfred von Richthofen, known as 'the Red Baron' because he led his own formation of hand-picked pilots in an aircraft painted red. Richthofen's reputation was not exaggerated, for in March and April he alone shot down thirty British aircraft.

Ball continued to operate in the only way he knew, cruising in search of the enemy, breaking up formations by means of reckless, head-on approaches, and then hunting down individuals by the sheer brilliance of his flying and his daring, innovative method of attack. His aircraft was frequently hit, and needed major repairs when he limped back to base; but never was he closer to disaster than on the evening of 28 April when, having shot one Albatros out of the sky, he attacked another and followed it down, not noticing how low he had gone. Suddenly he was in a storm of fire from the ground: exploding shells sent shrapnel ripping through the SE5 and cut all his control wires except one, leaving him only his left rear elevator with which to keep the aircraft flying. Somehow he managed to nurse his crippled machine back to Vert Galant, and landed by winding his adjustable tailplane up and down.

He always flew so safely and accurately that his colleagues, watching him come in, could not understand why he was making such an awkward, floating approach; but when he taxied up to the sheds, they saw that his elevators were flapping loose, and realised that his controls had been shot away. 'It was incredible he had not crashed,' Lewis remembered:

> His oil tank had been riddled, and his face and the whole nose of the machine were running with black castor oil. He was so angry at being shot up like this that he walked straight to the sheds, wiped the oil off his shoulders and face with a rag, ordered out his Nieuport, and within two hours was back with yet another Hun to his credit![12]

Writing to Flora next day, Ball reported that Trenchard had come to congratulate him, and had offered him two weeks in England – 'but dear I think I had better stay until all is OK and the month is up'. And yet, even though his sense of duty was unimpaired, his diary betrayed the strain he was feeling. 'It is all trouble and it is getting on my mind,' he wrote that night. 'Am feeling very old just now.' Clearly he recognised the need for a period of rest and recovery, but as so often with holders of the highest gallantry award, his sense of duty and commitment prevailed over all else.

On 5 May he had yet another hair's-breadth escape. Again, he shot down one Albatros, but then its companion came at him, head-on, guns blazing. Ball replied in kind – held his course and kept up continuous fire with his Vickers until collision seemed inevitable. At the last instant the German flared up over his windscreen, but a bullet ruptured his oil tank, and suddenly his vision was blacked out by the thick, dark fluid. Desperately he pulled up and scrubbed the oil from his eyes. Looking round, he could see no sign of his opponent, but when he flew lower, he spotted both his victims smashed on the ground, close to each other. The German, he felt certain, had been mortally wounded, and in his dying seconds had tried to ram him. The encounter left him in a state of such agitation that when he returned to the squadron, he could hardly talk. As the Recording Officer, Wing Commander T. B. Marson, wrote later,

> Flushed in the face, his eyes brilliant, his hair blown and dishevelled, he came to the squadron office to make his report, but for a long time was in so over-wrought a state that dictation was an impossibility to him. 'God is very good to me. God must have me in His keeping.'[13]

In a letter he told Flora that his total of kills to date was forty-two, and that General Trenchard had telephoned to say that he was going to be presented to General Sir Douglas Haig tomorrow. But he also echoed the theme to which he had held throughout his operational career: 'Oh, won't it be nice when all this beastly killing is over, and we can just enjoy ourselves and not hurt anyone.'

By the very next morning, 6 May, in an amazing recovery he appeared to have regained his equilibrium, and after flying to the repair depot to collect his refurbished SE5, he took his Nieuport up on an evening patrol and shot down yet another Albatros. That night he wrote to his father:

> Don't work too hard, Dad, for it will be so rotten when I come home if you cannot share my happiness . . . Please give my mother a huge cheerio from me, and tell her I am doing my best for her . . . Do send me a few plants for my garden . . . One of the Huns tried to ram me after he was hit, and only missed by inches. Am indeed looked after by God, but Oh! I do get tired of always living to kill, and am really beginning to feel like a murderer. Shall be so pleased when I have finished.

He wrote of finishing because he had served all but one day of the month of active service to which he had been committed, and he must have been hoping for a return to England in the near future. What he did not know was that, during the day, his wing commander had written to his squadron commander, asking for a full report on what he had achieved since he came out to France – his combat reports, observations of other pilots, the condition of his aircraft when he returned to base, and so on. The letter, ending 'I would like this as soon as possible', strongly suggests that he was about to be recommended for a Victoria Cross.

The last letter Ball wrote was to Lol:

> Received your topping letter and cake. It is so good of you to think of me so much. Today we drew lots for leave, and I came out last, but Lol, it was a sporting chance . . . I made my 42nd Hun yesterday, so am now four in front of the French . . . Was shot down yesterday, so am getting a new machine today. Must close now. Tons of love, Albert.

The seventh of May dawned bright and clear. Ball took off for his first sortie at 12.30 along with two other SE5s, escorting some Sopwith two-seaters on a photographic patrol. During the mission he attacked a formation of Albatroses, but had to pull out when his Vickers jammed.

The main business of the day was an offensive sweep, ordered by wing headquarters, in which eleven SE5s took part – three in A Flight, four each in B and C Flights. Ball was commanding A Flight, and in overall command of the formation.

The hunters lifted off from Vert Galant at 5.30 p.m., in a scene memorably described by another of the pilots, Cecil Lewis:

> Eleven chocolate-coloured, lean, noisy bullets, lifting, swaying, turning, rising into formation, two fours and a three, circling and climbing away steadily towards the lines . . . The May evening is heavy with threatening masses of cumulus cloud, majestic skyscapes, solid-looking as snow mountains, fraught with caves and valleys, rifts and ravines – strange and secret pathways in the chartless continents of the sky.[14]

It was the tremendous clouds, more than anything else, that caused confusion and disaster. One British pilot, Gerald Maxwell, lost sight of his fellows in the middle of a cloud-mass, never found them again, and turned for home. Another, Lieutenant Musters, disappeared as the formation was entering a cloud-bank, and was seen no more (he was later reported shot down and killed). The real battle started when four Albatros DIII Scouts appeared suddenly from a cloud on the SE5s' level, and Ball immediately launched an attack on one of them, only to pull off, apparently because – yet again – his gun had jammed.

From that moment the combat developed and spread over a huge area, with aircraft vanishing into the clouds, then popping out again, and others joining the swarm from every direction. Captain 'Duke' Meintjes, the South African commander of C Flight, destroyed one Albatros, but was then himself shot down with a shattered control column and a smashed wrist, just managing to bring his stricken machine safely to earth. Lieutenant John Leach of B Flight was severely wounded in the leg (which later had to be amputated) and although weak from loss of blood managed to land near a Canadian hospital. Lewis survived only by desperate manoeuvres, spinning and twisting down under attack from two more Scouts.

Even if Ball had lived, he could never have brought that great battle to life in writing, never put over the chaotic urgency of the dogfight with the clarity that Lewis achieved in *Sagittarius Rising*:

> A pilot, in the second between his own engagements, might see a Hun diving vertically, an SE5 on his tail, on the tail of the SE another Hun, and above him another British scout. These four, plunging headlong at 200 miles per hour, guns crackling, tracer streaming, suddenly break up. The lowest Hun plunges flaming to his death, if death has not taken him already.
>
> His victor seems to stagger, suddenly pulls out in a great leap, as a trout leaps on the end of a line, and then, turning over on his belly, swoops and spins in a dizzy falling spiral with the earth to end it . . . But such a glimpse, lasting perhaps ten seconds, is broken by the sharp rattle of another attack. Two machines approach head-on at breakneck speed, firing at each other, tracers whistling through each other's planes, each slipping sideways on his rudder to trick the other's gunfire.
>
> Who will hold longest? Two hundred yards, a hundred, fifty, and then, neither hit, with one accord they fling their machines sideways, bank and circle, each striving to bring his gun on to the other's tail, each glaring through goggle eyes, calculating, straining, wheeling, grim, bent only on death or dying.
>
> But, from above, this strange tormented circling is seen by another Hun. He drops. His gun speaks. The British machine, distracted by the sudden unseen enemy, pulls up, takes a burst through the engine, tank and body, and falls bottom uppermost down through the clouds and the deep unending desolation of the twilight sky.[15]

No one has ever known for certain what happened to Ball. Lewis believed that he was the last to see his red-nosed SE5 going east at 8000 feet. As it flew straight into the white face of an enormous cloud, Lewis followed, but when he came out on the other side, Ball was nowhere in sight. By then darkness had started to gather: visibility was failing, and drizzle had set in. One of the last pilots to leave the scene was Captain Cyril Crowe, commander of B Flight:

he too went looking for Ball, until shortage of fuel forced him to head for home.

By 2030 only five of the eleven SE5s had returned to base. At first nobody on the squadron would believe that Ball was dead: they hoped against hope that he had been forced down and possibly captured. Lewis remembered the leaden atmosphere:

> All next day a feeling of depression hung over the squadron. We mooned about the sheds, still hoping for news. The day after that, hope was given up. I flew his Nieuport back to the Aircraft Depot.
>
> It was decided to go over Douai and drop message-bags containing requests, written in German, for news of his fate. We crossed the lines at 13,000 feet. Douai was renowned for its anti-aircraft. They were not to know that the squadron was in mourning, and made it hot for us. The flying splinters ripped the planes. Over the town the message-bags were dropped, and the formation returned without encountering a single enemy machine.[16]

That evening the squadron held a sing-song in a barn near the airfield – 'Anything to raise the morale', Lewis remembered. The old songs were sung – 'Swanee River', 'Pack up Your Troubles' – and Lewis gave a rendering of Stevenson's 'Requiem':

> Under the wide and starry sky,
> Dig the grave and let me lie.
> Glad did I live and gladly die,
> And I laid me down with a will.
>
> This be the verse you grave for me:
> Here he lies where he longed to be;
> Home is the sailor, home from sea,
> And the hunter home from the hill.

The poem was so intensely apposite that, as Lewis recorded, 'the men applauded huskily; they understood'.

By then Albert Ball was not only dead, but buried too. Weeks passed before his comrades heard about his final moments – and even when news came, it left vital questions unanswered.

The only people who saw him crash were four German air force officers and a Frenchwoman. One of the Germans, Leutnant Franz Hailer, heard an aircraft engine, and through his binoculars saw Ball's SE5 emerge from a cloud upside down, already at low level and falling, with its propeller stopped and black smoke trailing behind it. As he watched, the biplane ploughed into some rising ground, still inverted, near a ruined farmhouse, a mile from the village of Annoeullin.

First to reach the wreck was Madame Lieppe-Coulon, who found Ball apparently still breathing in his shattered cockpit. She lifted him out and held him in her arms, but by the time the four Germans ran up he was already dead. Hailer had no difficulty in identifying 'the English Richthofen': the red markings on the aircraft, and items found in the dead man's uniform, left no doubt. Hailer was certain that Ball had not been hit by gunfire: his multiple injuries – broken back, arm, leg and foot, and crushed chest – had been caused solely by the impact. Except for a bruise on one cheek, his face was unmarked.

Hailer suggested to his commanding officer that Ball's body should be wrapped in a flag and dropped by parachute behind British lines, so that his comrades could bury him with due honour; but this idea did not find favour, and he was interred in a wooden coffin – a mark of exceptional respect for burials near the front lines – and accorded a military funeral in the village cemetery at Annoeullin. His grave was marked by a plain wooden cross bearing the inscription '*In Luftkampf gefallen für sein Vaterland Engl. Flieger Hauptmann Albert Ball, Royal Flying Corps*' ('Fallen in air combat for his fatherland English pilot Captain Albert Ball').

Experts have speculated endlessly about the cause of Ball's crash. Lothar von Richthofen, younger brother of the Red Baron, claimed to have shot him down, but undermined his own report by saying that Ball's aircraft was a triplane (which of course it was not). Nevertheless, his account received strong support from Leutnant Wilhelm Allmenroeder, who was flying with him that evening in a patrol of four fighters. As the light faded, Allmenroeder watched two biplanes, one German, one English, circling in a dogfight close below him, and in a vivid letter (translated here) he described the action:

> Below me each opponent tried to better his position by wide left turns; however, no one gained an advantage, and not a shot was fired. Meanwhile, it became darker and darker. Off to the north-east Douai was barely visible, and a dense haze was forming . . . The sun had just gone down. Suddenly, as if both had received an order, the two left the circle and flew straight away, Lothar to the south, his opponent to the north.
>
> I had believed that they both wanted to stop the fight because of the darkness, but then both turned and rushed at each other as if they intended to ram. Lothar dipped under the other, and then both turned and rushed again at each other, only a few shots being fired. At the third frontal attack Lothar came from the south and his opponent from the north. I waited. The machine guns peppered again. This time Lothar's opponent did not give sideways, but dived down to the ground . . .
>
> When, some days later, we heard that England was mourning the death of its ace, Captain Ball, we knew that Lothar's opponent could only have been Ball, who had, at the beginning of the fight, dived on Lothar and wanted to make a fight of it to the bitter end.[17]

As a result of the battle Richthofen's own Albatros was certainly forced down into an emergency landing, but there is no evidence that the SE5 or its pilot were hit by disabling enemy fire, and it seems more likely that Ball, exhausted after three hours' flying, became disoriented by the cloud, and did not realise that he was upside down until his engine flooded, and it was too late for him to recover.

At the end of May the Germans dropped messages over the British lines confirming his death and saying that he had been buried at Annoeullin. His Victoria Cross was announced in a supplement to the *London Gazette* of 8 June:

For the most conspicuous and consistent bravery from the 25th April to the 6th May, 1917, during which period Captain Ball took part in twenty-six combats in the air, and destroyed eleven hostile aeroplanes, drove two down out of control, and forced several others to land.

In these combats Captain Ball, flying alone, on one occasion fought six hostile machines, twice he fought five and once four . . . On returning with a damaged machine, he had always to be restrained from immediately going out on another.

In all, Captain Ball has destroyed forty-three German aeroplanes and one balloon, and has always displayed most exceptional courage, determination and skill.

When a memorial service was held on 10 June at St Mary's Church, Nottingham, huge crowds turned out and watched the procession in silence. Albert's father and his brother Cyril – by then also a pilot in the RFC – were present, but their mother had been prostrated by grief, and could not bring herself to attend: never reconciled to his loss, she withdrew from most of her husband's civic functions, and died in 1931.

Soon after Ball's death a fund was opened for public subscriptions so that a permanent memorial to him could be created: various difficulties delayed the completion of the project, but eventually, on 8 September 1921, Sir Hugh Trenchard unveiled a commanding statue on a plinth in the grounds of Nottingham Castle. After the war Albert Senior made several trips to France, to establish exactly where his son had died: he bought the field in which the SE5 had crashed, erected a memorial plaque on the spot, and laid a path from the impact point to the nearest road – the route along which the body had been carried from the wreck.

Ball once said to his commanding officer on 56 Squadron, Major Richard Blomfield, '"Two jobs a day are no good to me. I want to be up all the time" . . . He was the first airman to go right into his man and fight him to the finish.' That was it: he was an absolute tiger for action, and in Blomfield's words, 'a striking example of what courage means'.[18]

6

Private Albert Jacka VC, MC and Bar

1893–1932

Those who glorify war have probably never experienced casualties on a significant scale, and therefore have little appreciation of the horror and waste of armed conflict. To echo Clausewitz, 'War is nothing more than the continuation of politics by other means.' In civilised and democratic countries an outbreak of war indicates the failure of politicians to solve international problems, and one thing is certain: it never resolves a political difficulty. Rather, it creates the environment for increasingly complex situations that can be resolved only by diplomacy. One has merely to examine the indeterminate outcome of the wars in the Middle East in 1991 and 2003 to appreciate this essential truth.

The two World Wars fought in the last century for political ends led to massive loss of life, particularly the first – a war in which courage took on a new meaning, in which life became devalued, and yet in which, arguably, Australia found its place as an independent state free from the yoke of British imperialism.

But at what price? During the Great War, from a population of five million, nearly 417,000 enlisted, 331,000 actually left Australia to fight, 59,330 were killed and 159,171 were wounded. Proportionately, the casualty rate was the highest suffered by any army in the conflict. Yet men went to join that war with hope and enthusiasm, fiercely determined to serve their political leaders and above all the nation state to which they belonged, even though at the time it was still part of the British Empire.

No one was more determined than Private Albert Jacka. He was one of the fortunate few who eventually returned to Australia, twenty times wounded, and gassed so severely that it brought on his premature death from kidney failure, but also winner of the Victoria Cross and two Military Crosses. Jacka epitomised the courage, the independence and the freedom that are the hallmark of Australia today.

He was born on 10 January 1893 to a typical outback family farming cattle on a modest and not particularly profitable scale some 140 kilometres west of Melbourne. One of seven siblings, he seemed to have limited prospects, and he faced a life of manual labour with the possibility of promotion to some junior management position in the State Forestry Commission. As happened to thousands of National Servicemen in Britain, military service changed all that and released his potential, giving him international fame and recognition – not that he relished it.

His education at Wedderburn Primary School was sound, and, as his personal diaries demonstrate, he displayed intelligence and aptitude. He excelled in football, cycling and boxing, and gained himself a reputation locally as an accomplished sportsman. The scope of his education was limited by the fact that the family expected him to start work early in life: he took his first job as an employee in his father's smallholding, and then at eighteen joined the Victoria State Forestry Department. He is depicted as a shy but determined young man, uncomfortable in the company of girls, and with neither the opportunity nor the prospects of achieving much outside his home state. From his early days he became impatient and frustrated when blocked by bureaucracy or incompetent superiors, and these two characteristics were both his strength and his limitation when he was subject to the constraints of military discipline. His innate intelligence and natural tendency to focus on problems also showed through, and contributed to his achieving such a distinguished record.

To judge from photographs, he was of slim, athletic build and average height – maybe 5′ 9″. He appears to have had a long head, face and ears, all accentuated by swept-back dark hair which was already receding in his early twenties. His other noticeable feature was a crooked nose, probably the result of his boxing.

It is not surprising that this ordinary country labourer attracted little attention when he enlisted at the Broadmeadows training camp near Melbourne on 18 September 1914. He was not considered officer material, and his posting as a private to the 14th Battalion of the Australian Infantry followed a standard pattern, as did his journey aboard the *Berrima*, which sailed from Melbourne on 22 December. (Later in the First World War the 14th achieved great renown, but then it was little known.)

En route to the Gallipoli campaign in Turkey, his unit underwent two months' training in Egypt, and then took part in the landing by the combined Australian and New Zealand Army Corps (Anzac) at Anzac Cove on 25 April 1915. The Gallipoli campaign proved a disastrous failure for the Allies, both politically and militarily. The Australians' sacrifices in lives were enormous, and in military terms the operation suffered from the overconfidence of British politicians and military commanders alike. The Turks were considered an inferior and ill-prepared enemy; they may have been the latter, but as anyone who has fought with them or – less fortunately – against them will know, they are certainly not the former, especially when defending their homeland.

The Turkish Ottoman Empire, led by the young Enver Pasha, saw the war in Europe as a chance to reclaim lands that had been absorbed into the Russian Empire. Enver Pasha feared that if the Allies won, they would deprive Turkey of even more of its territory – and so on 31 October 1914 he took his country into the war on the side of the Germans.

The Gallipoli peninsula protects the Dardanelles, the strait which gives access to the Sea of Marmara, at the eastern end of which the Bosporus leads to the Black Sea. When the Turks closed both straits, Allied aid could not reach Russia, and Russian wheat could not be exported. Throughout the winter of 1914–15 the combined British and French fleets bombarded the Turkish batteries at the entrance to the straits, but the attack had not been pressed home, and the Turks had had time to strengthen their forces with German military equipment.

The Allies' plan was that the Anzac Division should land at Gaba Tepe, some 25 kilometres north of Cape Helles, at the southern end of the Gallipoli peninsula, where British and Irish landings were also scheduled. The forces at Cape Helles would drive the Turks northwards to a point at which the Anzac Division would create a block, and the enemy forces would be defeated in an anvil-and-hammer manoeuvre while the peninsula was secured.

In the event, possibly due to a navigational error, the Anzac Division was landed five kilometres north of its objective at Ari Burnu (renamed Anzac Cove, with Turkish consent, after the war). Although its arrival surprised the home forces, the cove was surrounded by steep mountains, easy to defend and expensive if not impossible to assault.[1]

At Ari Burnu disaster set in as the invaders attempted to break out through the high ground immediately surrounding the cove. Delays ensued, and the Turks built up a significant opposing army: the protracted stalemate that resulted led to a withdrawal of the Anzac forces from Gallipoli almost eight months later, in December 1915. What Kitchener had described as 'a cruise in the Marmara' turned into defeat, withdrawal and the loss of over eight thousand Australians and New Zealanders dead and eighteen thousand wounded.

It was into this stalemate that 14th Infantry Battalion found themselves deployed. Before landing, Private Jacka of D Company had not stood out from his contemporaries, but once ashore he showed eagerness to get stuck in and start winning the war.

As a soldier he epitomised the Australian fighting man in many ways. And yet, tough and independent as he was, he had demonstrated his individuality in his reluctance to frequent the bars of Cairo when opportunity presented itself – he was a practising Rechabite (a member of a total-abstinence society).[2] He judged his superiors by their performance rather than by their rank. Like all natural leaders, he showed an early tendency to ask nothing of his contemporaries that he would not do himself – he led by example. There is no record of him demonstrating any military ambition, and even in later life he would accept only those promotions and positions which he considered he had earned. When down on his luck after the war, he was offered a sinecure as a Member in a safe Labour seat in the Federal Parliament, and he refused with the words, 'No – they're not my style, and if I did accept, they'd say, "Look at Jacka – a failure in business climbs into a safe job as an MP."'[3]

Like most of his comrades at the start of the Dardanelles campaign, he was confident that the Australian forces were the best in the world and would be more than a match for the Germans, let alone the Turks. What he failed to appreciate was the price they would have to pay in lives to justify their self-confidence. His own 14th Battalion suffered savagely in the campaign, and only fifty members of the 800-odd who left home in 1914 returned alive to Australia after the war. During the conflict as a whole, forty-two officers and 1008 other ranks had been killed.

When he became a non-commissioned officer, his first principle of leading by personal example blended well with his 'rough justice' administration of discipline and insistence on the highest standards from his subordinates, coupled with unstinting care for their welfare. His methods were practical if unofficial. He accepted a certain amount of wild behaviour when out of the line, but would use his fists to bring tough miscreants to heel, and when briefing a new draft towards the conclusion of the Gallipoli campaign he warned them he would not 'crime' them for misdemeanours, but would give them a bloody nose.

On the battlefield he became totally focused on the task in hand, and had no regard for anything that might distract him from fighting, least of all worries about his own safety. His attitude to the enemy, Turks or Germans, seems to have been cold rather than a feeling of hatred. In one incident at Gallipoli he crept into no man's land and recovered a dead enemy officer: the feat required courage and risk-taking of a high order, and emphasised his respect for the enemy – but it was respect without pity. It is suggested that this combination was a common characteristic among men of the 1st Australian Imperial Force (AIF).

The Turkish forces were prepared to take enormous losses, reflecting their determination to defend their homeland. According to the Turkish General Staff, during the first day of the landings at Anzac Bay they suffered casualties amounting to 50 per cent of their strength of about four thousand. The Australians knew how to kill.[4] Such sustained slaughter of an enemy throwing unlimited manpower at a defensive position is not a tactic used in war since the Chinese adopted it in Korea. In modern warfare, with air power and increased effectiveness of warheads and weapon systems, it would be unlikely to succeed. At one stage three thousand dead Turks were counted in front of the Australian positions in one afternoon, and an armistice had to be called for sanitary reasons.

The Australians established precarious positions on a ridge in sight of the sea as the forward point of their bridgehead. On a seaborne assault such as this, it is the first essential that such a 'secure' zone be immediately put in place to facilitate the landing of stores and reinforcements, just as the landings in Normandy were crucial to the development of the Allied assault on Europe in 1944. However, the Turks fought back with such determination, courage and disregard for losses that the Australians spent the next eight months achieving nothing more than maintaining their positions at enormous cost to themselves. That they even managed this against increasingly effective Turkish assaults is a credit to their courage and their reputation as formidable fighting soldiers. They have maintained the Gallipoli spirit in many actions and wars ever since: it may be said to be the 'spirit of Australia'.

These forward positions, or outposts, as they became, gained names from the senior commanders of the time, and it was to Courtney's Post that Jacka and his platoon found themselves deployed. It is not difficult to imagine the hell that was life in the forward edge of the battle area (FEBA), and the critical importance of each of these mutually supporting posts is easily appreciated.

Jacka won his VC during the night of 19–20 May 1915, in an important but localised action at the key position of Courtney's

Post. He was twenty-two years old, and still held that great rank from which all the best army careers develop: acting lance corporal.

The Turkish forces had regrouped and reinforced to the point at which they had halted the advance of the AIF and were determined to push them and other invaders back into the sea. In his diary he gave a laconic description of his role in the Courtney's Post battles:

> Great battles at 3a.m. Turks captured large portion of our trench. D Coy called in to front line. Lieut. Hamilton shot dead. I led a section of men and recaptured the trench. I bayoneted two Turks, shot five, took three prisoners and cleared the whole trench. I held the trench alone for 15 minutes against heavy attack. Lieut. Crabbe informed me that I would be recommended.[5]

The Turks had succeeded in infiltrating the trench system; had they secured and reinforced it, they would have posed a severe threat to the whole 14th Battalion position. Jacka probably realised the importance of ejecting them, but was on his own, with his companions dead at his feet.

The truth was somewhat more complex than he suggested in his brief journal entry, and even more extraordinary. The following account appeared in the issue of *Pageant* magazine for April–May 1993:

> Jacka had been standing on a fire-step – a platform for riflemen – cut into the front face of a trench he was guarding, along with ten other men from his platoon. He was on the extreme left, and there was a communications trench running up behind him. A Turkish patrol crept up unobserved within a few metres of the trench and lobbed grenades into it, killing three Australians and wounding most of the rest.
>
> Jacka was not hurt, but when the Turks jumped into the trench, the remaining Australians fled past him. He, however, stayed in his position, firing to prevent the Turks from proceeding any further. Nevertheless they now held ten metres of firing line, and the stretch had to be recaptured. But the

Turks were in an invidious position: they were blocked by Jacka to the north and couldn't move any further south because the trench passed another communications sap [trench].

Other members of the 14th Battalion were trying to cut them off. Lieutenant Hamilton ran forward and made his way into a reserve trench running parallel to and five metres behind the line. He shot at the Turks with his revolver, but a bullet fired from the front trench hit him in the head.

Now Jacka was the only man stopping the Turks from advancing to the north. When another officer, Lieutenant Crabbe, approached him, he shouted, 'Back out! Turks in here!' Crabbe asked Jacka if he was all right. 'Yes,' he replied. Crabbe asked him if he would charge the Turks if he could get men to back him up. Jacka said he would need two or three.

Crabbe returned a little later with three volunteers, Privates Howard, Poliness and de Arango. Jacka jumped across the front trench from the fire-step into the mouth of the communications trench to join the trio. Crabbe had a simple plan. The four would try to fight their way into the front line from the communications trench. Jacka asked the men to fix bayonets. He would lead the counter attack himself.

The small force crawled up the mouth of the communications trench. The Lance Corporal jumped across it and found shelter once again on the fire-step. Howard, the next to try, was badly wounded before he was halfway across. Jacka abandoned the plan for a frontal assault.

With the Turks' rifles aimed at the mouth of the communications trench, he took the risk of jumping back to rejoin the two men. His luck held. He was not hit, and dragged Howard back to the safety of the communications trench.

The first attempt having failed, Jacka decided to do the job himself. He asked Crabbe to continue firing up the communications trench to create a diversion while he crept around to the rear of the Turkish position. Crabbe, with no other plan in mind, gave his approval. Jacka took a long swing around the trench system, coming up into the front trench about fifteen metres to the south of where the Turks had got in.

> A slight bend in the trench meant that he could not be seen by the enemy. He left the front trench near the bend and crawled out into no man's land. As Poliness threw two grenades and de Arango fired shots at the wall, to make the Turks think they were coming that way, Jacka leapt to his feet and jumped down into the trench, shooting five Turks and bayoneting two others. Poliness shot two more as they tried to crawl over the parapet.
>
> This part of the battlefield, Courtney's Post, now fell silent as Crabbe waited for the dawn to find out what had happened. For this time Acting Lance Corporal Jacka held the position alone. At sun-up Crabbe entered the trench and found it littered with dead Australians and Turks. Jacka had a cigarette end in his mouth when he told the officer: 'Well – I managed to get the beggars, Sir'.[6]

It is of course remarkable that he was neither wounded nor killed, but such is the fortune of war – and as he showed later in the conflict, luck was indeed on his side. There is no doubt that by his leadership, his intelligent use of ground and complete disregard for his own safety he restored the integrity of 14th Battalion's defensive position and made a contribution out of proportion to his rank and position. His valour is without question: what is surprising is that he sustained this high level of courage for a further three years of unremitting front-line operations.

His VC was gazetted on 19 August 1915 and changed his life militarily, although promotion came grudgingly and was limited in nature. By the conclusion of the Gallipoli campaign he had moved up through the ranks to company sergeant major, the senior non-commissioned officer in an infantry company. But he was not commissioned until his appointment as second lieutenant on 29 April 1916. Ultimately, after many further successful actions, he reached his ceiling of captain in August 1916.

At home, the first award of the VC to an Australian in the First World War attracted immense publicity. Even though Jacka was thousands of miles away, the news of the reaction at home alarmed him, and his discomfiture was further exacerbated by the way the

Government used his photograph for propaganda to sell the idea of conscription (his father was against conscription, and Jacka himself had reservations).

The Australian Prime Minister, William Hughes, tried to bring him back to spearhead the recruitment campaign, but Jacka resolutely refused: his place was in action, fighting, and his award made him all the more determined not to take the comfortable option of returning home. He maintained this stance throughout the war, and even in 1918, when General William Birdwood, the commander of the 1st Anzac Corps, personally wrote instructing him to return, he steadfastly refused – and thereby enhanced his reputation for disregarding his superior officers.

Holders of the VC are the first to admit that many others on the field of battle could have qualified for the medal but for the vagaries of luck. Certainly fortune played its part in Jacka's success. After his Courtney's Post action he was recommended for the award by Lieutenant Crabbe, but the records indicate that the suggestion was not followed up by his commanding officer, Lieutenant Colonel Courtney, who was ill at the time, and soon afterwards was evacuated to Australia. However, when Major-General Godley, the Anzac divisional commander, came to hear of Jacka's action, he instructed that follow-up action should be taken.

The intervention by such a senior officer emphasised the importance of Jacka's action in determining the security of the whole Anzac position. It would not be normal for a commander, five command levels above the man involved, to take such a detailed interest in a local patrol action unless it had held particular significance. This, however, begs the question of command arrangements within 14th Battalion: even if the commanding officer was unwell, the system allowed for the next senior officer to assume responsibility, and one can only speculate why it was left to the divisional commander to take the initiative.

At the conclusion of the Gallipoli campaign the Australian forces redeployed to Egypt. By this time, after eight months' combat, Jacka was indeed an experienced and battle-hardened soldier, and as a company sergeant major he held a position of some authority, which gave him the opportunity to demonstrate his leadership qualities.

These were formidable, but his natural inclination was still to support his soldiers against his superiors. His fearlessness on the battlefield was equalled by his fearlessness of and disrespect shown to his superiors if he felt they were not matching up to his own high standards, or if he strongly disagreed with an order.

In Egypt, the 14th Battalion was ordered to post selected old hands to a new battalion in order that it might have a core of experience among its inexperienced reinforcements. As a company sergeant major, Jacka had the invidious responsibility of deciding who should be posted, and it seems he carried out this inevitably unpopular and sensitive task with no mean moral courage, amid strong criticism and understandable dissent within his company.

When the restructured 14th Battalion moved with the AIF to support the Allied forces in France in March 1916, Jacka was selected for a commission as second lieutenant, which gave him his first opportunity to command a platoon. His bias towards his soldiers did not mean he was soft with them: rather the reverse. He exercised unremitting discipline, supported by the threat of a 'good thumping'. His soldiers appreciated the direct and instant discipline and were grateful to him for his insistence on high standards – always the essence of survival in combat.

Apart from periods in hospital when he was wounded, he stayed with the AIF until the end of the war. At no time was his courage diminished, although he suffered from severe shell shock during his recovery from wounds after the battle of Pozières, during the Somme offensive. His performance there was of the very highest order, and many considered he should have received a bar to his VC, rather than the Military Cross.

The abortive attack on the Somme had started on 1 July and had been foreseen at the time as a 'bloody holocaust' – an all too accurate assessment, as it proved. A surviving officer described it as 'ghastly' and went on:

> Everyone I care for gone: all four officers of my company

> killed: dear Harold died most splendidly before the German lines. He was shot through the stomach and Lawrence killed behind him by the same shot. Iscariot was shot through the heart and all his staff killed around him; Smiler killed about the same place, getting his bombs up. No single officer got through untouched. The men did grandly – going on without officers.[7]

The Australian Division had spent four days attempting to push past the village of Pozières to a windmill on top of the next ridge. They made some progress, but the Germans prepared for a counter-attack, and preceded it with a massive artillery bombardment which left the Australians concussed and bewildered. The enemy then followed through with an attack in depth which overran the Australians' positions, cutting off many of them and taking them prisoner.

Jacka did not realise that the Germans had passed over and beyond his position until he and some members of his platoon looked out during a lull in the artillery bombardment and saw that they were surrounded by enemy. Rallying the survivors, he tried to attack the Germans in his immediate vicinity. He himself was wounded, as were other members of his platoon, and he pulled back to regroup.

He then realised that despite his small numbers he held some advantage of surprise, and identified potential targets in the form of some Germans bringing back a group of Australian prisoners, who would pass within a few metres of his dugout. Despite being strongly outnumbered (at least twenty to one), he attacked the German escorts and freed the captives. In the skirmish he was hit some seven times, one bullet passing through him beneath his right shoulder. Despite this, he continued his assault until all the German guards were either killed or fled from the fury of his attack.

He was reported as having personally killed at least twenty Germans, some of them with his bayonet. The sheer ferocity and surprise of his brilliant counter-attack proved overwhelmingly successful, and the Australian prisoners released by it themselves managed to capture a large number of the enemy. This dramatic and fine piece of leadership had an exhilarating effect throughout his battalion, and the German advance was halted.

There is no doubt that 5 Platoon under Jacka had taken immense toll of the enemy, but at great expense to themselves: with only five members remaining unwounded, the platoon and its leader were effectively removed from battle. Another important product of his action was the encouragement that it gave to the rest of the battalion, and not least of course to the prisoners who were so unexpectedly freed. His brilliant leadership and courage of the very highest order also had an important tactical effect on the Australian forces. C. W. Bean, in the official War History, commented: 'Jacka's counter attack . . . stands as the most dramatic and effective act of individual audacity in the history of the AIF.'[8]

He was carried from the field of battle on a stretcher and was not expected to live. Yet his innate determination and refusal to give in kept him going, and he was evacuated to the United Kingdom with a 'Blighty' wound. Once in the UK, he attracted attention from the press, despite his attempts to avoid it. He arranged for one journalist to be told that he was dead – a fib which was subsequently reported and provoked a short obituary in *The Times*. This, however, rebounded, because his family also received the news, and his mother, not surprisingly, became extremely distressed. Eventually he moved to Perham Down Rehabilitation Centre in Wiltshire, where he convalesced while acting as assistant adjutant.

The terrible casualties suffered by the Second Australian Division in the battle for Pozières – some three and a half thousand killed and wounded in four days – meant that Jacka was promoted to lieutenant while he was still recuperating. The rest period also allowed him to accept an invitation to Buckingham Palace, where King George V invested him with his Victoria Cross.

Five VCs were awarded to the Australians in the battle for Pozières Ridge, and there is little doubt that Jacka's action could have qualified him for a bar. Once again he seems to have been the victim of inadequate and weak reporting, but it is possible that the lack of communication stemmed in part from the enmity he had created between himself and his company commander, and indeed his brigadier, by standing up to them on other occasions.

After the war Jacka described the action in modest terms to an old friend, and Edgar Rule recorded his comments.

> There were four Huns in a shell-hole. All I could see were their heads, shoulders and rifles. As I went towards them, they began firing point-blank at me. They hit me three times and each time the terrific impact of the bullets fired at such close range swung me off my feet. But each time I sprang up like a prizefighter, and kept getting closer. When I got up to them, they flung down their rifles and put up their hands. Shot three through the head and put a bayonet through the fourth. I had to do it – they would have killed me the moment I turned my back.
>
> I think another fellow must have fired at me, and missed. I looked around and saw a Hun who must have weighed seventeen or eighteen stone. I aimed at his belly and he almost fell on me . . . A stretcher-bearer came, took off my tunic and fixed me up. I asked him to go and bring a stretcher. He went away and I never saw him again. I lay there for a long time, and then began to think of the wounded that were never found. I made up my mind to try and get back by myself. I don't know how I managed it, but I got back quite a way and some men found me.[9]

These reflections were no doubt watered down by the passage of time – but they illustrate Jacka's sense of commitment and focus and his concern for others suffering on the battlefield at a time when he himself lay at the point of death from his injuries.

His wilful and often public disagreements with his senior officers were a major shortcoming and perhaps his greatest fault. It is difficult to see why he could not have been more tactful, when he must have known he was damaging his own position, and with it his chances of promotion. He failed to appreciate that by limiting his own seniority he was denying himself the opportunity of leading and representing the men to whom he was so loyal – a misjudgement I have experienced in some excellent long-term platoon commanders in my own career. Seen though he was as one of the greatest fighting soldiers in the AIF, Jacka was particularly insensitive, and blunt to a fault. Despite outstanding war records, no Australian has been awarded a bar to the VC, and it is arguable that Jacka's conduct cost him the chance of a glorious double.

Although he made a remarkable recovery from his many physical wounds, the effects of the bombardment at Pozières left him close to a nervous breakdown. For a while he became incapable of signing his name, and any small, unexpected noise would throw him into a fit of shaking which lasted for hours. Rest was the main factor that enabled him to regain his mental stability, but a further element in his recovery was his courage in recognising his condition and making a determined effort to overcome it.

It is now an accepted fact that individuals suffer from battle exhaustion when they have burnt up their mental reserves. There are horrendous stories from the First World War of soldiers who had conducted themselves with valour and distinction, only to run out of these necessary reserves, and then to be court-martialled or in some cases shot for cowardice.

A sergeant typist recalled how the noise of a box lid hurriedly closed would set up a physical shaking that would continue for hours at a stretch, during which time Jacka was incapable of signing his name to an order or memo. Realising what a state he was in, he himself took action to combat it. Yet at no time did it cross his mind to become LOB (left out of battle). It was to his superiors' credit that they tried to send him back to Australia, and only his own fervent expostulation prevented him returning. On rejoining the battalion he was well aware of the threat to his mental health and worked with his customary determination to overcome it. He did so with success where another man might have failed.

Despite his physical weakness, Jacka considered the idea of joining the Royal Flying Corps but discarded it, and concentrated on making a full recovery so that he could go back to his battalion for the next stage of operations. No matter that he had already achieved all that might reasonably have been expected of any man, he still refused all opportunities of retiring to Australia.

Returning to 14th Battalion, he was delighted to find a new commanding officer in the form of Lieutenant Colonel John Peck. For the first time he felt he had a CO who understood him and whom he could respect and work with. Jacka's habit of talking freely about what he considered to be the faults of senior officers had naturally led some of them to doubt his loyalty and his ability to carry out orders. Peck, however, saw his true value and determined to build on his strengths while ignoring his weaknesses. Furthermore Peck himself developed a fine reputation as a leader who put his men before himself. All this met with Jacka's unstinting approval.

Peck promoted Jacka to captain and appointed him the battalion's intelligence officer. Most men might have seen this as a chance to limit front-line activity and concentrate on the collation and dissemination of information. Not Jacka, who, at the first opportunity, once again thrust himself into no man's land at the Battle of Bullecourt in April 1917.

In the early spring of 1917 the German commander-in-chief withdrew from the Somme Line to the recently constructed and tactically more tenable Hindenburg Line. In April the British forces planned a major assault, and the Australian Division was instructed to carry out a diversionary attack at Bullecourt. 4th Brigade, which included 14th Battalion, was to play a leading role. During the night before the attack Jacka, as intelligence officer, went forward to test the German defences and their barbed wire in particular.

Together with one other man, he moved cautiously into no man's land and laid out a white tape which would act as a start line for the battalion. On the way back to his own lines he came across a German officer and a soldier. Since they were likely to discover the tape and give warning of the impending attack, he drew his pistol to shoot the officer but it clicked on an empty chamber – whereupon he hit the man with his pistol and took him and his orderly prisoner.

His assessment of the German defences was grim. The wire was some of the thickest he had seen, and had not been broken up by Allied artillery fire. It was clear that an attack would result in enormous Australian casualties unless the barriers could be breached by tanks – but only twelve tanks were available, and in the event even these proved mechanically unreliable. Furthermore, the armoured command system was separate from that of the infantry, and the whole operation lacked cohesion.

Jacka submitted a detailed report, couched in typically forthright terms, predicting that the results would be disastrous, but his warning was largely ignored and served only to gain him yet further criticism from his superiors. When the attack went in, the Australian divisional commander attempted to call down additional artillery support, but this was refused on numerous occasions. Many men were killed by their own gunners, who eventually opened up too late to be of use during the battle, but at a time when prisoners were being marched to the rear of the German lines.

Without fire support, and with the destruction of its limited armoured support, the task was beyond the capability of the 4th Australian Brigade. In the ensuing action they lost 2339 men, of whom nearly a thousand became prisoners of war – the largest number of Australians captured in a single battle throughout the First World War. The action destroyed the brigade's combat effectiveness – and the real fault lay in the failure of the British senior command to supply adequate artillery support.

After the battle 4th Brigade was placed in reserve to regroup and rebuild. Almost at once, however, an emergency developed and the brigade was ordered back into the line, missing its promised rest and recuperation. When 4th Brigade Commander Brigadier General Brand arrived to brief 14th Battalion, Jacka, who was furious about the planned deployment and loss of R & R (rest and recuperation) – not so much for himself as for the men under his command – argued with him in public and accused him of deliberately breaking his promise. A non-commissioned officer present at the time wrote in his diary that Jacka subsequently commented:

> These people make me sick. They go running after the heads, volunteering for everything. 'My men will do this' and 'My men will do that!' They take fine care they are not in it themselves.

(After the war Brand became one of Jacka's greatest supporters in Australia, and spoke with eloquence on his death; but during the conflict he was one of his *bêtes noires*.)

This was only one of several similar incidents, and it is not difficult to see why such a confrontational attitude undermined Jacka's chances of further promotion. The losses were so severe

A momentous occasion: Queen Victoria presenting the Victoria Cross to some of the first winners in Hyde Park on 26 June 1857. (*The Royal Collection*)

Field Marshal Sir William Slim distinguished between moral courage and physical courage, and suggested that physical courage 'is an emotional state which urges a man to risk injury or death'. (*TRH Pictures*)

Lord Moran – Medical Officer to 1st Battalion Royal Fusiliers 1914–17 and subsequently physician to Sir Winston Churchill. He wrote of courage that 'a man's willpower was his capital . . . when his capital was done he was finished'. (*Dimitri Kessel/Time Life/Getty Images*)

Private Bill Speakman VC, Black Watch attached to the King's Own Scottish Borderers – in Korea in 1951 'he led countercharge after countercharge' against the attacking Chinese. Speakman was a man fired by 'hot' courage. (*Imperial War Museum*)

Leading Seaman Mick Magennis VC – a diver aboard HMS Midget Submarine XE3 – ripped his hands to shreds as he fixed six pairs of timed charges to the Japanese heavy cruiser *Takao* in 1945. Magennis exemplifies 'cold' courage. (*Imperial War Museum*)

Captain Noel Chavasse VC and Bar, MC: Chavasse served in the trenches from 1914 to 1917, never killed anyone nor did he fire a shot in anger. This portrait, commissioned by the Chavasse family, was painted posthumously. (*St Peter's College, Oxford*)

Noel and his twin brother Christopher as athletics Blues at Oxford. (*Imperial War Museum*)

The pauper's grave of Colour Sergeant John Byrne VC, DCM, 68th Light Infantry, at St Woolos Cemetery, Newport, which was refurbished in 1985, some one hundred and thirty years after Byrne won his VC at the Battle of Inkerman.

In November 1854 an Anglo-French force was besieging Sebastopol in the Crimea. On 5 November a Russian army attacked at Inkerman. The Russians had numerical superiority, perhaps fifty thousand men against fifteen thousand, but were eventually forced to withdraw, having lost some twelve thousand men to the Anglo-French force's three and a half thousand. (*AKG Images*)

Albert Ball VC, DSO and two Bars, MC, when a 2nd Lieutenant. Ball fought with superhuman determination and destroyed or forced down nearly seventy German aircraft. (*Imperial War Museum*)

Albert Ball in his SE5, A4850, in 1917.

Australian forces at Gallipoli, where there were over thirty-three thousand Australian casualties. Lance Corporal Albert Jacka, Australia's first VC of the First World War, won his award here. (*Camera Press*)

a1Captain Albert Jacka VC, MC and Bar: one of Australia's greatest heroes. (*Imperial War Museum*)

Lieutenant Commander David Wanklyn VC, DSO and two Bars with his bride, Elspeth 'Betty' Kinloch, 5 May 1938. Wanklyn was the first submariner to win a VC in the Second World War.

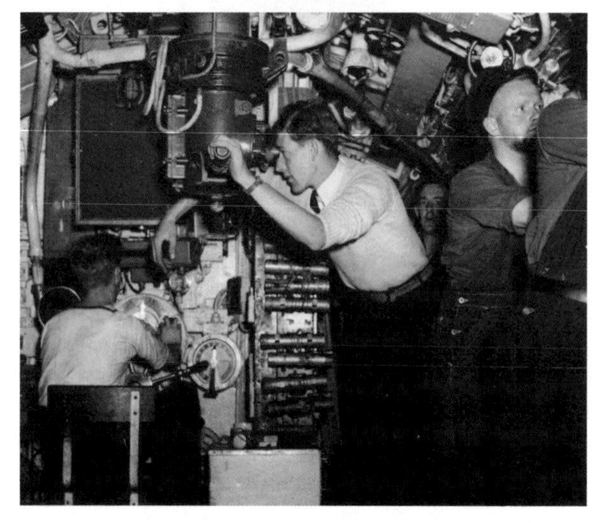

Control Room of *Upholder*'s sister ship *Utmost*. It was in similarly claustrophobic surroundings that Wanklyn when under attack remained imperturbable. (*Royal Navy Submarine Museum*)

that additional promotions were ordered, but once again Jacka himself was excluded and remained a captain. Colonel Peck did, however, appreciate his contribution and the importance of his reconnaissance and report, and saw that along with several other officers he was awarded the Military Cross. Sadly Peck himself then ran out of personal reserves: becoming exhausted, he collapsed from strain and had to be invalided home.[10]

Although Jacka was never one to advertise his own accomplishments, he nevertheless had a simple expectation of reward for his undoubtedly outstanding service, and when that reward was not forthcoming in the form of medals or promotion (particularly the latter), he felt deeply aggrieved. His stubbornness and habit of speaking his mind were both his greatest asset and his greatest enemy. 'Jacka vacillated between being the most popular and the most unwanted officer in the AIF,' wrote Ian Grant in his biography.[11] 'It is little wonder that his bitterness grew.'

Despite the pressure he had been under, Jacka continued to operate aggressively with the battalion until on 7 July his luck ran out and a sniper wounded him in the thigh severely enough for him to be sent to the United Kingdom. Yet he recovered within weeks and in late August rejoined the battalion, only to find it had acquired a disastrous commanding officer, resulting in disarray and a severe dip in morale. Even worse, the second-in-command had lost the confidence of the soldiers, while the adjutant was considered a coward and incompetent.

At one stage members of the battalion, encouraged by Jacka, submitted mass resignations to the brigadier – an act bordering on mutiny. A further public argument with Brand must finally have finished Jacka's prospects of promotion – if any still existed. 'Sparks flew,' wrote one of the officers present. 'The rest of us were amazed to think of a captain airing his views in this manner to a general. It was too much for most of us – we were thunderstruck.'[12]

Meanwhile the Germans, bolstered by massive reinforcements from the now-defunct Eastern Front, threatened a major advance based on the Hindenburg Line. The Allies countered by making a series of limited advances on a wide front with the intention of 'stealing' bits of territory from the enemy.

The battle of Polygon Wood may well have been Jacka's finest moment. On 26 September his brigade was ordered to press forward some 1400 metres. Once again he fell out with Brigadier Brand, and to his own shame refused to offer him advice on the forthcoming attack – on the basis that whenever he disagreed with him, he was threatened with arrest. It seems that even he was becoming tired and somewhat unbalanced at this stage of the war – hardly surprising after three years of intense fighting and having suffered seventeen wounds. His recalcitrance may well have been to the detriment of the overall plan, and of course ironically of his own soldiers.

Three battalions attacked, supported this time by a substantial artillery barrage. Jacka himself, leading aggressive assaults on enemy pillboxes containing machine-gunners, captured prisoners and killed many of the occupants, enabling his battalion to gain their objective with fewer casualties.

Showing leadership well beyond his role as a company commander, he noticed that the next-door battalion appeared to be on the verge of breaking backwards in the face of a ferocious German counter-attack. The Australians' difficulties were exacerbated by the fact that shells from their own artillery were falling short on to their position. At huge personal risk he recovered flares from his runner, who had been killed in no man's land, and let them off to signal for a switch of the artillery fire, sending the battalion a message: 'If the Hun attacks the 15th, we shall hop out and meet the blighters. Advise the 15th.'

His leadership undoubtedly played a major role in keeping the battalion together. His commanding officer, who was subsequently dismissed, put him and others in for Military Crosses, but none was granted, probably because the overall action was not deemed a success.

Nevertheless, the Australians themselves made such good progress that they created an opportunity to break through the German lines and secure ground beyond. This, however, was outside the scope of the plan and would have run the risk of isolating elements of the forward troops. Jacka had to be restrained – and probably correctly so.

His leadership indicates that he had matured in recent months, and that he showed the potential to command at a level higher than company. But, true to form, he had again become embroiled in an argument with his brigade commander before the battle – and clearly senior officers found it unacceptable to have such acrimony added to the stresses of an intense conflict.

Jacka's inability to accept decisions with which he was at variance indicates that he would have been a hopeless soldier in peacetime. Even so, he won the right to lead from his own reputation and from the respect that his own men held for him – and this is a critically important aspect of leadership in war. When Napoleon demanded 'lucky generals', he really meant generals who succeeded by whatever means. As Lord Moran aptly summarised: 'The secret of success in war is success', and Jacka was nothing if not successful. He was successful at surviving (the first requirement), successful as a tactician, successful as a manager of his men, and, most importantly, successful at destroying and defeating the enemy, be they Turks or Germans.

This success gave him a reputation that inspired the whole of the AIF; the inspiration spread to the Australian homeland; and this in turn added to the illustrious combat reputation of the Australian forces. Indeed, I believe it played a significant part in inspiring the Australian nation to appreciate that it was capable of standing on its own feet and did not need to be a puppet of the United Kingdom. There is a case for saying that Jacka also opened the way for Australia to become an independent member of the Commonwealth and a leader in world affairs, the Pacific region in particular.

After the Polygon Wood battle he served on in command of 'D' Company and took part in a variety of smaller actions, many of them at patrol level. At no time did his aggressiveness and focus on defeating the enemy waver, and it was only when his luck finally ran out on 15 May 1918 that he retired, not through his own choice but due to further wounds.

He was with his men in the forward trenches when the German artillery delivered mustard-gas shells. The gas not only damaged his lungs and burnt his face and eyes but also infected his old wounds.

When evacuated from the front line, he was in such a serious condition that he could not be moved back to the United Kingdom for proper hospital treatment for several days.

The injuries sustained in his gassing all but killed him: there was no question of him returning to duty, and he spent nearly four months in hospital, much of it at the Third London Hospital, where he underwent major surgery and was downgraded by a medical board to 'Light Duties', which in military parlance means administrative and sedentary work. In the words of his biographer, Ian Grant, 'The spirit was unbroken but the flesh could no longer carry him.'[13]

Although he had obvious claim on an early passage to Australia, he nevertheless chose to remain in the United Kingdom for a further year, giving as his reason his belief that married men should have priority. His arguments do not sound convincing, for men were being repatriated by ship, and the odd extra passenger would have made no difference at all.

On 28 August 1918 the Australian Imperial Force Headquarters instructed its London HQ:

> In view, however, of Captain Jacka's long service in the AIF and the fact that he has been wounded a number of times, the GOC directs that he should be returned to Australia on leave when he is fit to travel. This will meet the wishes of the Australian Government and the trip to Australia will ensure for Captain Jacka a well earned rest.[14]

But the man himself remained unimpressed by government or military instructions, and a month and many exchanges later the AIF relented:

> Dear Captain Jacka,
> The General has asked me to drop you a note to let you know that your remaining in England has been approved. I expect the official notification will be through in about two days.[15]

This was the last major battle that Jacka won before his discharge. He spent his time in the United Kingdom carrying out administrative duties at Depot Number 1, in London, where he took a keen interest in organising sporting events. He had no intention of sitting back and relaxing or taking any privilege that might come his way as a result of his fame. He did go on leave, but one can only speculate about his reasons for delaying, for a further year, his return to Australia. Maybe he felt insecure about the position he would hold when he returned to his birthplace with few civilian qualifications and a short track record in forestry. During his period in Europe he had probably developed greater ambitions, but it is also likely that he feared the glorification and idolatry he expected he would receive. The humble side of his nature told him to avoid this if possible, and he mistakenly saw a delay as the means of keeping out of the limelight until his name was forgotten.

Perhaps he also wanted time to reflect – which would have been a wise option after the intensity of the war. Certainly it was during this period that he conceived the idea of running his own business. Like any soldier, he little appreciated the complexities and cutthroat nature of business life; but running his own show, and not having to suffer the interference and bureaucracy of senior people in the hierarchy, appealed to his independent nature. He may also have felt that the follow-up treatment for his wounds would be better in the UK than at an Australian hospital less experienced in treating war wounds.

He eventually embarked on the *Euripides* on 7 September 1919, and his reception in Melbourne took him by surprise: far from being forgotten after his delayed repatriation, he became an instant hero and received overwhelming acclaim the moment he stepped ashore. The crowds, even children allowed out of school, surrounded his car, and it took a section of old 14th Battalion hands to protect him.

Like many winners of the ultimate award for gallantry, he felt that the medal represented not his own efforts but those of the men with whom he had served and faced the dangers of war, and above all of those who had died. He could not understand why he himself should be treated as a hero above all others, nor did he wish to be. However, his very reluctance to return home had added to his stature and made him a national hero.

In military parlance Jacka 'had a brilliant war'. His survival itself was an achievement of significant magnitude, and luck, as so often in military operations, played an important part in it. But luck alone does not win the Victoria Cross. His courage and his ability to focus totally on the operation in hand, together with his tactical skill, were the key factors in his military achievements.

It is tempting to imagine that he wandered around the battlefield with complete impunity, as if protected by some shield. But this was not the case. There may have been occasions when he took personal risks in order to inspire those under his command to even greater efforts, but he must also be credited with an outstanding comprehension of the use of ground to enhance his own protection and the effectiveness of the troops under his command. These instinctive military attributes automatically gained him the respect and following of his men. He had all the instincts, and later the experience, to succeed in his small battles, and to do so without squandering the lives of those under his command. As a soldier he was a man of outstanding and unique ability.

With the passage of time and the chance to assess his achievements in the context of Australia's important contribution to the Allied cause in World War I, it is probable that Jacka's real place in Australian history will become increasingly recognised. As Ian Grant wrote in his biography: 'His safe return to Australian shores revealed that it was possible for essentially Australian characteristics of bravery, resourcefulness and modesty to triumph in the European war. His return marked the physical culmination of the war effort for many people.'[16]

I would go further, to suggest that his return also marked a new era in Australian history, when his fellow people understood their own worth and potential for greatness, and moved forward towards independence from the British to develop into what is now one of the most influential nations in the Pacific region.

Like Charlie Upham (chapter 9), Jacka had no time for fame and glory. He refused to apply for government returnee grants, and in the difficult time that culminated in the great recession of the early 1930s never sought to use his reputation as a passport to an easy life.

At the start of the war a successful but somewhat sharp Australian businessman, John Wren, had offered £500 and a gold watch to the first Australian VC winner. The prize money was clearly due to Jacka, but according to his family he refused it. However, Wren was nothing if not persistent, and he saw the potential of exploiting the hero's fame by bringing him into a business venture.

When Jacka finally managed to detach himself from public adulation, he fulfilled his dream of becoming an independent businessman in a set-up where he was the boss. After demobilisation in January 1920, having refused many offers of employment from others (including, it is reported by his family, one as chief commissioner of the Victoria Police Force), he established an import-export business, Roxburgh Jacka & Co. Pty Ltd., to purvey imported electrical household equipment. At long last he was in charge of his own show, with the one vital exception that he did not have financial control: that was held by Wren, who had made a significant investment in the company.

Servicemen are brought up on a different set of ethics and principles from their civilian counterparts. Strengths that may have helped build a successful service career and battle reputation frequently become the very weaknesses that lead many of them to be unsuccessful in business. In the services, trust and loyalty are two of the great principles of management, but in business they are liable to be overwhelmed by financial imperatives, and are of little value when a commercial venture comes under pressure.

A further shortcoming in a serviceman's upbringing is the lack of a comprehensive understanding of accounts and financial management. Even today, when service commanders have greater responsibility for managing budgets, they do not face their civilian counterparts' ultimate sanction of going bankrupt or of losing their jobs and income at no notice.

I suspect that Jacka had little understanding of accounts and cash management, although he would have been astute enough to take the advice of others, so far as it could be trusted. Success in business depends on an individual's ability to contribute towards the bottom line. No such materialistic expectation is placed on a serviceman, and certainly Jacka had never had to achieve such commercial priorities in battle.

And so the outstandingly successful service leader, with an excellent tactical brain and a national reputation behind him, moved into the shark-infested waters of post-war commercialism in Australia. No doubt he took Wren's advice on the financial structure of his new company, and he was only too happy to let him invest in it.

For some years it proved a success and benefited from the euphoric post-war boom of the early 1920s. Jacka himself seems to have grown more at peace with himself and the world, and was able to apply his instinctive leadership qualities for the benefit of his customers and clients. However, once the recession began to bite, the loyalty of others withered around him.

By then other aspects of his personality had asserted themselves. He was still a member of the Rechabite Order, which kept him teetotal, and throughout his life he had been ill at ease and lacked confidence in the presence of women. While there is no suggestion that he resorted to drink, he did relax sufficiently to find himself a wife, Francis Veronica Carey (known as Vera), whom he married in 1921. They produced no children of their own, but they adopted a daughter, Betty. The marriage gradually deteriorated to the point at which he and Vera parted company, at the very time when perhaps he needed her most, in the late 1920s, with his health declining almost as rapidly as his financial security. (In spite of the break-up, they remained in contact.)

Wren and his brother Arthur had a majority shareholding in the company, and once they saw the financial downturn looming, they sold out, at a stroke destroying the financial structure of the business. In September 1930 the company moved into liquidation. Jacka had to sell his house to help cover the financial deficit, and the cold truth and stark reality of business 'loyalty' made itself apparent.

Those who have shared true hardship and danger together create a bond that transcends social and other differences in later years. Jacka maintained a close interest in his previous military associates and played a leading role in founding the 14th Battalion

Association. Here, he was able to bring companionship to those survivors of the war. He also involved himself in the Returned Soldiers' League, and this association kept him fully aware of the plight and poverty of many erstwhile associates.

His innate desire to help those less well off than himself moved him towards local politics. Intellectually this proved of great satisfaction and some comfort in the last days of his life. He was elected to the council of St Kilda, his home parish, where he pressed, among other issues, for improved recreational facilities, and campaigned for them to be made available over weekends – the only time that working-class people had to themselves. He had some success, and certainly made a name for himself within the council ranks and among the local populace. In 1930 he was elected mayor of St Kilda. From this position he spent his last months devoting himself to the relief of the ever-increasing unemployment and poverty produced by recession.

That same year his own business collapsed, and he became unemployed for most of his period of office, relying on the mayoral allowance of £500 a year to keep him and his family. Despite this, he is reputed to have scraped together such money as he had to pay for the reconditioning of second-hand boots for the unemployed. This and many other efforts made for the poor gained him their affection and respect, just as he had gained the affection and respect of his soldiers during the war.

He eventually obtained a job marketing soap for the Anglo Dominion Soap Company, but this gave him little satisfaction, and he was even less happy when he found himself working under the direction of others once again. Increasingly poor health, caused by his war wounds and gas in particular, added to his financial difficulties. Eventually in December 1931 he was admitted in a state of collapse to Caulfield Military Hospital for urgent treatment, but he never recovered: his kidneys began to fail and blindness set upon him until, like all good soldiers, he faded away into death, on Sunday, 17 January 1932, at the age of thirty-nine, on his eleventh wedding anniversary. In one of his final communications to his father, he said, 'I'm still fighting, Dad.'

After his death his greatest supporters – his former comrades and the poor of St Kilda – came forward in their masses to give him the acclaim and fame that he had attempted to avoid ever since his arrival home after the war. The *Melbourne Herald* reported the Secretary of the Unemployed, Mr T. Morgan, as saying, 'No man in Australia has done more for the unemployed than Captain Jacka.'[17]

It was perhaps in death that he made his greatest contribution to his country. His funeral attracted national leaders and senior officers, including Brand, the former brigade commander with whom he had often fallen out. His coffin was carried by eight holders of the Victoria Cross, and a crowd reported to number fifty thousand turned out to line the route. After his funeral local subscribers raised enough money to help his wife and child have a home of their own once again.

So at last the life and achievements and memory of Albert Jacka reached their rightful prominence, and he came to be seen as one of Australia's greatest heroes. In my opinion he was one of the founding figures of a modern nation.

7

Lieutenant Commander David Wanklyn VC, DSO and two Bars

1911–42

Not only was David Wanklyn the first submariner to win a Victoria Cross in the Second World War: in terms of enemy vessels destroyed he was also one of the highest-scoring underwater Allied commanders, and he is regarded by many naval experts as the most skilful and courageous submariner of all time. He combined a total lack or suppression of fear with an almost uncanny talent for attack and evasion, and between early 1941 and April 1942 his Unity-class submarine *Upholder*, operating out of Malta, sank an astonishing tonnage of enemy shipping in the Mediterranean, estimated at 90,000 tons of warships, liners and merchantmen.

A tall, lean beanpole of a man, Wanklyn was inevitably known in the Navy as 'Wanks'. With his commanding height of 6′ 2″, his thick, dark beard, his strong eyebrows and prominent, crooked nose (broken in a riding accident), he looked the archetypal naval officer – an impression reinforced by his habit of smoking a briar pipe.

His most obvious characteristic was his imperturbability: no matter how dangerous or stressful the situation, he never lost his cool. He never showed fear, and his steadfastness imparted tremendous confidence to his crew. He did not swear or shout at defaulters, and if he had to rebuke someone, did so in a quiet voice. Another valuable asset was his ability to get on with people of every rank and class: in an era when the Royal Navy observed sharp distinctions between officers and men, off duty he often enjoyed a closer rapport with the denizens of the lower deck than with those of the wardroom.[1]

His character and methods could hardly have been more different from those of his celebrated contemporary Lieutenant Commander (later Rear Admiral Sir Anthony) 'Crap' Miers, another winner of the Victoria Cross. Miers also secured powerful loyalty from his crews, but in ways all his own. He had a fierce temper, swore atrociously, and, when a punishment was awarded, gave the man the option of boxing with him for three rounds. Such was his reputation in the ring that very few miscreants dared take him on. Wanklyn, in contrast, always kept himself under strict control, and it is impossible to imagine him challenging one of his own sailors to a fight.

He was born on 28 June 1911 in Calcutta, the third son of William and Marjorie Wanklyn. William, an engineer, had worked in many countries, and by 1911 had become Consul General for Sweden in Calcutta. Marjorie, formerly Rawson, was a high-spirited girl and an enthusiastic rider to hounds. The couple had married in 1906, when he was thirty-five and she twenty-one. In 1915 William came home to join the Royal Engineers, and while he was away at the war the family lived for a while in Monmouthshire, where his family had been based for generations. After the armistice in 1918 they began to go for holidays to Knockinaam, a remote house in Wigtownshire, in the south-west of Scotland, and there in the wilds young David took to fishing, shooting and boating. He tended to be so quiet that he was known in his family as 'Mouse', and his mother noticed that whenever she took him and her three other children on expeditions, he would lag behind, carefully weighing things up before joining in.

Boarding at Parkfield, a preparatory school in Sussex, he kept himself to himself – except when singing, for he had an excellent voice, and had learnt a good deal of music from his mother. When sufficiently provoked, he would also perform an extraordinary physical contortion, wrapping his long legs round his neck and supporting himself on hands and backside – a trick which he was still supple enough to perform twenty years later.

From the age of six, at least, he set his sights on going into the Navy, but his hopes were temporarily dashed when one of the masters at Parkfield realised that he was colour-blind, unable to distinguish between red and green. It says much for his strength of character that, with careful coaching, he managed to circumvent this crucial disability, which would have ruled out a service career for anyone less determined.

At the Royal Naval College, Dartmouth, he again struck colleagues as a solitary fellow: rather than take part in hearty team games, he collected stamps, watched birds and photographed them, keeping meticulous records. He was not unpopular, but equally he was not very sociable, and he worked hard enough to pass out top in five subjects, before being promoted midshipman. Although shortage of pocket money restricted his leisure pursuits, he often went sailing, and became a whipper-in to the Britannia Beagles.

In the autumn of 1931, when he was nineteen, his father died suddenly of pneumonia, leaving the family in such financial straits that Marjorie had to sell many of her possessions. The disaster apparently reinforced David's solitary nature, and may have encouraged him to opt for the submarine branch of the Navy, where he earned an extra six shillings a day, and so was able to give his mother some meagre financial support.

Whether or not he was influenced by considerations of money, he told his brother Jack that he believed the future of the Navy lay in the submarine service, and his views were shared by many contemporaries, who saw the value of a relatively cheap underwater fighting force. He knew that in the dark days of 1917 it had been the German U-boats in the North Atlantic, rather than the Kaiser's armies on the Western Front, which had almost knocked Britain out of the war, and he was uncomfortably aware that the days of enormous – and very expensive – surface warships were numbered. He also knew that since the Armistice of 1918 the Admiralty had done little to build up Britain's submarine strength. All but two types of patrol boats had been scrapped, and during the early 1920s only a few experimental submarines had been commissioned. Then, in the second half of the decade, the Admiralty had begun construction of better-designed conventional models; but in the words of one naval historian, by the time Wanklyn began training, 'a sense of reality was only just beginning to seep through'.[2]

Having passed his training course at Gosport in the summer of 1933, he joined his first boat, HMS *Oberon*, as fourth hand (the most junior officer, responsible for signals and navigation) and it was in her that he first served in Malta in 1934. A year later he rose to become first lieutenant, the rank known to the crew as 'Jimmy the One' or simply 'The Jimmy', and to the officers as 'Number One' (the origins of 'Jimmy' are lost in the mists of the ocean). Already he was reputed to be a strict disciplinarian, but one who got on particularly well with his crew, because he was always completely natural with everybody regardless of their rank or position. Contemporaries saw him as a loner, dedicated to his profession, but considerate, and with a good sense of humour underlying his serious manner.

In 1937, serving in the brand-new S-class *Shark*, he returned to Malta, and there during a picnic he met Elspeth Kinloch (always called Betty), a Scottish girl from Perthshire. Family and friends were amazed by the speed at which he fell for her – a gentle but lively girl who had gone out to the Mediterranean to look after an old lady. She was a year younger than David, and although immediately fascinated by him, she was level-headed enough to return to the United Kingdom to think things over – but fate sealed the matter when *Shark* was sent home for a refit. The couple promptly became engaged, and they were married on 5 May 1938.

David's next appointment was to HMS *Porpoise*, in which he served as first lieutenant to the captain, Commander G. W. G Simpson (always known as 'Shrimp', because of his stocky frame), who was ten years older than him, but with whom he quickly established a close rapport founded on mutual respect and admiration. Early in 1939 *Porpoise* returned to home waters, where she spent much of the summer, and Wanklyn transferred to HMS *Otway*, the training submarine based at Gosport.

With the prospect of war looming ever larger, naval officers became uneasily aware that, like their counterparts in the RAF, they were underequipped and undertrained for a major conflict. Exercises were belatedly stepped up, but they were limited by absurd peacetime precautions which denied servicemen the opportunity of training under realistic conditions. One telling illustration of the prevailing naivety was the rule that submarines were supposed to surface at dusk, for safety reasons, and keep their navigation lights switched on until dawn.

On 24 August 1939 *Otway* was dispatched to the Mediterranean to relieve one of the more modern S-class boats for service nearer home, and when Wanklyn reached Malta again at the beginning of October, he learnt that he had become the father of a boy, Ian, who was already five weeks old. 'I am so delighted at receiving a son,' he wrote to Betty. 'Isn't it great . . . I hope the war won't affect him in any permanent way.'[3] He managed to get home at the end of the year to take the Commanding Officers' Qualifying Course – known then, as now, as 'The Perisher' (a corruption of its original title, The Periscope Course, with a connotation pointing at the number of failures) – on which he learnt how to observe through a periscope, how to judge range and launch attacks by firing torpedoes. He also began to absorb the elusive skills and attributes specified a generation earlier by the Inspecting Captain of Submarines:

> The military value of a submarine lies in the skill of her captain and in his powers of leadership. If you can add the hunter's instinct to a first-class, steady nerve, you will probably have a first-class submarine captain. But skill in attack is not enough. Unless the captain has the absolute confidence of his crew, you will not have a first-class submarine.[4]

Wanklyn soon showed that he could win the full confidence of his crew, and that he possessed the hunter's instinct as well. His first command was *H31*, one of the small H-class boats built in 1918;

with her, patrolling off the Dutch coast in July 1940, he not only sank an enemy trawler but evaded the inevitable counter-attack put in by his victim's companions.

Thus blooded, he went across to Barrow-in-Furness, on the west coast, where Vickers Armstrong were building the new U-class submarines. Designed for short-range patrolling in northern waters and the Mediterranean, these were small, slim vessels, 190 feet long and with a maximum beam of only 16 feet, fitted with six torpedo tubes, four internal and two outside the hull. They had two periscopes. One, for searching, was bifocal, with a large-diameter top tube; the other, for attack, had a much thinner (and less conspicuous) top tube, with a low-magnification lens.

Wanklyn's particular task was to supervise construction of HMS *Upholder*, to which he had been assigned. At 540 tons she had only half the displacement of a T-class (1090 tons); her speed on the surface was only 11 knots – half that of German U-boats – and her fastest underwater pace 8 knots, which she could maintain for less than an hour. Her single skin meant that the deepest she could dive was 200 feet – hardly enough to conceal her from aircraft prowling above the clear waters of the Mediterranean, even when she was painted in the local camouflage of deep blue.

For propulsion, she relied on a combination of diesel and electric power: the diesels, which needed air for their combustion, ran when the boat was on the surface, driving the twin propellers and charging the batteries. Electric motors took over when the submarine dived. The endurance of the batteries depended on the speed at which the boat was travelling: if she was creeping at 2 or 3 knots, they might last for sixty hours, but if full speed was needed, they would give out in a far shorter time.

Even on the surface, *Upholder* was barely fast enough to overhaul merchant ships, which generally travelled at between 8 and 15 knots, in a straight chase. Still less could she catch an enemy warship capable of 20 knots or more. This meant that she had to intercept, rather than pursue, and to position herself accordingly. Successful hunting would depend on receiving good intelligence of enemy convoy movements.

Accurate positioning was one thing, accurate shooting another.

To aim his torpedoes, the captain had to be able to see his target: this meant that the submarine had to be within 12 feet of the surface, and any speed greater than about 3 knots set up an easily detectable wash around the periscope. This in turn made precise control of the boat's depth difficult, especially in rough water, for U-class vessels were very sensitive and hard to hold steady. The torpedoes, 21 inches in diameter and known as 'fish', travelled at 40 knots, and could cover 1000 yards in about 40 seconds, but they carried no homing device, and could be aimed only by pointing the submarine in the right direction. The captain had a small rangefinder built into the periscope, and a primitive calculating apparatus known as 'the fruit machine' to help analyse all the information available; but much depended on his own judgement of range, and of the angle and speed at which the target was moving.

Internally, with an operational crew of thirty-one, *Upholder* was extremely cramped. In the tiny wardroom the four officers had bunks, two of which were fixed, and two hinged so that they could be let down. The captain had no privacy: as one former officer put it, 'He just rolled out of his bunk and sat down for breakfast at the table in the middle.' In the forward compartment, which housed the torpedoes, the stokers and junior ratings barely had room to move: whenever a salvo was fired, their hammocks had to be dismantled before the tubes could be reloaded. Every available space was packed with food, stores and equipment, and whenever the submarine dived, the air became ever fouler with the stink of fuel oil, decomposing vegetables, human sweat and the effusions from the chemical lavatory, until it was as thick as a London fog. Even for the officers, washing facilities were extremely limited, and scarcely any of the crew shaved during patrols.

(For a soldier like myself, it would have been intensely claustrophobic to live and fight in such a confined environment. When serving in the Falkland Islands as the Military Commissioner and Commander of British Forces, I had the privilege of visiting a submarine lying off the islands (it is always a privilege for a 'Pongo', as the Navy irreverently describe soldiers regardless of rank or position, to visit a Royal Navy ship on patrol). Delivered by helicopter,

I was winched on board the sleek, fish-like body in a moderate sea and taken below. Even a modern submarine, in non-hostile waters, seemed exceedingly cramped, and I can well imagine how stressful life must have been in *Upholder* during the war: clearly there was no room for anyone temperamentally unsuited, or for anything other than the most outstanding leadership from the captain.)

Once *Upholder* had been launched, trials at sea and in sea lochs showed up her strengths and weaknesses. The trials also revealed some of the captain's qualities. Michael St John, the Number One, was amazed by what he called Wanklyn's 'intuitive perception' – his almost uncanny ability to anticipate problems or danger. This was illustrated by an incident during torpedo trials in Loch Long, where patches of fresh water, flowing down among the salt, each with a different buoyancy, made it difficult to keep the boat trimmed (balanced, and maintaining a steady depth). At one point Wanklyn disconcerted St John by giving a sudden order, 'Blow main ballast', to lighten the load. Normally, a captain did not interfere when his Number One was on the trim, but somehow Wanklyn had sensed that they were about to enter a pocket of fresh water, which would have made the submarine plunge suddenly, had not pre-emptive action been taken.

Between trials Wanklyn took to the rivers with his fishing rod and to the hills with his shotgun. One day he brought back a hare, which he insisted on hanging on the bulkhead door that separated the fore-ends from the seamen's mess, with a cup under its nose to catch the blood – and so noisome did the corpse become that after a week the sailors, who could not stand the smell any longer, threatened to mutiny. In the end Wanklyn himself cooked the hare, and the crew got some of it to eat as a reward for their stoicism.

That autumn, in the Lake District and the western Highlands of Scotland, he and Betty managed to spend a good deal of time together. She too was keen on fishing, and they took little Ian with them when they went down to the river. She can have had no inkling that once David had sailed on his next voyage, she would never see him again.

Just before *Upholder* left home waters, to Wanklyn's great vexation Michael St John was snatched from him, to go on The Perisher, and replaced by First Lieutenant M. L. C. Crawford, universally known as 'Tubby' – partly from his comfortable frame, but also from the wide and friendly grin with which he greeted the world. At twenty-three, he was already usefully experienced, having served in submarines in the Mediterranean and the North Sea; and although it was annoying for Wanklyn to be deprived of an officer with whom he had got on exceptionally well and with whom he had developed an excellent working relationship, he soon realised that in Tubby he had another winner.[5]

On 10 December 1940 *Upholder* slipped out of Portsmouth harbour, and after a slow passage lasting a month reached Malta, where Wanklyn once again came under the command of 'Shrimp' Simpson, who had just been appointed the local Commander Submarines. By the time he arrived, in January 1941, the island had become a key point in the struggle for supremacy in the Mediterranean. Lying immediately south of Sicily, it was an ideal base from which Allied ships and aircraft could intercept the Axis convoys heading southwards and eastwards to supply their forces in North Africa. In particular, the island was vitally important to the defence of Egypt, the Suez Canal and the Middle East oilfields. From 10 June 1940, when Mussolini declared war on Britain, Malta had repeatedly come under increasingly ferocious air attack, as the Axis powers made desperate attempts to wrest it from the Allies (in March and April 1942 more bombs were dropped on Malta than on London during the entire Blitz). But the islanders, reinforced by the Royal Air Force and the Royal Navy, held out heroically, and submarines and torpedo bombers continued to operate despite the constant assaults.

This maritime campaign had no mean success, and was an example of joint operations in their infancy. The Royal Navy, and the submarine service in particular, together with the Royal Air Force, denied Rommel vital supplies and troop reinforcements. Later, in 1942, nearly a third of the supplies shipped to his *Panzerarmee* were sunk crossing the Mediterranean, and as the war went on, losses became even greater. Artillery ammunition ran so short that little was available for use against the British. Above all, the sinking of oil tankers left the Axis forces with only a tenth of the fuel they needed and severely disrupted their build-up for the critical battle of El Alamein, where, in October and November, the Allies scored one of the greatest victories of the war.

Yet the impact of the operations such as those carried out by *Upholder* was wider still, and had far-reaching political effects. Much of the shipping bound for North Africa was Italian or sailed from Italian waters, and in German eyes Italy was to blame for the losses – causing Hitler to widen the rift that had already opened up between the two Axis nations.

As a relatively junior commander, fighting as a small cog among the big wheels of an overall campaign, Wanklyn must have found it difficult to appreciate how important his apparently minor operations would become; but it was only through the combined efforts of the many elements of the Allied forces that the major military and political objectives were achieved.

The Malta boats were based in Lazzaretto Creek, off the former isolation hospital of that name on Manoel Island, a peninsula just west of the capital, Valetta. The building had large, high-ceilinged rooms, ideal for a barracks, and bomb-shelters could easily be tunnelled out of the underlying sandstone; but the idea of cutting submarine pens out of the rock had never been implemented, with the result that boats in harbour became vulnerable to air raids.

Upholder had scarcely arrived before she came under intensive air attack. On 16 January 1941 she was moored astern of the aircraft carrier *Illustrious* when a swarm of Axis fighters and bombers came pouring in at low level. A hail of defensive fire, including some from *Upholder*'s Lewis guns, did little to deter them, and *Illustrious* suffered a direct hit on her quarterdeck. A still worse fate befell the merchantman *Essex*, moored at the far end of the creek: a bomb landed in her engine room, killing or wounding thirty-eight men – but luckily the 4000 tons of torpedoes and ammunition in her hold did not explode. Had they gone up, carrier and submarine would both have been destroyed.

Upholder began her first patrol on the evening of 24 January, and she was on the surface the next night when the operator working her Asdic listening device picked up his first contact – the hydrophone effect of propellers turning. (Asdic is an active sonar device that sends out pulses of high-frequency sound to detect enemy ships. A pulse bounces off a steel hull (or off a whale or big fish) and returns as an echo or 'ping', which a skilled operator can analyse. Asdic remains in use to this day, but because the emission of pulses betrays a vessel's position, modern submarines tend to 'listen' for sounds of enemy movement with passive sonar devices.) As Wanklyn moved towards the source, he made out the dim shape of a merchantman escorted by one destroyer. Opting for a surface attack, he closed to a range of 2500 yards and fired two torpedoes at eight-second intervals. When he realised from the lack of any explosion that both had missed, he fired two more, only to be disappointed again.

Two days later he had better luck. At 0430 he launched two torpedoes at a large merchant vessel, and one struck home. As the boom of a distant explosion buffeted the submarine, the entire crew cheered. When Wanklyn surfaced to take a look at his victim, the ship was down at the bows and appeared to be sinking – but later he was disappointed to hear that the 8000-ton German transport *Duisburg* had only been damaged and had been towed into harbour at Tripoli.

Then on the afternoon of 30 January *Upholder* detected two large supply vessels, escorted by two destroyers, approaching from the west. Again a torpedo hit one of the targets, and this time the attack provoked immediate retaliation: a destroyer had seen the submarine and sped towards it. Wanklyn dived to 80 feet, but, as Jim Allaway wrote in his book *Hero of the Upholder*,

> Now his crew was to experience the horror of depth charging for the first time. The detonations crept nearer and nearer, each one a huge tremor hammering the hull, and Wanklyn began the deadly game of cat and mouse. As the destroyer stopped, he stopped too, and when he heard the sound of movement above, he moved in turn on a new course, diving deeper, full speed ahead. In the interval, the deck plating shuddered, light bulbs tinkled into splinters.[6]

This time he got away with it. Other captains used other tactics. Some thought their best bet was to keep moving in the same direction, dead slow, thereby making the least possible noise, and to accelerate only if depth charges were making enough disturbance to confuse the enemy's listening devices. But everyone agreed that luck played a large part in any escape.

Upholder's first bombardment lasted fifteen minutes, during which twenty-five depth charges rained down near her. The submarine not only survived; she came out of the encounter with the morale and confidence of her crew much enhanced by the calm manner in which their captain had handled the crisis.

A glimpse of his foresight can be gained from the fact that he worked out a simple code, for use in letters if he were taken prisoner. This consisted of his normal signature, M. D. Wanklyn, embellished with a variety of dots and dashes beneath it. Thus a subscript of '_ . . .' meant 'Hands safe ship destroyed all secrets burnt or lost'; '. _ _' indicated 'Not all secrets burnt', and other combinations revealed that the submarine had been mined, caught in defence nets or depth-charged.[7]

Anthony Kimmins, a well-known actor, and writer and broadcaster on naval affairs, remembered Wanklyn thus:

> He was tall and lanky, with a keen, studious face and a rather untidy black beard, which gave him a definitely biblical appearance. At sea he wore one of the most disreputable uniforms I've ever seen; torn and patched and with only a few wisps of what had once been gold lace hanging from his sleeves. He wore no medal ribbons.[8]

Kimmins was rather naive in his sartorial observations. In diesel boats it was common practice to wear 'pirate rig' at sea, and this continued until the advent of nuclear submarines, in which everyone is supposed to wear proper uniform. Pirate rig was a useful way of wearing out old clothes, both civilian and uniform, which could no longer be tolerated in respectable society. The older and tattier, and the greener the lace on the uniform jacket, the better – and no one would have dreamt of wearing medal ribbons.

Kimmins was struck by the racket and confusion when the submarine was on the surface, with the diesels grinding away at full-ahead and the boat pitching into the swell; but he noticed how, when she dived, everything changed:

> The noise and vibration of the diesels stopped and gave way to the quieter hum of the electric motors . . . As the needles of the depth gauges passed the 20-foot mark we lost the effect of the surface swell. The boat stopped creaking and settled down to her steady underwater course. The sudden silence was quite uncanny . . .
>
> The routine seldom varies: sleep – eat – a spell on duty – sleep and eat . . . The amount of sleep you put in is quite amazing – it's largely the lack of oxygen when submerged . . . There is, of course, no exercise to be had in the terribly cramped quarters, and during the twenty-four hours you'll probably only move a few paces – and yet you're always tired and always hungry. And, oddly enough, by the end of a patrol you've probably lost weight.[9]

This was the strange environment in which Wanklyn eventually flourished; but after that reasonably successful start, his performance in *Upholder* became so poor that senior officers nearly dispatched him to another theatre. His commander at Malta, Captain Sydney Raw, Captain of the First Submarine Flotilla, reckoned that his first patrol had been 'extremely well carried out', and reflected 'great credit on the determination and resource of the Commanding Officer'. Thereafter, he continued to give Wanklyn good reports – but when *Upholder*'s next three patrols brought no further success, official patience wore thin.

Wanklyn pressed home several more attacks, but all his torpedoes missed, most of them because they were fired from too great ranges – 4000, 3000 and 2500 yards. Even though 'Shrimp' Simpson never lost faith in his protégé, he could not help wondering whether somebody who seemed to be such a poor shot should stay in command. As 'Tubby' Crawford put it, Simpson 'was beginning to wonder whether he could afford to retain a Commanding Officer who was using up valuable torpedoes with no result'. Simpson saw that Wanklyn himself was bitterly disappointed by his failures, but that, in spite of the setbacks, the morale of his crew remained high – a tribute to his personality and leadership at a time that was clearly very difficult for him. 'The ship's company had every confidence in him,' Crawford wrote, 'and they went all-out to give him the best support they could.'

It was an anxious time for 'Shrimp' Simpson also: in 1941 alone five of his U-class submarines were sunk – his worst losses so far – and Kimmins recalled what a strain there was on a senior officer waiting for his boats to return:

> Sometimes there's an agonising twenty-four or even forty-eight hours when, for some reason or another, a boat has been delayed. Sometimes it's even longer, and eventually you'll read a short paragraph in your papers: 'The Admiralty regrets to announce that one of our submarines is overdue and must be considered lost.'[10]

On Wanklyn's fifth patrol, which began on 21 April 1941 when he sailed for the coast of Tunisia, things at last went right. Having found a heavily laden merchantman, he closed to within 700 yards at periscope depth and fired two torpedoes, one of which hit and went off with an explosion that buffeted the submarine, sinking his victim. Next *Upholder* was sent to finish off a merchant vessel and a destroyer which had grounded in the shallows off Kerkenah, the aim being to prevent them being salvaged. Creeping alongside the stranded merchantman in the moonlight, the crew saw that she was the *Arta*, and that her decks were packed with trucks, cars and motorcycles bound for the Afrika Korps. A boarding party had a lively few minutes, described by a member of the crew:

> On blowing the safe they set fire to the ship but managed to get her papers all right. Had to come off quick as the ship began to blaze up but managed to bring off with them a few Tommy guns, a few tin hats, a Nazi ensign and a lot of other junk.[11]

As they drew away, the ship erupted in a series of explosions and flared up like a colossal bonfire. At first light *Upholder* cautiously approached the destroyer, but the warship proved to be out of reach: as the submarine closed on it, she herself ran aground when still 4000 yards off, and spent some nerve-racking minutes fast on a sandbank before her screws, threshing in reverse, pulled her clear. (There is no useful tide in the Mediterranean which will lift a ship off after a beaching such as this.)

The patrol culminated when *Upholder*, along with *Ursula* and *Upright*, lay in wait for a convoy of merchantmen, escorted by destroyers, which was known to have left Naples. The submarines were lined out east and west at ten-mile intervals, and after two days of anticipation, Wanklyn sighted the convoy of five transports and four destroyers during the afternoon of 1 May. A salvo of torpedoes scored three hits out of four, sinking one of the merchant ships outright and crippling another: the destroyers retaliated with what Wanklyn described as a 'moderate counter-attack', but at that stage of the war they had no Asdic, and with only passive hydrophones they could not track their quarry accurately as long as it lay still.

Once they had moved on, *Upholder* sank the damaged ship with her last two torpedoes, and she returned to base flying the Jolly Roger – a black flag bearing a white skull and crossbones, embellished with four white bars, indicating her quadruple hits – above the German ensign captured from the grounded merchantman.

Between patrols crews could usually unwind and recuperate, provided an intercepted signal warning of further enemy ships in the area did not immediately send them to sea again. Wanklyn had plenty of chances to indulge his passion for fishing, and he sometimes drove about the island in a pony-trap. On 10 May he wrote to his brother Peter on paper headed 'The Palace, Malta' – the official residence of the governor:

> Dear Old Peter,
> Don't get startled by the address, I'm only a guest here for a few days' rest which I feel I have earned and certainly need. His Excellency has been extremely kind giving an open invitation to any submariners who care to come and stay . . .
>
> I have at last been recommended for a decoration. So here's hoping.

When *Upholder* sailed again on 15 May with orders to patrol off the southernmost coast of Italy, things rapidly went wrong: a torpedo which sprang a leak had to be changed with another, causing chaos in the ratings' quarters, and then the Asdic broke down, leaving the submarine without any listening device. A less determined captain might have returned to base, but Wanklyn pressed on, and on the 19th he learned that a southbound convoy had left ports on Italy's west coast. On the evening of the 20th the Officer of the Watch spotted them, and although the closest Wanklyn could approach was 7000 yards – just over four miles – one of the three torpedoes he fired hit and sank a tanker. Three days later he had yet another success when he sank a Vichy French vessel on charter to the Italians.

Two victims would have made the patrol a good one, but the climax was still to come. At last light on 24 May, as the submarine headed for base, 'Tubby' Crawford, the Officer of the Watch, spotted a large vessel on the horizon to the west. Closer investigation revealed that it was one of four troopships escorted by five destroyers, steering a zigzag course. Several factors militated against an attack: the convoy had a powerful escort; the submarine's Asdic was still out of action; a heavy swell was making it difficult to control the boat precisely; and in any case they had only two torpedoes left.

In spite of all this, Wanklyn decided to launch an assault. He reckoned that in the gathering darkness the destroyers would not see his periscope approaching, and that he should be able to get close enough for an easy shot at one of the troopships. Escaping afterwards would be another matter: clearly the risks were high, but he was determined to take them.

In the event he went in *so* close, inside the screen of escorts, that he found one of the destroyers suddenly filling the lens of his periscope as it crossed his bows. Diving as fast as she could, *Upholder* missed ramming the enemy warship by a few feet – and now she was in an extremely dangerous position, inside the destroyer ring. Sure enough, her torpedoes had hardly been fired when one of the enemy spotted their track and sent up an alarm flare.

The warning came too late for the troopships to take avoiding action, and one of them blew up with a huge blast, but the strike threw the submarine into acute danger. Now, as never before, the hunter was hunted, and the next twenty minutes were as terrifying as any the crew had known. *Upholder* dived again, but the surface above her was alive with destroyers, and soon depth-charges began raining down, to explode with horrible thumps all round the boat. Some were so close that the submarine shuddered violently, lights went out, particles of cork insulation fell from the deck-head, and the needles on gauges flickered wildly. The crew tried to reassure themselves with the knowledge that in the vast depths of the sea their vessel was a tiny target, and that unless the enemy managed to explode a charge within 30 feet of their half-inch steel hull, they would survive.

Most of them, powerless to help, could only tense themselves and wait. So heavy was the bombardment that several men crouched down with their knees bent, bracing themselves for the next thunderclaps. One, Leading Seaman George Curnall, afterwards confessed, 'Pretty shaky, could not stop legs from shaking but did not let any body notice it.'[12] The worst moments of all were those when the thudding beat of a destroyer's engines passed close overhead. One man lost his nerve, rushed to the conning tower and started trying to open the hatch, before he was seized and restrained.

The only person with the power to save the boat was the captain, and he did not fail. Standing in the control room, Wanklyn quietly gave out orders as he constantly changed depth, speed and course. His manoeuvring was entirely intuitive: except when a destroyer passed close overhead, he could not tell exactly what was happening on the surface, yet his experience and flair, backed by his extraordinary control of fear, somehow guided him to the most effective decisions.

Sometimes he lay doggo, sometimes he moved stealthily, sometimes he accelerated, sometimes he changed course. Throughout the ordeal his outstanding leadership steadied the whole crew. 'Tubby' Crawford never forgot the absolute stillness that prevailed in the submarine as they lay low between attacks. 'There was complete silence apart from a few inspired quiet words from Wanklyn as he stood in the Control Room characteristically stroking his beard from time to time.'

In all they counted thirty-seven detonations, the last four particularly loud and close. Then, just as they began to think they had got away with it, they heard a sinister noise, as if wire was scraping along the hull. Confident as ever, Wanklyn told everyone not to worry: what they could hear (he assured them) was the noise of their victim breaking up. When the submarine surfaced two hours later, there was nothing in sight, but a smell of oil drifted over the water, and Wanklyn, allowing himself a smile of satisfaction, called for a cup of tea. It is possible that the submarine was saved by the fact that she had sunk a troopship: the need for all available German surface craft to join in the rescue of passengers may have deflected them from searching out their quarry and forced them to move on with the remains of their convoy, to avoid further losses of reinforcements vital to an army already undermanned.

Back in port, Wanklyn found that he had sunk the *Conte Rosso*, an 18,000-ton troopship, and that 1300 Axis soldiers had perished – yet it was not for nearly six months that he learned that the action had won him the Victoria Cross.

The man whose nerve had failed was deemed temperamentally unsuitable for work in submarines and returned to general service. He pleaded to be allowed to remain, but Simpson upheld Wanklyn's decision, which was not a vindictive one, but thoroughly humane, and indeed represented the very highest standard of operational leadership. Unlike the infantry officers in the First World War who had defaulters shot for cowardice, he recognised that the man had had enough and needed time to recover.

By midsummer 1941, even before the announcement of his VC, Wanklyn was regarded as the most brilliant submarine captain operating from Malta. The change from his earlier failures was remarkable, and his new reputation inevitably excited some jealousy among rival commanders. After a rest period at the beginning of June, he took *Upholder* out again on the 24th, but for once he drew a blank, unable to find the troop convoy which had been reported leaving Naples, and after only three days the submarine was recalled. On the 28th he went out again, and this time had better luck, finding three merchantmen escorted by a destroyer and an armed merchant cruiser. The escorts were both zigzagging well wide of the convoy's course, and when the destroyer dropped a depth-charge, Wanklyn felt sure he had been spotted. Seconds later the destroyer turned and headed straight towards him at high speed – whereupon he dived to 45 feet and made off, until he heard the warship go past.

Coming back up to periscope depth, he manoeuvred into a good position and at 1142 fired three torpedoes at the second of the three ships – a grey cargo vessel, heavily loaded, its deck covered with wooden packing cases. Eighty seconds later came a loud explosion, followed in twenty seconds by another. As *Upholder* moved away, down came a hail of depth-charges, nineteen in all, some of which even Wanklyn admitted were 'moderately close'. Once more he brought his submarine away with no serious damage, and on the morning of 8 July she was back in harbour, with the 6000-ton *Laura C* to her credit.

On his next patrol, which began on 19 July, Wanklyn brought off one of his most startling coups by disabling the 8000-ton cruiser *Garibaldi*, one of the stars of the Italian Navy. *Upholder* set out from Malta to take part in Operation Substance, an attempt to replenish the island's dwindling stocks by means of a large convoy. For the first two days the submarine guarded the southern approach to the island of Marittimo, but when no enemy ships appeared, Wanklyn moved off towards the western tip of Sicily and there found a destroyer escorting a supply vessel of some 6000 tons. A volley of three torpedoes, fired at 5000 yards, scored only a single hit, but that was enough to sink the merchantman; enough also to provoke a sharp counter-attack from the destroyer, which dropped seventeen depth-charges without ever getting very close.

On the evening of 28 July *Upholder* found two cruisers forging steadily along with an escort of destroyers zigzagging on either side. From the Asdic reading of the big ships' propellers, turning at 230 revolutions per minute, Wanklyn calculated that the cruisers were travelling at 28 knots, and after making rapid calculations, he fired a salvo of four torpedoes, at 12-second intervals, from a range of 4000 yards. Four minutes later he was rewarded by the sound of two major explosions, with twelve seconds between.

One destroyer immediately put out a smokescreen round the stricken *Garibaldi*, but the other came straight towards *Upholder*, spewing out depth-charges. Once again Wanklyn executed a masterly escape, somehow surviving an attack which lasted forty-five minutes: the crew counted at least thirty-eight explosions, some perilously close, and at least once they heard the sickening beat of propellers as a destroyer passed directly over their heads. Back in harbour, Simpson was astonished by the accuracy of Wanklyn's shooting. 'I cannot recollect a previous instance of a 28-knot target being hit by torpedoes,' he reported.

On 1 September the submariners on Malta received a powerful boost when the base was given official status as the Tenth Submarine Flotilla, and its commander, 'Shrimp' Simpson, was promoted captain. On the same day numerous awards were announced in the *London Gazette* – eleven to the crew of *Upholder*, including a DSO for Wanklyn and a DSC for 'Tubby' Crawford. The general euphoria was reflected by a budding versifier in the torpedo depot, who wrote Wanklyn a poem:

Sir I humbly beg to offer,
Or perhaps I should say proffer,
Heartiest congratulations
On the well-earned decorations
Recently bestowed on you
And the members of your crew.

No one could be any bolder
Than the submarine *Upholder*,
Nor could any tradesman wish
Better advert for his fish . . .[13]

In the middle of September information derived from an intelligence intercept revealed that a convoy of troop-carriers was on its way from Italy to Tripoli. Along with three other submarines – *Unbeaten*, *Upright* and *Ursula* – *Upholder* was deployed to intercept it. While she was on passage, her gyro or main compass broke down, leaving her only the less reliable magnetic compass with which to navigate; nevertheless, she reached her allotted position by midnight on 17 September, and within a couple of hours *Unbeaten* sighted the enemy ships heading straight towards her. By then *Upholder*'s SST (Subsonic Transmission) system had also broken down, and it was nearly half an hour before she could be alerted by a radio message relayed from base.

Ten minutes after receiving the signal, as *Upholder* wallowed and bobbed on the surface in the choppy water, yawing from side to side, the Officer of the Watch, 'Tubby' Crawford, spotted the convoy outlined against the rising moon. The three large liners, escorted by five or six destroyers, were passing at long range – about 5000 yards, or 3 miles – and the short, choppy waves made aiming extremely difficult. Nor was there time to work out the angle of attack on the fruit machine: in such conditions, the Mark 1 eyeball was the only effective aid they had.

None of this deterred Wanklyn. Having given the order to attack, he waited until there came a moment when two of the liners were overlapping each other, thus doubling the width of the target. With his submarine pointing at the bow of the first ship, he ordered a torpedo to be fired. As *Upholder* swung to starboard, he fired another, and then, as she swung back, two more.

On the bridge he and Crawford waited, tense with anticipation and soaked by flying spray. The interval can only have been six or seven minutes, but it seemed an age. At last they heard a distant explosion, followed by another. Crawford, supposing they would dive at once to escape any counter-attack, turned to go down the conning tower into the control room; but Wanklyn asked him where he was off to, and although he did consent to go below, he obviously wanted to stay on the surface to savour the effects of his salvo.

This time, to the huge relief of the crew, no counter-attack came in. At 0445 Wanklyn raised the periscope and saw that one of the liners was stationary, with two of the destroyers milling round her as they picked up survivors. A second liner was sailing slowly into the distance, with one destroyer for escort, and the third had disappeared.

At once Wanklyn moved in for the kill, easing forward with the low sun behind him; but he came so close that, just as he was about to launch another torpedo, he was almost rammed by one of the destroyers. His only option was to dive immediately, pass under his target, turn beyond it and fire from the opposite direction. Again his torpedoes found their mark, and the ship went down in eight minutes. Unknown to him, *Unbeaten* had also seen the crippled liner, was also closing in on her, and had been about to open fire when *Upholder*'s torpedoes exploded.

Wanklyn later learned that he had sunk the liners *Neptunia* and *Oceania,* each of 19,500 tons. In a report to Admiral Sir Andrew Cunningham, commander-in-chief of the Allied Mediterranean Fleet, Captain Sydney Raw reckoned that Wanklyn's 'devastating accuracy at 5000 yards' range in poor light and with his ship yawing badly was almost unbelievable and shows the highest skill, not altogether unexpected in this most able officer'.[14]

Wanklyn himself was dissatisfied with the attack, reckoning that his strikes had been due to luck rather than to skilful tactics or aiming. In fact they showed that he had developed an extraordinary knack, using his submarine almost as he would wield a shotgun, of giving moving targets the right amount of lead. The fact that so many of the enemy had died in the attack weighed heavily on some of *Upholder*'s crew; but they were bolstered by the knowledge that their job was to stop Axis reinforcements reaching North Africa, and also that, with every German or Italian killed, they might be saving Allied lives.

In November, to his keen disappointment, Wanklyn was again deprived of his Number One, when 'Tubby' Crawford was sent home to train as a future commander. In a letter to Betty, which Crawford himself carried to England, he wrote,

> I am very sorry to lose him, he has done marvellous work and is a great friend. Well, my darling, I wish it was me who was coming home today. All my thoughts are going anyway, and it's only a matter of time till I follow them in person. How I long to see you and Ian again.

Crawford himself was sad to be leaving such a successful and well-motivated crew – but, as things turned out, the posting saved his life.

The citation for Wanklyn's VC, published on 16 December 1941, praised the winner for his 'great valour and resolution', and after describing his attack on the *Conte Rosso* in May, went on:

> The failure of his listening devices made it much harder for him to get away, but with the greatest courage, coolness and skill he brought *Upholder* clear of the enemy and safe back to harbour.
>
> Before this outstanding attack, and since being appointed a Companion of the Distinguished Service Order, Lieutenant Commander Wanklyn has torpedoed a tanker and a merchant vessel. He has continued to show the utmost bravery in the presence of the enemy. He has carried out his attacks on enemy vessels with skill and relentless determination.

When Wanklyn belatedly heard the news, he did not at first believe it. By his own account – which he gave to the *Times of Malta* – he was woken at 0600 one morning by a knock on the door, and, expecting to be ordered to sea, got an agreeable surprise. That, however, seems to have been a fiction concocted for public consumption.

In fact he was out on patrol when word reached Malta, and when he returned to Valetta, nobody mentioned it; but that night 'Shrimp' Simpson surreptitiously arranged for his tunic to be filched from his cabin and the VC ribbon to be sewn on the breast. In the morning Wanklyn got dressed without noticing the addition – and only at lunchtime did he walk into the mess angrily asking who had played such a distasteful trick on him. Simpson owned up, and huge celebrations broke out. Wanklyn's telegram home revealed his own delight:

> BETTY DARLING I HAVE GOT TWO TAILS AND THEY ARE BOTH WAGGING HARD ALL MY LOVE.

In a letter of congratulation from his headquarters in London, Admiral Sir Max Horton, Flag Officer Submarines, told Betty:

> Everybody in submarines will be equally delighted as I am, for we know better than others the measure of his sustained courage and skill.[15]

On 24 December 1941 the *Times of Malta* carried a brief report, letting on to its readers that 'Lieutenant Commander Wanklyn is a man of resolute character, quiet speech and has penetrating brown eyes. He is over six feet in height and like most submariners in wartime, sports a beard . . . He is a Scot by birth [not so] but best known in Cheltenham.' When asked what quality was most needed in submarine warfare, he replied, 'That's a nasty one, so I will use a long word: "Imperturbability".'

He might also have said 'luck' – and his own was still in at the end of the year when, for once, *Upholder*, set forth without him, although only on a day's exercises, commanded by his new Number One, Pat Norman. Just as the submarine was about to re-enter Sliema Harbour, she was suddenly attacked by a Messerschmitt 109. Before she could dive – before Norman could even get down the conning tower – a cannon shell exploded on the bridge behind him, knocking him out and leaving him quite badly wounded, with lacerations to the back of his head and arm, and his back full of shell splinters. The submarine survived, but when Wanklyn came into the sickbay ashore and saw a doctor working on his colleague, he toppled to the floor in a dead faint.

'Shrimp' Simpson now made the first of two attempts to send *Upholder*'s commander home for a rest – but Wanklyn refused absolutely. It is to Simpson's credit that he realised his star commander needed a break, and that this would refresh him for further operations; at the same time it is easy to identify with Wanklyn's wish to remain with his crew. His submarine was scheduled to complete twenty-five patrols before she went for a refit, and he was determined to take her back to Britain himself. Shared experience had forged strong bonds of loyalty between him and his crew, and he had no intention of prematurely leaving them in someone else's hands.

On his first patrol of the new year he scored another major success, sinking the brand-new Italian submarine *Amiraglio St Bon*, almost three times the size of *Upholder*, and thus winning a bar to his DSO – the decoration automatically awarded for the destruction of an enemy submarine, reflecting the importance of the target. His next patrol drew a blank, through no fault of his own, and when he came back from it on 24 January, Simpson again tried to persuade him to return to the United Kingdom. Rebuffed once more, he insisted that Wanklyn at least stand down for one patrol and hand over command to Norman. To this he reluctantly agreed: in his absence Norman did him proud, adding to *Upholder*'s tally by sinking an armed trawler, and Wanklyn himself at last got a four-week break.

By the beginning of February Malta had been pounded into such a state by Axis bombers that the submariners were almost glad to go on patrol, for it meant leaving the wrecked harbour and the continual alerts, and escaping to the relative peace of the sea. The air raids seemed relentless – on 7 February alone there were seventeen attacks within twenty-four hours – and in the towns whole streets had been reduced to chaotic wastelands of rubble. Submarines in harbour were forced to moor on the bottom in deep-water berths, manned by skeleton crews, and when part of the Lazzaretto hospital was demolished by parachute mines, ratings had to sleep on bunks in a huge disused oil tank deep underground, picking their way on duckboards between stinking pools of sludge. Officers and ratings messed together in the roofless shell of the old hospital building.

Some historians have suggested that by then, in spite of the time off that he had enjoyed, Wanklyn was suffering from cumulative exhaustion. Yet there is no sign of this in his letters home. Nor is there any hint that he had developed a fatalistic outlook, still less a death wish. On the contrary, he was making active plans for the future. In a letter to Betty dated 21 February he urged her to go ahead and 'take the cottage for June and July', when he would be on leave. She could expect him in London on 1 June: by then, he promised, he would cut off his beard, and he ended:

> You won't get too prickled, darling. All my love to you both. Keep smiling and cheerful. Ever your loving David.

That same evening he went to sea yet again, and yet again he scored, sinking a merchantman, the *Tembien*, of 5500 tons. On *Upholder*'s twenty-fourth patrol, which began on 14 March, he was ordered to the Adriatic, where he lay in wait off the entrance to the harbour at Brindisi and sank the submarine *Tricheco* as it was returning to base. This scalp brought him a second bar to his DSO, but Simpson felt that he had taken too many risks, and refused to let him revisit the same area, rich though it was in targets. Again, Simpson was correct to order this, as excessive risk-taking is a sign of misjudgement that comes from strain.

Instead, for *Upholder*'s twenty-fifth patrol, the last before her refit, he sent Wanklyn southwards with the initial task of landing two Arab agents on the coast of the Gulf of Sousse, near Carthage. In charge of the pair was a sabotage expert, Captain Robert Wilson, DSO, an officer in the Royal Artillery, known as 'Tug', and a good friend of Wanklyn's, who was due for leave in the UK but had agreed to do one more job for Simpson on his way.

The plan was that 'Tug' should ferry the agents ashore in a Folboat (a collapsible dinghy), return to *Upholder* as she waited out to sea, and then transfer to *Unbeaten*, which was proceeding straight to Gibraltar. All this he accomplished, and when the two submarines met at their prearranged rendezvous in the early hours of 11 April, he changed ship, taking with him a letter which Wanklyn had just written to Betty. The commander was evidently in good spirits, and thinking of home:

> Would you like to come to Anchor Bay with me on Wednesday, or perhaps Sunday would be better? I can't produce a car these days but perhaps someone would lend us bicycles for the day . . .
>
> Well, darling, count the days, they are not so many. Only fifty-nine.

In a postscript he added, 'You would be amazed if you knew just how this one is going to reach you.'

On 15 April 1942 *Upholder* should have taken her place, along with *Urge* and *Thrasher*, in a line designed to intercept a convoy sailing out of Tripoli – but she failed to come on station. At 0651 on 14 April Lieutenant Commander Tomkinson, the captain of *Urge*, heard the distant explosion of a depth-charge, followed by others at regular intervals, and then by sporadic outbursts of depth-charging which continued all day. Later it seemed probable that these attacks were made by the Italian destroyer *Pegaso*: at 0615 that day, alerted to the presence of a submarine by a reconnaissance aircraft, the crew spotted a periscope, detected a submarine by echo-sounder, and attacked with depth-charges. The Italians saw no evidence of a hit, but their quarry had disappeared.

To this day some naval officers maintain that, with all his experience and accumulated cunning, Wanklyn would never have allowed himself to be caught unawares in such a fashion. They prefer to believe that *Upholder* hit a mine. Either way, nothing more was heard or seen of her, and after an increasingly anxious wait Simpson could only conclude that she had gone to the bottom with all hands.

Nobody will ever know whether Wanklyn at last made a fatal mistake, or whether his luck simply ran out. But it can safely be assumed that in his last minutes he faced a horrible death – by drowning or gradual asphyxiation – with the fortitude he had shown in life. He must have imagined such an end a thousand times, yet he had never flinched or thought of giving up. After he had gone, the enemy struck one last blow against him: his effects, and those of his crew, were put aboard her sister-ship HMS *Urge* for transport to the UK, but she too was lost only a fortnight later. (With her went the impressive collection of stamps that Wanklyn had amassed. A keen philatelist, he had been the first into action when HMS *St Angelo*, the shore base in Malta, was bombed: together with a naval doctor, he had salvaged all the Victorian and Edwardian envelopes in which correspondence had been posted.[16])

In her brief service life his little submarine had established an extraordinary record. She had sunk two U-boats, damaged a third, damaged a cruiser and a destroyer, and sunk or damaged nineteen supply ships with a total displacement of 119,000 tons. In a letter to 'Shrimp' Simpson, Admiral Sir Henry Harwood, the recently arrived commander-in-chief in the Mediterranean, wrote, 'Her brilliant career was an inspiration, not only to the Mediterranean Fleet, but to the people of Malta as well.'[17]

Reporting her disappearance to the Admiralty, Simpson wrote:

> I hope it is not out of place to take this opportunity of paying some slight tribute to Lieutenant Commander David Wanklyn, VC, DSO, and his company in HMS *Upholder*, whose brilliant record will always shine in the history of the Mediterranean Fleet in this war.[18]

When the Admiralty announced the loss of the submarine on 22 August 1942, the communiqué included an unusual tribute:

> It is seldom proper for their Lordships to draw distinction between different services rendered in the course of naval duty, but they take this opportunity of singling out those of HMS *Upholder*, under the command of Lieutenant Commander David Wanklyn, for special mention. She was long employed against enemy communications in the Central Mediterranean, and she became noted for the uniformly high quality of her services in that arduous and dangerous duty.
>
> Such was the standard of skill and daring set by Lieutenant Commander Wanklyn and the officers and men under him that they and their ship became an inspiration not only to their own flotilla, but to the fleet of which it was part, and to Malta, where for so long HMS *Upholder* was based. The ship and her company are gone, but the example and the inspiration remain.[19]

In a letter to Betty dated 11 May 1942, Simpson wrote:

> I have lost a friend and adviser who I believe I knew better than a brother. His record of brilliant leadership will never be equalled. He was, by his very qualities of modesty, ability, determination, courage and character, a giant among us. The Island of Malta worshipped him.[20]

Betty was presented with his medals by King George VI at an investiture held at Buckingham Palace on 2 March 1943. She did not marry again; but Ian followed his father into the Navy – followed him to Malta, as well – and rose to the same rank, lieutenant commander, before leaving to go into business.

In the eyes of the Royal Navy, the crew of HMS *Upholder*, thirty-two strong, are still on patrol, and will continue to be so for the rest of time.

8

Wing Commander Guy Gibson, VC, DSO and Bar, DFC and Bar

1918–44

Every schoolboy with an interest in military history knows about the Dambusters – the force of Lancaster bombers, led by Wing Commander Guy Gibson, which on the night of 16/17 May 1943 breached the Möhne and Eder dams and sent disastrous floods coursing through Germany's industrial heartland, the Ruhr. The raid has passed into history as one of the most stirring episodes of the Second World War. For the outstanding leadership and courage he showed that night, at the age of twenty-four, Gibson was awarded the Victoria Cross, and he at once became a national hero.

On the surface he seemed the archetypal Royal Air Force pilot: young, fair-haired, good-looking, apparently fearless and highly skilled, always cheerful. 'Not a cerebral man', wrote the military historian Max Hastings, 'he represented the apogee of the pre-war English public schoolboy, the perpetual team captain, of unshakeable courage and dedication to duty'.[1] Even at the time few people realised what difficulties he had confronted during his short life, and today hardly anyone remembers how he struggled with the deficiencies in his character. In the end he fell victim to his own compulsions – yet he remains a hero, driven by his unquenchable desire to carry the war to the enemy.

Many of his problems seem to have stemmed from the fact that, unlike the Chavasses (chapter 3), he never enjoyed a stable family background during his formative years. His father Alexander James Gibson – always known as 'A.J.' – was an official in the Indian Forest Service, and his mother Nora came from the Strike family, a clan of Cornish mariners. Alick, the couple's first son, arrived in 1915, their daughter Joan in 1916, and Guy was born in Lahore on 12 August 1918.

Nora was twenty years younger than her husband, good-looking and lively, and she revelled in her role as a memsahib, with comfortable homes in Lahore and Simla, and a small army of servants to run the household. Guy, pampered by an *ayah* (nanny) and several bearers, also enjoyed his earliest years; but by 1924, when he was only six, the family had started to disintegrate: with the marriage under stress, his mother returned to England, taking the children, and A.J. continued his work in India.

From that point Guy spent at least two-thirds of each year in boarding schools – first in Cornwall, then at St George's prep school at Folkestone, then at St Edward's, Oxford. This meant that he saw relatively little of his mother – and, harsh as it seems, maybe that was as well, for she became an alcoholic, prone to outbreaks of embarrassing behaviour and constantly shifting her abode. During the holidays he, his brother and his sister sometimes stayed with her wherever she happened to have settled, often in a hotel, and at other times they went to her parents' home in Porthleven; but the children's existence was essentially rootless.

At St Edward's Guy's performance was adequate, though not outstanding. At first he depended heavily on the comradeship and support of his brother Alick, but gradually his self-confidence increased, and masters discerned in him unusual strength of character, as well as extraordinary determination: once he had put his mind to something, he would concentrate on it intently. At the same time, he seemed curiously insensitive to the feelings of other people, or to the impression that he was making on them. His academic record was moderate, and, being sturdily built, he was only fairly good at games; in the Officer Training Corps he never rose above lance corporal.

Even at school his burning ambition was to fly. By his own account, at that stage he thought little of the Royal Air Force, and it was not the glamour of the armed forces that attracted him. He simply wanted to become a civilian test pilot – but because he was told that the best way of learning to fly was to join the RAF, he applied for a short-service commission, only to be rejected. One reason may have been that he was considered too short in leg and body; another, that he suffered from attacks of migraine. Nevertheless, he persisted, and at the second attempt was accepted.

In July 1936 he left St Edward's, aged eighteen, a stocky, fair-haired lad, and in November that year he joined the Bristol Flying School at Yatesbury, in Wiltshire. Along with thirty-three other beginners, he learnt the basics of aviation; but high winds and bad weather often grounded the students, and their course, which should have ended at Christmas, was extended to New Year's Day 1937. Six of the young men failed, but Gibson, although again not distinguished at desk work, passed out with a flying rating of 'average'.

He went through the rest of his training at much the same level, never failing, never shining. After only a few weeks at the RAF depot at Uxbridge, he passed out as a fully fledged acting pilot officer. Then he progressed to more advanced training at Netheravon – again in Wiltshire – and on 24 May 1937 he won his Flying Badge. Fellow students and instructors remembered him as immensely enthusiastic about flying, and excited by it; but he was not one of those people who master new skills with apparently effortless ease. No natural pilot, he had to work hard at whatever task he tackled, and he soon showed exceptional tenacity. Off duty, he was not altogether likeable, for although he had a lively sense of fun, and was a bit of a daredevil, his childhood in India had left him inclined to treat lesser human beings with undisguised contempt. Just as in Lahore he had habitually given orders to his *ayah* and his bearers, so in rural England he referred to farm workers condescendingly as 'peasants' or 'yokels'. The result was that although his friends loved him dearly, others found him insufferable.

His next station was Sutton Bridge, in Lincolnshire, where he opted to fly multi-engined bombers, in preference to fighters, and in September 1937 he was posted to A Flight of 83 (Bomber) Squadron at RAF Turnhouse, a few miles west of Edinburgh. The unit was equipped with the Hawker Hind – a light bomber which was easy to handle, but old-fashioned, with its fixed undercarriage and open cockpit. Going up at first in company with a more experienced pilot, then on his own, Gibson enjoyed himself enormously and began to develop a taste for – not to say an addiction to – low flying, which soon gained him the reputation of being very daring. Yet in the mess he cut an awkward figure, prone to bore colleagues with boastful descriptions of his flights, and – as usual – failing to sense the poor impression he was making.

His original contract with the RAF expired in April 1938: had the political scene been calmer, he would have left the service and become a civilian test pilot. Yet with war clouds gathering, he felt that he had no option but to stay on.

Life on the squadron in many ways resembled the one he had known at St Edward's. Most of the pilots were officers in their early twenties who came from middle-class backgrounds and had been to minor public schools, and there was an easy community atmosphere. Off duty, much drinking took place, either in the mess or at any agreeable pub, hotel or nightclub within reach. 'Gibbo' drank as much as anyone, and after a few pints was inclined to attract attention by jumping on to the piano or the bar and leading a chorus. In his autobiographical memoir *Enemy Coast Ahead*, which he wrote in 1943 and 1944, he boasted unattractively of wild evenings and gargantuan hangovers. ('Then, after a few more drinks, I was almost literally poured into the train.'[2])

In March 1938 the Squadron moved to Scampton, in Lincolnshire, within easy reach of the bombing and gunnery ranges on the east coast. That autumn, as Hitler flexed his muscles in Czechoslovakia and Neville Chamberlain flew to meet him at Munich, the unit was re-equipped with new bombers, the twin-engined Handley Page Hampdens.

With their enclosed cockpits and retractable undercarriages, these were hailed as a huge advance on the feeble Hinds; nevertheless, they were still primitive and pitifully inadequate for the war that was looming. The cockpit was so narrow that it had room for only one pilot: when a novice was learning, a more experienced man had to stand behind him and shout instructions into his ear. Even worse limitations were the fact that the bomb-load was extremely small, and that the aircraft were not equipped to fly at night.

Mock attacks and defence exercises, sometimes in conjunction with fighter aircraft, gave a superficial impression of effectiveness, but Gibson himself was openly critical of the RAF's weakness. In his book he looked back contemptuously on the force's capability in 1939. 'We had very few bombers,' he remembered. 'None of these could carry many bombs and only a few could even find their targets. Navigation was at a very low ebb.'[3] Describing his Hampden, C Charlie, he wrote: 'She was my own aeroplane, and a lousy one at that. On take-off she swung like hell to the right and flew in the air with her left wing low. Sometimes an engine died out, but that was nothing. We loved her because she was ours.'[4]

At the start of September, with the outbreak of war imminent, he confessed to a feeling of 'dull, pent-up excitement', yet colleagues sensed that he was positively thrilled by the promise of fighting. They also felt that he already had a fatalistic outlook. As he drove back across England after a holiday in Wales, he told his companion that if war broke out, 'I don't suppose we will live long enough to know much about it, or care.'[5]

Even if he rated his own chances of survival low, he was driven by a ferocious hatred of the Nazis, which he later expressed with characteristic lack of finesse: 'How I loathed the Nazis . . . a world-conquering crowd of gangsters . . . Ruthlessness and swaggering, domineering brutality, that was their creed.'[6]

His first live sortie came on 4 September 1939, when the war was one day old. A force of six Hampdens, each carrying four 500lb bombs, was detailed to attack German pocket battleships lying in the Schillig Roads, at the entrance to the Kiel Canal. None of the pilots had taken off with a bomb-load before, and there was some doubt as to whether the Hampdens would leave the ground with such a weight. Gibson became exceedingly nervous before departure: 'My hands were shaking so much that I could not hold them still,' he wrote.[7] Once airborne, he felt calmer, but he was bitterly disappointed when low cloud and rain forced the raiders to abort their mission, turn for home and jettison their bombs before they reached their target. Gibson later conceded that their leader was right to do so, but at the time (he wrote later) 'now our blood was up, we were young and keen, and we wanted to go on alone'.[8] He was denied a second chance to damage the enemy on the way home, when the RAF pilots spotted a single Dornier flying boat on patrol: Gibson longed to attack it and shoot it down, but he was not allowed to break formation.

As his experience increased, he grew more and more addicted to low flying, and A-flight, to which he belonged, became known as the 'low-level kings' in the squadron. He and his co-pilot developed a technique of diving at a steep angle from 6000 feet and pulling out at 2000, a height from which they had more chance of bombing accurately.

In December 1939 he took part in an exercise which, in a curious way, prefigured the Dambuster raid. When the Air Ministry decided that Scampton airfield must be enlarged, it became necessary to get rid of a farmhouse which was in the way, and one of the wing commanders on the station decided to carry out the demolition by means of a low-level bombing competition between two squadrons. Running in at only 100 feet, the pilots were surprised by how difficult it was to hit the target. Some of their 500lb bombs overshot, and several of those that fell short bounced clean over the house, to explode a quarter of a mile beyond it.

Live operations were still relatively amateurish. Many crew members were volunteers, and when a night bombing raid was planned, the pilots were allowed to take off at any time they chose, follow whatever route they liked and bomb from any height they fancied. Thus on the night that Gibson was detailed to attack an oil refinery at Hamburg, he decided not to take off until 0330, so that dawn would be breaking by the time he reached his target, and he and his bomb-aimer went to watch a film first.

After every sortie the aircrews dissolved their tension in prodigious bouts of drinking. Gibson drank as hard and fast as anyone; many of his colleagues admired his high spirits and energy, but some disliked his apparent need to attract attention.

Boozing apart, his other main relaxation was the pursuit of women. He had a strong sexual appetite, and his main aim was usually to hustle a new conquest into bed. Yet occasionally he was attracted by someone older, who perhaps took the place of the mother he had scarcely known.

Contact with his family – tenuous at the best of times – had practically ceased, for the clan had scattered. His mother had succumbed to drink, and was in and out of hospital. His father was about to get married again – this time to a woman thirty years his junior. His brother Alick also had married, and his sister Joan, though unmarried as yet, had given birth to two children, one of whom had died.

Just before Christmas 1939 Guy's isolation was increased by a horrifying accident. By then his mother was living in a guest house in Kensington, and on the evening of 23 December, as she prepared to go out for supper, she stood too close to an electric heater, which set fire to her dress. Her screams quickly brought help, but she suffered such extensive burns that she died next day in hospital. How Guy heard about her death, or what he felt about it, is not recorded, for he made no mention of it in his memoirs.

Providentially, he had just met Evelyn Moore, a fair-haired, long-legged professional dancer, who came from Penarth in South Wales, and whom he saw performing in a revue at Coventry. She was nearly eight years his senior – twenty-eight to his twenty – but from first glimpse he was fascinated by her: he sent a message to her dressing room and met her backstage. She, though initially surprised by the brashness of his approach, found him attractive and amusing.

In June 1940 the tempo of operations increased: every night between 100 and 150 bombers were setting off from England to attack targets in Germany. Between the 9th and the end of the month, Gibson flew on almost every other night, to raid railways, oil refineries and warships. As he himself wrote, 'it was a question of bombing as often as possible: as often as humans could possibly take the strain'.

One mission demanded particularly bold and accurate flying. Two crews were detailed to block railway tunnels near Aachen by dropping bombs that would roll into the entrances and explode a few seconds later. The first attack went perfectly, but on the second the flare with which Gibson tried to light up the target would not drop off, so he approached at treetop height along the railway line, with his bomb-aimer shining an Aldis lamp forward like a spotlight. For a few minutes he flew on, 'watching the shiny surface of the railway lines', then, as a white cliff-face loomed ahead, he released his bombs with pinpoint accuracy and hauled the Hampden upwards.

It is no disparagement of his courage and skill to say that he had astonishing luck. As mission followed mission, one crew after another was shot down, and very few of the men survived; yet he – who courted danger more than anyone – kept escaping unhurt. Once, when a shell went right through his cockpit, severing the intercom and cutting him off from his bomb-aimer, his response was typical: he pressed home the attack and dropped the bombs himself.

Other pilots became dangerously stressed, worn down by the strain of night flying and the lack of sleep, and some had to be taken off operations until they recovered their equilibrium; but Gibson seemed extraordinarily impervious to either fear or strain. Far from seeking respite, he was so competitive that he volunteered for extra raids, and in July 1940 he was awarded a Distinguished Flying Cross – not for any single achievement, but in acknowledgement of his persistently tenacious flying.

In his memoirs he tried to explain why he preferred bombing sorties to all other operations. By the time he wrote, he was referring to Lancasters, but his feeling was the same for all types. Bombers, he wrote,

> have a crew of about seven chaps, all of whom depend on the captain for their lives. They fly aircraft weighing about thirty tons and costing £35,000 sterling. They have to combine the skill of the night fighter with the guts of the day-sweeper. They

> have to face all the hazards of bad weather, icing and low cloud. They have to endure the sagging effect on morale of high casualties due to enemy action, they have to wait weeks, perhaps, to know what has happened to their comrades.[9]

Defending his frequent accounts of drinking sprees, he emphasised that 'in a squadron the boys live, eat, sleep and face death together', and that for pilots 'the one and only plan is to go out with the boys, drink with them, lead them into thinking they are the best; that they cannot die'.[10] Then as now, operational aircrew – here today and dead tomorrow – were of necessity a tightly knit group, and had Gibson stood back, he would have lost some of that close relationship. There were good leadership arguments to support his joining the lads at the bar.

Unknown as yet to the boys in the front line, a new strategy was being developed at the highest level, by the prime minister, Winston Churchill, and the senior officers of Bomber Command. Their idea was not so much to assault individual targets as to launch what Churchill described as 'an absolutely devastating, exterminating attack by very heavy bombers . . . upon the Nazi heartland'. So it was that on the night of 23 September the first massed force set out to bomb Berlin – a swarm of 129 Hampdens, Whitleys and Wellingtons that included eleven aircraft from 83 Squadron.

As Gibson himself recorded, the raid 'looked as though it was going to be a good prang on the German capital'. His particular target was the railway station at Potsdam, on the south-western outskirts of the city, but the difficulties proved formidable:

> Cloud all the way, flak all the way; no one knowing where Berlin was, our loop bearings continually being jammed by the enemy, and general chaos all round. Needless to say, we had to bomb at the end of our dead reckoning position where we estimated Berlin might be. Down below were several American journalists, and one of them, William Shirer, said afterwards that not many bombs actually dropped in Berlin itself. I can well believe it.[11]

The raid left him profoundly depressed, for one of its victims was Squadron Leader Anthony Bridgman, a key member of the unit. In fact he had survived being shot down and had been taken prisoner, but Gibson did not know this, and next day he lay in bed thinking how many of his colleagues and friends were dead. He knew he was lucky to have survived, and he gloomily predicted that operations 'would go on and on until the whole squadron was wiped out'. As for himself (he wrote later) he 'did not see any point in living'. Depression of this kind settles on men in all three services when they suffer the strain of continual operations, death and the loss of friends. Gibson's bank balance of courage had been overdrawn: he was in urgent need of a rest, to avoid long-term nervous damage.

He was rescued by the intervention of Air Vice-Marshal Arthur Harris, the officer commanding 5 Group, who had marked him down as 'the most full-out fighting pilot' in the whole of the group. Now Harris had Gibson withdrawn from the front line and posted as an instructor to No. 14 Officer Training Unit at Cottesmore, in Rutland, where pilots, wireless operators and air gunners received their final training. This, however, proved only a stepping stone, for Britain was coming under increasingly severe night attacks from German bombers, and there was an urgent need to improve the skill of the RAF's own night pilots. Gibson had been at Cottesmore less than a fortnight when Harris moved him on again, this time as the result of an unusual bargain: if Gibson would forego his rest period at the training unit and fly night fighters, Harris would reward him later with the best command within his power. So it was that in the middle of November 1940 Gibson joined 29 Squadron at Digby in Lincolnshire.

His arrival was inauspicious. Morale in the squadron was low, largely because its pilots had found it impossible to locate, let alone to shoot down, the German bombers which were causing havoc with their nocturnal raids. On the night of 14 September – only the second after he had arrived – Gibson sat in the operations room at Digby, watching and listening in frustration as Hurricanes and Beaufighters were launched against an armada of 400 bombers attacking Coventry: the defenders were so inept, and so poorly equipped, that only one of the pilots even saw an enemy aircraft, and by morning the city lay devastated by high explosive and fire.

Gibson's reaction was typical: he immediately threw himself into the task of learning a new kind of flying, a new form of warfare. His aircraft, now, was a Beaufighter, a powerful twin-engined machine which he described as 'the new aeroplane of the day', armed with four cannons and six Browning machine guns. The squadron was also equipped with the faster Hurricanes, but the pilots of both types were crippled by the inefficiency of their airborne radar, which was so feeble that they could rarely, if ever, find other aircraft at night.

Before Gibson could make much progress learning new skills, he took a few days off. For the past year he had persistently courted Eve Moore, travelling to meet her whenever he could snatch a day's or even a few hours' leave, and on 23 November 1940 the couple were married at the Anglican Church in Penarth. Rationing or no rationing, Eve's parents laid on a splendid show, with a champagne reception at the Esplanade Hotel. Guy's father A.J. was there, together with his second wife, Diana, and after the party the honeymooners were driven to a hotel in Chepstow which looked out over the Severn.

Cynical colleagues wondered why Gibson bothered to get married at all, for he knew that Eve could never have children, and he already had a reputation for sleeping around. Back in Lincolnshire after only a couple of days, they took a room in a village near Wellingore. Before long Eve became bored, sitting around all day without much to do, but Guy was immersed in his training, and soon the pair began to quarrel. For him, the new aircraft and new type of operations presented a major challenge, psychological as well as physical. In Hampdens he had been very much the boss, giving the rest of the crew orders, but in Beaufighters he depended heavily on the skill of his Aerial Intercept operator, who worked the primitive radar and sat several feet behind him. Only by trusting each other fully and cooperating closely could the two members of the crew hope to find the Heinkels and Dorniers which were coming across to hammer Britain every night.

Gibson found an excellent partner in the form of Sergeant

Richard James (whom he called Sam in his book), and by constantly flying together the two raised their interception skills to a new level; even so, it was not until the middle of March that they at last scored a kill. One night, out to sea off Skegness, their radar picked up an aircraft heading for Glasgow: James guided them in until Gibson could see 'a fat Heinkel' flying north some 400 yards ahead. Easing in to within 150 yards, he fired a burst of shells, only for his cannons to jam. The German aircraft turned away, but Gibson pursued it, and in the end, when James got the cannons going again, more bursts sent the bomber plunging into the sea. Gibson screamed over the radio in exultation, and recorded that he and James were so excited that they could hardly speak.

More kills followed, and the hit rate rose even higher in May, when 29 Squadron was redeployed to West Malling, near Maidstone in Kent, right under the flight path of bombers heading for London. At first both Guy and Eve benefited from the move – he because he got more action, she because social life in the south was better than in the wilds of Lincolnshire, and she was within reach of her friends in London. Someone gave the couple a black puppy – a mongrel, mainly Labrador – which Guy called Nigger and often took aloft with him on patrol. Looking back on that summer, he described the time as 'really enjoyable', and 'no matter what happens . . . in many ways . . . the happiest I have ever had'.

Gradually, however, he became bored: as the intensity of German bombing raids decreased, opportunities for combat dwindled, and he spent many sorties on what he called 'stooge patrols', flying fruitlessly up and down over the Channel. He reckoned that in the past twelve months he had flown seventy night sorties and thirty day patrols, and yet had seen in total only twenty Germans.

His chief worry was the uncertainty of his own future. He knew that his next posting would be to another training unit – and to be removed from any chance of action was the last thing he wanted. It was small comfort that in the autumn he was awarded a bar to his DFC. The citation, published on 12 September, declared that he continued to show 'the utmost courage and devotion to duty':

> Since joining the present unit [29 Squadron], Squadron Leader Gibson has destroyed three and damaged a fourth enemy aircraft. His skill was notably demonstrated when, one night in July 1941, he intercepted and destroyed a Heinkel 111.[12]

What he longed for was a return to bombers, and in his attempt to fix it he was brash enough to go straight to the top. On 15 December he flew north to the headquarters of 5 Group at Grantham, but his mentor Air Vice-Marshal Harris had become Deputy Chief of Air Staff, and was no longer there to keep the bargain he had made in September the year before.

Gibson had no option but to proceed, as ordered, to 51 Operational Training Unit at Cranfield, where he became the Chief Flying Instructor. Because he was determined to move on again as soon as possible, he sent Eve back to her parents' home in Penarth until he could be more certain of his own future.

As he had expected, he hated Cranfield, but his posting there proved mercifully short. On 22 February Harris became Commander-in-Chief of Bomber Command, and on 12 March Gibson received a telegram ordering him to report for interview that afternoon. In a letter to Air Vice-Marshal John Slessor, Harris wrote, 'Gibson has only been a S/Ldr a year, but I desire to give him acting W/Cdr rank and command of a Lancaster squadron as soon as he can convert . . . You will find him absolutely first class.'[13]

A wish from Harris was as good as an order, and this one produced the usual rapid reaction. Two days after the interview another telegram told Gibson that he had been posted to command 106 Squadron, which was equipped not with Lancasters but with Avro Manchesters, and was based at Coningsby, in the Lincolnshire fens.

He was naturally thrilled to have his first command, and as he went into the officers' mess for the first time, he felt as if he were 'walking on air'. He soon found, however, that the pilots were disillusioned with the Manchesters, whose engines had proved unreliable, and when he himself flew one of the bombers, he found it heavy on the controls. Luckily, by the time he joined the squadron, the larger, faster and more reliable four-engined Avro

Lancasters were already on the way, and the new aircraft started to arrive in May.

Meanwhile, he set out to mould the squadron into the shape he wanted, drinking with 'the boys' to get to know them, but taking a rigidly disciplinarian line when on duty – and because he was inclined to be overzealous, he soon became known as 'the Boy Emperor'. His aim, as he said, was to make Coningsby 'a crack station'. In spite of his tendency to officiousness, he showed admirable pertinacity in protecting his crews from the excessive demands that Harris had started to make of all bomber units. In his efforts to mount enormous raids on Germany – the beginning of the strategic bombing offensive – the commander-in-chief was calling for increased sortie-rates all round; but Gibson, determined not to throw his young pilots into the heat of battle until they were fully trained, and seeing that some of his older pilots were already almost at breaking-point, resisted with a degree of obstinacy that might have landed less favoured young leaders in trouble.

Whenever he had dispatched a force of bombers on a mission, he found it a tough task to sit up in the ops room all night, waiting for his aircraft to return, hoping against hope that all would clock in. He much preferred to fly, and although he was nervous before every departure, once the door of the aircraft had 'clanged shut', he felt fine, because it was 'just another job'.

In the words of Max Hastings, the Lancaster was 'indisputably the great heavy night-bomber of the Second World War':

> The Lancaster looked superb. Its cockpit towering more than 19 feet above the tarmac, the sweep of its wings broken by the four Rolls Royce Merlin engines with their throaty roar like a battery of gigantic lawnmowers. The green and brown earth shadings of the upper surfaces gave way to matt black flanks and undersides, the Perspex blisters glittering from the ceaseless polishing of the ground crews. The pilot sat high in his great greenhouse of a cockpit.[14]

One drawback of the Lancasters was that they needed larger crews – seven men, to the old Hampden's four – and their arrival brought on a manpower crisis, for there were not enough trained personnel available. When 106 Squadron began to get its new aircraft, five at a time, the crews had to train themselves, because there was no conversion unit to instruct them.

Compared with later bombers, Lancasters were quite small – 70 feet long, with a wingspan of 102 feet, as against the 185-foot length and 158-foot wingspan of the American B-52s, which came into service in 1954 and are in service to this day; but to Gibson they were 'huge': the landing wheels were 'huge', the propellers were 'huge', the acceleration on take-off 'terrific'. After his first training sortie, on which he accompanied an experienced pilot, he reported enthusiastically:

> Our air-speed was about 210 [mph]. Pretty fast for a big bomber. She was flying perfectly, hands off. On the controls she was as light as could be. This ship was certainly a honey.[15]

He missed the first of Harris's grand-slam attacks – the thousand-bomber raid on Cologne, which was carried out on the night of 30 May. Eleven of 106 Squadron's aircraft took part, but Gibson, to his chagrin, was in hospital, prostrated by what seems to have been an ear or sinus infection. Even when discharged in the middle of June, he was still not fit, and was sent on convalescent leave, most of which he spent with Eve at Portmeirion in North Wales, swimming in the sea, lying in the sun and walking in the mountains during a fortnight of glorious weather.

Back at Coningsby, he led and trained the squadron with energy so intensely focused that sometimes it alarmed his colleagues. The mainspring of his motivation was hatred of the Nazis, and he expected everyone to share his fanatical loathing of the enemy. When any of his aircraft were shot down – as three were one night in the middle of September – he felt the losses deeply and wrote personal letters of condolence to bereaved families, channelling his grief into even greater determination to exact revenge. Under his leadership, 106 Squadron rapidly achieved the reputation of being an outstanding unit.

At the end of September the squadron moved to a new base at

Syerston, in Nottinghamshire, signalling their departure from Coningsby with a 'shoot-up' or fly-past so low that the shock waves produced by the bombers were alleged to have broken windows. As autumn advanced, their operational tasks became more and more varied: a daylight attack by ninety-four Lancasters on the Schneider arms factory at Le Creusot, in south-east France, raids on the docks at Genoa and on various military objectives in Milan. The sortie to Le Creusot was carried out at extremely low level, the Lancasters cruising at between 50 and 500 feet, before pulling up to 4000 feet as they approached their target.

For his part in these raids Gibson was awarded a DSO, which was gazetted on 17 November 1942. After a brief description of the attacks on Le Creusot and Genoa, the citation concluded: 'On both occasions Wing Commander Gibson flew with great distinction. He is a most skilful and courageous leader whose keenness has set a most inspiring example.'

On the evening of 8 December there occurred a dreadful accident, of which, for obvious reasons, Gibson gave only a perfunctory account in his memoirs. At 1730 bombers were taking off for a raid on Turin, and a reserve Lancaster was standing by on the far side of the airfield, loaded with small incendiaries and a single 4000lb bomb known to the crews as a 'Cookie'. Shaken by the vibration of other aircraft engines, some of the incendiaries fell out on to the hard standing and burst into flames.

It was obvious that they might touch off a devastating explosion at any moment. The station commander, Group Captain Gus Walker, who had been watching with Gibson from the control tower, raced out to his car and hurtled across towards the conflagration. Grabbing a long-handled rake from the crew of the fire-tender, he was trying to drag the burning incendiaries out of the way when the 4000lb bomb went off. The explosion was colossal: the Lancaster simply vanished, and Walker was blown backwards so violently that Gibson thought he must be dead. In fact he survived, minus half his right arm, which was severed by a piece of flying metal, but seven of the fire crew had also been severely injured, and one of them died three days later.

For Gibson, the vital result of the accident was that it put him in contact with Corporal Margaret North, one of the nurses from the nearest Crash and Burns unit who were rushed to the scene in response to Coningsby's emergency call. He was immediately attracted to her, and, ignoring the protocol of the day which laid down that he, an officer, should not make assignations with an NCO, asked her out for a drink. Over the next few weeks he saw a great deal of her, taking her out to country pubs, occasionally to a film, and even to a dance. She reciprocated his interest and affection, yet their relationship never became sexual: for Gibson, Maggie was more of a mother-substitute than a girlfriend – a wise and warm-hearted young woman in whom he could confide, and on to whom he could unload some of the multiple anxieties that beset him. He often talked to her about Eve and the difficulties of his marriage, and once after he had lost highly valued colleagues he broke down sobbing in her arms.

For her, attractive as she found him, their relationship obviously had no long-term future; and in February 1943 she agreed to marry one of the suitors who had been courting her. This development gave Gibson a severe shock: several times he asked her – more or less ordered her – to call the wedding off, in the vague hope that he and she could somehow eventually come together, and when she went through with it, he was bereft.

He made no mention of Maggie in his memoirs, but his need of an emotional outlet had become great, for by the end of February his stock of courage was running low. To his colleagues he seemed the same as ever: unquenchably optimistic and full of fight. Yet in truth he was on the verge of exhaustion. In all he had flown 170 combat sorties – ninety-nine in fighters, and the rest in bombers. As he himself wrote, 'No matter how hard you try, the human body can take so much and no more.'

His final mission with 106 Squadron was a raid on Stuttgart in the second week of March: on the outward journey one of his engines failed, but, rather than abort the sortie, he eased the Lancaster down out of the formation, carried on to the target at low level, dropped his bombs and nursed the labouring aircraft home. On the way back he looked forward to the leave that was due – only to discover, the morning after he had landed, that he had suddenly been posted to 5 Group and that his leave was cancelled.

Summoned to Group Headquarters at Grantham, he met the Air Officer Commanding, Air Vice-Marshal the Hon. Ralph Cochrane,[16] who congratulated him on the bar to his DSO and then asked an enigmatic question: 'How would you like the idea of doing one more trip?' Gibson replied that he would do it, expecting immediate action – and he was puzzled when nothing further happened for two days. Then he got a still greater surprise. Cochrane now told him that the trip which he had mentioned was 'no ordinary sortie', and that it could not be made for two months. Moreover, it was so unusual that Harris, the commander-in-chief, had decided that he, Gibson, was to form a special squadron, based at Scampton, to carry out the task.

Such was the conception of 617 Squadron, and its birth and consolidation were incredibly rapid. Aircraft, equipment, munitions and five hundred personnel were assembled in a week, much of the work being done in the first three days. At first, as Gibson himself wrote, the unit 'had no name and no number', and then was known for a while as 'Squadron X'. Later he claimed that he picked all the pilots himself, from his personal experience, but other authors have shown that this was an exaggeration: some were men he did not know but had only heard about. Nevertheless, he formed twenty-one highly skilled crews, comprising 147 men, and because the order to create the squadron had come right from the top, anyone he called for was posted to 617 immediately. He also stretched the truth a bit when he described how he walked into the hall of the officers' mess and found all his nominees waiting for him: in fact some of them joined later – but it is easy to condone his compression of events:

> These were the aces of Bomber Command . . . From all over the world they had come, from Australia, America, Canada, New Zealand and Great Britain. All of their own free will. All with one idea: to get to grips with the enemy. As I stood there, talking to them and drinking beer with them, I felt very proud; surely these were the best boys in the world.[17]

Foremost among them were Pilot Officer David Shannon, an outstanding 21-year-old Australian who had often flown with Gibson on 106 Squadron, and Flight Lieutenant John Hopgood, another 106 Squadron pilot whom Gibson thought exceptional. Both were holders of the DFC.

In his memoirs Gibson made much of the heavy secrecy in which preparation and training for the mysterious mission were cloaked: he had been told it would have 'startling results', and not much more – but he must have been told that it involved water, for one of his first actions was to send a crew to fly over every lake they could find and take photographs of them all.

It is now common knowledge that the objective was to breach the major dams in the Möhne, Eder and Sorpe valleys, and so to flood large areas of Germany's industrial heartland, the Ruhr. But at the time the project was so sensitive that Gibson was initiated into its secrets only step by step. Sent southwards by car towards some unnamed destination, he caught a train, was met by a senior test pilot and driven to an old country house. There he found a man he described as 'Professor Jeff', a 'scientist and very clever aircraft designer' with thick spectacles, who told him that he had been developing a bomb or mine that could be dropped from very low level over water so that it would bounce along the surface and explode when it came to rest against a vertical wall.

'Jeff' was Barnes Wallis, an engineer at Vickers who had spent months trying to devise ways of bursting large dams and breaching the sides of warships. Although embarrassed by the fact that he was not allowed to reveal the nature of the target, he asked Gibson whether it would be possible to bring a Lancaster down in a steep dive from 2000 feet, then fly at 240 mph 150 feet above the surface, to release a bomb at precisely the spot required. Gibson replied that he hoped he could manage it, and said he would report back after some experimental flights.

At Scampton he started all his crews on low-level training, and on 29 March he was told what his targets would be. Lancasters roared about the country at treetop height, at first in daylight, then mainly at night, skimming over big lakes in the hills of northern England, Scotland and Wales. There was so much low flying that public complaints poured in. Gibson himself, in a series of runs over Derwentwater, in the Pennines, found it relatively simple to position his aircraft during the day, but he had great difficulty at night:

> The water, which had been blue by day, was now black – we nearly hit that black water. Even Spam [the bomb-aimer] said, 'Christ, this is bloody dangerous', which meant it was . . . Unless we could find some way of judging our height above water, this type of attack would be completely impossible.[18]

After many experiments, a solution was found. Two spotlights were mounted on each bomber, one under the nose and the other under the tail, and aligned so that their beams converged at exactly 150 feet. The system worked so well that within a week all the pilots could fly within two feet of the necessary height. Then came an unpleasant surprise. Because trial mines were breaking up when they hit the water, Barnes Wallis revised his calculations and told Gibson that the optimum release height was not 150 feet but 60, the optimum speed 232 mph. As Gibson remarked, 'At that height, you would only have to hiccough, and you would be in the drink.' Nevertheless, he said he would try it, and found it perfectly feasible.

As the crews trained, Avro was feverishly building new Lancasters adapted to carry and drop the huge mines, code-named Upkeeps. The mid-upper turrets were removed, as was some of the armour, to save weight, the bomb bays were cut away to accommodate the outsized bombs, and equipment was installed which started them spinning backwards before their release – a trick which made them bounce better when they hit the water.

The haste was caused by the fact that a tight deadline had been set. With the spring floods, the water level in the dams was rising, but for the mines to have maximum effect, it had to be at its maximum – and this, it was calculated, would be reached some time late in May.

When each new aircraft arrived at Scampton, its crew had to learn all its idiosyncrasies against the clock. Reconnaissance sorties revealed that the German dams were filling fast: time was running out.

The whole squadron was under intense pressure. Men were becoming exhausted, so Gibson sent them off on three days' leave. He himself (by his own account) became irritable and bad-tempered, troubled by a large carbuncle on his face, and by gout, which made his feet very painful. Yet when a doctor told him to take two weeks off, he 'just laughed in his face' – although he did submit so far as to take a recommended tonic. Almost always he was firm and fair in dealing with his men, but now and then his underlying tension broke through – as when a sergeant courteously held open the door for people coming to a briefing, and then, entering the room last, found himself on a charge for being late.

On Saturday, 15 May, the order came for Operation Chastise to be launched the following night – but on Saturday evening there occurred an event which some of the participants saw as an evil omen: Gibson's beloved Nigger, the squadron's mascot, was run over and killed, leaving his master profoundly distressed. Alone in his room that night, he looked at the scratch marks Nigger had made on the door whenever he wanted to go out, and felt 'very depressed'. Next day he gave instructions that the dog was to be buried at midnight, when he himself would be crossing the German coast:

> And while he was being buried, I hoped that we would be going over to give his friendly little soul an uplift with the job we were about to do.[19]

Sunday dawned clear, and by midday the air had become baking hot. Final briefings took place in the cool of the evening – and so complex was the operation that it took Gibson over an hour to run through the final plan. His force was divided into three formations: the first, consisting of nine aircraft led by himself, would make the Möhne dam its principal target; if that were breached, they would go on to attack the Eder. The second formation, of five aircraft, was to attack the Sorpe, and the third, of four bombers, was a rear echelon which would 'fill in gaps left by the first two'.

The first Lancaster took off at 2128, and the whole force flew away at low level, out over the sea. One aircraft hit the water and bounced off: with both outboard engines out of action and its mine wrenched clear by the impact, it had to turn back. Another was so badly damaged by flak that it too had to return to base. Closer to the targets, a third came to grief when the pilot was blinded by searchlights, lost control and crashed. The aircraft burst into flames, and a few seconds later the mine it had been carrying went off with a colossal explosion. The remaining fifteen forged on, using a canal and the Rhine as direction markers.

Gibson's own account of the raid is extremely vivid – by far the best part of his book. When he reached the Möhne lake, 12 miles long and holding 140 million tons of water, his first sight of the dam was daunting: 'It looked squat and heavy and unconquerable; it looked grey and solid in the moonlight, as though it were part of the countryside itself and just as immoveable.'

As Gibson went in for the first attack, down moon, the other aircraft dispersed to prearranged hiding places among the hills. Diving towards the lake, he levelled off at sixty feet and ran straight for the dam. Green, yellow and red tracer shells came looping up at him.

> The gunners had seen us coming. They could see us coming with our spotlights on for over two miles away. Now they opened up and their tracers began swirling towards us. Some were even bouncing off the smooth surface of the lake. This was a horrible moment . . . I thought to myself, 'In another minute we shall all be dead – so what?' I thought again, 'This is terrible, this feeling of fear – if it is fear.'
>
> By now we were a few hundred yards away, and I said quickly to Pulford [the flight engineer], under my breath, 'Better leave the throttles open now and stand by to pull me out of the seat if I get hit' . . .
>
> We skimmed along the surface of the lake, and as we went my gunner was firing into the defences, and the defences were firing back with great vigour, their shells whistling past us. For some reason, we were not being hit.
>
> Spam said, 'Left – little more left – steady – steady – steady-coming up'. Of the next few seconds I remember only a series of kaleidoscopic incidents.

The chatter from Joe's front guns pushing out tracers which bounced off the left-hand flak tower.
Pulford crouching beside me.
The smell of burnt cordite.
The cold sweat underneath my oxygen mask.
The tracers flashing past the windows . . .
The closeness of the dam wall.
Spam's exultant, 'Mine gone.'
Hutch's red Very lights to blind the flak-gunners.
The speed of the whole thing.
Someone saying over the R.T. 'Good show, leader. Nice work.'[20]

As Lancaster AJ-G hurtled over the dam, behind it an enormous column of water and spray leapt into the air, and the surface of the lake boiled and seethed. Gibson's mine had been dropped in precisely the right spot, but the wall held. He circled for ten minutes, watching to see what would happen, then called up the second aircraft, M Mother, piloted by 'Hoppy' Hopgood.

In he came, on the same track, with Gibson flying parallel and slightly ahead to distract the gunners; but then someone called over the radio, 'Hell, he's been hit!' A lucky shell had penetrated one of M Mother's inboard fuel tanks and instantly set it on fire. The bomb-aimer released his mine, but afterwards Gibson thought he must have been wounded, for the device bounced over the dam and went off behind the powerhouse on the end, with a tremendous explosion. Struggling to lift his stricken aircraft, Hopgood flew on, but he had reached only about 500 feet when M Mother blew up and cascaded to the ground in flaming pieces.

Shaken but resolute, Gibson called in his third aircraft. Again he ran in beside the attacker, to draw off the flak. The third mine went in dead on target: the aircraft got through, but was hit several times. When the water had stopped seething, Gibson started to fly about beyond the dam, distracting the defenders, switching on his identification lights in a deliberate attempt to draw fire, even though he was probably out of range. Then he called in Melvyn Young in D Dog.

Yet again the mine went in on target. This time a colossal wave of water swept over the top of the dam and kept going. Melvyn called, 'I think I've done it. I've broken it.' Gibson, who had a better view, could see that the wall was still not breached, but he 'screamed like a schoolboy', 'Wizard show, Melvyn! I think it'll go on the next one.'

In came No. 5, piloted by David Maltby: again the bomber flew into a storm of flak. There was a huge explosion, and a deluge of water went over the top. Coming in close to the dam wall, Gibson got a clear view of what had happened:

> It had rolled over, but I could not believe my eyes. I heard someone shout, 'I think she has gone! I think she has gone!' Other voices took up the cry and quickly I said, 'Stand by until I make a recco' . . . We had a closer look. Now there was no doubt about it: there was a great breach one hundred yards across, and the water, looking like stirred porridge in the moonlight, was gushing out . . . We began to shout and scream and act like madmen over the R/T, for this was a tremendous sight, a sight which probably no man will ever see again.[21]

At 0056 Gibson told Hutch, his radio operator, to send back the code-message 'Nigger', meaning that the Möhne had been breached. In the headquarters of 5 Group at Grantham, where Bomber Harris, Air Vice Marshal Cochrane, Barnes Wallis and others had been waiting breathlessly, jubilation swept through the operations room: there were handshakes and congratulations all round, and even Wallis – normally so quiet and reserved – threw his arms in the air.

Above the Möhne Gibson watched incredulously as a colossal surge of water swept down the valley, carrying away buildings, bridges and viaducts, overtaking vehicles that tried to flee from it. As the flood engulfed them, their headlights turned light blue, then green, then purple, and finally they vanished.

Setting course for the Eder, sixty miles away, Gibson sent home two of the aircraft which had already dropped their mines and led the remains of his force over the mountains. His other formation, meanwhile, had attacked the Sorpe dam, without success: the barrage was of different construction – basically an immense mound of earth with sloping sides – and the bouncing mines could not shift it.

The Eder proved to be undefended. Nevertheless, it was the most difficult target of all, for the lake lay cradled among steep hills, and to put in an accurate attack run the Lancasters had to dive precipitously before levelling out; then, having cleared the dam, they had to climb under full power to clear the mountain beyond.

Having found the right lake – itself a difficult task, with mist forming in the valleys – Gibson fired a red Very light as a marker, and Dave Shannon started his first approach. Four times he tried to line up on the target, and four times he was not satisfied. Gibson then called in Z Zebra flown by Henry Maudslay. He ran in accurately, but dropped his mine fractionally too late, so that instead of sinking down the dam face it hit the parapet and exploded immediately, with the aircraft close overhead. The Lancaster reared into the air and vanished. Gibson tried to call Henry on the radio telephone, asking, 'Are you OK?', and at the third attempt thought he heard a faint, tired voice reply, 'I think so – stand by.' But that was all.

> There was no burning wreckage on the ground; there was no aircraft on fire in the air. There was nothing. Henry had disappeared. He never came back.[22]

Next, Dave Shannon ran in again, and after one more dummy approach, placed his mine right on the spot. Again an immense explosion flung a column of water into the air, but the dam held. Then came the Australian Les Knight. He too found it difficult to align his Lancaster correctly, and made several abortive runs. Gibson felt that time was running out and told him to try once more. At last, on his final attempt, Knight got everything right – and Gibson was flying close enough to see the mine's effect:

> We saw where it sank. We saw the tremendous earthquake which shook the base of the dam, and then, as if a gigantic hand had punched a hole through cardboard, the whole thing collapsed.[23]

Even then Gibson had not finished. Telling the others to head for home, he himself flew back to the Möhne to assess the damage. He found that 'the map had completely changed': the water level had fallen enough to reveal old bridges, and below the dam a long, narrow, slow-moving lake had formed. With the eastern sky already starting to lighten, he turned for home, and he touched down at 0415.

At Scampton tremendous celebrations broke out; but delight at the success of the operation was tempered by grief at the heavy casualties it had cost. Of the 133 young men who had flown out to launch Chastise, fifty-six did not return. In fact three of the missing crew members had survived, but fifty-three were dead – and no one was more shocked than Barnes Wallis, who had been so absorbed in calculating and weighing the possibilities of his invention that he somehow had not thought much about the possible loss of life.

Before the raid, Gibson had been warned that news of it might be suppressed, for security reasons, until the war ended. In the event exactly the opposite happened: the Government decided to make propaganda use of it, and authorised maximum publicity. Within days Gibson had become a national hero, and when his award of the Victoria Cross was gazetted on 28 May 1943 – less than two weeks later – his fame pervaded the entire country.

After a brief summary of his career, the citation recorded that under his leadership 617 Squadron had just 'executed one of the most devastating attacks of the war', and gave an outline of the action. This, inadvertently, incorporated two major inaccuracies. One was the remark that over the Möhne he 'circled very low for thirty minutes, drawing the enemy fire on himself'. He did, it is true, circle, but that was mainly in attempts to see what was happening. His far more courageous action was to run in low, repeatedly, parallel with other attacking aircraft and slightly ahead of them. Another error was the report that, over the Eder, where there were in fact no defences, 'he once more drew upon himself the enemy fire'. Nevertheless, the citation saluted him as an 'outstanding operational pilot who, by his skilful leadership and contempt for danger . . . has set an example which has inspired the squadron he commands'. The citation concluded:

> Wing Commander Gibson has completed 170 sorties, involving more than 600 hours' operational flying. Throughout his operational career, prolonged exceptionally at his own request, he has shown leadership, determination and valour of the highest order.

There can be no doubt that during the dams raid he showed the most extraordinary courage, of the cool, protracted kind. As his own writing revealed, he was by no means immune to fear; yet he controlled his fear and overcame it. That night he flew a heavy bomber for more than six hours, and for almost all that time he was in danger of being shot down. For two hours over the Möhne the danger was acute, yet he ignored it and led from the front throughout the raid, when he could well have stood off and directed his supporting aircraft from a safer distance. Yet it must also be said that he had extraordinary luck: the fact that he made at least three low-level passes over the dam, through storms of flak, and was never hit, seems miraculous.

One can only guess at his motivation. Hatred of the Germans certainly played a large part in it, and he was fuelled by a burning desire to avenge the deaths of the companions he had lost, that night and earlier. He was also driven by his strong sense of responsibility for his team – his determination to look after the members of his squadron as best he could, and bring them safe home. And even if the dams raid was the peak of his achievement, it was only the latest in a huge number of sorties that had demanded the highest standards of bravery and resolution.

Operation Chastise caused widespread havoc in the Ruhr. Over 1300 people were killed, along with thousands of farm animals; railways were brought to a halt, roads cut, and industry disrupted. Yet if the physical damage was less than the planners had hoped, the psychological effect of the raid was incalculable, both in Britain and in the United States. The triumph came at a moment when Bomber Command was in need of some major success to justify its operations and its losses. In America critics were questioning the effectiveness of the Allied bombing campaign – in which the US 8th Air Force was heavily involved – and Gibson's master stroke went a long way towards restoring service morale on both sides of the Atlantic. Churchill, who was on a visit to the United States when the raid took place, was able to reassure not only the Americans, but also the Canadians, that the campaign was proving effective.

The remainder of Gibson's story can be briefly summarised. Taken up by Churchill, he sailed for Canada and America aboard the liner *Queen Mary* early in August, when the prime minister set out for the Quadrant conference in Quebec – the meeting with President Roosevelt and the Combined Chiefs of Staff held to discuss future Allied strategy. Unlike Albert Jacka, who refused to have his award of the VC exploited for propaganda purposes, for the next four months Gibson readily acceded to Churchill's request and gave speech after speech in which he extolled the achievements of the RAF, but also judiciously praised the skill and courage of Canadian and American aircrews. His youth and good looks, reinforced by his unparalleled combat record, made a powerful impression on his audiences, and he attracted much favourable coverage in the press.

Arriving back in England exhausted, he rushed up to Scampton, only to find that 617 Squadron had moved to Coningsby, and that it was now commanded by Squadron Leader Leonard Cheshire. He made an abortive attempt to secure another operational posting, but because of his run-down state he was sent on a month's leave, and then, in January 1944, posted to the Directorate for the Prevention of Accidents in the Air Ministry, with the suggestion that he should spend his time there writing a book. The result – in the end – was *Enemy Coast Ahead*.

Air historians have surmised that his posting to London was designed partly to keep him away from further operations, and partly to produce a personal vindication, by one of its most glamorous participants, of Bomber Command's Strategic Air Offensive. At first Gibson bitterly resented being cooped up in a small room away from the war, but later he came to enjoy writing, and seemed to relish the challenge of capturing some of his experiences on paper.

Soon, in any case, he was seduced away, by – of all things – the lure of politics. During his trip to Canada Churchill had seen a good deal of him, and had come to admire him greatly. Gibson, for his part, revered the prime minister. Now Churchill backed a suggestion that Gibson should be encouraged to stand for Parliament, and as a result he was adopted as the prospective candidate for Macclesfield, in Cheshire. Already he had become a practised speaker, and, by nature a Conservative, he found it easy enough to propound Tory ideas at public meetings.

For a while the cut and thrust of the hustings kept him well occupied, but the war was constantly on his mind, and when Operation Overlord – the invasion of Normandy – was launched on 6 June 1944, the news goaded him into appealing to Harris for a return to some form of active service. A few days later he was posted to the staff of 55 Base at East Kirkby, a bomber station in Lincolnshire, with the role of understudying the operations officer. This was only an office job, but it put him back among aircrews who were flying every day and fuelled his own determination to fly again. This he soon managed, going up first in a Lancaster on a test sortie, and then joining a live mission to attack a V1 flying bomb site in France.

On 4 August he was transferred as air staff officer to 54 Base Headquarters at Coningsby, the scene of his first command, and by then the home of 627 Squadron, whose speciality had become the dropping of low-level markers for bombing raids. From there he wrote an apologetic letter to the Macclesfield Conservative Association, asking to be released from his candidature on the grounds that the demands of his service career were so exacting that he could not combine them successfully with politics.

At Coningsby, meetings with former colleagues, and rumours that the war might end within weeks, sent him into a state of agitation which grew worse as time went by. Occasionally his pent-up aggression broke out in a display of arrogance – as when he walked into the officers' mess and, when people did not greet him with enough deference, asked loudly, 'Don't you know who I am? I'm Wing Commander Guy Gibson.' His reward was to be debagged and thrown outside without his trousers.

During the summer he had engineered another meeting with Margaret, gone to see her, played with her little son Michael (his godson), and promised that after the war he would come to find her. Soon afterwards he had sent a note saying, 'I love you now and for ever.' On the other hand, in August he found lodgings for Eve in Skegness, on the coast within easy reach of Coningsby, hoping to spend some time with her; but as things turned out he did not see much of her, and their last meeting was on 12 August, when they went out to supper on his birthday.

By then his addiction to flying had become irresistible, and through sheer persistence he began to go up in Mosquitoes, the small, fast fighter-bombers, made largely of wood, which were then being used for precision target-marking. When Cochrane visited the station, Gibson pressed for permission to return to operational flying, but the air vice marshal told him, correctly, that he would have to go through full training on Mosquitoes before he did so.

Nevertheless, on 19 September, to the amazement of the regular crews, he was selected as controller of the Mosquito force which was to mark targets for a complicated raid that night by Lancasters on industrial targets at Mönchengladbach and the neighbouring town of Rheydt, in the Ruhr. Controversy has smouldered ever since about who authorised his participation, for he had flown Mosquitoes for a total of fewer than ten hours, he had never taken one up at night, and his experience of target-marking was minimal.

In any case, he took off just before 2000 hours in Mosquito KB 267, having for some reason rejected another aircraft which had been specially loaded and prepared for him. With him, as navigator, went Squadron Leader James Warwick. The briefing officer advised them that as soon as the raid had been completed, they should fly south-west into French airspace – only ten minutes away from their target – at medium height, and then head for home. Gibson, however, insisted that he would come straight back at low level.

The raid duly went ahead, and it was completed after a fashion, but Gibson's inexperience at that kind of operation contributed to its relative lack of success. He was let down partly by a technical failure – at the critical moment his target indicators would not detach from the aircraft, so that he could not do his marking – but he also gave contradictory orders which confused several of the bomber pilots.

He was last heard of at about 2200, when the raid was over, circling the target to assess results. He then set out, as he had insisted, low-level for home, but half an hour later his Mosquito caught fire in mid-air and crashed outside the Dutch town of Steenbergen with such a violent impact that both crew members were blown into small pieces. Scarcely any of their body parts were recovered. At first the Germans, who sealed off the area, thought the remains were those of one man only, but the discovery of a third hand revealed that two men had died. Warwick was identified from his identity disc and from a letter found in his wallet, and his name was inscribed on the plate of a single coffin. But before the interment could take place children playing near the site of the crash found a sock with the name-tag Gibson on it, so the plate was taken off and reworked, with both victims' names on the other side.

To this day nobody is certain why the Mosquito came down. Many theories have been advanced. Gibson never reported being hit during the raid, but his aircraft may have been damaged by anti-aircraft fire over the target, with the result that one of the engines ran hot and eventually caught fire. He himself may have been wounded during his homeward run, and perhaps passed out. One or more of the hung-up target indicators may have detonated in the bomb-bay. Gibson may have been trying to switch from one fuel tank to the other, and temporary starvation may have caused his Merlin engines to backfire and belch sparks, besides cutting off electrical and hydraulic power.

The puzzle will probably never be solved. Yet there is little doubt about the ultimate cause of Gibson's death. Bomber Harris blamed himself for authorising his protégé's return to the sharp end, writing, 'I quite wrongly allowed him to return to operations.'[24] But Harris acknowledged that 'he would not stop fighting. He resisted or avoided all efforts to rest him from operations.' As Gibson's biographer Richard Morris aptly remarked, he died 'not because he was sent back to battle, but because he refused to be left out of it'.[25]

Enemy Coast Ahead was published in 1946 and at once achieved immense success. In spite of restrictions on the supply of paper, the publishers, Michael Joseph, printed 50,000 copies, which rapidly sold out, and the book has since gone through numerous further editions, remaining in print for almost fifty years. Its quality varies widely, from naive social and political comment to brilliantly vivid descriptions of action in the night skies. Some of Gibson's colleagues doubted that he had written it all himself, but his widow Eve insisted that he did. It seems that he may have had help or advice from some professional author – possibly Roald Dahl, whom he met in Washington, or H. E. Bates, who was working in the Ministry of Information: certainly his text was heavily edited, partly by Eve, partly by official censors, and partly by the publishers. His original draft has survived, and an unexpurgated edition has recently been published: many changes are evident, often designed to tone down his criticisms of people he regarded as lesser beings – farmers, Jews and elderly politicians among them – although no attempt was ever made to disguise his hatred of 'the Nazi master race'.

In writing an introduction to the book, Harris sought to excuse the wild behaviour of RAF personnel off duty:

> Remember that these crews, shining youth on the threshold of life, lived under circumstances of intolerable strain. They were in fact – and they knew it – faced with the virtual certainty of death, probably in one of its least pleasant forms.

He praised Gibson lavishly, declaring that 'his personal contribution to victory was beyond doubt unsurpassed', and he came up with a ringing epitaph, calling him 'as great a warrior as these Islands ever bred'.[26]

9

Captain Charles Upham VC and Bar

1908–94

An Officer and a gentleman – determination and singleness of purpose personified – loyal, constructive, quiet, unassuming and friendly.[1]

A loving father, a dedicated farmer who put his animals and his land before himself, a born leader and fearsome fighting soldier: such was Charles Upham. He was the only combatant ever to win a bar to the VC, the other two holders of the double being Noel Chavasse and Arthur Martin-Leake, both of whom were doctors.

Upham never aspired to become a hero. His two leading characteristics were his modesty and his ability to focus on the task in hand with the greatest intensity. His acute dislike of publicity haunted him throughout his post-war days when, driven by his high sense of duty, he had to carry the public burden of being a Second World War hero. On one occasion, when asked about the actions for which he had been decorated, he replied, 'The military honours bestowed on me are the property of the men of my unit.'

He came from typical New Zealand stock that represented the finest of nineteenth-century British middle classes, who, finding no opportunities in England, left home voluntarily and, against tremendous odds, established the immigrant population in New Zealand. His father, Johnny Upham, practised as a prominent barrister and solicitor in Christchurch, and his mother, a clergyman's daughter, was descended from William Guise Brittain, who arrived on one of the first four ships at Lyttelton in 1850, to colonise Canterbury. As a couple they were gentle and shy, but with high principles and an exceptional devotion to work and service to the community.

They had three daughters and a son, Charles Hazlitt Upham, born on 21 September 1908. His boyhood was undistinguished, and his upbringing typically virtuous in the Victorian mode: discipline and family routine guided his schoolboy days. His parents had no great wealth, but in line with the times wished to see their children educated in the best establishments that their meagre income could afford.

Charles was far from a model student: indeed he made little impression either scholastic or athletic during his days at a boys' preparatory school near Timaru. However, his personality and strength of character did begin to show through. He developed a single-minded obstinacy that gave him an unusually powerful grasp of whatever project he had in hand, and convinced him that his vision and his way of doing things were right.

He would always question what he saw about him, and repeatedly challenged the authenticity of school books – driving the masters to the point of exasperation. He would accept an idea or instruction only if he considered it was the best, and right. On his eleventh birthday he was given a watch which was claimed to be 'boy-proof': he was immediately sceptical, and as soon as the guests had left he went upstairs and threw the watch out on to the gravel below. As he picked up the shattered remains, he nodded wisely to a friend and said, 'That shows how boy-proof it was.'

He developed an almost fanatical belief in what he saw as the difference between right and wrong – even though the gentle side of his nature mitigated these principles. This came out at school in his hatred of bullying and his courageous support of any boy he found suffering at the hands of classmates. It also came through in his love of animals.

For his secondary schooling he returned to Christchurch, attending Christ's College as a boarder in Flower's House, and won class prizes in English, history, science and divinity. His housemaster wrote of him:

> He was a quiet and unassuming boy, despite his nickname of 'Puggie'. Rather shy, not a very good mixer, he would walk over to school with a group of boys, not talking and chatting with them, but head down and brow furrowed, completely wrapped up in his own thoughts. He took things more seriously than others. He was a lone ranger. Though normally placid, now and then he showed he was capable of a deep fierce temper if he were aroused. But you could rely on him implicitly. I would risk anything on his word – and once having been given his word, nothing would budge him.[2]

He was an extremely good-looking man, about 5′ 9″ tall and of medium build, with extraordinarily clear, ice-blue eyes that seemed to bore right through anyone he disapproved of. His chosen career as a farmer, and the training he went through, further developed the self-reliant and uncompromising traits in his make-up. He spent time as a musterer (a shepherd on a ranch) – a tough way of life almost beyond the comprehension of cosseted, modern society. His son-in-law, Forbes MacKenzie – himself a courageous man who has overcome more than his fair share of physical adversity and setbacks in life – gave a fine description of musterers:

> These men from Canterbury and Westland, were all outdoor men – musterers and lumberjacks, men who were used to living and working in the open, from bush to shingle screes, wet or fine, day or night. They knew how to save water and limit rations and move quietly and inconspicuously when hunting. And of course they were all damn good shots, using .22 rifles until about the age of eleven when they were strong enough to move on to the .303.

This was the stock and background that formulated Charles

Upham's personality and character. He was a natural with small arms, an instinctive man of the outdoors, whose years in the remote, rugged and beautiful country of New Zealand's South Island equipped him ideally for infantry training later.

In 1928, as preparation for the career on which he had set his heart, he enrolled at Canterbury Agricultural College (now Lincoln University) to assimilate the practical and theoretical sides of farming. He shone in this field as he had not managed to do in his school years, and gained Firsts in Veterinary Science and Economics. He developed a singular forthrightness of speech, and the frequent use of swear words became a natural outlet for his emotions – a habit which stood him in good stead when rousing his men to action in the desert. He dressed in a manner typical of a soldier who puts action ahead of career and ambition: his turn-out was, in short, scruffy, and would never have stood him in much stead had he served as a peacetime soldier. In 1941, in Egypt, when he went to the formal parade at which he was presented with his VC ribbon by the commander-in-chief, General Sir Claude Auchinleck, he chose to turn out in bright yellow socks, visible beneath his puttees.

Having completed his Diploma of Agriculture, he began learning about life on the land in the 1930s, and lived up to the best of his son-in-law's description of musterers. He revelled in the free existence, governed only by self-discipline and the need to get a job done without any bureaucratic or parade-ground niceties to interfere. He developed a passion for horse racing, and it was one Saturday at the races in 1935 that he first met Molly McTamney, who was on the medical staff of Christchurch Hospital.

With his accustomed determination and refusal to be put off, he pursued her intermittently right through the war to his marriage some ten years later. But in 1939, like all his generation, he watched the political situation deteriorating in Europe: with New Zealand at that time a colony of the United Kingdom, he felt bound by powerful loyalty to King George VI and the mother country, and had no difficulty in identifying his duty as that of supporting England in her confrontation with Nazi imperialism. His sentiments were exactly those of his prime minister, who told the nation: 'Both with gratitude to the past, and with confidence in the future, we range ourselves without fear beside Britain. Where she goes, we go. Where she stands, we stand.' On 3 September 1939 New Zealand was at war with Germany.

Even before he joined up, Upham saw that the British Empire, including New Zealand, was threatened by German aggression, and he began to develop the loathing of the Nazis that inspired him throughout the war. In 1939, at the age of thirty-one, he was among the first to enlist at Burnham Camp, near Christchurch, with the earliest draft of New Zealand's First Echelon. His erstwhile tutor, Professor Hudson from Lincoln College, quite exceptionally wrote a letter of commendation:

Canterbury Agricultural College,
Lincoln.

To the Commanding Officer,
Burnham Military Camp,
Burnham.

Dear Sir,
A young man by the name of Upham has left the College to join your unit. I commend him to your notice, as, unless I am greatly mistaken, he should be an outstanding soldier.

Yours faithfully, E. Hudson.[3]

And so Private Upham was launched on a military career that became as momentous as it was effective in destroying Germans. He was in no mood to hang around basic training and the draft reinforcement system, and when identified by Colonel 'Kipp' Kippenberger[4] as a potential officer, he turned down the opportunity for advancement, hoping that by so doing he would obtain an operational posting more quickly.

No one in Burnham Camp was more delighted than Corporal Upham when told he would be among the fifty-two-man advance party selected for overseas service. Six days before he sailed, he was promoted to sergeant – and so in early 1940 he set off for action with the New Zealand Expeditionary Force, which formed an important element of the Allied armies in the Middle East.

After his rapid departure from home shores, he was disappointed to find himself bogged down in a lengthy period of training and routine soldiering under the Egyptian sun, while Rommel's army and the Allies deployed into their positions for the battle to control the North African coast. During the delay he was finally selected for, and persuaded to go on, an officer-training course, from which he managed to pass out near the bottom. His low placing was due less to his lack of professionalism than to his determination to question the outmoded tactics he was taught, which reflected First World War practice: only with the experience and enlightenment of a few senior generals was the Army adjusting to mobile armoured warfare in the wide-open expanses of the desert.

When told by an instructing officer where to deploy his platoon on an exercise, Upham refused to comply, giving sound tactical reasons for sticking to his own plan – and he held out so obstinately that in the end the instructor was obliged to give way. His stubbornness, and his refusal to modify his beliefs, were the very ingredients that later made him a candidate for the Victoria Cross; but on this occasion they annoyed his superiors, which led to his grading out near the bottom of his course. Fortunately Colonel Kippenberger realised what had happened, and insisted on his returning to command 15 Platoon of C Company, 20th Battalion New Zealand Infantry. This proved a perceptive decision.

During the work-up and training Upham developed, probably subconsciously, the principles he applied to his personal leadership. He exhibited outstanding professionalism, ensuring that he became the platoon expert in weapon handling. Having achieved a pinnacle in his own standards, he ruthlessly insisted that his soldiers, all tough and unforgiving men who had learnt their skills growing up on both sides of the 'Main Divide' – the Southern Alps – should strive to emulate him: this was true leadership through personal example.

His own striving for perfection shone through in all that he did. He would never allow himself to achieve less than any of his men, and if danger or risk was involved, it was always Upham to the fore. However, he balanced this unremitting imposition of standards with a devoted concern for his men's welfare. Nothing was ever too much trouble if he saw they were not receiving the very best available in whatever spartan conditions they found themselves. This mix of robust professionalism and sympathetic leadership is the essence of military command in battle – and Upham practised it par excellence, with the result that his tough platoon soon became the most loyal, hardened and battle-worthy unit in the division.

He based his relationships with his soldiers almost entirely on respect and little on discipline – and his attitude to his batman is as good an example as any of his man-to-man contact. When Upham came across him, Leggy LeGros had been 'discontinued' as a batman to another officer in the battalion. Talking to him, he received cheeky and what some would certainly describe as insubordinate responses, but these, far from putting him off, encouraged him to take on the challenge of working with an awkward customer.

He offered the man employment, which Leggy accepted on 'condition that he would be excused guard duties'. With this somewhat irregular start, the two built up a close rapport, fuelled on the one hand by Leggy's courage and loyalty to his officer in battle, and on the other by his all but total disregard of regulations when in reserve. Typically, he would regularly return late from leave, and frequently expected Upham to make the tea, rather than carry out this customary batman's duty himself.

Officers were normally equipped with revolvers, and indeed Upham himself carried one in battle; but any sensible infantry officer would complement his handgun with a weapon possessing a bigger punch and longer range than the 15 metres at which a pistol is effective – perhaps a sub-machine gun or a rifle. Upham, however, believed in close-quarter fighting, and as his personal weapon selected the grenade, keeping his pistol as a back-up, just in case.

With a maximum range of about 30 metres – the distance that he was able to throw a grenade – his choice implied that for him battle started only when in the closest proximity to the enemy. Yet, as always in his life, he developed and thought through his tactics, using the whole of his platoon to support him in his ferocious assaults.

The normal issue of grenades was about two per man, the assumption being that they would be used only in the final assault, when hand-to-hand fighting developed, and not many would be needed. Upham always liked to carry a sackful, and it was his platoon's task to forage round the ammunition reserves and acquire enough to keep him supplied. He and the grenade became synonymous, and it is unfortunate that on the statue put up in 1996 in Amberley, 25 miles north of Christchurch, he has had his grenade replaced by binoculars. The grenade was Charlie's personal weapon in battle, and his trademark.[5]

In the spring of 1941 the Germans decided that they needed to secure the Balkans and the Thracian Peninsula before concentrating their forces to attack Russia. The British Government, and Churchill in particular, had promised the Greeks that the Allies would come to their aid, although this made little military sense, as it weakened the forces available for North Africa, and the defence of Greece was always likely to be unsustainable.

On 6 April 1941 the Germans attacked Greece and Yugoslavia and, using their well-practised Blitzkrieg tactics, overran Sabrinica. On 13 April 1941 German forces occupied Belgrade and began their southward advance towards the Aliakmon Line, which the Allies were holding in an attempt to stop the German advance into Greece. The Allied commander-in-chief, General Sir Archibald Wavell, deployed such troops as he could to man the line, and these included the New Zealand Division, despite reservations expressed by General Bernard Freyberg (himself VC, DSO and three Bars), who was in command of the defence forces. His anxieties were passed on to the British Government by New Zealand's Prime Minister Fraser, who foresaw disaster looming and pointed up the risks in a cable to London:

> The operation, which has always been regarded as highly dangerous and speculative, is now obviously much more

> hazardous . . . Pressure by the Germans might perhaps lead to a rapid collapse of the Greeks, which would leave the British force in the air.[6]

There is no doubt the Germans expected to walk through Greece with little or no opposition. Their optimism was partially justified when on 17 April, after eleven days of fighting, the Yugoslav Army surrendered and the Greek prime minister committed suicide. It became clear that the Aliakmon Line could no longer be held, and the withdrawal of the Allied forces was put in hand.

The collapse of Yugoslavia gave the Germans a clear run into Greece by the central route, which brought them into direct conflict with the New Zealand Division. The Kiwis were forced to move back, but fought long and hard to delay the German advance. Defence turned into an ordered withdrawal, in which limited offensive operations were designed to delay the invading forces; but with the Germans having overwhelming air superiority, casualties mounted.

Unchallenged in the skies, the Germans were able to deploy reconnaissance planes with great effect. Upham, reckoning camouflage to be of little value in these circumstances, told the divisional commander, Major General Kippenberger, that he considered defensive action to be a waste of time. Kippenberger dismissed this typically insubordinate and dogmatically expressed view. But as the German air attacks increased, so Upham exhorted his platoon to challenge them with their light machine guns, ineffective as they were: as always, his instinct was to take the fight to the enemy, whatever the odds. He demonstrated his personal leadership in action for the first time when he seized a machine gun to return fire. Moving from section to section, he exhorted the men to take on the aircraft and not to become dispirited, cowering in trenches, where their morale and determination to fight would be worn down through continued and unchallenged air assault.

With commendable speed decisions were taken to withdraw the forces so recently deployed, and the New Zealanders found themselves moving back in the face of an overwhelming German armoured attack. The evacuation began on 24 April, and for seven days German dive-bombers attacked troop transports in attempts to prevent the Allied forces pulling out. Many thousands of men were killed, and at sea two destroyers carrying 650 men were sunk.

There were, apparently, moments of light relief to raise their spirits. The story goes – although it is possible that it is apocryphal – that at one point, as they went in convoy through a deserted town, they suddenly came on a bank with two huge, beautiful wooden doors. The men persuaded Charlie to halt the column, and although he himself stayed in his jeep, he gave them six minutes. A tank blew open the doors; the men rushed in, grabbed armfuls of drachmas, and a grateful soldier brought Charlie two great wads of notes, which he stuffed into his leg pockets. Later, as they went out to the destroyer which had come to evacuate them, he fell asleep in the bow of the tender, and when he woke, he found he was the sole passenger, heading back to the Greek harbour. With the money from the bank he was able to bribe the boatman, who reluctantly took him back out, and even then he only just managed to scramble up the nets as they were being pulled back on board. But for that cash, he would never have reached Crete.

As the withdrawal continued, he was suffering from severe dysentery, which plagued him for the rest of the campaign. Despite his weakness, he continued to command and fight with total conviction. No illness, however debilitating, would restrain his determination to kill the enemy with every means at hand, and he refused any suggestion of reporting sick or taking a rest during which he might recover. Eventually he became so run down that his platoon acquired a donkey for him to move around on.

The withdrawal from Greece resulted in a significant loss of equipment and artillery, which hindered the New Zealand Division's fighting capability well into the desert campaign of 1942. In Crete Upham and his platoon were sadly underequipped – they were even short of ammunition – but at once they found themselves involved in yet one more ill-fated operation.

Crete was of critical strategic importance, and the Allies expected that once the Germans had consolidated their positions in mainland Greece, they would attack the island from the sea. Major-General Freyberg, the New Zealand general officer commanding, promoted the widely held view that a sea attack was the most likely method of assault. 'Cannot understand nervousness,' he reported on 5 May. 'Am not in the least anxious about airborne attack.'

The Germans, however, had other ideas and decided to invade Crete from the air – an excellent example of why one should never take anything for granted in war. Their parachute delivery of troops, despite its many shortcomings, was probably the most successful use of airborne forces in the whole of the Second World War: on 20 May 1941 some three thousand men dropped in. Yet the surprise effect was greater than the efficacy of the assault itself, which became disjointed, with troops landing in the wrong locations – as could so easily happen in the early days of parachute operations, when navigational aids were primitive, and troops had to rely on the judgement and skill of individual aircrews.

The main defenders were British, Australian and New Zealand troops, along with two Greek divisions. And so once again the New Zealand Division was thrust into a defensive battle, which was from the start more than likely to end in yet another withdrawal, this time to Egypt. In the initial stages 20 Battalion, of which C Company was a part, were held in reserve and deployed only when the parachute assault enabled the Germans to seize Maleme airport, which they used as a reinforcement airhead. The battalion launched a counter-attack, and for the next eight days they were closely engaged with the German forces.

The New Zealanders had to advance uphill across open ground, with the sea on their right. They started in the dark, but as day broke they were so exposed to enemy fire that the scene remained printed for ever in the mind of Jim Burrows, who took part in the assault. Returning to Maleme forty years later, and moving up the same hill, he remembered:

> Out at sea there were gun-flashes and searchlights, telling us that the British Navy had intercepted the German convoys, but with what success we did not know . . . We ran into the first enemy posts. Bursts of fire from automatics, flares fired into the air and lines of tracer bullets streaming across our front made our men pause for a moment, but not for long . . . With

> daylight came enemy planes called up from Greece. They surged back and forth machine-gunning us . . . and it was about there, when we were encountering aimed fire deadly in its effect, that I realised that if we went much further over the open ground ahead, we would hardly have a man left.[7]

Such were the circumstances of the battle in which Upham excelled himself. His personal contribution is best recorded in the words of Lieutenant Colonel Kippenberger's citation for his Victoria Cross:

> During the operations in Crete this officer performed a series of remarkable exploits, showing outstanding leadership, tactical skill and utter indifference to danger.
>
> He commanded a forward platoon in the attack on MALEME on May 22 and fought his way forward for over 3,000 yards unsupported by any other arms and against a defence strongly organised in depth. During this operation his platoon destroyed numerous enemy posts but on three occasions sections were temporarily held up.
>
> In the first case, under heavy fire from a MG nest he advanced to close quarters with pistol and grenades, so demoralizing the occupants that his section was able to 'mop up' with ease.
>
> Another of his sections was then held up by two MGs in a house. He went in and placed a grenade through a window, destroying the crew of one MG and several others, the other MG being silenced by the fire of his sections.
>
> In the third case he crawled to within 15 yards of a MG post and killed the gunners with a grenade.
>
> When his Company withdrew from MALEME he helped to carry a wounded man out under fire, and together with another officer rallied more men together to carry other wounded men out.
>
> He was then sent to bring in a company which had become isolated. With a corporal he went through enemy territory over 600 yards, killing two Germans on the way, found the

company, and brought it back to the battalion's new position. But for this action it would have been completely cut off.

During the following two days his platoon occupied an exposed position on forward slopes and was continuously under fire. 2/lt UPHAM was blown over by one mortar shell and painfully wounded by a piece of shrapnel behind the left shoulder by another. He disregarded this wound and remained on duty. He also received a bullet in the foot which he later removed in Egypt.

At GALATOS on May 25 his platoon was heavily engaged when troops in front gave way and came under severe mortar and MG fire. While his platoon stopped under cover of a ridge 2/Lt Upham went forward, observed the enemy and brought the platoon forward when the Germans advanced. They killed over 40 with fire and grenades and forced the remainder to fall back.

When his platoon was ordered to retire he sent it back under the platoon Sergeant and he went back to warn other troops that they were being cut off. When he came out himself he was fired on by two Germans. He fell and shammed dead, then crawled into a position and having the use of only one arm he rested his rifle in the fork of a tree and as the Germans came forward he killed them both. The second to fall actually hit the muzzle of the rifle as he fell.

On 20th May at SPHAKIA his platoon was ordered to deal with a party of the enemy which had advanced down a ravine to near Force Headquarters. Though in an exhausted condition he climbed the steep hill to the west of the ravine, placed his men in positions on the slope overlooking the ravine and himself went to the top with a Bren Gun and two riflemen. By clever tactics he induced the enemy party to expose itself and then at a range of 500 yards shot 22 and caused the remainder to disperse in panic.

During the whole of the operations he suffered from diarrhoea and was able to eat very little, in addition to being wounded and bruised.

He showed superb coolness, great skill and dash and

complete disregard of danger. His conduct and leadership inspired his whole platoon to fight magnificently throughout, and in fact was an inspiration to the battalion.

It is clear that Upham and his platoon played an outstanding role in prolonging the defence of Crete, and in ensuring that the final withdrawal was successful. Stirring as it is to read this summary of his leadership and activity, one might underestimate his achievement. To demonstrate great courage and leadership in defeat and withdrawal, rather than during the high note of an attack or when one is obviously winning, demands quite exceptional strength of character. Add to this the fact that Upham was wounded in the foot and in the shoulder, and one begins to understand his extraordinary drive and disregard for his own well-being. No doubt there were many other gallant actions in the hard-fought withdrawal, but surely there can have been nothing to equal his.

In the action on 20 May at Sphakia, not only was he wounded and ill: he and all the men with him were utterly worn out, undernourished and dispirited by the withdrawal. Yet Upham managed to lead them on a long and arduous climb away from the safety of the evacuation harbour, to regain the heights from which he could overlook the German troops filtering down to intercept the withdrawal. Such leadership, drive and determination to remain on the offensive during a withdrawal operation are exemplary. During the climb of the steep hill some of his party urged him to stop and tackle the Germans from less tactically favourable positions halfway up, but he pushed them further ahead until, by crawling and clambering over the rocks, a small group positioned themselves at a point on the Germans' flank where they had full observation and surprise.

Firing their small arms and particularly their Bren gun with devastating effect, they picked off the enemy one by one, with Upham himself grabbing the Bren gun and having a go, until all the Germans were in disarray and retreat, or, in most cases, dead.

It was in these operations that he finally developed his technique as a human grenade-launcher. Each of the specific acts of valour mentioned in the citation required him to move ahead of or separate from his own troops and to rely on personally lobbing grenades into German positions. He and his platoon worked superbly as a team. The platoon would direct fire on all identified enemy positions while Upham headed out in front of them, using his tactical expertise, his fieldcraft and his instinct to work his way to the German strongpoint causing the most trouble. Then, with deadly accuracy he would hurl his grenades, whereupon his men would follow through and move on to the next objective.

There was no crude, heat-of-the-moment courage here: every time, he ignored the risk to his own life, and exercised the professional skill, leadership and determination that singled out 16 Platoon and its leader for special recognition. There is no doubt that Upham's personal gallantry saved many New Zealand lives, and in the final withdrawal ensured the integrity of the beach, enabling the evacuation to be completed without German interference. His contribution to the successful withdrawal from Crete was out of all proportion to the size of his platoon command.

When his Victoria Cross was announced, he was overwhelmed with embarrassment at the thought that he should have been singled out from the many other men who fought at Maleme. He expostulated that the VC was not for anything that he himself had achieved, but rather represented recognition of all the New Zealanders who fought in that battle. What is more, he believed this, and to his dying day set an example in modesty that can rarely have been equalled. In due course he came to terms with both his VCs, if only by appreciating the honour and respect they brought to New Zealand.

After the withdrawal from Crete, Upham was eventually persuaded to enter hospital, where he had his chronic dysentery treated and his various wounds patched up. Much to his chagrin, this treatment, coupled with the need for him to unwind mentally, led to him being LOB (left out of battle) when the New Zealanders took part in Operation Crusader, the dramatic assault on Tobruk. The decision to rest him was taken by Kippenberger:

> Because of the mood he was in, from his experiences in Greece and Crete, he had developed a hatred for the enemy. He was bitter about army shortcomings and about the two miserable withdrawals. Yet he believed his men were superior to the Germans in fighting ability. He was fretting for more action. He was really too anxious to get at the enemy again. I thought his mood was too dangerous. I left him out because I thought he would get himself killed too quickly.[8]

Kippenberger's judgement was absolutely correct. Had he not taken that decision, the New Zealanders fighting in the Second World War would never have had a bar to a VC awarded to one of their countrymen. This was a classic example of a commander having the experience, the judgement and the wisdom, not to mention the moral courage, to back-seat an officer who clearly needed a rest, not so much to recover from his physical wounds as to recharge his mental batteries. Such command judgements and decisions are exceedingly difficult to make, and can only come with battle experience. Upham's was a classic example of how such a decision preserved a gallant soldier to fight another day, when other senior officers might have sent him straight back into battle, to be killed through his own lack of judgement and mental balance.

He spent a year retraining and standing by as reinforcement, including some time in Syria. He finally rejoined 20 Battalion before the New Zealand Division's major battles at Ruweisat in July 1942. The rest period was punctuated by minor incidents, but gave Upham a valuable opportunity to recuperate.

The announcement of his first VC came through at an appropriate moment, when he found he had 'misplaced' his pistol and binoculars during an exercise. They had been 'acquired' by a third party – but that is no excuse in the army, where losing your personal weapon is the ultimate crime, for which dire punishment is liable to be meted out. Charlie's whole company rallied round to search the desert for the missing weapon, but although they discovered some ancient Roman coins and other interesting memorabilia, there was no sign of the pistol or binoculars. His reaction was typical. He considered the loss to be unfortunate but inconsequential in the light of the vast quantities of guns, equipment and ammunition that had been written off during the withdrawal from Greece and Crete. I have to agree that there was some merit in his argument – but in the army the loss of your personal weapon is a serious matter of principle rather than a question of intrinsic value. Fortunately his predicament was alleviated when on the news that evening he heard the BBC announce that 'the Victoria Cross has been awarded to an officer of the New Zealand Military Forces, 2nd Lt. Charles Hazlitt Upham, for gallantry in Crete'.[9]

Abhorring the fame the award would bring, along with what he considered to be thoroughly unwelcome publicity, he immediately adopted a defensive approach – and his reservations, which he maintained for the rest of his days, were totally genuine. They are best expressed by his response in later years, when he had come to terms with his duty of being a public figure, but not with the distinction it gave him: he commented that he wished he had never been awarded the Victoria Cross, and once said, 'I wasn't a brave man. It was just circumstances that won those medals.'[10] Others will make a different judgement and draw their own conclusions as to who it was who created the circumstances.

His true modesty came through both at home and in public. Only once in a letter to his future wife Molly did he make mention of his VC, and even then his sole instruction was, 'Please don't put VC on your envelopes.' On the home front in New Zealand he fought a losing battle. His reputation quickly spread throughout the forces and from there to the newspapers. It inspired others to great deeds, and reassured people that their contribution would not be forgotten. Thousands of men could see that Upham had set them a challenge, and given them a set of standards to live up to in battle. In the award of medals, most of which have little or no intrinsic value, it is perhaps this morale factor which makes them so important and inspiring to individuals and their regiments. Certainly Upham's VC brought a glow of self-confidence and pride to the New Zealand forces: it helped to soften the blow of the defeats in Crete and mainland Greece, and to mitigate the hurt felt over the huge loss of life in these operations.

*

On their return from Crusader, the New Zealanders were in very poor shape after the severe mauling they received during the German counter-attack, and required reinforcements. Upham, to his delight, found himself posted back to 20 Battalion and given command of C Company and the rank of captain.

And so on 27 June 1942 he played a leading role in the break-out from Minqar Qaim and the subsequent gallant but disastrous battle at Ruweisat Ridge. Once again, over a period of more than two weeks, he displayed the most outstanding gallantry, raising his finely honed tactics of acting as a human grenade-launcher, supported by covering fire, from platoon to company level.

With a more senior command, and responsibilities for three platoons over a wider area, he had to spread his leadership more thinly, but reacted with ever greater energy and drive. Over these two and a half weeks he performed no fewer than five acts of conspicuous gallantry and finally sealed his place in history books as the only New Zealander, indeed the only combatant, ever to be awarded two VCs.

In the North African desert the New Zealand Division was given a more fluid role on the southern flank of the Eighth Army, and 20 Battalion was tasked with providing cover for engineers laying some nine thousand mines in the path of Rommel's advance. There was heavy fighting, and at dusk the New Zealanders were surrounded by four German divisions; unless something dramatic was done that very night, they would be cut off by the following morning and captured. General Freyberg had been seriously wounded, leaving Brigadier Inglis to command the division and organise a breakout during the night of 27–8 June.

This proved an amazing operation, and one that is secure in the annals of New Zealand's military history. To a man, 4 Infantry Brigade spontaneously rose up and with blood-curdling yells, led by the Maoris, struck at the weak spot in the Germans' besieging force. With complete disregard for personal safety, shouting war cries, using bayonets and grenades in hand-to-hand fighting, they broke through, each man for himself and every man for the success of the brigade. 'As soon as the Maoris reached their start line, 4 Brigade advanced,' the official history recorded. 'Probably definite orders to move were received by companies poised on the line. No one remembers them. The start seemed to be automatic, as if a familiar spirit had whispered that there was a rendezvous to keep and it was time to be on the way.'[11]

Upham was in his element. In the bright moonlight, with a sackful of grenades and his high-pitched voice screaming above the noise to encourage his men, he led his company through the gap. At one point he and a corporal ran forward to a truck full of Germans and hurled in grenades, wiping out the entire lorryload and leaving the truck in flames. So close to the target was he that he took wounds from his own grenades. As on previous occasions, he refused to report sick until the break-out was completed and his men had settled into new defensive positions.

Yet this was only the beginning of two weeks of exceptionally heavy fighting to check the German advance and maintain the integrity of what was to be the start line for the battle of El Alamein. The New Zealanders regrouped, and C Company formed part of the reserve for 20 Battalion. Already Upham's commanding officer, Colonel Burrows, had sown the thought that he should receive another VC for his action at Minqar Qaim, and the man himself soon reinforced the recommendation with yet further extraordinary deeds.

The New Zealand Division, with 20 Battalion in reserve, was tasked with seizing an insignificant feature some tens of feet high in the desert – Ruwaisat Ridge. On 14 July they carried out a frontal attack, and Upham again starred. When communications broke down, he was asked to send forward a small patrol to establish how the leading battalions were getting on. No delegation for him. With total disregard of the obvious risks, he went forward alone, using a captured machine gun mounted on a jeep to work his way round the enemy's forward positions.

When the jeep became bogged down in the confusion and darkness, he even managed to bluff enemy soldiers into helping to push it out. Then, firing the gun himself, he drove his ad hoc reconnaissance vehicle across the German lines, shooting up any opposition he came across. Thanks to the information he brought back, the brigade commander was able to reassess the situation.

In the meantime, however, Upham had lost two of his platoon commanders and many men. As dawn came up, four enemy machine-gun posts and about five tanks were identified. Quickly rallying his company, he directed an attack against the two nearest machine guns, crawling forward on his own, as always, to fling his grenades. During this assault he was shot in the arm – a severe wound – but remained with his men until the objective had been captured and the position consolidated. Only then did he return for treatment, but he refused to remain and rest, and moved forward to take command of his company once again.

The New Zealanders, lacking armoured support, were open to a counter-attack. This was successful, and over a thousand men were taken prisoner. Among them was Upham, wounded once again, this time so badly that he could no longer walk.

For most, becoming a prisoner at least meant the end of the war and fighting the Germans. Not for him. His initial induction into captivity proved perhaps the most traumatic and unsettling experience of his life. Certainly, his time in the so-called 'ward' for terminally wounded officers almost proved a death sentence. However, his first concern was to see that his own soldiers had enough water, and as he himself could not move, he instructed his batman Leggy LeGros to see that water was provided for wounded men. Such thoughtfulness, even in moments of greatest adversity, was typical of his leadership. Upham himself counted for nothing in his own list of priorities: other people mattered to him above everything else.

Never was his suffering more acute than when he was moved to a cellar in which all medical cases considered near terminal appeared to have been collected. As Kenneth Sandford recorded in his book *Mark of the Lion*,

> He found that down here was where the actual operations were done. There was no privacy. It was all just one filthy communal operating theatre, where those waiting for the surgeon lay cheek by jowl beside those writhing fresh from the scalpel and those for whom mercy had at last gratefully intervened. There were no drugs, no apparatus, little water. For victims it was life or death and it was mostly death.

> The continental doctor approached his amputation patients with a surgeon's knife, a little machine like a hinged paper cutter, and a saw. As the orderlies closed around the victim the dreadful details of the operation were spared those others looking on; but Upham saw with cold horror the blood-encrusted saw being wiped again and again across the doctor's trousers.[12]

Upham saved his own life by refusing any treatment under these conditions, despite his agony and the threat of gangrene that must have hung over him. Gradually he recovered and gained better treatment as he was put on a ship to Italy; and as his health improved, so his mind switched to trying to get away. Yet for many months he was not fit, and even he could not countenance the rigours of escape, although he seriously considered it in July 1943, during the gap created when Italy surrendered and German guards replaced the Italians at his camp at Modena near Bologna. The senior British officer had issued instructions that there were to be no escapes, and for once in his life Upham conformed to regulations, in the interests of good order and on the promise that arrangements would be made for him and his fellow prisoners to be handed back to Allied authorities.

It was too late when he realised that he had made a gross misjudgement and he found himself back under control, this time of the Germans, who increased security and discipline. This, however, served as nothing but a challenge, and throughout the rest of his captivity he made persistent attempts at escape, many of which can only be described as daring beyond the point of common sense. For instance, on the way from Italy to Germany he broke away from a convoy guarded with machine guns, and then missed being shot, due solely to the kindness of a German guard, who recaptured him alive instead of shooting him, which he had every right to do.

At his new camp in Weinsberg he helped dig several tunnels, and in pure frustration made a daring attempt to climb out over the wire in broad daylight; the first wire, on which he was poised to jump to the second, collapsed, and he finished between the two fences. Again he could have been shot, but this time his quick wits saved his life: a German corporal was about to shoot him when he pulled out a cigarette and lay there helplessly having a smoke – an action which unnerved his captor. He then attempted to escape from solitary confinement, and it is not surprising that in the end the Germans transferred him to Colditz. He took this as a compliment and continued his attempts to get away; but Colditz defeated him, and the end of the war fortunately came to his rescue.

This extraordinary man created a legend – and yet he would have denied that he was anything out of the ordinary. His selflessness became a byword among New Zealand forces. Apart from his bravery, which stretches belief, two qualities stand out in his war service: his complete focus, and his total disregard for his personal welfare or safety. When he was engaged in operations, nothing stood between him and the need to kill Germans and win his local battle. His courage was of the cold variety, long-lasting and permanent. It is incredible that through all his trials, tribulations and many wounds he only once needed a rest, which Kippenberger insisted on his having during the relief of Tobruk.

Perhaps he was obsessive – but then that is what is needed for success in battle. Perhaps he was *over*focused – but then a clear and simple aim and objective are the essence of a successful military operation. Perhaps he took unnecessary risks – but then war is all about risk-taking, and certainly nobody wins the Victoria Cross twice over unless he excels in this dangerous art. Perhaps he was lucky – but then we all need luck to see us through life; it's just what you manage to do with the opportunities that luck puts in front of you that makes you what you are.

I believe Upham saw opportunities and grabbed them; and accounts of his courage and risk-taking show that they were usually based on judgement, intelligence and quick reactions – as when he was caught between the two fences in the camp at Weinsberg. Who else would have had the nerve to light a cigarette at that desperate moment? Most people would never have thought of doing so until long after the event, had they survived it.

No one who has fought in a war comes out of it unchanged. Some people find their personalities destroyed and weakened, depending upon the extent and horror of their experiences, the stresses to which they have been subjected, and how far their personal courage bank has been depleted. One can only sympathise with such sufferers, and acknowledge that everyone possesses a different level of resilience. Others come out of battle apparently unchanged, but one can be sure that unless they had little experience of fighting, any pretence to normality is just that.

War changes everybody: it kills people in large numbers and matures survivors overnight. Its full horror and destructiveness can be appreciated only by those who have experienced it. People who have managed to control the shock of war, and discipline the alterations it has wrought in their personalities, emerge as perhaps the strongest and best-adjusted: they are also the fewest. Upham fell into this latter category. Most people who fought like he did in one ferocious battle after another would have either died or become mentally broken. When you consider, also, his defiant and consistently confrontational attitude during almost three years as a prisoner of war, it is clear that only a truly remarkable, balanced and intelligent person could have survived the mental stress which he must have suffered.

So what sort of a person did he become after the war? Undoubtedly the most important event was his marriage to Molly on 20 June 1945, which was followed by a blissfully happy but all too short honeymoon in Scotland. That autumn testimony about his actions went up to the Military Secretary, General Sir Henry Wemyss, who supported the award of a bar to his VC, and sent his papers on to Sir Alan Lascelles, private secretary to King George VI. Returning the submission on 19 September, Lascelles wrote, 'If there is any likelihood of Upham being in London, so that HM could see him, perhaps you would let me know.' But their man had already departed for New Zealand, and his fame had moved ahead of him. Molly, who had served in the Red Cross throughout the war, was offered a place on the aeroplane – a rare opportunity in those days – so that she could accompany her new husband on the journey home. Both of them refused this privilege:

Upham went back on his own, and she returned by sea some months later.

Arriving in New Zealand, he found himself a national hero – and, in his eyes, things became even worse one day in Christchurch when he was having his portrait painted and a cable arrived from the Ministry of Defence in London telling him he had been awarded a bar to his Victoria Cross. Without a word he stuffed the cable in his pocket and continued the sitting. It was not until the afternoon that a reporter barged into the studio and demanded an interview: only then did the artist, Archibald Nicoll, find out the content of the telegram. And so Upham was created the first and only VC and Bar awarded to a combatant since the inauguration of the medal in 1856.

The people of the quiet town of Christchurch could not contain their enthusiasm for their new hero, and there was a deep yearning to express their pride and enthusiasm in some way. Led by the mayor, they set up a committee to raise funds for the purchase of a farm, so that Upham, despite his family's lack of money, might be able to return to the land and the life he loved.

No one could have been more dismayed by this suggestion of special treatment. Countless families had lost their next of kin, and many men, like him, had come home in comparative poverty. The New Zealand Government was spending millions of pounds to help returning soldiers rehabilitate themselves, and there was a generous distribution of land. In this difficult and challenging resettlement period Upham could not face being singled out for any favours. He wrote to the mayor of Christchurch, Mr E. H. Andrews:

> I am deeply conscious of the honour intended to be bestowed upon me and I shall always carry with me the knowledge in my heart that the people of Canterbury wish to pay me such a wonderful tribute.
>
> The military honours bestowed upon me are the property of the men of my unit as well as myself and were obtained at a considerable cost of the blood of this country . . .
>
> Under no circumstances could I consent to any material gain

> for myself for any services that I, in conjunction with a hundred thousand more, rendered to the Empire in her hour of peril, and I most humbly request that you will understand my position in having to decline the province's most generously intended gift.[13]

The people of New Zealand respected his modesty, and admired him all the more because of it. However, £10,000 was soon subscribed, and a committee, which included Upham himself, decided that the money should go to a fund for the young people of New Zealand. So was established the Charles Upham Scholarship Fund, which would award scholarships to the sons of servicemen attending either Lincoln College or Canterbury University.[14]

Meanwhile, Upham applied like all other servicemen to the Land Settlement Board for a grant to help him purchase Rafa Farm, a hundred miles from Christchurch, in remote and grand country, and he paid for it like any other person. Bucolic by nature and by upbringing, he at last took up the life he had always wished to lead.

The farm had to be developed and opened up, and even the farmhouse had to be built. There was no electricity or running water, and one can only admire Molly for her willingness to put up with the deprivations of her first years there, after they had both suffered the hardships of the war. She was perhaps the one person strong enough to control her husband.

Together they created a home, converted the farm and at the start were fortunate in having some of the best years for wool prices. Above all, they had the happiness of producing twin girls, Amanda and Virginia, and their younger sister Caroline. These three remember their father as a kind and loving person, devoted to his farm and family. That said, he made no unnecessary concessions to creature comforts, and in Virginia's memory, 'He didn't need comforts. He could survive on whatever was going. If he went to the ski hut, he didn't have a bath for a week, and we had to cook on a coal range. He could cope easily.'

His main hobbies were fishing, riding, racing and breeding horses. He had his obsessions, the first of which was the development and success of the home and farm; but probably the most important priority in his life, outside his family, was his concern for young people – and despite his reluctance to be a public figure, he valued the opportunity it gave him to help them. As Virginia said, 'He always told his family and friends to look after the children of New Zealand, because they are the future.'

Perhaps the five years after resettlement, with their challenges and privations, were the happiest and most rewarding of his life. He seldom discussed the war, except in the company of his former military compatriots and particularly his own soldiers. With them, to quote Jack Hurran, his batman at the battle of Ruwaisat, 'Charlie was more or less the same man. He didn't change, really, although he came to life a little more if he was with us alone.'[15] In Jack's view, Upham's greatest attribute, so far as his soldiers were concerned, was his sincerity and his habit of thinking of others more than he thought of himself.

Upham was the sort of man that any fighting soldier aspires to be, but few indeed become. He had a supreme ability to calculate risks and run them to the limits at which they might be overcome. He would be the first to admit that he often had luck on his side, but his courage in battle was no foolhardy, rash, adrenalin-fuelled testing of fate. His training of his platoon to support him as he threw his cherished grenades was a classic example of his intellectual approach to overcoming risks.

He also possessed an unusual ability to concentrate on the task in hand, whether it be the actions which led to his winning two VCs and a Mention in Despatches (awarded in recognition of his escape attempts and for courage when in captivity), or developing a wild and largely decrepit property into a prosperous farm. He was typical of many great wartime soldiers in that he would have had difficulty fitting into the bureaucratic, career-driven routine of peacetime military service: he was a wartime soldier, nothing more and nothing less.

Fear played only a passing role in his life. His determination to win the battle overcame any sense of apprehension in action. He became so bloody angry with the Germans who threatened his Empire and caused so much suffering that his rage overruled fear, and nothing mattered but to win the war. At the same time, he had the highest respect for those under his command who fought alongside him. In return he earned their respect for his own courage, and in particular for his self-sacrifice and overriding concern for others. Even his soldiers commented on the occasion in the middle of a battle when he gave his remaining water to a wounded German he had captured.

He possessed a dogged determination to live – and indeed he survived to the age of eighty-six. When he died on 22 November 1994, the nation responded with an unaccustomed show of respect, and over five thousand people thronged the streets of Christchurch for his funeral. As one commentator remarked, 'New Zealanders like to cut their heroes down a peg or two, but in Charles Upham we found a man with whom it was difficult to find fault.'

10

The Bradford Boys

Thomas Andrew Bradford, DSO	1886–1966
George Nicholson Bradford, VC	1887–1918
James Barker Bradford, MC	1889–1917
Roland Boys Bradford, VC, MC	1892–1917

Some clans seem to breed medal-winners. Whether acts of extreme bravery are sparked by a particular gene, or provoked by a spirit of competition between brothers, there are many striking instances of VCs, DSOs and MCs being won by members of the same family. In this respect no record is more remarkable than that of the Turner brothers: Alexander and Victor both won VCs in the First and Second World Wars, Mark a DSO and an MC – and Cecil, who won no medal, was known in the family as 'The Coward'.[1]

A harsh upbringing undoubtedly forged the steel in the characters of the four Bradford boys – Thomas (born in 1886), George (1887), James (1889) and Roland (1892) – who between them created the astonishing record of winning two VCs, a DSO, two MCs and three MiDs during the First World War.[2]

Their father George was a rough, tough manager of collieries in County Durham, who frequently beat, cuffed and kicked his sons, believing that corporal punishment was not only a valuable corrective when they misbehaved, but also a beneficial influence in the general development of character. His uncompromising regime had the effect, which he probably intended, of teaching the boys to control themselves: he taught them never to succumb to fear or pain, and thus helped make them all outstanding leaders.

Their mother, Amy, was entirely different. A gentle, timid woman from Kent, as disorganised as she was attractive, she lived in dread of her thuggish husband, who criticised her sarcastically for failing to maintain the standards of housekeeping which he thought were his due. Getting little comfort from him, she bestowed her love on her children. Yet in a curious way she, too, prepared them to become fighters, for she fired their imagination by reading aloud stories of war and adventure in which patriotic heroes always triumphed, and classics such as *Tom Brown's Schooldays*. Among their favourites was Macaulay's epic poem *Lays of Ancient Rome*, and in particular the story of

> How well Horatius kept the bridge
> In the brave days of old.

In the garden they often acted out the sagas which excited them, taking sides to recreate battles in far-flung corners of the British Empire, and struggles in which clean-cut English soldiers invariably overcame the heathen.

They were of good Border stock, and for their first few years their home was Carrwood House, a substantial dwelling that stood on its own among green fields outside the village of Witton Park, three miles south-west of Bishop Auckland. Then in 1894 the family moved to Morton Palms Farm, near Darlington, where the healthy outdoor life helped all the brothers grow up fit and strong. Thomas (aged eight) and George (seven) walked to and from the Primary Department of the Queen Elizabeth Grammar School in Darlington – four miles there and four miles back. Luckily for them, and for the peace of the household in general, their father was often away on business; but one of the few positive contributions he made to their development was to encourage them in sporting activities: cricket, rugby and above all boxing. It was presumably their mother who inculcated a strong religious faith, and a habit of regular attendance at church.

In 1898 the family moved to Milbank House, in Darlington itself, and there it was augmented by a late arrival in the form of a daughter, Amy, born in 1901. Sometimes known as 'Ginger', she became very close to her brothers, and frequently corresponded with them when they went to war. As the boys left home, one by one, they escaped their father's influence to a great extent, and he died in 1911, aged sixty-six, before any of them had won a medal.

At the risk of sounding macabre, it is easiest to describe them not in the order in which they were born, but in the order in which they died.

James Barker Bradford, MC, 1889–1917

The Bradfords' third son – known in the family as 'Jimmie' or 'Sling' – was no academic. He appears to have gone to three schools in Darlington, but he left the last one at the end of 1902, when he was only thirteen, and never showed intellectual promise. On the other hand, he was musical, and a successful, wiry athlete: he boxed and wrestled, played cricket and soccer, swam, and hunted with the Hurworth hounds. After serving an apprenticeship, he qualified as an engineer, but he seems to have had no firm idea about what career he wanted to follow, for at one point he joined the Navy Reserve as an able seaman, and in 1913 he signed on as a private in the Northumberland Hussars. Next summer, with war looming, he became an active recruiter, and taught many men to ride, giving them lessons in the garden at home on his own mare Kitty and Ginger's pony.

When war broke out in August 1914, the Hussars were attached as mounted troops to the 7th Infantry Division, and they sailed from Southampton to Zeebrugge on 5 October. One of the division's early tasks was to cover the retreat of the Belgian army from Antwerp. Then in the middle of October it reached Ypres, just as the first battle for the town was beginning, and at once it was swept up into vicious fighting. There is no record of Trooper

Bradford's part in the various battles which the Hussars fought, but the Northumberlands distinguished themselves in action, suffering numerous casualties, and his first experience of trench warfare must have been extremely frightening.

He seems to have been curiously lacking in ambition, and he would have been content to carry on in the ranks, had it not been for the urging of his brothers, all of whom had become commissioned officers and felt that he too had the qualities necessary to command men. At their behest he applied for a commission, and in September 1915 he became a temporary second lieutenant in the 18th (Service) Battalion of the Durham Light Infantry.

By June 1916 he had been appointed Bombing Officer, and he took part in the disastrous initial assault that opened the battle of the Somme on 1 July. At dawn that morning he led his special bombing parties up to an assault trench, and he was there when the infantry went over the top at 7.30 a.m. – but exactly what he did, or how he survived the annihilating fire from German artillery and machine guns, will never be known. Like the other regiments alongside them, the DLI suffered terrible casualties, yet James somehow came through unscathed.

He was not so fortunate when, after a period of rest, and reinforcement by new drafts, the battalion again went into action on 27 July in the Neuve Chapelle sector of the front line. Having put down a ferocious artillery barrage, the Germans launched infantry attacks before being eventually driven back, and on 1 August James was hit by small-arms fire in the arm and right ankle.

Back in England, recovering, he married Annie Wall, a girl from Darlington, always known as Nancy, who had been a friend of his sister Amy at boarding school. Little is recorded of her, except that she was, and remained, a good friend of the family. The two were married late in the summer – but the time that she and James had together was pitifully short, for in October he rejoined his battalion on the Somme, where the Durhams were again in the front line.

In the spring of 1917, when the Germans began a planned withdrawal to the heavily fortified trench system known as the Hindenburg Line, the 18th Battalion harassed them repeatedly, and on 3 March they pushed forward, trying to take a strongpoint known as the Garde Stellung, which was still occupied in force. The Durhams were held up by wire entanglements and blocks in the trenches, and for a while the attack was suspended so that an artillery barrage could be put down on the enemy position. The moment it lifted, the attackers dashed forward again and overpowered the garrison, capturing thirty-five prisoners and two machine guns.

Evidently James played a vital part in the action, for the Battalion History recorded that the victory was largely due to 'Second Lieutenants H. E. Hitchen, MM, and J. B. Bradford showing fine leadership'. Moreover, it is clear that this was by no means the first time he had distinguished himself in the trenches: his brother George, writing home to Amy three weeks later, told her that

> Jimmy has been doing very well, and I trust a grateful country may give him a decoration. I think he strongly deserves it for his all-round ability and most important of all, tenacity, or in the homely expression but unladylike phrase, 'guts'.

The family did not have to wait long. On 17 April 1917 the *London Gazette* announced that James had been awarded the Military Cross 'for conspicuous gallantry and devotion to duty':

> He gallantly led his men into the enemy trench, capturing many prisoners and two machine guns. He himself killed three of the enemy. Later, he succeeded in repelling a determined enemy counter-attack.

For a few weeks after the capture of the Garde Stellung, his luck held. He took part in several more attacks – notably the intense fighting during the assault on the German positions at Gavrelle, which took place on 3 May. The next night his battalion was relieved, but on 7 May it returned to the front-line trenches east of Gavrelle, and there, on 10 May, he was hit by small-arms fire in the left shoulder and thigh. On paper the wounds do not sound life-threatening, as they were not in any vital area; but, after an operation, he died on 14 May. His family, and particularly Nancy, were deeply shocked, not just at losing him, but because they felt that the doctors had killed him by operating too soon, before he had regained enough strength.

Only when he was dead could his buttoned-up brothers express their feelings about him. On 21 May from Fermoy, in Ireland, where he was stationed, Thomas wrote to their mother:

> You will know that poor old Jimmie has gone out, it is a very sad business, he was a great fellow.
>
> I think Kipling's words are more true of him than most of us.
>
> He scarce had need to doff his pride or slough the dross of earth.
> E'en as he trod that day to God so walked he from his birth,
> In simpleness and gentleness and honour and clean mirth.
>
> There is little consolation to be got except that his life has been quite happy and he went out of it a great fellow, and we must remember that he would want us to meet this blow with a firm face and try to do the extra amount of good in this world that he himself would have done, had he been spared.

On the same day Roland wrote to Nancy, now a widow, invoking the family's religious faith:

> Keep a brave heart, and think of the noble and gallant way in which he fought for our righteous cause; and remember that one day we shall all meet again and will attain a happiness far greater than that we are now capable of conceiving. How thankful I feel that he and I met last April. I shall never forget the true manly look in his dear eyes when we parted from each other.
>
> May God help you, as he is helping me, to bear up under your grief.

George also wrote to Nancy, saying 'We can both be absolutely certain that poor old Jimmie died a hero's death,' and to Amy he wrote:

> I suppose you have heard the sad news of poor old Sling. No matter, he was a hero and we can be certain faced his end like the fine large-hearted fellow he always was.

The esteem in which the Durhams held him came out in a letter to Nancy from Captain Chappell, chaplain of the 18th Battalion:

> I hardly know what to write to you. One always feels, of course, that in a home where a soldier falls, there is deep sorrow. But, somehow or other, knowing your husband so well, I feel that your grief must be intense to a degree.
>
> I write chiefly to give you comfort on this point – that your husband always lived a life very near to the Saviour. He was always regular in his communion, and carried the strength he received at the altar in all his duties. He was a truly magnificent man, and I can't put it into words how deeply his loss is felt by all ranks.

Roland Boys Bradford, VC, MC, 1892–1917

Youngest of the four brothers, Roland was also by far the liveliest, endowed with an excellent mind and an ebullient sense of fun. His sister Amy remembered him as 'a tremendous tease', who used to invent lurid crimes that her dolls had committed and then sentence them to death, either having them hanged or chopping off their heads (but generally replacing casualties). He grew up a complex character, simultaneously full of imagination and yet excessively casual. He resented the fact that he was the junior member of the family, and (according to his brother Thomas) 'disliked being suppressed on account of his youth'. The result was that he argued energetically with his elders, always determined to make his point – and yet he did not often annoy them, for he was blessed with a great deal of natural charm.

Although so intelligent, he had little interest in most academic subjects, and after various schools in Darlington he went on to Epsom College in Surrey, but left prematurely in 1909 without matriculating. Yet he loved language and literature, both English and French, and spent countless hours learning poems which he would recite by heart to the family or to himself. As a boy of fourteen he compiled a notebook in which he kept meticulous records of his tame pigeons. Admiring them greatly, he was upset when the cat got one of their squabs, and at the end of the year he quoted from *Antony and Cleopatra:*

> The following lines of Shakespeare are worthy of the hen:
>
> > Age cannot wither her, nor custom stale
> > Her infinite variety.
>
> Total at close of season, eight eggs. Two birds lived.

His passion was physical exercise. Not only did he excel at rugby, winning his First XV colours at Epsom, and playing cricket and hockey, he also boxed and hunted, and wrote instructional pamphlets on how to keep fit, among them 'Neck Exercises' and 'Trunk Bending'. 'It is quite common to see a well-developed body attached to the head by a thin and weedy neck,' he wrote:

> A bull neck is still more unsightly, but a neck obtained by physical exercise is shapely and handsome. As the neck gets very little freedom, being encased in a stiff collar during the day, I think it of special importance that it should receive exercise.

Having left school at seventeen, he had no clear ideas about a career, and for a few months he drifted aimlessly; but at Epsom he had much enjoyed the activities of the college Cadet Corps, and it was no surprise to the family when, in 1910, he joined the 5th Battalion of the Durham Light Infantry (Territorial Force). After two summer camps, in 1910 and 1911, he attended a month's course at Colchester, and this, it seems, persuaded him to aim for the regular army. Having joined the Special Reserve, he went to a military crammer in London, worked hard there through the winter, and in March 1912 passed the examination for a commission – which enabled him to join the 2nd Battalion of the DLI as a second lieutenant.

From the start senior officers were aware that they had recruited a subaltern with a strong personality and exceptional gifts as a leader. As one of them put it, he was 'all keenness and enthusiasm in the right direction', with a streak of originality and a strong sense of humour thrown in. He was never a teetotaller, but drank sparingly, smoked very little, and spent much time trying to develop minor inventions. One of these was an aluminium body-shield, light enough to be carried into battle by an infantry soldier. It seemed a good idea, but Roland was disappointed to find that on the range rifle bullets easily penetrated the metal.

The outbreak of war in August 1914 found the 2nd Battalion at its annual camp in Wales, but within three days it was on the move, and by 20 September it was on the right of the British front line in France, on the ridge north of Troyon. Roland by then had become one of D Company's platoon commanders, and nobody can have had a more ferocious baptism of fire. In bitter fighting, the Durhams found themselves enfiladed (fired on from the side) by Germans who had broken through on their flank, and even though in the end they drove the enemy back, their casualties were appalling. D Company alone lost five officers and thirty-six other ranks dead, besides six officers and ninety-two other ranks wounded. Among those killed was the company commander, Major Robb, and Roland was the only officer to survive unscathed.

He again became involved in heavy fighting at the end of October, when attacks and counter-attacks continued almost without a break for several days. On 28 October his platoon was manning a road barricade when enemy troops began to outflank them in an attempt at encirclement, and he held the position until the last possible moment, with a tenacity never forgotten by an unnamed NCO, who wrote the following morning:

> We had another big do at Bois Grenier, and Lieutenant R. B. Bradford proved at this period one of the finest officers I have

> ever had the pleasure of being with. We fought continually for two days and nights, but on the third night we were almost surrounded, and he gave me orders to watch the main road to Lille with three men; and when I gave my report to him, he brought us out, and it was owing to his skill and valour that we got safely through.

As a result of this action, Roland received a Mention in Despatches 'for gallant and distinguished services in the field'. This was published in the *London Gazette* of 17 February 1915, and on the following day the journal announced that he had won a Military Cross, 'for services rendered in connection with operations in the field'.

The Durhams suffered further heavy casualties during that winter, but again Roland came through unharmed. In March 1915 he was promoted to temporary captain, and on 3 May he was posted as adjutant to the 7th Battalion of the DLI, a territorial unit which had recently come out to France, and was commanded by Lieutenant Colonel E. Vaux, of the brewing family. Two days later, at a parade drawn up before General Sir John French, commander-in-chief of the British Expeditionary Force, an anonymous witness caught a revealing glimpse of him:

> Captain Bradford MC stood in striking silhouette to those who noticed him, alongside our Colonel. A pleasanter smile no man could have seen than Lieutenant Bradford [wore] on that particular day, and he was among strangers of whom he could know nothing.

On paper the 7th Battalion was a pioneer unit, whose function was to build and repair trenches, excavate dugouts and so on; in practice, during the summer of 1915, it was often thrown into the front line. But between such crises, when things were relatively quiet, Roland found time for self-improvement, polishing his French, learning Spanish, taking elocution lessons by correspondence with a London teacher, and practising his public speaking by delivering words and gestures in front of a mirror.

By the end of the year many senior officers had discerned his outstanding qualities, and one promotion rapidly followed another. In December 1915 he moved to the 6th Battalion, DLI, again as adjutant; then in February 1916, after a spell of home leave, he became Brigade Major of 151 Brigade, and on 8 May he was transferred as second-in-command to the 9th Battalion, DLI, with the rank of temporary major, still aged only twenty-four. Colonel Vaux, his former commanding officer, wrote him a warm tribute:

> Our year together has been, in my opinion, a very wonderful one. Never since you joined me have you and I had a single wrong word, and honestly I feel deeply all the things you have done for me.

The 9th Battalion was the unit in which Roland made an indelible mark. As soon as he arrived he threw himself into the task of training, bringing all ranks up to a high standard of fitness. Yet he was also still involved in front-line patrolling, and on 15 June the *London Gazette* announced his second Mention in Despatches. Such was the impression he created that on 4 August he was promoted to acting lieutenant colonel and given command of the battalion.

Contemporaries bore witness to his exceptional ability and character: they described his magnetism, his efficiency, his dedication to training, his capacity for giving clear orders, his skill as a tactician, his attention to detail, his personal courage – all of which made him an outstanding leader. Also, as one fellow officer, Major E. H. Veitch, recorded,

> He had an extraordinarily charming personality. His smile and greeting on meeting you actually made you feel that there was nothing he liked better than to see you. His first thought for everyone, officers and men, was their comfort. His attention to details was extraordinary. He saw to everything himself, even to superintending a working party.

Yet he was also a strict disciplinarian, who insisted that his men shaved every day, even if they were in the line, and kept their trenches free of rubbish. When he realised how many of them suffered from skin disease – often exacerbated or brought on by lice – he took the advice of the regimental medical officer and decreed that they should sunbathe naked for an hour every day. The order produced unfortunate repercussions, for some of Roland's colleagues thought it odd that he should enjoy the sight of young men's bodies: they had already remarked on how little interest he showed in girls, and some even said that he hated women in general. Now word went round that he was homosexual. The rumours seem to have been unfounded: it was true that he sometimes appeared unsociable, preferring his own company to that of his fellow officers, and withdrawing to his tent, where he would practise his public speaking or pray; but there is no evidence of homosexual inclinations – and in any case, the order to sunbathe merely specified that the men should take their shirts off.

In fact he loved his men, in very much the same way as did Noel Chavasse (chapter 3), and he did all in his power to promote their physical and moral well-being. Passages from the speech with which he greeted new drafts to the battalion give some idea of his priorities:

> You must always do the best work of which you are capable, try hard and conscientiously to keep yourself fit, happy and efficient. Make yourselves masters of your own particular job as soldiers; do your duty willingly and thoroughly.
>
> The call of duty is a sacred one. We must do our duty, not merely to gain praise and advancement thereby, but because it is a duty to ourselves, our comrades, our battalion, our country, our King and to the God who made us and who will help us in our work . . .
>
> My friends, I am going to arrange for the band to play one verse of the hymn 'Abide with Me'. I would like all of you to join in the words. It should mean more to you than the singing of a well-known hymn. 'Abide with Me' should be no mere catchphrase with us.
>
> It means that we realise that there is Someone who really

abides with us and who will help us to help ourselves: Someone who is with us in all our sorrows and hardships – and every man in the world has their fair share of that.

Under his command, it became the battalion's custom to sing 'Abide with Me' before going into action, and every evening at dusk. This remained the regimental hymn to the day the DLI was disbanded.

Roland was never one to lead from behind, and when the 9th Battalion was swept into the dreadful battle of the Somme, which began on 1 July 1916 and developed into weeks of slaughter for both sides, he was always in or near the action. At 2100 on 15 September his battalion was ordered to take part in an attack on a German position known as the Starfish Line. They were met by heavy machine-gun and rifle fire from both flanks, and most of the leading men were killed. Roland himself was hit by shrapnel, badly enough for the wounds still to require treatment two months later, but he carried on directing operations regardless. When another assault was launched next morning, he was in the front line (according to an unnamed officer) 'continually moving about with the most surprising vigour'. Again the Germans held out – as they did against a third attack on 18 September – and at 2000 that day the 9th Battalion was relieved, having lost nearly half their strength: four officers dead, nine wounded, forty-four other ranks killed, twenty-seven missing and 219 wounded.

Bitter, close-range fighting continued to rage intermittently, and the Starfish Line eventually fell to the British, but neither side was making much progress. A heavy artillery bombardment, starting on 30 September, softened the enemy up for yet another attack, to be carried out by the 6th DLI on the following day; but before this had even started their commanding officer was wounded by shellfire and had to make his way back to the casualty clearing station. On the way he met Roland, and suggested that he should take command of the 6th as well as the 9th – a proposal rapidly endorsed by the Brigade Commander.

So it was that during the afternoon of 1 October Roland crossed open ground under heavy fire to join the attacking battalion.

Finding them pinned down, he ordered two of his own companies forward in reinforcement, and by 0100 on 2 October the first and second German lines had been captured. The Durhams' right flank was unprotected, however, and Roland established blocks in both lines, to prevent infiltration from the side. Fighting raged through the night and into the next day, much of it with bombs (grenades), and Roland was in the forefront of the desperate struggle. Thanks largely to his obvious courage, his quick tactical thinking, his leadership, and above all to his galvanising, inspiring presence, the Durhams held the enemy off and saved the front from being rolled up.

In the morning, minutes after he had returned to his headquarters, an officer of the 8th DLI was astonished to find him looking 'as though he had just stepped out of his tailor's'.

> It was all in keeping with his strong belief in the moral effect of his presence and appearance on those he came into contact with. He certainly inspired confidence in everyone who saw him at that time, when things were decidedly uncomfortable and very uncertain. It was a little thing, but I came away feeling that everything was all right. In other words, it did all of us good to see him.

Such was Roland's conduct in the battle that he was immediately recommended for a DSO; but when the full details of the night became known, the recommendation was revised upwards into one for a VC, which was gazetted on 25 November. The citation praised his 'most conspicuous bravery and good leadership in attack, whereby he saved the situation on the right flank of his brigade and of the division . . . By his fearless conduct under fire of all description, and his skilful leadership of the two battalions, regardless of all danger, he succeeded in rallying the attack, captured and defended the objective, and so secured the flank.'

At the beginning of June he was on leave, and went to Hyde Park for the investiture by King George V. He recorded that he made 'a hard fight' to get out of going, but was told by a general that he could not disobey a direct order from the King. At home in

Wing Commander Guy Gibson VC, DSO and Bar, DFC. Gibson was twenty-four when he led the Dambusters Raid on the night of 16/17 May 1943. (*Imperial War Museum*)

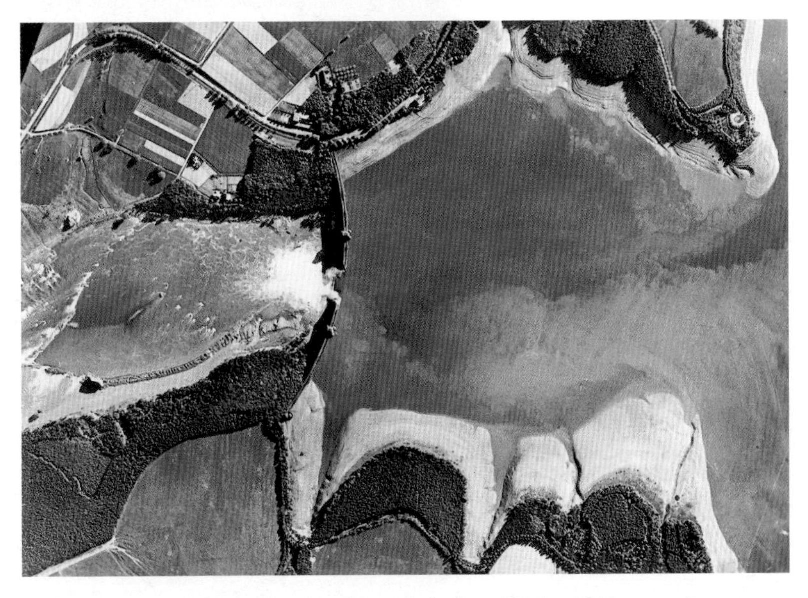

The breach in the Möhne Dam – photographed on 17 May 1943 – sent disastrous floods coursing through Germany's industrial heartland. (*Imperial War Museum*)

Captain Charles Upham VC and Bar in unwonted formal pose. A modest New Zealander, Upham is the only combatant of the three men to have won a Bar to their VCs: Noel Chavasse and Arthur Martin-Leake were both doctors. (*Imperial War Museum*)

Major Anders Lassen VC, MC and two Bars: the only SAS VC ever awarded. Lassen was a warrior with a calm, deadly courage. (*Imperial War Museum*)

The Fighting Bradfords: Roland, VC, MC; Thomas DSO; George VC; and James MC.
(*Courtesy of the Bradford family – taken from* The Fighting Bradfords (*County Durham Books*))

Lieutenant General Premindra Singh Bhagat VC, Corps of Indian Engineers. Bhagat won his Victoria Cross in Eritrea in 1941 for clearing mines, which required a special type of courage and self-control and facilitated the pursuit of withdrawing Italian troops. (*Imperial War Museum*)

Captain Rambahadur Limbu VC, 2nd/10th Gurkha Rifles. Limbu won his Victoria Cross in Borneo in 1965, where, having seen a fellow rifleman wounded, he decided that 'blood for blood and nothing but blood could settle the account'. (*The Gurkha Museum*)

Petty Officer William Hall VC, the son of a slave, was the first Canadian sailor, the first black man and the first Nova Scotian to win the Victoria Cross. (*Canadian War Museum*)

The relief of the siege at Lucknow, 25 September 1857, during the Indian Mutiny, where William Hall won his Victoria Cross. (*Getty Images*)

Piper James Richardson VC, who asked permission to pipe the demoralized men of the Canadian Scottish over the top at the Somme. Galvanised by the braw skirling notes, the men rushed the wire, broke through it and captured their objective. (*Canadian War Museum*)

2nd Lieutenant Barker VC, DSO and Bar, MC and two Bars. It was an amazing display of aggression and courage despite shocking wounds that won Barker his Victoria Cross while the Canadian was serving with the Royal Flying Corps.

The VC and Bar won by Noel Chavasse. The medal is awarded 'only to those Officers or Men who have served Us in the presence of the Enemy and shall then have performed some signal act of valour or devotion to their country'. (*Copyright Imperial War Museum, London/medal illustrated with the permission of the Master and Fellows, St Peter's College, Oxford*)

The reverse of the Victoria Cross and Bar of Noel Chavasse, who epitomises the selflessness of the VC winner. (*Copyright Imperial War Museum, London/medal illustrated with the permission of the Master and Fellows, St Peter's College, Oxford*)

Darlington, the mayor wanted to arrange a public welcome, but Roland, entirely in character, refused, threatening to take the first train to London if the idea went ahead. He disliked the idea of any pomp and ceremony, and felt that celebrations should not take place until the war had been won.

In November, when the award was gazetted, the 9th DLI were resting at Millencourt, on the Somme: some of the men hoisted their young colonel on to their shoulders and carried him round, refusing to put him down until he acceded to their cries of 'Speech! Speech!' Again his reaction was typical: he told them that the award was not merely for him, but for the good work of the whole battalion – and he took up the theme in a letter to Lord Northbourne, the unit's Honorary Colonel:

> The men of this Battalion fought conspicuously well and with great gallantry. In all we had seventy officers and men killed and 400 wounded . . . The men are all happy and fit and eager again to meet the accursed Germans.

In the same letter he told the Honorary Colonel that he had organised a band, 'which is a great boon to all ranks', and asked for music to be sent out. He also said, 'Do you think that during the winter you could send out a weekly parcel for the men of, say, polonies, cakes, kippers, condensed milk and a few socks? In the cold weather the great thing is to be able to feed the inner man.'

In making requests on behalf of his men, he was absolutely fearless. He once told a general that leave which ought to be given to the fighting troops was being appropriated by staff behind the lines. For a while the senior officer glared at him, as though about to place him under arrest, but then softened, and eventually said he was glad to find someone else as interested in the matter of leave as he was himself.

The weather, that winter, was atrocious: gales, rain, hail, snow. The ground in no man's land became churned into a morass of glutinous mud, knee-deep in some places, thigh-deep in others, so treacherous and sticky that men could hardly advance across it. On the morning of Guy Fawkes day, in bitter cold, the 9th DLI took part in an attack on the German positions round La Butte de Warlencourt, a chalk mound some forty feet high, reputed to be an ancient burial tumulus like those on Salisbury Plain. The ensuing battle lasted for fourteen hours, and its ebb and flow were vividly illustrated by the reports that Roland sent back:

> [At 3 p.m.] We have been driven out of the Gird Front Line, and I believe my posts there are captured. I have tried to get back, but the enemy is in considerable force and is still counter-attacking. It is taking me all my time to hold Butte Alley. Please ask artillery to shell north of Bapaume road in [map references] M 10d to M 11c, as Germans are in considerable force there . . .
>
> About 6 pm the Germans made a determined counter-attack, preceded by a terrific bombardment, and were able to get to close quarters. A tough struggle ensued. But our men, who had now been reinforced by the Reserve Company, and who showed the traditional superiority of the British in hand-to-hand fighting, succeeded in driving out the enemy.
>
> [7.15] The enemy still has a post on the northern slope of the Butte, but I am trying to scupper this . . .
>
> [Midnight] At about 11 pm battalions of Prussians delivered a fresh counter-attack. They came in great force from our front and also worked round from both the flanks. Our men were overwhelmed. Many died fighting. Others were compelled to surrender. It was only a handful of men who found their way back to Maxwell Trench, and they were completely exhausted by their great efforts and the strain of fighting.

The casualties suffered by the battalion were again severe: six officers dead, eight wounded and three missing; thirty-six other ranks killed, over 220 wounded and 154 missing.

Goaded by the carnage in this and similar engagements, which ended in stalemate, with no advantage gained by either side, Roland set about introducing new tactics and formations to be used in infantry attacks. Only an officer of exceptional originality could have driven through such revolutionary ideas in the middle of the war.

Until then infantry attacks had been launched with the troops advancing all together, spread out in line abreast – easy targets for the German riflemen and machine-gunners. Over the next few weeks Roland refined a new method, whereby men scuttled forward in small sections, a few at a time, and dropped down into shell craters for protection, while colleagues covered them with small-arms fire, and rifle grenadiers engaged enemy machine-gun posts. He also encouraged the men to fire their rifles and launch grenades from the hip as they went forward, even loosing off with their Lewis guns – something that had apparently not been done before. In a letter to his brigade commander he particularly recommended a policy of rushing forward from one shell hole to another: 'Select your next position before you advance, and point out this position to your section.'

His own energy was unquenchable. When his battalion was in the line, he was for ever moving about the trenches, encouraging his men – but although supremely brave, he was never reckless. A vivid glimpse of him survives from a meeting on the night of 13 April, when the 9th DLI relieved the 10th in the line. Around midnight, in a blizzard, he arrived at the dugout of Colonel H. H. S. Morant, the 10th's commanding officer, who had earlier been his own CO in the 2nd Battalion.

> After greeting me most respectfully, though we were of similar rank [Morant recorded], and after a brief and modest account of his recent doings in the war in answer to my enquiries, he asked me to excuse him whilst he issued orders to his Second-in-Command, Quartermaster and Transport Officer. The way he gave these orders impressed me greatly. Though he had come up in the dark and in a blizzard to a perfectly strange locality, he had noticed positions for cookers, transport lines and everything and everyone, and proceeded to give clear and brief but comprehensive orders to each one. This lad, who barely five years previously had been attached to me for preliminary training, was now, unconsciously no doubt, giving me a lesson as to how things ought to be done.

Roland's new infantry tactics were well tested, and triumphantly vindicated, in a raid on the German position known as Narrow Trench which took place on 15 September. His planning was meticulous, and he gave his companies special training over a system of trenches which he called 'the Replica', with the Army, corps, divisional and brigade commanders watching. One of his special weapons was deception: during the attack a dummy tank – a wooden and canvas silhouette – placed in front of the trenches, and dummy men set out in no man's land, both drew a useful amount of enemy fire.

For the assault itself, in the wake of a ferocious creeping barrage the attackers moved forward in a series of rushes, from shell hole to shell hole, firing from the hip, and Roland himself almost had to be physically restrained from taking part. An eye-witness described how

> One figure stood out prominently on the parapet at zero-hour, that of our beloved Colonel, who was helping the men out of the trench. He went forward into No-man's land to see his boys reach their objective, and afterwards doubled back through the enemy barrage to telephone his report to the General. He had asked permission to lead the men over, but had been forbidden to do so. But he would not be denied the pleasure of seeing the boys enter the enemy line.

The 9th DLI reckoned they killed seventy Germans and captured twenty-five, for the loss of only eight dead and twelve wounded, and the raid was judged a huge success. Together with his Action Report, Roland compiled a list of several 'lessons' learnt in the action, among which were:

> *Hip Firing*. All ranks attach great importance to firing from the hip during the advance . . . Firing on the move gives confidence to our men and takes their attention from the dangers which surround them . . .

> *Training*. The practices over the Replica were of paramount importance . . .

The success of the raid drew high praise from the Third Army Commander, and only ten days later Roland was ordered to take over temporary command of 151st Brigade. In effect he was being promoted to brigadier – the youngest in the British Army, at the age of twenty-five. 'My good luck continues,' he wrote to his brother George, 'although a CO now has no better chance of surviving than any of his men.'

He was still with the 9th DLI on 4 November when the battalion moved up into the line in the Ypres Salient. As always, he visited the men in their shell-hole posts, and was talking to one of the company commanders when a German machine gun opened fire on them. About the third bullet pierced his companion's steel helmet, and splinters from it wounded Roland in the face. All he did was get up and say to the company commander, 'Are you hurt? What an idiot I was not to get down when I heard the first shot!' Once satisfied that the other officer was all right, he walked back to have his wounds dressed, and remained on duty.

When notice of his appointment to command a brigade was sent to him, and he was ordered to report to divisional headquarters, two or three days passed before he put in an appearance. In the end an irate officer rang through and asked, 'Where the devil is Bradford? We've been trying to get him a brigade for the last six months, and now he's got one, he won't go to it!'

Roland insisted on remaining with his regiment until it was relieved, and then at last he took up his new command. Leaving the 9th DLI was a great wrench. In a generous letter to Major Crouch, his second-in-command, who was taking over from him, he described his transfer to 186th Infantry Brigade as 'sad news', and in another, written on 9 November, he reported:

> Today I said *au revoir* to the Battalion. You can understand what my feelings were. It is like leaving home . . . The Division I am going to is a long way from the Battalion, but you may be sure that I will come over and see you at the first opportunity.

He went on to say that he was having a 'souvenir picture' made, and that he would send Crouch 2650 copies of it, together with envelopes, so that one could be presented to 'each NCO, Officer and Man who has ever served in the Battalion'. The care with which he planned this memento gives a good idea of his attention to detail. Writing to Messrs Raphael Tuck & Sons, the publishers who were producing the card in the City of London, and had commissioned the artist Pio Ximenes to paint a picture of Christ appearing to a soldier in a trench, he made several small requests:

> There is one alteration I wish. The soldier should be wearing a box respirator in the 'alert' position – that is, in front of his chest . . . You will notice I have put a diamond on right sleeve. In my Battalion we wear a small green diamond patch on the arms. If this could be added, I would like it to be done – although it is not important.
>
> I wish the words 'Abide With Me' to be written over the top of the picture . . . The DLI crest should be put above the words . . . Only the crest need be shown, and not the number of the Battalion.
>
> Then underneath – copied from my own handwriting which you will now find at foot of picture:
>
> 'With best wishes from Roland Bradford'.
>
> I think the DLI crest would be better done plain than embossed in gold, as gold would make it look rather gaudy . . .
>
> I do not now wish the card to be a Christmas Card, but a souvenir picture from me to my Lads. So there will now be simply the DLI crest, 'Abide With Me', and 'With best wishes from Roland Bradford' to be shown.[3]

He said goodbye to his beloved battalion on 9 November. With officers and men formed up in a shell-holed field, he rode up, dismounted, and made a heartfelt speech:

> Comrades – we have endured many hardships together, and it is against my wish that I leave you; but as a soldier I must obey orders. I asked permission to stay with you till the end of the war, and no honours or promotion can ease the ache in my

> heart on leaving you. When the war is over, I hope we may meet again to talk over the days when we fought together.

He then shook hands with every officer and man, and was so overcome with emotion that he was forced to jump on his horse and gallop away before anyone could offer a reply.

He took command of the 186th Brigade, 62nd (West Riding) Division, the next day, and in his introductory speech he asked the men to look on him not merely as their brigadier, but as their friend:

> By the help of God I will try to lead you to the best of my ability, and remember – your interests are my interests. As you all know, a few days from now we are going to attack. Your powers are going to be tested. They must not fail you. Above all, pray! More things are wrought by prayer than this world dreams of. It is God alone who can give us victory and bring us through this battle safely.

His new appointment was an immediate success, due not least to the energy with which he went round learning names and faces: his charm and enthusiasm inspired confidence in everyone he met, and, as one officer recorded, 'his men would have gone anywhere for him', even though they scarcely knew him. Another huge advantage was that he appreciated the value of tanks – primitive though they were – and of the immense support which they could give infantry advancing across no man's land. Many officers were suspicious of the mechanical monsters, which had just arrived in force, but Roland had long seen their potential, and immediately began training his men to cooperate with them in the coming assault.

This was the battle of Cambrai, the first major tank battle in history, which began on 20 November 1917. The aim of the 62nd Division was to capture the Hindenburg Line and various other objectives: the attack was to be led by 185th Brigade on the right and 187th Brigade on the left, with Roland's 186th in reserve, ready to pass through the other two when they had reached their first objectives.

The night before the battle, Roland told the divisional commander, Major-General Walter Braithwaite, that he was very anxious to advance early on the 20th and take up a position far more forward than the one he had been allocated. At first Braithwaite thought it was merely 'the ardour of youth' speaking, and did not agree with his plan; but then he came round to the extent of allowing 186th to move up and push through earlier than in the original plan. As the general himself recorded,

> It was taking a bit of a risk, but if it came off it was well worth it. As a matter of fact, it did come off and had a tremendous effect on the fortunes of the day alone, because Bradford was a born leader, and led his men with conspicuous success.

On the morning of 20 November the Germans were caught completely off guard when, without any preliminary bombardment to put them on the alert, the British tanks crawled forward in front of advancing infantry. The first two brigades quickly cleared the Hindenburg Line, and the 186th, following up, leapfrogged through towards the further objectives. Roland kept moving around the battlefield all day, directing moves with such skill that the brigade advanced over four miles – probably the greatest single gain made since the early days of the war.

That night, in the catacombs of the church at Graincourt, which were serving as his headquarters, Roland was visited by the tank commanders with whom he would be working next day: they were all soaking wet, and he insisted that they ate, drank and warmed themselves before getting down to plans for the capture of Bourlon Wood and village. In his book *Cambrai: the First Great Tank Battle, 1917* A. J. Smithers recorded the verdict of one Colonel Oldfield, who remarked that his brigadiers in the 51st were 'the best in the Army', and yet, admirable as they were, there was one who 'stood head and shoulders above the rest'. Roland Bradford, he wrote, 'was not of the common run of men . . . [He was] the ideal General for work of this kind.'[4]

In the event 186th Brigade did not quite manage to take Bourlon Wood. In two days of intense fighting they captured eight officers and 1130 other ranks, as well as a great number of weapons, but in the end were driven off by determined resistance. From 23 to 25 November, while they were resting in reserve, some parts of the wood did fall to the British, and on the 26th the 186th were again called up to try to finish the operation. In the dense undergrowth every yard had to be bitterly contested, and at 1630 on the 28th it was decided that the positions which the brigade had occupied were untenable. That night the brigade was relieved, and Roland marched back with his men to positions near Lock No. 6 on the Canal du Nord.

There his luck finally ran out – and a brilliant career could hardly have ended in greater anticlimax. Between 0900 and 1000 in the morning of 30 November he walked out of his headquarters, as was his habit at that time of day, to visit his troops, and for a few hours his staff were not worried by the fact that he did not return. Then in the early afternoon a search party went out and found him lying dead, his spine pierced by a splinter from a stray shell.

His death sent shock waves through his brigade, his division and above all through his regiment. That evening the 9th DLI were in a training area west of Arras. The troops were ordered to fall in on parade, and the band was present. Lieutenant Colonel Crouch, visibly distressed, told the men that Roland had been killed. After reciting the Lord's Prayer, the band played, and all sang 'Abide with Me'. Lance Corporal King, who had been Roland's servant for the past five years, was on leave at the time, but when he rejoined on 2 December he was overcome by the news:

> The first words I spoke when I got back were to some of the men in his Brigade, asking if he was all right. And they gave me the sad answer, and I can tell you it nearly broke my heart, after being with him so long. I have been back nearly a fortnight and I can't get settled down at all. I feel as though I don't know where I want to be.

Tributes from senior officers poured in. General Braithwaite issued an order saying, 'The 62nd (West Riding) Division is the poorer by the loss of so gallant and determined a leader, and the

Army can ill afford to lose a soldier of real genius such as was our late comrade.' Later, in letters, he wrote:

> He was a very exceptional man, though only a boy, and might have risen, in fact would have risen, to any height in his profession. His power of command was quite extraordinary. He certainly knew every officer in his Brigade, although he had only commanded it for quite a short time, and I honestly believe he knew every non-commissioned officer, and a great many of the privates. He had extraordinary personality, and that personality, linked with his undoubted military genius, made him a very extraordinary character and a very valuable commander of men. His services during the battle can hardly be too highly appraised . . .
>
> He was quite indefatigable, he infused the whole Brigade with his own fine spirit of determination and of dash tempered with sound judgment . . . Personally I think he is the most remarkable character that I have met during this war. He had an absolute genius for war, and a fine tactical instinct.

His death devastated the family. Trying to console their mother, George wrote on 5 December:

> I received your telegram and am truly sorry for you. Roland has died a hero's death, and we should all be honoured and proud that he was able to do so much for his country. You have the greatest honour of all, to have produced such a son and to have given him the home training that has made him capable of so much.
>
> We may be certain that he is not sorry, and we must try and bear it with the same kind of fortitude he always displayed. He leaves a mark on British history that will go on for ever.

During the 1920s a public subscription raised £3000 – over £100,000 in today's terms – and on 19 July 1925 a monument to him was unveiled in St Cuthbert's Church, Darlington. The service included an appreciation by the author John Buchan:

> In the long roll of young dead, Roland Bradford is in some ways the most conspicuous figure. In three years of war he had made a great career, and he fell at the age of twenty-five, the youngest general in the British Army. His family, which contains both Durham and Kentish strains, had a battle record which few can equal.

Let the final word on him rest with Sir Douglas Haig, commander of the British Army in France, who wrote in 1918: 'The example of his unselfish courage and devotion to duty is, in my opinion, very worthy of being kept in continual remembrance by a nation he died to serve.'

George Nicholson Bradford, VC, 1887–1918

After schools in Darlington, the Bradfords' second son went, in 1901, at the age of fourteen, to the Royal Naval College at Eltham, where he remained until he joined the Royal Navy in 1902 as an officer cadet. Like his brothers, he was athletic and good at sports, cricket and rugby among them; but his main love was boxing, at which he became highly skilled – winner of numerous prizes, and welterweight champion of the Navy. Even during the war years he fought in many tournaments and exhibition bouts organised between ships.

Maybe boxing was the means whereby he worked off his aggression. Out of the ring he seems to have been a cheerful, easygoing fellow, much liked by his contemporaries, who saw him as the best sort of English gentleman. He was particularly fond of his young sister Amy, to whom he wrote jokey letters:

> You are quite right about the canoe, the stern is the place to steer from – only great men like me can do it from forward. I suppose you like David Copperfield. Dombey & Son is one of my favourites . . . The enclosed is a somewhat fantastic crest. The animal is actually a flea. It strikes one as rather heavily misplaced wit . . . Mother sent me the book Whyte Melville, what I wanted was the song though I stupidly did not say so.

> Good luck to you at school, keep the Bradford name like that of Bayard *chevalier sans peur* – possibly misquoted but conveys the right idea.

He also wrote loving letters to his mother, particularly at times when he knew she was ill or distressed (even to her he always signed himself 'G. N. Bradford' – never 'George'). Other members of the family attributed his affectionate, relaxed attitude to the fact that, leaving home at fourteen, he escaped his father's baleful influence earlier than his brothers, and so was less inclined to see people and events in terms of black and white.

One of his most attractive characteristics was his optimism. Wherever he happened to be, he felt sure that the war was going well. 'I think the allies have never been in [a] stronger position than now and am very confident in the result,' he wrote to Amy in February 1917. When James died of wounds on 14 May, he told her, 'You should give your mother an optimistic letter from time to time. She has been much shaken by her illness and by [losing] Jimmy.' Then he immediately went on to say, 'Weather here glorious, winning the war, in fact everything going splendidly. No aches, no pains, a pleasure to be alive.'

Until its very last moments, when suddenly his courage blazed up in glory, his naval career was worthy but undistinguished. Nevertheless, there was one incident which gave a good indication of his mettle. In 1909 he was serving as a sub lieutenant on the destroyer HMS *Chelmer* when she and her sister destroyer HMS *Doon* were ordered to Dover to collect King George V and ferry him to Calais for an official visit. At 0320 on the morning of 3 March the *Doon*, steaming at 15 knots, collided in mid-Channel with a trawler, the *Halcyon*, slicing open her port side.

Under George's command, the *Chelmer*'s whaler was launched and went to rescue the trawler's crew. In about fifteen minutes the open rowing boat had taken three men aboard, and it had pulled away when a signal came from the *Doon* saying that there was a fourth member of the crew – a boy who had fallen into the hold. With the *Halcyon* about to sink, the whaler pulled back to the stricken vessel: George jumped aboard and vanished into the black cavern of the hold, reappearing with the unconscious boy in his arms. Scarcely had he regained the whaler when the *Halcyon* up-ended, with only her bow above the surface, and then sank. His courage, physical fitness and decisiveness were noticed by senior officers, and on 30 July, as a reward for his gallant rescue, he was promoted to full lieutenant.

He served throughout the First World War in the battleship *Orion*, and was present at the great battle of Jutland – the titanic yet inconclusive clash between the British and German fleets on 31 May 1916; no records of his conduct survive, but he must have proved an efficient officer, for, as he informed Amy in a letter dated 5 August 1917,

> *Moi*, I am a Lieutenant Commander, having completed eight years as Lieutenant, and as the designing mothers of Portsmouth would say, 'He gets another shilling a day now.'

Then, in April 1918, came the naval raid on the port of Zeebrugge, in Belgium, which made his name. For months the Admiralty had been gravely worried by the strength of the German naval presence at Zeebrugge, which stands at the seaward end of a six-mile canal leading inland to the harbour at Bruges. Enemy warships based there, and submarines in particular, were posing a severe threat to Allied shipping: attempts had been made to put Zeebrugge out of action by heavy naval bombardments, but the port's defences were extremely strong, and by the end of 1917 it had become clear that only drastic action would bottle up the ships using the base.

A complex raid was planned, chiefly by Vice Admiral Roger Keyes. The principal objective was to sail three blockships into the harbour and sink them in the mouth of the canal, so as to shut it off completely. To give them a chance of getting past the guns on the mole, an infantry force would launch a diversionary attack to distract the defenders, and at the same time two submarines loaded with high explosive would ram the pillars of the viaduct which formed part of the mole and blow a gap in it, thus preventing any reinforcements coming up to the critical area. A flotilla of fast motor launches would follow the bigger vessels, to take off the crews of the blockships and submarines once they had reached their resting places.

The vessel chosen to lead the assault was the light cruiser HMS *Vindictive*, which would sail straight to the mole and land the assault parties on it. Three other ancient light cruisers – HMS *Thetis*, *Intrepid* and *Iphigenia* – were prepared as blockships. Recognising that the mission was going to be extremely hazardous, and that many of those taking part would not return, Keyes insisted that the crews should all be single men, and volunteers.

More men came forward than were needed, and among those chosen to sail with the storming parties was George Bradford. We can only guess at his motives for volunteering. He had never before shown any signs of suicidal recklessness; on the other hand, his war until then had been fairly dull, and already two of his brothers had been killed fighting the Germans. Perhaps he saw the raid as a means of inflicting retribution on the enemy.

Much depended on the weather. One essential element was an onshore wind, which would carry a smokescreen into Zeebrugge and blind the defenders – and the first attempt, on 11 April 1918, had to be abandoned when the wind changed with the attacking force still twenty miles out to sea. Two days later a second attempt also had to be aborted when a gale blew up. The third and final attempt was made on the night of 22 April, the date of the next high tide.

This time everything seemed propitious. The weather was good, the breeze on-shore, and the task force closed on its objective unobserved. Then at the last moment, when the *Vindictive* was barely a quarter of a mile from the mole, the wind changed and blew the vital smokescreen back out to sea. As the cruiser headed all out for the mole, the defenders opened fire with a variety of weapons, and many of the assault force were killed before they ever went ashore. Then the captain, Alfred Carpenter, had the greatest difficulty positioning his ship alongside, as her fast approach through shallow water had built up an enormous surge, and she bucked and reared in the turmoil.[5]

Another of the assault vessels, the *Iris II*, on which George had sailed, went past her and tried to go alongside the mole, but she too pitched and rocked wildly, thrown about by the turbulence of the water. Under the high sea wall she was relatively safe for the moment, since the defenders could not depress their guns enough to hit her; but it was obvious that anyone appearing on top of the mole would be a close and easy target.

The motion of the ship was so violent that scaling ladders could not be kept steady against the wall, and several of them were smashed. With incredible courage, Lieutenant Claude Hawkings went up a ladder held at a steep angle by several colleagues, balanced on the top rungs, leapt for the wall and tried to secure the ladder, but it was dashed to pieces just as he left it. He was last seen firing his revolver at the defenders, but almost immediately was shot and killed.

The situation was desperate. Unless the *Iris* could be steadied enough for several ladders to be set up, her assault parties would not be able to help their hard-pressed colleagues on *Vindictive*. In this extremity George did not hesitate. He was in command of the storming party, but it was not his job to secure the ship, and nobody ordered him to try. Nevertheless, he climbed one of the violently swaying derricks, which carried a large parapet anchor. As the derrick swung over towards the top of the wall, he judged the moment perfectly and jumped the gap, taking the anchor with him, and tried to hook it into place – a feat which only a man of great strength and fitness could have managed. According to one witness, he lay there on top of the parapet for two or three minutes, struggling to secure the anchor. Then, inevitably, he was riddled by machine-gun bullets and fell into the water between the mole and the ship's side. Petty Officer Michael Hallihan dived into the sea in an heroic attempt to save him, but he too was lost.

The raid was partially successful. After chaotic close-quarter fighting on the mole, and the loss of many men, two of the three blockships were sunk in the mouth of the canal, and for a while – until they dug a new route round the obstructions – the Germans were satisfactorily bottled up. The British public hailed the operation as a great victory, even though it had incurred heavy casualties.

George's body was washed up on the beach near Blankenberge,

five miles down the coast to the west, a few days later, and he was buried with full military honours by the Germans in the town's communal cemetery. His extraordinary heroism was at first acknowledged only by a Mention in Despatches, but on 23 February 1919 Keyes recommended him for a Victoria Cross, and in his letter to the Admiralty wrote:

> Lieutenant Commander Bradford's action was one of absolute self-sacrifice; without a moment's hesitation he went to certain death, recognising that in such action lay the only possible chance of securing *Iris II* and enabling her storming parties to land.

On 14 March Keyes wrote to Mrs Bradford:

> You may hear before my letter reaches you that your very gallant son George has been awarded the posthumous Victoria Cross which he so heroically earned on his birthday. I *knew* he would eventually get it, because although many actions were performed on that night by officers and men who survived, and by others who gave their lives, amongst the latter your son's act of glorious self-sacrifice stood out, I thought, alone . . .
>
> I know how deeply you have suffered in this war, but to have been the mother of such splendid sons must have been some consolation to you.

George's award was gazetted on 17 March 1919. Initially, five other officers and men who took part in the raid had won VCs, but after reconsideration, another was awarded to Lieutenant Commander Arthur Harrison, who led the *Vindictive*'s assault parties on to the mole. Petty Officer Hallihan, who dived into the sea trying to rescue George, received a posthumous Mention in Despatches.

The tributes sent in by other officers were of quite exceptional warmth and sincerity. Admiral the Lord Jellicoe declared that he had 'admired his [George's] character as well as his great personal ability . . . He died, as one would have expected him to die, under circumstances of the greatest gallantry and supreme sacrifice.' Captain Fullerton, who had commanded the *Orion*, wrote to his mother: ' I can truly say a more honourable, straight and gallant English gentleman never lived . . . he was loved by all,' and the *Orion*'s chaplain added: 'He was so magnificent, so firm and patient and kind that we all, both officers and men, looked to him for guidance and advice.'

When Captain Carpenter, who commanded the *Vindictive*, began to give lectures about the raid, people kept asking him to put the whole story into a book, and he did just that. *The Blocking of Zeebrugge* was published in 1922, and brought the hazards of the operation vividly to life; but in a letter to George's mother, Amy, the author confessed that he had found it extremely difficult to do him justice,

> because my enthusiasm concerning his gallantry cannot be measured by mere words. His death was a terrible blow to us all. We feel, however, that we should be better men for having known him. He was a great gentleman and loved by all with whom he was associated, and his name will go down in history and act as a spur to the coming generations whose emotions will be bestirred deeply whenever his splendid deed is mentioned.

Such plaudits, and the fact that the family had won its second VC, may have given poor Amy some comfort. But the loss of a third son within the year overwhelmed her: she became fairly eccentric, and went to live for the rest of her days with her two sisters in Kent. Although she seemed to want to shut off her past, she appeared at every Remembrance Day ceremony in Folkestone wearing two Victoria Crosses and one Military Cross. She died in 1951 aged ninety-one.

Thomas Andrew Bradford, DSO, 1886–1966

Cricket was Thomas Bradford's forte. His three younger brothers were all useful performers, but he excelled them by a distance.

Playing for Chester-le-Street in the Durham Senior League, he soon established a reputation as a stylish, aggressive batsman, once scoring 207 runs in 90 minutes in a league game. From 1909 to 1914 he played for the Durham county team, for some of the time as captain, and averaged 39.97. A big, well-built fellow, he also represented the county at rugby, as a forward, and was proficient at squash.

Like his brother George, he was sent to the Royal Naval College at Eltham when he was fourteen; but the prospect of life at sea did not attract him. Nor did academic work, and when he finished college he went to live with an uncle on his farm in Northumberland, before qualifying as a land agent. Then he joined the 4th Volunteer Battalion of the Durham Light Infantry, and was commissioned as a second lieutenant in 1906, with a reputation for being very direct and a stickler for detail.

By the time hostilities broke out in 1914, his unit had become the 8th Battalion of the DLI Territorial Force, and he was a captain, in command of D Company. After rigorous training and guard duties in the north of England, the battalion marched to Newcastle Central Station on 19 April 1915 and were given a high-spirited send-off to war by crowds of relatives and well-wishers.

Most units reaching the war zone for the first time were given a gentle run-in, with at least a few days to acclimatise; but the Durhams arrived at a moment of crisis, and were thrown into the horrors of the front line with no time to adjust. After launching gas attacks in the north-east sector of the Ypres Salient, the Germans had broken through the Allied lines, and the Second Battle of Ypres was under way, as the British and French desperately tried to contain their advance.

A hellish approach march through the shattered town of Ypres left the 8th DLI out in drenching rain, already exhausted, for most of the night. Then, towards dawn on Sunday 25 April, they went on, and two companies, A and D, occupied trenches which had been held by Canadian troops, and before them by the French. The dugouts were full of dead Canadians, and everywhere half-buried French bodies were protruding from the ground. A few Canadians had volunteered to stay behind and bolster the newcomers' firepower with their machine guns (which the Durhams lacked), and their support proved invaluable.

Daylight revealed that the German trenches were less than 200 yards away. Soon enemy shellfire severed communication with battalion headquarters in a farm a few hundred yards behind the line, and the two companies were cut off for the rest of the day. About mid-morning they saw German marines working round D Company's left flank, and then an enemy observation aircraft dropped glittering paper over their positions. This accurate marking brought down a heavy bombardment which at once began to kill officers and men.

The trench was protected in front by a reasonable breastwork, but it had no parados, or bank at the back, so that any shell landing close behind it caused havoc. What made matters worse was that the Durhams, at that stage, had no steel helmets, and so were particularly vulnerable to shrapnel. In the words of Harry Moses, author of *The Fighting Bradfords*,

> The scene was one of chaos and destruction, with the screams of frightened and wounded men merging with the ear-shattering noise of exploding shells which rained down upon them. The dwindling number of officers and NCOs vainly tried to make themselves heard above the din. There was nothing the men could do but take this hell that broke over them, cowering in what little shelter the disintegrating breastworks could give. There was no way they could fight back.
>
> Some men, a few, cowered against the breastwork, their nerves shattered, unable to control their shaking limbs and the tears streaming down their faces . . . All they could do was curse, cry and pray. Men were literally blown out of existence. Those badly wounded tried to crawl to shelter in the dugouts already crowded with Canadian wounded. Comrades tried to stem the flow of blood from ugly, gaping wounds with inadequate shell dressings.

Yet in this hell on earth, discipline never broke down. The men continued to obey orders – and the fact that they did so was due in no small measure to Thomas, who, in his first battle, showed astonishing courage and powers of command. Moving back and forth along the trench with apparently complete disregard for his own safety, giving out stentorian commands, he rallied the survivors so effectively that during the course of the day they beat off no fewer than three German infantry attacks.

Even so, by evening the survivors' position had become desperate. D Company – originally 200 strong – had only thirty men left fit to fight, and they could again see Germans working round their left flank. They were almost out of ammunition, and no relief could be expected. Thomas took the only decision open to him – to withdraw – and he gave the order to retire through A Company's positions on their right. He himself was the last to leave, and he eventually reached battalion headquarters wounded in the hand. Of the 200 men he had led into the line that morning, seven officers and 173 NCOs and men had been killed or wounded, or were missing.

In May the remnants of the battalion fought several more actions, in which Thomas played a leading role. In an advance on the 24th they found that the way ahead was blocked by wire entanglements on the railway line, so Thomas, crawling ahead under heavy fire, cut a way through, and the men were able to dash across in small parties to the shelter of the embankment. He then led on along the line, taking casualties from enemy rifle fire, and in the end had to cross 200 yards of open ground to relieve the 3rd Battalion Royal Fusiliers.

It was feats of this kind that won Thomas two Mentions in Despatches and a DSO. Unfortunately his movements after the middle of June 1916 are not well documented, and one cannot tell exactly which actions he took part in. Casualties had been so high that early in June the survivors of the 6th and 8th DLI were amalgamated into a single battalion, and Thomas took command of the new unit's A Company. He and his men were repeatedly chosen to lead the rest of the DLI into difficult situations, and this fact alone gives an idea of the high esteem in which he was held.

In August, at Armentières, fresh drafts enabled the 6th and 8th to revert to their separate identities, and Thomas continued to command a company. In bitter weather, that December, the 8th was back in the front line in the Sanctuary Wood sector, where they beat off a gas attack. Details of Thomas's involvement are lacking, but on 14 January 1916 the *London Gazette* announced that he had been awarded a DSO for distinguished service in the field.

That, it seems, was the culmination of his active service. In 1916 he became a staff captain and then a brigade major, and while on leave in England married Rebe, daughter of Lieutenant Colonel C. B. Blackett, a former commanding officer of the DLI. In 1917, for reasons unknown, but perhaps because he was suffering from the after-effects of a wound, he transferred into the Yorks. & Lancs. Regiment, in which he took a regular commission, and was sent to Fermoy in Ireland as an instructor training young officers. When the war ended he left the army to farm in Northumberland, but later moved to County Durham. He and Rebe had one son, George.

When Rebe died prematurely, Thomas married again, once more (as it were) into the Durhams. This time his bride was Kitty Percy, widow of Brigadier Jos Percy, who had commanded the 9th DLI. Thomas twice stood for Parliament, without success, but nevertheless in 1939 was knighted for political and public services. In 1942 he was high sheriff for the county of Durham, and he held numerous directorships. He remained close to the DLI all his life, working energetically for the Regimental Association. In his spare time he shot and fished, and he died at home in 1966, aged eighty, greatly loved and respected by all in the county.

His bravery, and his excellence as a fighting leader, have never been in doubt. Yet the sudden switch in his military career remains something of a mystery. What was it that saved him from the fate which had overtaken his brothers, and would surely have claimed him too, had he continued to serve with such selfless courage in France? It may well be that he was posted out of the war zone because his three brothers had already been killed.

It is good to know from his nephew Jonathan Cremer, son of his sister Amy, that neither she nor Tommy appeared to hold any grudge against the Germans. Even when the Second World War broke out, they showed no animosity against the race that cut the heart out of their family in the earlier conflict: it was as if their mother's quiet compassion had triumphed over their father's anger.

11

Major Anders Lassen VC, MC and two Bars

1920–45

Any soldier who knocks out his commanding officer while drinking with him in a public bar, and then escapes unpunished, clearly must have outstanding virtues. Anders Lassen once did just this, flattening Major the Earl Jellicoe without warning in a drinking den in Tel Aviv because he took exception to something that had been said. Jellicoe, though in his own words 'rather surprised', forgave him, not wanting to have him court-martialled and so lose the services of an invaluable fighting soldier – a morally courageous piece of insight on his part.

Lassen was extraordinary in many ways – a tall, blond Dane whose devastating good looks and normally smiling demeanour concealed a ruthless killer, he was dedicated to the extermination of his country's enemies, the Germans. He is the only member of the SAS ever to have been awarded the Victoria Cross, which, with his three Military Crosses, made him the highest-decorated SAS soldier – although Colonel Paddy Mayne, with four Distinguished Service Orders, all for gallantry, ran him close.

Lassen came from warrior stock. His grandfather Axel Lassen, who made a fortune from tobacco in the Dutch East Indies, married into the Schau family, one of Denmark's great military clans, which lost all seven sons in the wars with Prussia of 1848 and 1864. Anders's father Emil became a captain in the Danish Lifeguards and was drawn to any conflict going – the Spanish Civil War from 1936 to 1939, then as a member of the volunteer brigade which fought for the Finns against the Soviet Union in the Winter War of 1939. As a final throw he took off for South America, where he became an honorary captain in the Chilean air force.

Anders was born on 22 September 1920 at Høvdingsgård, a fine country house with fifty rooms and a pillared portico near Mern, in South Sealand; but when he was nine the family moved to another manor house, Baekkeskov, only ten miles away, which stood on high ground, with open grassland sloping away in front towards marshes and the sea. It was there that he grew up, running loose in the surrounding estate with his younger brother Frants and their Great Dane, Rufus. His mother Suzanne, who made a name as an author of children's books, often lost track of the boys for days and nights on end, and only when she looked out of her window and saw a column of smoke rising could she tell where they had camped out, with bundles of spruce branches for their beds.

The freedom with which Anders roamed the woods and fields surely encouraged the wild elements in his character, and at the same time developed his fieldcraft and shooting skills, which saved his life on many occasions during the Second World War. He was quick in everything he did, with almost animal-like reactions, and Magnus, husband of the housekeeper at Baekkeskov, remembered that 'he could go down the stairs in the main building as quick as lightning and without a sound; he was like a panther – a second, and he was down'. From an early age he was a killer, his favourite weapon being the bow and arrow, with which he achieved phenomenal accuracy: explaining that he never really aimed, but simply looked where he wanted his arrow to go, as if throwing a stone, he could hit birds on the wing, fish in the water, and running targets from mice to full-grown fallow bucks. Another prized possession was his hunting knife, which he sharpened fanatically and threw with deadly precision.

In school he had little time for lessons, and distinguished himself only in running. At the first opportunity he left, and signed on as cabin-boy, aged eighteen, aboard the *Fionia*, which sailed for Bangkok in January 1939. When the ship returned to Copenhagen in May, he went back to Baekkeskov, where he left an indelible impression on a friend, Varinka Wickseldt:

> I remember very clearly his incredible beauty, the looks of the perfect hero – but I was repelled by his aggressive, macho behaviour. He had a gun and was shooting gramophone records to pieces, using them as clay pigeons.[1]

Already wanderlust had infected him, and in June he enlisted as a cadet on the 16,000-ton tanker *Eleonora Maersk*. In spite of the filthy work at sea – washing down the tanks, which were coated with an inch-thick layer of solid oil and sand – he enjoyed the voyage to Mexico, and when the ship came back to Hamburg, his mother joined him for a few days there. As he prepared to re-embark, she felt an inexplicable sadness and had to hold back her tears; but they had already planned to meet whenever he returned to Europe, and she had no premonition that she would never see him again, despite the poignancy of the parting.

The *Eleonora Maersk* sailed again on 11 August 1939, and by the end of the month she was in Curacao. When the Second World War broke out at the beginning of September, she came back to Europe, put in for a few days at Weymouth, and called at Antwerp; but then, instead of heading for America, as the crew expected, she was ordered to the Persian Gulf, and she was there on 9 April 1940 when the Germans invaded Denmark.

Lassen, not yet twenty, was outraged by the fact that his homeland had been violated, and from that moment his mission in life was to exact revenge. No matter that his Aunt Jenny had married a German, Baron von dem Bussche, and that his cousins Axel and Kuno von dem Bussche were officers in the regular German Army:

to him, Hitler's action was unforgivable, and his own immediate ambition was to hurry to England and join in the fray.

'Mutinied in the Persian Gulf', he wrote in his diary, demanding, along with most of the crew, to be taken to a British port. Under pressure the skipper headed first for the island of Bahrein, then proceeded to Colombo, where Lassen tried to enlist in the Royal Air Force, but was rebuffed, being told that foreigners were not wanted. His spirits lifted when the ship was fitted with a 4.7″ anti-submarine gun and he was given some instruction in firing it, but in Cape Town he deliberately made himself so objectionable that he got himself paid off. In November 1940 he joined the crew of the *British Consul*, an English tanker bound for Scotland, and after a tough four-week voyage, during which the convoy several times saw action, he landed at Oban, in the north-west of Scotland.

Still his ambition was to join the RAF; but after hanging around for two or three weeks in Newcastle, he met a young second mate called Hammer who suggested that they both should go to London that night to join the army. 'To hell with your army,' Lassen told him. 'I want to be an airman.' Nevertheless, he agreed to go, and so met Captain Michael Iversen, who had served in the Danish Army during the First World War, and who now was recruiting young Danes to fight for their country.

On 25 January 1941, along with fourteen others, Lassen swore an oath on the Bible, 'sword in hand', pledging loyalty to their king, Christian IX, and vowing that they would 'fight together with their allies for the liberation of Denmark from foreign yoke'. After an initial diversion, in which he tried to return to the sea, he found himself training with a small group of his countrymen at Arisaig, a desolate wilderness of bog, rock and mountain on the west coast of the Scottish Highlands. Although the young Danes did not know it, they were under assessment by SOE (Special Operations Executive), the secret organisation which trained agents and infiltrated them into occupied countries as saboteurs and spies.

The commando training at Arisaig was notoriously hard: forced marches through the hills, rock-climbing, swimming, live firing, landings on the coast. Then, and later, Lassen could out-walk any of his companions: he was outstandingly fast and fit, and had an extraordinary power of moving so stealthily in the dark that he seemed to be making no contact with the ground. One day he caused a minor sensation by killing a red deer stag with his knife. An account of the incident, given to his mother by one of his contemporaries, does not quite ring true: the man claimed that Lassen, spotting two stags about fifty yards off, shouted 'I want that one!', ran round some 'small patches of bushes', got up close and stabbed the animal to death. Anyone who knows Highland deer may well doubt the accuracy of this report: if Lassen had shouted within fifty yards, the stag would have been away like the wind (unless it was ill). It seems more likely and in character that the beast was lying down asleep, and he stalked it carefully. In any case, the feat immediately confirmed his reputation as a lethal hunter who possessed exceptional skills in fieldcraft.

When it came to drill, his performance was less satisfactory. Itching for action, he had no time for square-bashing, and kept complaining that he had joined the army to fight, not to prance about a parade ground. He was becoming more and more difficult when, luckily for all concerned, he was taken on by Captain Gus March-Phillipps, who, with his second-in-command Geoffrey Appleyard, had been given permission by Sir Colin Gubbins, the executive head of SOE, to form a small unit and train it for guerrilla operations.[2]

March-Phillipps, from the Royal Artillery, was thirty-two, Appleyard, from the Royal Army Service Corps, twenty-four. They had first met under fire on the dunes at Dunkirk, and, forming an immediate rapport, had teamed up to train B Troop of No. 7 Commando for special duties. Intensely patriotic, contemptuous of red tape, ebullient and explosive, they were described by Gubbins as 'full of initiative, bursting to have a go . . . quite determined to get into the war just as soon as they could'. For the wild and determined Anders, they were ideal leaders.

The transport they chose for their first venture was a Brixham trawler called the *Maid Honor*, seventy feet long, strongly built of wood, with an outside skin of planks four inches thick, which made her impervious to magnetic mines. She had dark red sails and a small auxiliary engine, but March-Phillipps hoped to avoid German submarines by never using it. His plan was to pose as a neutral Swedish yacht and sail unaccompanied to Freetown, in West Africa, and from there launch raids on the bases which the Germans were reported to have established along the coast. The boat was fitted with a two-pounder cannon hidden in a dummy deck-house, and twin machine guns which could fire through the scuppers.

Besides March-Phillipps, the crew on the outward voyage consisted only of Lassen and three others; the rest of the force, under Appleyard, travelled on another ship. On 12 August 1941 the *Maid Honor* sailed out of Dartmouth, and after a passage of forty-one days arrived safely in Freetown. Life on board was none too comfortable – the temperature in the galley once reached 135°F – but the little ship made excellent progress, and the skipper described the voyage as 'a magnificent trip with no particular excitements'.

Reunited, the force marked time for much of the next three weeks, camped on the edge of a tropical bay, in which the men swam and speared fish in the intervals of training and maintaining their trawler. But idleness never appealed to Lassen, and he was glad when they sailed on to the south and east, heading for Lagos and then, 400 miles beyond it, for the Spanish island of Fernando Po, which lies right in the elbow of West Africa. There in the harbour reconnaissance aircraft had spotted an ocean-going liner, the *Duchessa d'Aosta,* and a tanker, the *Likomba*. SOE strongly suspected that although Spain was a neutral country, the *Duchessa* had been acting as a supply ship for German U-boats operating in the Atlantic, and ordered March-Phillipps to kidnap her.

In Lagos he strengthened his little force with a number of local volunteers, and with two tugs, the *Nuneaton* and the *Vulcan*. The flotilla left Lagos at first light one morning and reached its destination at midnight. The officers of both the target ships had been lured ashore to a dinner party given by a Spanish doctor – an SOE agent – who made sure his guests stayed late by lighting oil lamps when the official blackout came into force and power was switched off at midnight.

In the velvet darkness the *Vulcan* edged quietly alongside the *Duchessa*, and Lassen, chosen for his agility, leapt across on to a dangling rope ladder, carrying a line attached to a heavier rope and a cosh made of an iron bolt encased in rubber. In a few seconds he was on deck and had flung the line across. At the call of 'All fast!' March-Phillipps and his raiding party swarmed aboard brandishing knives and pistols, while an independent cable-party fixed charges to both ships' anchor chains.

There was no fighting. The sole watch-keeper jumped over the side, and down in the boiler room the African stokers, though scared out of their wits when explosions blew the chains, were induced to get up steam as fast as possible. The raiders aboard the *Nuneaton* found themselves with two prizes rather than one, for a motor yacht was moored alongside the *Likomba*, and they took that too.

Away went the flotilla, while the Spanish anti-aircraft gunners, confused by the loud bangs, opened fire skywards on what they supposed to be enemy bombers. Next day a Royal Navy corvette met the little fleet and escorted it back to Lagos, where the raid was reckoned a triumphant success. March-Phillipps was awarded a DSO, and Appleyard received a bar to his MC. No citations were published, for the awards had been made for a secret operation.

Such was Lassen's first live action, and he followed it by spending two months training natives in various aspects of warfare. He won no medal, but so well had he performed in Africa that on the way back to England March-Phillipps, knowing SOE would bypass all normal channels and back him in promoting such an exceptional operator, simply told him, 'Put your pips up, Andy,' and in England, to his amazement, Lassen found himself, at the age of twenty-one, a second lieutenant in the British Army. His sole disappointment was that he had failed to clinch negotiations to buy 'an exceedingly pretty wife'. At first, he reported in his diary, the father had demanded 'the shocking price of £15'. Lassen was prepared to take the girl on trial, and, 'if she was any good', he was willing to pay £10 and two bottles of trade gin. If she was no good, he would still hand over the gin. Alas, he sailed for home before the deal went through.

In England again, he visited his Aunt Estrid, who gave a revealing glimpse of him in a letter:

> Anders looks remarkably well, tall and slim, broad-shouldered, strong as a lion, healthy and charming . . . I find him absolutely wonderful, a law unto himself – he is a mixture of a mercenary, Viking, pirate, little boy – naughty little boy and man. He swears fluently and in a hair-raising manner in all languages . . . He, who has really gone through a lot and is as tough as nails, becomes child-like and gentle when we talk about Høvdingsgård and Baekkeskov.[3]

Aunt Estrid's 'in all languages' meant Danish, English and German. Lassen never bothered to perfect his English accent or grammar, pronouncing 'v's as 'w's and generally mangling his syntax; but his German, which he had learned partly at school and partly in the family, proved an immense asset on operations, whenever he suddenly came up against enemy sentries and had to bluff his way past.

The African expedition had created a close bond between him and March-Phillipps: the young man had become fiercely loyal to his boss, and was delighted to serve under him again when he formed a new group, known for cover as 62 Commando, but in fact called the Small Scale Raiding Force, or SSRF. Other wild characters flocked to join the unit, which was based at Anderson Manor, a seventeenth-century house in Dorset set in lovely gardens and grounds, where all ranks got down to the usual hard commando training – assault course, cross-country night marches, rowing and canoeing in Poole Harbour. One of Lassen's new colleagues was Lord Francis Howard (later Baron Howard of Penrith), who recalled being paired off with him for a sixty-mile march:

> We slept out on Exmoor under the stars and arrived in Lynmouth so very hungry that we went down to the sea and began eating winkles and molluscs that we prised off the rocks with our knives. Andy was a very pleasant companion to have on that sort of a walk. Not only as a nice person to be with, but as one of those physically extraordinary people who are completely tireless . . . He gave me the impression of being an adventurer, and I feel that being in the same unit as Andy

> Lassen was rather like serving with Achilles . . . Other people were very good on the assault course. They were all so fit, but Andy, without seeming to take any trouble, was much the best. He just floated everywhere, up the ropes and then along them.[4]

Training included the frequent use of explosives, grenades, pistols and sub-machine guns, but Lassen was particularly fascinated by methods of silent killing, especially with a knife or with his favourite weapon, a bow and arrow. In a personal plea to the War Office he argued the merits of bows and arrows, claiming that a trained archer could fire up to fifteen noiseless shots per minute, and kill 'without shock or pain, so it is unlikely, shall we say, that a man would scream or do anything like that'. (The official reaction was typical: the War Office sent down two bows and arrows, but gave no permission for them to be used against the enemy.) Howard felt that Lassen had a real hatred of Germans, and wanted to get at them by any means he could: his colleagues sensed that the only way he could work off such bitter enmity would be by killing them with a knife, with arrows or with his bare hands.

The SSRF's initial operations were amphibious cross-Channel raids, designed to test defences, take prisoners and generally alarm the enemy on the mainland and the Channel Islands, which had surrendered to the Germans in June 1940. Lassen did not go on the first, Operation Barricade, which attacked an enemy gun position on the Cotentin peninsula; but he certainly played a part in the second, Operation Dryad, on the night of 2 September 1942, when a team led by Appleyard landed on the island of Les Casquets, eight miles north-west of Alderney, seized the seven-man crew of the lighthouse and radio station, smashed the radio equipment, and carried off code-books, rifles and an Oerlikon cannon – all without a shot being fired.

Four nights later Lassen was again in action, one of a six-man team that carried out a reconnaissance of the Channel Island of Burhou. The rocky outcrop turned out to be uninhabited, but Lassen's participation in the raid earned him a weekend pass – and so it was that on the night of Saturday, 12 September, he was off duty in Bournemouth when March-Phillipps led yet another raid on Normandy, Operation Aquatint.

Lassen spent that night with friends called Knight, who reported that after dinner he was very restless: he kept pacing about and peering out at the weather. He slept on a divan in the sitting room, but suddenly in the middle of the night he gave a loud yell. When Mrs Knight went to see what the matter was, he told her he was convinced that his commanding officer had been killed.

His premonition proved all too accurate. Aquatint went hideously wrong. The raiders had hardly gone ashore before they were detected by a dog belonging to a German patrol, and after a vicious fire-fight they were driven off. They tried to return to their motor torpedo boat, which was standing off the coast, but none of them made it: of the eleven, eight were captured and three killed; the dead included March-Phillipps.

The SSRF had sustained a damaging blow, but its response was characteristically robust. Appleyard took over command, recruited new members, carried on training as before, and less than a month later launched Operation Basalt, a raid on the Channel Island of Sark aimed – once again – at capturing prisoners. One of the party, Bombardier Redborn, wrote a long and vivid account of the night's events.

Having rowed ashore and landed on a beach, seven of the raiders ascended a cliff, leaving one to guard the boat. All had been told to choose their own weapons, and Lassen had opted for his commando knife, whose blade had two razor-sharp edges and a stiletto point. Their target was the hotel annexe in which they thought some German engineers were billeted. As they approached the building, they became aware that one guard was patrolling: lying still in the moonlight, they caught glimpses of him moving out and back, out and back. Then, in Redborn's words,

> Andy crept on – alone. There was a kind of sinister atmosphere, but suddenly the silence was interrupted by a muffled groan. We looked at each other and guessed what had happened. Then Andy returned, and we could see that everything was all right.[5]

The five engineers, taken by surprise in their sleep, at first offered no resistance. In a few minutes they had been bundled into a corridor, their thumbs tied together behind their backs with strong grey cord brought for the purpose. But as soon as they were hustled outside, they all started yelling for help and running off. In the ensuing fight four of them were shot, and as reinforcements came pouring out of the hotel, the raiders ran for their lives.

They escaped unscathed, and afterwards Churchill congratulated Appleyard; but the long-term result of the attack was disastrous, for the Germans were incensed by the fact that in tying up their prisoners the commandos had violated international law, and used the raid as an excuse for chaining their own prisoners thereafter.

Lassen recorded the episode with a laconic entry in his journal: 'Was at it again the other night. The hardest and most difficult job I have ever done – used my knife for the first time.' Soon he heard that he had won a Military Cross for his generally outstanding conduct in the cross-Channel operations. The secret citation, signed by Lord Louis Mountbatten, Chief of Combined Operations, described him as 'an inspiring leader . . . and brilliant seaman possessed of sound judgement and quick decision'. In a personal letter of congratulation, Mountbatten told him, 'Any decoration won with the Small Scale Raiding Force is thoroughly well deserved. Good luck to you on your future ventures.'

Early in 1943 Lassen's reputation reached the ears of 24-year-old Earl Jellicoe, son of the celebrated First World War admiral, and himself a distinguished operational soldier who was to win the DSO and MC with the SAS. Jellicoe was home on leave from the Mediterranean, where he had recently established the Special Boat Squadron – an offshoot of the original Special Air Service – and no sooner had he interviewed Lassen than he asked him to join. So it was that Lassen went out to the SBS's training base at Athlit, south of Haifa on the coast of Palestine, and one night when he went drinking at a bar in Tel Aviv, he laid his new commanding officer out cold.

As Jellicoe recalled, 'I must have said something that offended him and ignited his quick fuse, and two or three minutes later I found myself getting up from the floor.'[6] Having already discerned exceptional qualities of leadership in his hot-headed recruit, Jellicoe simply took him back to camp, where Lassen apologised. Many less perceptive officers would have resorted to the *Manual of Military Law*, and the war and the SAS would have lost a unique fighting soldier to the cells.

Lassen's next action came in June 1943 when he landed on the south coast of Crete. For the past two years the island had been in German hands, and the aim of the raiding party, commanded by Major David Sutherland, was to destroy as many enemy aircraft as possible before the impending Allied invasion of Sicily. Lassen's particular destination was Kastella Pediada airfield, near Heraklion, on the north coast of the island.

The approach march itself was something of an epic – a sixty-mile scramble through the jagged mountains, with the days scorching hot, the nights freezing, and all the way the possibility of being betrayed by Greeks collaborating with the occupying forces. The raiders' luck held: passed from one guide to another, they carried iron rations but were fed mainly by country people who brought them whatever they could spare – eggs, bread, wine, vegetables – and hid them whenever enemy patrols were in the neighbourhood.

The Germans were highly vigilant, for the airfields had been raided by Jellicoe and Sutherland the year before, and Lassen had to move with extreme caution. For the last stage of his approach he had, as guide, Nereanos Georgios, who lived in a village near the airfield, and took him to lie up in a cave about half a mile away. There he spent two days with his raiding partner, Corporal Ray Jones, observing German traffic on the road outside the narrow entrance, and waiting for the night of 4 July, set for the attack.

That evening he went out for a final reconnaissance, then sent Georgios back to the cave, to bring up Jones and their supply of bombs, and for the last hour they lay hidden in a vineyard just outside the perimeter fence. The entire raiding party was only four strong: Lassen and Jones were to go in from the western side, while Sergeant Jack Nicholson and Corporal Sidney Greaves attacked from the east. Lassen described his part of the operation as a 'diversion', but the others reckoned it turned out more in the nature of a full-scale assault.

At 2330 he and Jones went forward, cut a gap in the wire and moved on to the airfield. The first sentry to challenge them, an Italian, died without a sound as Lassen gripped him by the chin with his left hand and with his right drove his commando knife down into the base of his neck. Close to the nearest hangar they were challenged again, but Lassen answered in German and bluffed his way past. Two more sentries were fooled in the same way, but the fourth stood off and raised his rifle. Before he could fire, Lassen shot him without drawing his pistol from his pocket.

The report let bedlam loose. The Germans sent up flares and rushed about yelling. Lassen and Jones ran for the fence, as one French report put it, *comme des chevreuils* – like roe deer. Back outside the perimeter, they waited till the commotion died down, then made their way back towards the hangars, and Lassen was climbing into one when he was spotted and challenged. Quick as a cat, he jumped down, but the guard fired at him, and immediately other defenders opened up. Once again he and Jones ran for their lives. In their haste they missed the gap in the wire and had to struggle through elsewhere.

Once outside, they ran straight into an anti-aircraft battery. '*Was ist los?*' the commander shouted. 'What's going on?'

'British troops inside the airfield!' Lassen called, in German. 'Swivel the gun and fire inwards!'

With that he and Jones disappeared into the night. But still he was not satisfied that he had created a long enough diversion for the other pair to place their charges, and he took Jones back to the hangars yet again. By then the defenders had called reinforcements across from the eastern side of the field, and inevitably he was challenged once more: the Germans formed a semicircle and drove the two raiders into the middle of an anti-aircraft battery, where they were fired at from all sides. That they escaped unscathed was a miracle – but even when the air was alive with bullets, Lassen found a moment to place a bomb on a caterpillar tractor, which was destroyed.

Recognising at last that the position was intolerably dangerous, the pair ran for it yet again. This time, however, they became separated, and when Jones did not appear at the agreed rendezvous, Lassen went back into the airfield in search of him. This time he crept so close to a group of Germans that he could overhear their conversation, from which he gathered that no prisoners had been taken. Reassured, he slipped away – but when dawn broke he was caught in the open, and had to spend the day lying full-length in a field of cabbages, without water in the baking heat of the Cretan summer. The next day he was again pinned down, this time in a field of onions, and only on the following night did he set out for the south coast. Villagers reunited him with Jones, fed the pair, concealed them and helped them on their way with courage and selflessness impossible to describe.

Lassen's audacity on the airfield had decoyed the guards away from the eastern side of the airfield and enabled the other raiding pair, Nicholson and Greaves, to plant their bombs unopposed. The result was that three aircraft and a fuel dump were destroyed – but the success was bought at a fearful price, for with characteristic barbarity the Germans executed fifty-two Cretans in reprisal. After the event, Nicholson was critical of the role played by Lassen: although acknowledging his courage, the sergeant claimed that the western prong of the attack had never been conceived as a noisy diversion. Rather, it was supposed to have been an infiltration as silent as his own, and Lassen had made a mess of it – although it is difficult to understand how an effective diversion could at the same time have been silent. Nevertheless, David Sutherland recommended Lassen for a bar to his Military Cross, and the citation, published on 21 July 1943, concluded:

> Throughout this attack, and during the very arduous approach march, the keenness, determination and personal disregard of danger of this officer was of the highest order.

Women of all nationalities found Lassen magnetically attractive, and that summer, in Beirut, he had a long affair with a nightclub singer and dancer called Aleca. He also picked up a small, mangy, woolly-coated mongrel dog which he named Pipo, and which he took with him everywhere, much to the disgust of his colleagues, who complained that the dog stank and piddled on their equipment as they dodged about the Greek islands packed into caiques. There was an immense difference between Lassen off duty – a vague, gentle charmer with a soft spot for dogs and children – and Lassen in action. Then, in the words of a radio script written by his colleague Commander Adrian Seligman,

> He was brave with a calm, deadly, almost horrifying courage, bred of a berserk hatred of the Germans who had overrun his country. He was a killer, too, cold and ruthless – silently with a knife or at point-blank range with pistol or rifle. On such occasions there was a froth of bubbles round his lips, and his eyes went dead as stones.[7]

Training at Athlit with Jellicoe's crew of what one officer called 'legitimised pirates', Lassen outmarched and outshot everyone else, demonstrating not only outstanding physical endurance, but also an unusual capacity for thinking fast and tactically. Some of the British SBS resented being given orders by a foreigner, and he himself sometimes gave the impression that he did not much care for the English. On the other hand, he got on very well with the Irish – and whenever he went into action, his conduct silenced all criticism.

The next major task assigned to the SBS, still in the summer of 1943, was to accelerate the departure of enemy forces from the islands of the Dodecanese, in the Aegean, and in these operations Lassen played a leading role. The Germans remained in force on Crete and Rhodes, but after the capitulation of Italy, in September 1943, the smaller islands were left with token Italian garrisons, and whenever an SBS group appeared out of the night in a caique or a motor boat, the Greeks went wild with joy.

Ever since his schooldays Lassen had suffered from kidney trouble, and in August he was admitted to hospital in Nazareth with hepatitis and a high fever. In the next bed was Canon Arthur Walter, a padre with the Parachute Regiment, who had a good chance to observe his volatile neighbour:

> He was very tense, tightly coiled, a wild young boy. Very often, in my impression, he was not aware of all that he was doing. Without denigrating the bravery, I think he was one of those people who act without foreseeing the consequences. Something has to be done, so they go and do it regardless of their own safety.
>
> I acted, more or less, as father confessor while he lay naked on the bed and poured out his inner pressures. In action, he would be physically alert but mentally relaxed; afterwards, it would be the complete reverse. He would be fatigued but taut as a spring, and then he would have to find someone with whom he could unwind as he talked over the men he'd killed. I don't know if the tension clarified the action as he tried to find faults in it; certainly, it didn't stem from guilt. A guilt complex was the last thing Andy had.[8]

By the middle of September he was back in action. On the night of the 17th he put into the harbour at Simi, a little island lying just north of Rhodes, in a small inflatable craft for a reconnaissance. When told that the water might not be deep enough to admit the two motor boats carrying his forty-strong party, his response was to jump straight overboard, fully dressed. He proved his point: having sunk far out of his depth, he came back to the surface and called, 'Bring them in!'

For the next three weeks he and his little force held the island, their defences strengthened by the acquisition of a 20mm Italian Breda gun which he himself had brought back from neighbouring Alimnia. Then, at dawn on 7 October, a force of 120 Germans managed to come ashore unopposed, because members of an RAF contingent who were on duty did not realise until too late that they were enemy.

In the ferocious battle that broke out, sixteen Germans were killed and thirty-five wounded. Lassen was in his element, leading the defence, compelling the reluctant Italians to fight partly by threats but mainly by sheer force of character, lurking with his knife in the alleyways of the old town to sniff out enemy infiltrators. It was he who led the counter-attack which drove the surviving raiders back to their caiques. Yet after this initial repulse, the Germans recovered the initiative, sending in wave after wave of Junkers 87 dive-bombers in low-level attacks that rendered Simi untenable, pulverising the stone-built houses and forcing the SBS contingent to abandon the island.

Throughout this brief but intense conflict Lassen displayed extraordinary leadership and courage, made all the more remarkable by the fact that he was far from well. As several of his contemporaries remarked, he should have been in hospital again, since he was suffering not only from dysentery, but also from festering burns on the backs of his legs.

His conduct on Simi earned him his third Military Cross, and the Most Secret citation which recorded it began:

> This officer, most of the time a sick man, displayed outstanding leadership and gallantry . . . He himself . . . stalked and killed three Germans at the closest range . . . The heavy repulse of Germans on 7 October 1943 was due in no small measure to his inspiration and leadership.

Those who knew Lassen took this to mean that he had three times used his knife to good effect – and the supposition was borne out by the evidence of the SBS sniper and Bren-gunner Hank Hancock:

> Once he'd got going, he'd kill anyone. He was frightening in that way – and his view of Germans was even more personal than ours, because his country was occupied. I think he was driven by the occupation, although it's difficult to assess if the killing instinct used the war as an excuse, or whether it sprang from genuine hatred of the enemy. But I do know that if he had the opportunity, he'd kill someone with a knife rather than shoot.[9]

The next island to fall was Leros, which the Germans attacked on 12 November with dive-bombers, paratroops and seaborne forces. The Allies had hoped to hold Leros, along with Samos to the north, but the enemy's complete air superiority gave them no chance, and after five days the garrison surrendered – though not before 250 Allied servicemen and fifty SBS (including Jellicoe) had slipped away to fight another day. Lassen, meanwhile, had been sent ahead to Samos with three colleagues to evacuate wounded servicemen, and if possible refugees, to the coast of Turkey, which lay only a mile to the east.

There were frantic scenes as Greeks and Italians swarmed aboard a boat and sank it, and Lassen spent a whole afternoon trying to set up a rope, buoyed by petrol cans, along which escapers might make their way to shore. When this failed, he had to wait until dark to resume ferry operations: then, plying a rowing boat and a small schooner during the night, the SBS men took 150 refugees safely to the mainland, before themselves embarking, the last to cross.

For all his courage, Lassen was by no means immune to fear. Several of his colleagues reported that he hated aeroplanes and parachuting, and that although he had completed his parachute training and gained his wings, he never jumped again. His fear was caught for posterity when Stukas dive-bombed Samos and he was photographed by a reporter from the forces' magazine *Parade*, huddled in a ditch, his face drawn with terror. A colleague who was with him remembered how 'his head was down and shaking', and he was 'sucking in his breath'. This incident humanises the man and reminds one that nobody is immume from fear. Rather than detract from Lassen's performance, it emphasises his control over fear and his amazing self-discipline and courage.

At the end of 1943 he was ordered into hospital in Alexandria for treatment, apparently for his chronic kidney trouble. As usual, he took Pipo with him, and when a doctor's visit was imminent, he shoved the animal down the bed of his neighbour, Hugh Stowell, who had been with him on Leros. For three or four days the two chatted, and Stowell found him still obsessed with the idea of killing as many Germans as possible. 'He was a tense fellow, very highly strung,' Stowell remembered. 'Not raving, though, but in very good form.'

In the middle of December he was promoted from acting to temporary captain, and on Christmas Eve he learned that his third

Military Cross had been confirmed – but, as his mother recorded, 'his manner of dress was altogether so haphazard and careless that it was not always easy for outsiders to see whether he was an officer or a private'. Although he had two makeshift rosettes cut from the lid of a tobacco tin, and wore them for a while on his medal ribbon as bars to his MC, one later fell off. He was inclined to go about with three pips on one shoulder and two on the other, thereby causing confusion among men who did not know him. His indifference to any form of sartorial discipline became legendary, and when inspecting officers rebuked him for the scruffiness of his men, he ignored their strictures.

In 1944 he took command of 'K' patrol – one of several patrols formed by the SBS as a means of fostering team spirit and rivalry. His men, who were Irish, included some formidably tough operators, among them 'Gyppo Conby', described by one contemporary as 'a semi-animal at times', and the wild, hard-drinking Sean O'Reilly, who was twenty years older than Lassen, but nevertheless happily became his bodyguard in all but name and fought alongside him for the rest of his life. Sergeant Porter Jarrell, an American medical orderly known as 'Joe', who attached himself to Lassen's retinue, remembered how

> Andy led the patrol by force of personality. On operations, there's no time for debate. Someone has to take the lead, and that's what Andy could do – he made decisions. And, where most of us worry about being brave or not, Andy always had courage . . . Basically, he was a sensitive, decent person whom the war made tough – and you had to be tough to gain the admiration of people like Gyppo Conby and Sergeant Sean O'Reilly.[10]

Such was Lassen's respect for O'Reilly, so keen was he to retain his services, that when the Irishman accidentally shot him in the leg, he did not even report the matter. Nor did he take any action to repair the damage until the wound turned septic and he needed an operation at the military hospital in Alexandria. By then – in contrast to this self-neglect – his attitude as an officer had started to mature: he was showing more concern about his men, and worrying about them when they were on leave.

His next target was the German garrison on Santorini, or Thira, southernmost of the Cyclades – the island with sheer cliffs and a spectacularly round harbour created by a volcanic eruption. There, after a three-night sail from a base in Turkey, Lassen landed on the night of 22 April 1944 with two other officers and fifteen men: their aim, to destroy enemy personnel and communications on Thira itself, and to 'destroy, capture or entice' enemy shipping in the area.

After lying-up in a cave, and collecting information from islanders, they decided to launch their main attack on the Bank of Athens, in Thira itself, where thirty-eight Italians and ten Germans were reported to be billeted on the first floor. On their advance to the town Lassen stopped his little force and made everyone swallow two Benzedrine tablets to ensure they were all wide awake.

In spite of dogs barking, they gained entry to the bank unobserved, but when they deployed upstairs to attack the rooms in which the garrison was quartered, things went seriously wrong. Lieutenant Stefan Casulli, a Greek officer, was killed almost instantaneously as he made the fatal mistake of standing in a doorway, and Sergeant Kingston, a medical orderly, was severely wounded by bullets in the stomach. Heavy fire forced the attackers out of the building on to the terrace, but, led by Lassen, they burst in again through the back, smashing windows, shooting out locks and hurling grenades.

During the two-hour battle one Italian jumped from a window and was killed on the rocks forty feet below, eight other Italians and three Germans were killed, and nine Italians and two Germans were wounded. In all, during the main fire-fight and other skirmishes, there were thirty-one enemy casualties. A separate party, meanwhile, had destroyed the German radio station and taken eight prisoners.

Carrying the wounded Kingston through the narrow streets, the raiders then withdrew to a house two miles away and hid there, awaiting pick-up at night; but during the next day their casualty died. That night their boat did not arrive and they had to hang on through another day, during which German aircraft made repeated passes over the island, searching for them. Finally, on the following night a small flotilla of three vessels took them off. The official report, probably dictated rather than written by Lassen, recorded:

> To avoid possible shooting of hostages, a strong note was sent to the surviving German commander, then a Leutnant Hesse, reminding him of the Allied views on hostages and war criminals. His name should be noted if any hostages are shot.[11]

In spite of that threat, the Germans executed ten Greeks, including the mayor. Lassen himself recorded a severe verdict on some of his own men:

> Hard training must be substituted for lack of experience, especially in street and house-to-house fighting, and the men should all be trained in how to look after themselves; for instance, not take up position in front of doors. The [cross-country] marching standard of recruits was poor and in many cases not what one would have expected.[12]

The official report makes little mention of the leader's own part in the raid; but Sammy Trafford, who was wounded in the upper arm and leg during the first exchanges of fire, remembered it as 'Andy Lassen's bloodbath – because he killed nearly every bugger'. Once again Lassen emerged unscathed, partly through luck, but more because of his uncanny ability to move stealthily and strike fast. Yet he was profoundly affected by the deaths of Casulli and Kingston, and, as another Greek put it, 'Captain Lassen drunk two days of sorrow – like a father.'

His luck held through the rest of 1944, and through an astonishing number of quick operations – on the island of Paros (the source of the finest white marble in antiquity), where a raid on an airfield went wrong; in Yugoslavia, where he blew up a bridge near Dubrovnik and ambushed a German column; and in Albania, where he captured a *Wehrmacht* Volkswagen and had it shipped back to Italy. The Balkans had become exceedingly dangerous, for in Yugoslavia the Partisans had started to resent the presence of foreigners (even those who were fighting for them), and in Albania the Ustashi – Croatian Nazis – were committing every kind of atrocity.

By then some of Lassen's colleagues thought that he had acquired a death wish. More probably, he had become immensely tired, mentally as well as physically, and his judgement was suffering as a result – a common effect in men committed to continual operations with no real break or rest. On Paros he behaved with relative caution and restraint, but elsewhere he seemed increasingly wild, and during the most flamboyant of all his exploits – the capture of Salonika, the major sea port and second-largest town in Greece, with a population of 150,000 – he exhibited a magnificent but almost lunatic disregard for his own safety.

Together with a naval officer, Lieutenant Martin Solomon, who had already won a DSC and bar, and had become a close friend, he sailed up through the islands of the Sporades in two caiques, taking his personal jeep and a force of about forty men. He was supposed to be carrying out a reconnaissance, but he extended his research northwards into the Potidia Canal. As the veteran war reporter Richard Capell remarked in his book *Simiomata*, 'The Germans had no notion of any British within a hundred miles', and, having landed, Lassen drove his jeep at high speed towards the town, startling the Communist-backed ELAS guerrilla fighters, who took him for enemy.

The Germans were on the point of pulling out of Salonika, and they had retreated to the western end of the city; but they were still present in battalion strength, and they were setting demolition charges, to destroy as many installations as they could before leaving. Yet when Lassen's colleague Captain Jim Henshaw sent them a note demanding that they surrender 'to the encircling British forces', they were comprehensively bluffed.

Rejecting the Germans' request for a forty-eight-hour cessation of hostilities while they retreated, Lassen launched an immediate victory parade along the waterfront, driving his jeep at the head of the city's four fire engines, with his men clustered on the ladders and the sides. As Richard Capell reported, 'his jeep and handful of men were magnified by mobility into hundreds'.

Girls bombarded them with flowers. Older citizens brought out cheese, wine and ouzo. The fire bells rang, the Greeks cheered, SBS men burst into song, and so the crazy procession continued . . . until, as it approached the Germans' position, the carnival atmosphere suddenly melted away. The hangers-on disappeared into alleyways, and the British realised that there were enemy somewhere close ahead.

When signs in German Gothic script indicated that they were approaching a fuel dump, Lassen saw an opportunity for action. Quickly the SBS abandoned their vehicles and split into two patrols, Lassen's and Henshaw's, to attack the party of Germans who had been setting demolition charges. In the fire-fight that followed, twenty-two Germans were killed, and in the morning the survivors abandoned the city, still believing they had been invaded by a huge force. The fuel dump was saved, and the only casualty suffered by the liberators was one man wounded in the shoulder.

'Have taken Salonika,' Lassen radioed his headquarters in Cairo, and for the next week he ruled the place from the commandeered Hotel Mediterranean. 'Andy and I were treated like gods,' Solomon wrote home. 'I shall never again have so much power or enjoy anything so much. Dictators for a week . . . Andy and I prevent riots and murder, we pass laws, we pardon and pass sentences. If we had not come and acted as we did, much blood would have been spilt.' Others confirmed that had it not been for Lassen's outrageous intervention, large parts of the city would almost certainly have been destroyed. So active were the SBS men, in and around the town, that Germans who had stayed behind reckoned that more than a thousand Allied troops must have arrived.

After three weeks' leave in Athens, where he went partying in high spirits, Lassen got himself sent to Crete as commander of Senforce, whose objectives were to maintain the peace among the feuding Greek irregulars, and to keep thirteen thousand Germans bottled up round Kania, in the north-west corner of the island. The first task proved harder than the second: for two months the Germans remained *in situ*, making no attempt to break out, but the factions of ELAS caused endless trouble, and one of the Greek snipers killed a British captain and a dispatch rider, as well as wounding another officer. Lassen was incensed by the murders, but showed (for him) unusual restraint, and vetoed a colleague's plan to shoot up the Communist area.

As his mother afterwards remarked, he could easily have spent the rest of the war in Greece, out of harm's way; but his demon drove him on. 'It was as if a fever were burning within him,' remembered the American medical orderly Sergeant Porter Jarrell:

> He defied death and exposed himself to the greatest dangers. He was like a restless dynamo, charged with energy. He had to do something to translate his thoughts into action . . . Life had become a race against death. He drove his jeep like fury. He drank big gulps, as if he were thirstily trying to find everything there was in life, in a wild chase after fleeting happiness. But then a strange calm would settle over him – as though he had lived for ever and knew everything.[13]

So it was that he volunteered for Italy, and at the end of March 1945 he was summoned to Ravenna, in the north-east of the country, where the British offensive had come to a halt. With him went his squadron, his dog, his Volkswagen and his normal retinue of cook, barber and other hangers-on. He had always wanted to take part in what he called 'the big war', and now he had his chance: instead of working on its own, far from conventional forces, the SBS was to create a diversion and draw off as many Germans as possible while the Eighth Army launched a major assault along the western shore of Lake Comacchio – a huge, flooded area, 20 miles across, more of a swamp than a lake, dotted with low islands which rose out of water in many places only 2 feet deep.

Because he was to take part in a large-scale operation, Lassen had to attend protracted briefings. These seriously bored him, and in the middle of one, as some colonel was in full flow, he suddenly stood up, announced, 'I go now,' and walked out of the room. Such was his renown, and the force of his personality, that no one tried to recall him or sought to pursue the matter afterwards.

During the first two nights of April the SBS carried out reconnaissances of the lake and its islands, on some of which the

Germans had established observation posts. Movement – by canoe or collapsible Goatley craft – was extremely difficult, as the heavily laden boats were continually grounding in mud beneath the shallow water or becoming stuck in weed. On the third night, taking all their stores with them, the sixty men rowed and paddled out to the island of Casone Agosta, where they spent the next day, with the boats camouflaged under nets and bracken, and they themselves lying in shallow scoops dug out of the grass. When dark fell again, they went forward once more, dropped one patrol under Captain Stud Stellin on a small island, and at 0200 reached the bigger island of Casone Caldirolo, on which there were two stone buildings.

The place was deserted, and the next day passed peacefully, without the enemy realising that the SBS were right under their noses. That night, however, some Germans approached in a boat, and after a short fire-fight the SBS captured five men, whom they locked up in one of the buildings. The firing betrayed the presence of the British, and for the next two days the Germans shelled both houses, scoring several hits but inflicting only one casualty – a corporal who was wounded in the leg.

On the afternoon of 8 April Lassen received coded orders from Second Commando Brigade. 'Attacks must rpt must take place tonight as planned whether reconnaissance has taken place or not stop every reasonable risk must rpt must be taken stop . . .'[14]

No satisfactory recce *had* taken place, because the two-man crew who set out by boat the previous night had been blown backwards by a high wind. So Lassen spent the evening in the main house, which was still under fire, planning his assault, and Stud Stellin, who had rejoined him, found him in cheerful mood. Nevertheless, Lassen talked for the first time about what would happen if one of them failed to return, and Stud thought he had had a premonition that he was going to die.

The raiders pulled silently away from Caldirolo just before midnight, with the force divided into three patrols. Never for a moment had Lassen thought of directing operations from the rear – which, as squadron commander, he might well have done. On the contrary, he led the first patrol himself, rowing out to a causeway or dam, and then advancing on foot along the top of it towards the town of

Comacchio. Next behind him came Fred Green, the squadron's interpreter, who spoke some Italian. The road was about five yards wide, and the only cover was afforded by the steep, slippery banks of the causeway, which sloped down a few feet into water on either side.

The outskirts of the town lay nearly two miles ahead, but they had moved up only about 500 yards when a shout came out of the dark ahead: '*Qui va la?*'

'Forward you go,' whispered Lassen to Green. 'Do the talking.'

'*Siamo pescatori di San Alberto*,' Green called. 'We're fishermen from San Alberto.' He repeated the phrase three or four times, but there was no reply, and suddenly firing broke out from the nearest of the German defence positions, which were described in official reports as 'pill-boxes' or 'block-houses', but were in fact low machine-gun emplacements built of stone and covered with turf.

Pushing Green down on to the road, Lassen ran forward and hurled grenades through the opening of the first pillbox. As Green said later, 'I'm sure something clicked in his mind at the sound of gunfire. He forgot who he was. He forgot about taking cover. He forgot every damn thing except going forward.'

Four Germans were killed in and around the first emplacement, but a hail of machine-gun bullets was still whistling down the road. Even Lassen's own men, who knew his methods, were amazed to see him taking on the machine-gun posts single-handed. But, as his sergeant major Leslie Stephenson recalled,

> All our success had come from stealth, but now we were being used for an infantry assault that, considering our type of soldiering, was a suicide mission. We were rushing along with him in front, blowing his whistle and shouting, 'Come on! Forward, you bastards! Get on! Get forward!'[15]

Ignoring the acute danger, Lassen ran on again and attacked the second pillbox with grenades, killing the occupants. Just after he had cleared it, Stephenson caught up with him, and during a temporary lull in the firing they both got down behind a slight rise in the road. By then Lassen had thrown all his own grenades, so he borrowed more from Stephenson, hurling them at the third pillbox. Already the patrol had captured two prisoners, and now, in the hope of getting more, Lassen shouted out in German for the occupants to surrender.

Someone called back '*Kamerad*' – an ambiguous response. Lassen told the rest of his men to stay where they were, stood up and went forward. There was a single burst of machine-gun fire, then silence.

To Stephenson, the silence seemed to last twenty minutes. In fact it can have been only a few seconds. Then he heard, 'SBS, SBS, Major Lassen wounded. Here.'

He found him lying beside the pillbox entrance, and tried to drag him away, but he was too big and heavy.

'Who is it?' Lassen asked.

'Steve.'

'Good.' A pause. Then, 'Steve, I'm wounded. I'm going to die.'

Stephenson got out a morphine tablet and put it on his tongue. 'Morphine,' he told him. 'We're going to take you back to the boats.'

'No use, Steve,' Lassen muttered. 'I'm dying, and it's been a poor show. Don't go any further with it. Get the others out.'

Again Stephenson tried to lift him, but both men were entangled in a telephone line, and Lassen collapsed unconscious. By the time another SBS man came up, he was dead.

With Lassen gone, the operation had lost its driving force. Pulling back, Stephenson relayed his last order to get the men out – and Lieutenant G. W. Turnbull, in command of the rear patrol, fired a red Very light, the signal to retreat. By 4 a.m. the survivors were back in the house on Caldirolo, too shocked and dispirited to sleep.

Three other first-class men had also been killed, three had been wounded, and one was missing; but it was the loss of their leader, who had seemed indestructible, that left them shattered. Corporal Richard Marsden of the Royal Army Medical Corps, who had stayed behind on the island to receive the wounded, remembered how 'they just sat and talked about what had happened, and about Major Lassen's incredible courage'. Sergeant Waite said that 'never in all his life had he seen anything so magnificent', and that they all owed their lives to Lassen. Later, Turnbull's operation report spoke of his 'magnificent leadership and personal courage'.

At dawn on 9 April Italian partisans found the bodies and carried them into the town, where they laid them at the foot of the old *campanile*. When the news reached David Sutherland, out on an operation in the wilds of Yugoslavia, he, by his own account, 'went white', and so did his companions. They simply could not believe that Lassen was dead.

Later, when Sutherland talked to the men who had been on the raid, it struck him that what Lassen had done was, even by his own standards, extraordinary, and he decided to try for a VC, the only posthumous award then available, apart from the Mention in Despatches. His first attempt, at the headquarters of Commando Brigade, was baulked, because the Commandos were already trying to obtain a posthumous VC for their own Tom Hunter, a twenty-one-year-old Scottish corporal who had been killed in the same theatre on 2 April, when, with his troop pinned down on a canal bank, he had charged alone for 200 yards, through intense small-arms fire, to clear enemy from a group of houses. The Commandos thought that a second request for a VC so soon after the first might prejudice their chances, so Sutherland bypassed them, wrote out a citation, and took it straight to the headquarters of the Eighth Army commander, General Sir Richard McCreery, at Klagenfurt, in Austria. His swift advocacy paid off without affecting the Commandos' recommendation: Hunter also received a posthumous Victoria Cross.

The citation for Lassen's VC was published by the War Office in London on 7 September 1945, and after an account of the night's actions, it concluded:

> By his magnificent leadership and complete disregard for his personal safety, Major Lassen had, in the face of overwhelming superiority, achieved his objects. Three positions were wiped out, accounting for six machine-guns, killing eight and wounding others of the enemy, and two prisoners were taken. The high sense of devotion to duty and the esteem in which he was held by the men he led, added to his own magnificent

courage, enabled Major Lassen to carry out all the tasks he had been given with complete success.

His heroism has never been doubted – and it was some consolation to his family, as well as to his comrades in the SBS, that his ferocious final action proved of considerable benefit when the main British assault on the Argenta Gap went in the following night, for the Germans had withdrawn many troops from their front line to cover what they took to be a major threat from the direction of Lake Comacchio. His personal sacrifice thus probably saved dozens, if not hundreds, of casualties.

But was it worth it? Should the SBS have been used in what was essentially an infantry task? Should such highly skilled and trained men have been sent in as decoys? The questions have been endlessly debated.

As it was, the family declined to bring his body home, and he lies buried in the British war cemetery at Argenta. There are memorials to him in four countries: Denmark, England, Scotland and Israel. The Freedom Museum in Copenhagen displays a full set of his medals – the VC, MC and two bars, the King Christian Honour, the medal of the Greek Sacred Squadron, and five British campaign medals – the 1939–45 Medal, the African Star, the Italy Medal, the Defence Medal and the War Medal.

There is no doubt that in terms of individual acts of gallantry he won his Victoria Cross several times over, and he made a contribution to the war out of proportion to his rank and position. His personal work in the Dodecanese diverted enemy troops and weakened enemy resistance in key areas of the main battlefield, while his seizure of Salonika, with a handful of men, must surely rank as an outstanding individual achievement.

His courage ran in the family, and, in my view, represented an accentuated personality trait. I am sure there are many others with similar characteristics who failed to survive long enough in battle for it to be recognised and rewarded. Luck plays a part as much as skill: luck, however, only offers opportunities, and it was Lassen himself who had the decisiveness and courage to grasp opportunities to fight.

One cannot help wondering what he might have done or become, had he survived the war. In peacetime his temper might still have been a problem, but his extraordinary wartime experiences would surely have mellowed his sharp and abrasive characteristics. He might just have gone on fighting, as a mercenary. He might have found fulfilment in charity work. He might also – as Lord Jellicoe (who knew him as well as anyone, except perhaps David Sutherland) told me – have played a leading role in politics or diplomacy. 'He had an astonishing talent for doing the things which really interested him. He loved his country, and I believe he would have played an important role in Danish affairs.'[16]

His mother Suzanne published her moving memoir *Anders Lassen VC* in 1965, and ended her book with the words:

> I feel that I owe it to him not only to be thankful but also happy that he, in the short time he was allowed on this earth, was to his country a courageous warrior and to us a good and loving son.[17]

12

Eastern Allies: Gurkha and Indian VCs

The Gurkhas

British people visit Nepal for many reasons: to climb or trek in the Himalayas, to go white-water rafting, to look for tigers and rhinos in the jungles of Chitwan, or merely to see the sights of Kathmandu, Pokhara and other centres. Whatever the purpose of their visit, they are immediately struck by the exceptional friendliness of the people – and this close, warm relationship derives largely from the fact that for nearly two hundred years men from the mountain kingdom have fought with outstanding tenacity and courage as members of the British Army.

In the nineteenth century only British officers serving in command of Gurkhas could win the VC: native soldiers qualified for lesser awards, such as the Order of British India, the Indian Order of Merit, the Indian Distinguished Service Medal and the Royal Victorian Medal. In 1911, however, a new warrant made native troops eligible for the highest honour, and since then thirteen Gurkhas have won VCs in theatres as diverse as North Africa, Italy, Burma and Borneo.

The British Army has always had a special rapport with the Gurkhas, and it was my good fortune to fight alongside them in the Malayan Emergency Campaign of the 1950s, when British armed forces helped local troops suppress a Communist insurrection, and again in the Borneo 'Confrontation' of the 1960s, when Indonesian forces mounted cross-border operations into Sarawak. In both theatres I witnessed their tough, adaptable soldiering, their skill at arms and their loyalty to those whom they respect. The latter does not come out of subservience, but is gained only by outstanding leadership – which is why British officers serving alongside the Gurkhas are only of the best that we have to offer.

The popular image of an award-winning Gurkha is of a man gone fighting-mad, galvanised by heat-of-the-moment courage and wielding his kukri with ferocious abandon as he hacks the enemy to pieces. Several VC winners have indeed fought with astonishing ferocity, but the popular idea is misleading, for in general the Nepalese are by no means aggressive. Rather, they are gentle, polite and easygoing, and only when roused do they become ferocious.

In battle, much of their aggression is sparked by team spirit and peer pressure, and in this respect they are little different from the British serviceman. Every small unit – every section or platoon – is immensely strengthened by the determination of its members not to let each other down. The men know and trust each other: living and working together gives them confidence and brings out the best in them. If they start taking casualties, their anger rises, but even when enraged they generally remain cool-headed. As one British officer who has commanded them remarked, 'It takes them some time to get aroused. But once they do – watch it.'

Above all they are practical. In his book *Defeat into Victory*, Field Marshal Slim recorded how, in Burma during the Second World War, some Gurkhas were once collecting up dead Japanese for burial:

> One Japanese . . . proved not to be as dead as expected. A Gurkha had drawn his *kukri* to finish the struggling prisoner when a passing British officer intervened, saying, 'You mustn't do that, Johnny. Don't kill him!' The Gurkha, with his *kukri*

poised, looked at the officer in pained surprise. 'But, sahib,' he protested, 'we can't bury him *alive*!'[1]

Slim delighted in the Gurkhas' robust attitude, and described how once, in Burma, some soldiers 'presented themselves before their General, proudly opened a large basket, lifted from it three gory Japanese heads and laid them on his table. They then politely offered him for his dinner the freshly-caught fish which filled the rest of the basket.'[2] Slim also relished the account given by twenty-year-old Rifleman Ganju Lama, who won a VC when he fearlessly moved forward in the open, through withering small-arms fire, to engage Japanese tanks with his PIAT grenade-launcher:

> He was shot in the hand, the shoulder and again badly in the leg, but he got to within thirty yards of the tanks and bumped off two of them. Later, when I saw him in hospital, I asked him why he had walked forward in the open like that. He replied, 'I'd been trained not to fire the PIAT until I was certain of hitting. I knew I could hit at thirty yards, so I went to thirty yards!' He had only one thought in his head – to get to thirty yards. Quite simple, if you are not bothered by imagination.[3]

Ganju Lama, although a splendid fighting man, had little time for the niceties of military conduct. On the first day of his employment as batman to Major Roy Gribble (winner of the MC and Bar) in Borneo, he appeared in his officer's dugout at 0400 with a mess-tin of tea. He did not bother to say 'Good morning', or even 'Sir'. He merely barked, 'Get up!' – and Gribble, though startled, took to him at once.[4]

Another aspect of the Gurkhas' character is their quiet humour. General Sir Walter Walker, who conducted the British 'Confrontation' operations of the 1960s, told the story of a battalion celebrating its imminent departure from Borneo with a hectic party in the officers' mess. The camp's guard commander, a sergeant, was briefing a newly arrived Gurkha rifleman in his duties. After he had checked the sentry's knowledge of the password and other essentials, the sergeant posed a hypothetical situation as a well-tried method of ensuring that his briefing had gone home. 'You're on sentry. It's one o'clock in the morning. Suddenly you see a strange figure crawling towards you through the long grass over there. What would you do?'

Instantly the soldier replied, 'Show him the way to the Officers' Mess.'[5]

The Gurkhas have a special place in the hearts of our nation – and never was this more manifest than at the 50th Anniversary of the end of the Second World War, when their detachment of veterans, led by four holders of the Victoria Cross, marched past the Queen in London and received the longest, loudest and most spontaneous acclamation. As a more permanent tribute to these great warriors, a recently erected monument of a Gurkha soldier, cast in bronze, stands outside the Ministry of Defence Main Building in Whitehall, and, appropriately for the subjects' rural background, a stone's throw from the Farmers' Club.

The Gurkhas are drawn from all the tribes in Nepal – and indeed some of them are not Nepalese at all, but come from neighbouring Sikkim and Bhutan (Ganju Lama was a Sikkimese). All derive from a mountain environment which naturally creates very tough people. A boy sent out on his own at the age of four or five to look after a herd of buffaloes grows into an intensely practical man who lives for the day and does not worry too much about what may happen tomorrow. Used as he is to living in the isolated community of his own village, and walking for days on end up and down precipitous slopes to reach the nearest town, he tends to be confident and self-reliant, not awed by authority or large organisations. As a soldier, one of his greatest strengths is his knack of seeing what needs to be done, and, in a crisis, of seizing the initiative without waiting for an order.

Before 1939 some 18,000 men had enlisted in the British Army, but during the Second World War the Brigade of Gurkhas expanded enormously, taking in another 105,000. The impulse came largely from the Ranas, the family who ruled Nepal at the time and wanted to reciprocate the help they had had from Britain. Given that the population of the entire country was then 4,500,000 – about that of Inner London – the recruiting drive meant that there was hardly a village which did not have every young man of martial age drained from it.

The men who poured down to the recruiting depots in India were mostly uneducated and illiterate – unsophisticated country boys who had never been to school. If anyone asked them why they had enlisted, they generally replied that they saw military service as an opportunity, a chance to escape from the village, which otherwise would have held them prisoner for life. It was true that pressure to join up had filtered down from Kathmandu, but the Gurkhas have always been volunteer mercenaries. So many of the men bore the same name that they were known by the last two digits of their army numbers: otherwise, with four or five Lalbahadurs in the same platoon, life would have been extremely confusing.

After rudimentary training, the boys who had walked out of the Himalayas were sent into battle, and it soon became apparent that they had various advantages over their British counterparts. One was their ability to keep themselves warm and dry even in dire weather, and another their aptitude for fieldcraft, which came naturally from their rural upbringing. They place a high value on medals, which they regard as tangible evidence of success. A man returning with a decoration receives a tremendous welcome in his village, no matter how remote it may be, and his arrival sets off great celebrations. The receipt of a Victoria Cross naturally generates the highest excitement of all. On the other hand, if a soldier does not get a medal when he thinks he should have won one, he is apt to voice his disappointment. Conversely, when a man does something of which he is not very proud, word quickly gets back to his village, and often he never goes home.

As with other nationalities, fortune seems to favour the brave: several Gurkha winners of the VC have had extraordinary luck – and none more so than Lance Corporal Rambahadur Limbu, who gained his medal in Borneo during 1965, fighting Indonesian terrorists in the campaign, or 'Confrontation' as it became known.

He came from Eastern Nepal and was then twenty-five. Uniquely among Gurkhas, he has published a simple yet touching autobiography,[6] recording a pattern of life shared by most of his fellow soldiers. 'My childhood was sad and unhappy,' he recalls, for it seemed that 'Death was determined to wipe out my whole family in no time.'

Seven of his parents' ten children died, leaving only three young brothers. Rambahadur was put to work in the fields at an early age, and 'one day when it was still dawn and the village was fast asleep', at the age of fifteen and only 4′ 10″ tall, he slipped secretly away from home with two friends to join the army. After walking for six days, the little party reached the border of India, and made their way to a recruiting depot; they were accepted for training as Boy Soldiers, and told that they would be travelling 'to that unknown land beyond the seven seas which we knew was called Malaya' – but they lost their nerve and ran away.

After many weeks wandering aimlessly, living off the country and charity, Rambahadur returned home. He tried to settle down, helping his brothers on the tiny, terraced fields, but presently he left again, and after various adventures joined the army on Man Service in 1957, just as the Malayan Emergency was entering its final months. By then he had grown to the fine height of 5′ 3″, and he spent ten months training hard in Malaya, gaining further in stature and fitness.

He then got his first taste of active service, taking part in jungle patrols and ambushes to eliminate those few terrorists who had remained to continue the fight against the British and the Malayan Government. 'We laid a few ambushes, but every time the enemy eluded us, thereby denying me the opportunity of seeing them alive,' he remembered. 'I had been lucky, however, to see some of the dead ones killed by our First Battalion.'[7] Little did he know how important this experience was to be in his developing military career.

Home on leave in 1961, he married a girl called Tikamaya, from his own village, who in due course bore him two children. The army rules of the day prevented her accompanying him on his return to Malaya, as he was too young, and he had to put in another unaccompanied tour before he reached the magic age when he would become entitled to an army quarter.

At the end of 1962 the Malaysian concept of an association of independent democratic states began to develop into a reality. In

December, however, an abortive rebellion took place in Brunei, and a short time later President Sukarno of Indonesia declared a 'Confrontation' with Britain in a military and political attempt to disrupt the planned creation of Malaysia. Indonesian patrols infiltrated across the border between Kalimantan, or Indonesian Borneo, and the newly formed Malaysia.

Fighting in the jungle is a very personal affair. Seldom is it possible to see further than 15 or 20 metres, and to spot something even at this distance requires an aptitude for looking through the undergrowth rather than at it. Much of the terrain in Malaysia is steep, and the ground is frequently wet and slippery from the constant rain. Background noise from wildlife such as monkeys and the numerous insects is continuous, night and day, yet to the trained ear any human or unnatural noise is instantly discernible. Conversation is conducted in whispers when there may be enemy near. Night movement is impossible, except if one takes the risk of moving along predefined tracks which will be known to both sides. So little sun penetrates the undergrowth that after a few weeks in the jungle British soldiers emerge as pale and wan as they might after a long, dark winter.

The atmosphere is claustrophobic and all-embracing. The men on either side of you are the only reality, and the rest of the environment has to be left to the imagination – until there is a burst of fire and an intense battle begins. Of course shellfire and bombing knock the tops off trees, and this in turn allows more light to permeate; but the thick tangle of dying and broken branches from the forest canopy impairs movement and vision even further, and can make progress impossible.

There were no men better suited to close-quarter operations in this dangerous environment than the tough, independent Gurkha soldiers who were flown in to help British and other nations' security forces repel the intruders. Rambahadur entered the fray in Borneo as a member of the 2nd Battalion, 10th Princess Mary's Own Gurkha Rifles, and at last got a chance to put his years of training into practice.

His great day came on 21 November 1965. The night before, he was troubled by a strange dream in which, as he and his section advanced with their weapons at the ready, he saw a glowing red arc of fire right in front of him. His men looked frightened and moved back, but he 'marched right forward to the arc, expecting to be burnt', only to feel, when he was inside it, 'a strange kind of happiness'.

Next morning his section was tasked to creep up on an enemy strongpoint near the border and seize a prisoner. This is one of the most difficult operations with which a section can be tasked. It requires all the skill and patience of a hunter, and one who is faced by an adversary who knows the ground better than you do. The enemy will have sentries out and will change them regularly every few hours so that they remain at maximum alertness. In other words, the odds are stacked against the snatch party.

It was in this context that Rambahadur's section set forth. Reveille was at 0300 hours and they moved off at 0400, feeling their way along jungle tracks in the dark before dawn. They followed a careful, covert uphill approach along a thickly forested ridge, which brought them extremely close to their quarry before they were spotted by a sentry who promptly opened fire from 10 yards' range. Immediately the plan for abduction was converted into one of full-scale attack – a form of warfare dear to the Gurkha heart. One rifleman was wounded – and Rambahadur reacted violently: 'I saw blood on his face. As soon as I saw his blood, my own blood began to boil. I swore that the enemy would pay for this with their blood. Blood for blood and nothing but blood could settle this account.'[8]

Rushing forward, Rambahadur killed the sentry – and in so doing brought down a storm of small-arms fire from the rest of the garrison who had instantly stood to to repel the assault. The Indonesians are robust and well-trained soldiers, and the ensuing battle was no walkover, as the sides engaged in an intense firefight. Ignoring the danger, Rambahadur called his group forward to a better fire position, then moved out into the open to report his intentions to his platoon commander. At that moment both his two remaining companions were seriously wounded, and over the next twenty minutes he made what his VC citation described as 'three supremely gallant attempts' to rescue them.

First he crawled forward under a barrage of fire, but when he realised how exposed he was, he decided that only speed would save him, so he got up, ran forward, dropped down beside one of the wounded men, picked him up and carried him to safety. With hardly a pause he set out again for the top of the hill, moving in a series of short rushes. Once he was pinned down for several minutes by automatic fire, which ripped up the ground all round him. At last he reached the casualty, picked him up, and ran back through the hail of bullets. That none hit him was something of a miracle: it was as if his amazing courage had acted as a shield.

With the rescue complete, he took part in the assault, which turned into a ferocious, hour-long battle, and himself killed four enemy as they tried to flee across the border. At least twenty-four Indonesians were killed, at a cost to the attackers of three dead and two wounded. In the words of the citation,

> His outstanding personal bravery, selfless conduct, complete contempt of the enemy and determination to save the lives of the men of his fire group set an incomparable example and inspired all who saw him . . . In scale and in achievement this engagement stands out as one of the first importance, and there is no doubt that, but for the inspired conduct and example set by Lance Corporal Rambahadur at the most vital stage of the battle, much less would have been achieved and greater casualties caused.
>
> He displayed heroism, self-sacrifice and a devotion to duty and to his men of the very highest order. His actions on this day reached a zenith of determined, premeditated valour which must count amongst the most notable on record and is deserving of the greatest admiration and the highest praise.

Rambahadur's own accounts of the action are extremely vivid, and give an exceptional glimpse of the chaotic nature of close-quarter fighting. He described the advance:

> I was in front, parting the undergrowth as I went and, using scissors [*sic*], cut the vines that got in the way. We were some 150 men strong. We got near the enemy camp. It was still

dark . . . On we went until we were about thirty yards from the enemy and we saw their mosquito nets. They were still asleep. The OC stopped us and I heard the platoon commander talking on the radio. Why had we stopped? Was it because the enemy was too strong for us? I only heard the platoon commander . . . say: 'No, sahib, we have reached as far as this, now it's on and kill them' . . .

One of the enemy woke up and, with his rifle slung, walked towards us as we were crawling towards the camp. He came near but did not see us. He had a piss and took the rifle off his shoulder as though he had seen us. We opened fire and killed him. Then 9 Platoon started with the covering fire and we moved forwards . . .

The man on my right was wounded, one of two new riflemen. The LMG 1 and 2 [first and second light machine-gunners] were on my left. Enemy fire then hit LMG 1 in the stomach and his guts fell out. His arm was also shot off above the elbow. He was still alive and gave his gun to the Gun 2. I put on a first field dressing but it took quite some time to get it out of its case as it was new and I had neglected to tear it open in readiness. Then the LMG had a stoppage. Gun 2 took the magazine off and changed it. As he was doing this I told him not to raise his head but he did and was shot in the forehead. He managed to say, '*Aiya, ustad,* a bullet', and died. He fell on top of me.

I did not know where the next enemy trench was and the enemy were firing at us. I took out a grenade and pulled the pin out with my teeth and threw it. It hit a tree and rolled back quickly on the slippery earth, towards us. I told the others to keep their heads down but I had to watch it. It slipped out of sight down the hill and exploded in a group of Indonesians who were moving round to infiltrate us. I threw more on to them and firing ceased.

I paid attention to the wounded man. He said, and I can never forget it, '*Ustad,* I won't live, please kill me.' I told him I was about to rescue him and detailed the other two to stay there and give me covering fire while I went back to get help. I saw my platoon commander down below and shouted to him:

'Gun 2 dead, Gun 1 wounded. Come and help,' but no one came so I went back to my section, crawled up to Gun 1 and brought him back. He was heavy and it was difficult. I went back a hundred yards to the first of the felled trees. He wanted water. I told him I'd come back and give him some, then I went back and brought the Gun 2 back. He was lighter and so it was easier. My hand was cut by the jutting bone of the broken arm of the wounded man but I only found that out later.

I did all that on my own. I saw a lot of dead enemy where we had fired before. The third time I went back and cleared the whole area then withdrew the rest of my men and the LMG. I called for help but no one came . . . While the medical orderly was coming forward the wounded man died.

Next morning when it was light I looked at the LMG and saw it was covered in blood but I had no idea about myself. I made my own tea with what was left of my water bottle water but no one came to sit near me. I wondered why not. They did not say anything. It was only an hour later, at 0700 hours, that I realised I was covered in blood, intestines and human skin, and my pouches were full of the same stuff.[9]

Rambahadur's award was announced by General Sir Alan Jolly, Commander-in-Chief of Far East Land Forces, at a special parade in Singapore in January 1966, and later that year he was presented with his medal by Her Majesty the Queen at an investiture at Buckingham Palace. He was accompanied only by his five-year-old son Bhakta, for, to his intense grief, his wife had died in the British Military Hospital in Singapore in January – an event which he described in heart-rending detail in *My Life Story.*

Another Gurkha who showed supreme courage in saving the lives of wounded comrades was Rifleman Kulbir Thapa, who served with the Third Queen Alexandra's Own Gurkha Rifles in France in the First World War. On 25 September 1915, after an Allied attack had petered out near Neuve Chapelle, he was the sole survivor of a party which had fought its way into the German trenches. He himself had been wounded, but when he found a badly injured soldier of the 2nd Leicestershire Regiment, he insisted on remaining with him for the rest of the day and through the night, even though the Briton urged him to save his own skin and make his way back.

At first light on the 26th, with mist giving him some cover, Kulbir brought the man out through the German wire and left him in a relatively safe place while he himself went back to rescue two wounded Gurkhas, one after the other. He then returned in clear daylight and carried the Leicestershire man to safety, drawing enemy fire for much of the way. The citation for his VC, published on 18 November 1915, praised his 'most conspicuous bravery'. He was twenty-seven at the time; having recovered from his wound, he was promoted to *havildar* (sergeant), and went with his regiment to Egypt.

The Gurkhas' most celebrated (and feared) form of assault was the silent attack, launched with kukris and bayonets, and a supreme example of this was the operation carried out by Subedar (Captain) Lalbahadur Thapa in Tunisia on the night of 5–6 April 1943. His unit, the 1st Battalion of the 2nd King Edward's Own Gurkha Rifles, was part of the 4th Indian Division, and the plan was to capture a feature called the Fatnassa Heights so that the Eighth Army could wheel round behind the Axis forces under General Erwin Rommel.

On the night assault, Lalbahadur led two sections up a corridor or chimney which ran between escarpments into the heart of the enemy's defensive position, gradually widening out from a narrow opening. The success of the entire operation depended on this first attack being driven home – and I cannot do better than quote from the admirably vivid account of the action which appeared in the regiment's official history:

> Enemy sentries in an outpost sangar [a small fortified emplacement] suddenly discerned figures leaping through the darkness. The Italians died to a man under the kukris. As the Gurkhas raced up the widening passage, the arena before them was swept by machine gun fire; grenades arced down from posts on both escarpments and shook the night with their blasts. A number of men fell, but the dauntless subedar headed

> the rush, which overwhelmed the next machine gun nest. He killed two enemies with his kukri and shot down two others [with a pistol].
>
> Gaining the twisty track leading to the crest of the escarpment, and followed only by Rifleman Harakbahadur Gurung and Rifleman Inrabahadur Gurung, he managed to close on the machine gun nest which guarded the top of the path. Again he struck two men dead with his kukri, while two others fell before the weapons of the riflemen. The corridor had been won and the way was open.
>
> Subedar Lalbahadur Thapa and the two riflemen stood guard at the top of the path while D Company passed through. Fanning out along the top of the escarpment, the Gurkhas, adhering to the technique of silent attack, fell on the machine gun nests and sangars. Plying kukris and bayonets, they quickly put an end to resistance . . . Many enemies, confronted by fearsome figures leaping upon them out of the dark, fell or were flung over the cliffside.[10]

In the citation for his Victoria Cross, which appeared in the *London Gazette* of 15 June 1943, Lalbahadur was commended for his 'unsurpassed bravery'. His 'outstanding leadership, gallantry and complete disregard for his own safety' were an example to his whole company, 'and the ruthless determination of this Gurkha officer to reach his objective and kill his enemy had a decisive effect on the success of the whole operation'.

Lalbahadur continued to serve with his regiment for another five years, also winning the Order of British India (1st Class) and the Star of Nepal (4th Class). He retired in 1948 with the honorary rank of captain, and died in 1968 at the age of sixty-two. Four of his sons followed him into his regiment.

For sheer, sustained aggression, no one will ever match the achievement of Rifleman Bhanbaghta Gurung, who served in Burma during the Second World War in the 2nd King Edward VII's Own Gurkha Rifles. On 5 March 1945, at the age of twenty-three, leading an attack on a hill known as Snowdon, he fought with such ferocity that he cleared the entire position of Japanese, and after the action sixty-six enemy dead were picked up.

Described by his company commander as 'a smiling, hard-swearing, gallant and indomitable peasant soldier, who, in a battalion of very brave men was one of the bravest', Bhanbaghta Gurung had been demoted from his rank of *naik* (corporal) for some lapse that was later established not to have been his fault, and colleagues felt that in fighting so furiously he might have been trying to prove himself. Whatever his motivation, his feat was astonishing – and the story of it was crisply told in his regiment's official history:

> Rifleman Bhanbaghta Gurung's section of a leading platoon had been held up in an exposed position, when man after man was picked off by a tree sniper. Spotting the marksman, Bhanbaghta Gurung sprang into the open, engaged him in a point-blank duel and killed him. The platoon pushed forward, only to be pinned down once more when within twenty yards of its objective. Whereupon Bhanbaghta Gurung again attacked.
>
> He reached the nearest Jap post, killing two enemies with a grenade and a third with his bayonet. He then flung himself on two other foxholes, destroying their defenders. The platoon moved up in his wake. There remained only a solitary bunker on the extreme eastern tip of Snowdon which continued to rake the advance with machine-gun fire.
>
> For the fifth time Bhanbaghta engaged the enemy single-handed. Leaping ahead, he gained the bunker, sprang on its roof and dropped smoke grenades down the air slits. As the blinded gunners staggered out, the Gurkha despatched them with his kukri. Yet from within a single machine-gun continued to spit defiance. Whereupon Bhanbaghta Gurung crawled inside; in the befogged bunker a last kukri stroke put an end to resistance.
>
> Nor did this conclude his amazing performance. A Jap group rallied and raced to regain the bunker. With a Bren gunner and two riflemen beside him, Bhanbaghta Gurung met the rush head on. Several enemies fell at close range, and the assault disintegrated.[11]

The citation for his Victoria Cross praised his 'outstanding bravery' and 'complete disregard for his own safety', but it hardly did justice to the exceptional initiative that he showed: the fact was that he captured Snowdon virtually single-handed. He was restored to his former rank of *naik*, but after the war he opted to return home to his young wife, rather than continue serving. When he left the army, he was given the honorary rank of *havildar*, and he made several return visits to his regiment in Malaya, Hong Kong and the United Kingdom. His three sons all served in the 2nd Battalion of his regiment.

As these stories show, Gurkhas at war display formidable courage. They also show complete dedication to carrying out orders, regardless of the personal risks involved, and are driven by a fierce sense of duty, combined with a will to kill the enemy. All this is emphasised by their selfless disregard of their own lives when a compatriot is wounded and in peril from the enemy, and they see it as their overriding duty to bring him to safety.

These qualities have gained Gurkhas the respect and love of the British people. Hence the inscription on the monument in Whitehall:

The Gurkha Soldier
Bravest of the Brave
Most Generous of the Generous
Never had Country
More faithful friends
Than you[12]

Indians

Indian formations were the spearhead of our first and much needed victories in the Western Desert[13]

By the end of the Second World War the Indian Army had provided the Allies with nearly two and a quarter million fighting troops, each one of them a volunteer. Field Marshal Slim, who gave a significant part of his life to service with the Indian Army and the Gurkhas, described their contribution as 'the greatest voluntary army in history. It was not in numbers only, but in achievement that it was great.'[14]

Since Indians became eligible to win the Victoria Cross in 1911, eighty-four have been awarded the medal – a proud record for a nation whose soldiers have often fought valiantly on behalf of Britain. The first winner was Sepoy Khudadad Khan, who continued to man a machine-gun post even when badly wounded at Hollebeke, in Belgium, on 31 October 1914. Another outstanding example from the First World War was that of Sepoy Chatta Singh, who gave cover to his commanding officer when he was lying wounded and incapacitated in the open. Although exposed to heavy rifle fire, Singh bound up the officer's wounds and dug a protective hollow with his entrenching tool, lying beside the casualty for five hours and shielding him from the enemy with his own body. At last, when night fell, he went back for help and took the officer to safety – having demonstrated phenomenal coolness and courage.

The Second World War produced another large crop of thirty-one Indian VCs, and the support given by native troops to the Allies was of incalculable value, especially against the Japanese – witness the feat of *Naik* Nand Singh on the night of 11 March 1944, when a Japanese patrol infiltrated an Allied position covering the main road between Maungdaw and Buthi-daung in Burma.

Singh was in command of the leading section of a platoon which was ordered to recapture the position at all costs. Leading the way up a steep, knife-edged ridge, he came under heavy fire from rifles and machine guns and was soon wounded by a bullet in the thigh. Undaunted, he rushed forward alone and stormed the first enemy trench with his bayonet. Again he was wounded, this time in the face and shoulder by a grenade which exploded a few feet in front of him, but on he went and captured a second trench.

Within a few minutes all the rest of his section had been killed or wounded – yet Singh dragged himself out of the second trench and captured a third, bayoneting its defenders. With that pocket of resistance eliminated, the rest of the platoon managed to regain possession of the hilltop. Singh's personal tally of Japanese was seven – an amazing tribute to his courage and determination.

Yet the most celebrated Indian VC winner – and a hero throughout the subcontinent – was Premindra Singh Bhagat, a Sikh officer generally known just as 'Prem', the first Indian commissioned officer to gain the award, and a man whose modesty, enthusiasm and ebullient good nature made him enormously popular with all ranks.

Prem was born on 14 October 1918, the third son of Surendra Singh Bhagat, an engineer and a strict disciplinarian. His elder brothers, Tony and Tutu, went to school normally, but he, being skinny and not very robust, was regarded as the runt of the family, and so had lessons at home from a private tutor. Although he did not seem particularly intelligent, he was much loved, his genial temperament causing him to be nicknamed 'Bhondu', a term of affection meaning 'idiot'.

When he was only nine, his mother died, but for him the blow was softened by the swift arrival of two aunts, sisters of his father, who took over the running of the household. The tragedy was worse for his elder brothers, who were away at school and were not told what had happened, because their father thought it better not to distract them from their studies. When they came home for the holidays, they were shocked to find that their mother had gone. In less than a year their father remarried, this time to an attractive woman of eighteen, scarcely older than Tony, whom the boys called Aunty, and who produced four children in quick succession.

Prem's formal education began in February 1930, when he went as an eleven-year-old cadet to the Royal Indian Military College in the Doon Valley, among the foothills of the Himalayas. The establishment was run on the lines of British public schools, with the aim of training boys for the army, and provided the best education of any school in India. From reveille, sounded on a bugle at 0620, until retreat at sunset and lights out at 2130, the routine was energetic: it included compulsory games and, for the senior cadets, was laced with military pursuits such as fieldcraft and weapon training. At meals in the mess only English was spoken.

At first Prem did not shine: his achievement was adequate rather than outstanding, but teachers praised his intelligence and his attitude, and saw promise in him. 'Talks all day and has a good command of English,' reported his Section Master, G. F. Wood.[15] At various stages of his school career he was accused of idleness, carelessness and untidiness, but by the time he was fifteen he had become more responsible, and was showing signs of being a natural leader, not least as an NCO in the cadet force.

In January 1937 he moved on to the Indian Military Academy – the local equivalent of the Royal Military Academy at Sandhurst – which had been founded only four years earlier. There the routine was even tougher than at the college, with cadets kept smartly on the move, either at the double or on bicycles, from 0600 until 2230. One colleague remembered Prem as 'a cheerful bloke', always ready to crack a joke; but once again he irritated his teachers, this time by failing to control his quick temper and having too high an opinion of himself.

It took the sudden death of his father – killed in a riding accident at the start of 1938 – to sober him up and make him more likeable. After the accident the tenor of his reports changed for the better: instead of carping, his instructors praised him for his hard work and powers of leadership, and in July 1939 he was commissioned into the Royal Bombay Sappers and Miners – the unit with which he was associated for the rest of his life, and of which he became enormously proud. With war threatening in Europe, Prem was posted to the Sappers' 21 Field Company – a natural berth for him, considering his father's engineering skills.

Stationed in Poona, he made a powerful impact on the local girls, with his high spirits, good looks, unselfconscious charm and delight in parties – although, oddly enough, the one person he did not impress at first was Mohini Bhandari, the sixteen-year-old daughter of a colonel in the Indian Medical Service. Mohini was reckoned the most beautiful girl in town, and Prem became fascinated by her, but he was kept at a distance by the hostility of her father, who was anxious that she should marry someone more distinguished than this rather erratic young officer.

Thus it was with a heavy heart that Prem took a train to Bombay in September 1940 and embarked with the rest of 21 Field

Company on the SS *Devonshire*, as part of 5 Indian Division, bound for Africa – a voyage made hellish by the disgusting food, intense heat and the overcrowding on board. Life on a troopship was never less than dreary routine, day on day and week on week, with the occasional twenty-four-hour call into port to refuel and revictual. Conditions were thoroughly uncomfortable, particularly for the soldiers who slept on the mess decks in hammocks, which had to be cleared at reveille.

On sea journeys that can take up to four weeks, the greatest problem is boredom. Training and fitness are vital if the military passengers are to arrive at their destination fit to fight, yet the facilities are limited. Firing small arms at balloons over the stern loses its novelty after a couple of days, as does the pounding of innumerable circuits running round the limited deck space; neither does more than slow the decline of skill at arms and personal fitness.

Prem sought solace in writing long letters to Mohini – an activity for which he had had to seek her father's permission. Although tightly controlled, and prevented by the threat of censorship from giving details of where he was, his words carried unmistakable hints of his infatuation.

'Well, here I am, still at sea,' he wrote on 6 October.

> This journey is getting a bit boring, hence the letter writing! Joking apart, a sea journey does get a bit exacting when there is a ship full of men with nothing to do . . . The region we are now in is exceedingly hot and at night when everything is closed (blackout), it is really frightful inside. I am glad to say the moon does make a difference, and at night it is really quite picturesque and romantic. But what romance, except in thought?
>
> Let me not bore you with my misfortunes. How are you getting on, and is the artistic and intellectual side of you progressing?[16]

When he wrote again two days later, he was still afloat; his tone was still facetious, but clearly he was longing to hear from her. 'Now please do reply, Mohini. I will be looking forward to your letters . . . Now do not forget about your promise and please do write. I will be very disappointed if you do not. Remember, a nice long letter.'[17]

His unit's destination was the Eastern Sudan, a barren and largely waterless land, sparsely populated but sustaining the vital Port Sudan. Egypt and Sudan were then British protectorates, and the Indian troops were sent to Africa to provide vital reinforcements to the British formations which were direly stretched in their fight against Italian forces attacking from neighbouring Abyssinia and Eritrea. In support of these operations the Axis forces achieved a logistic miracle in opening up communications within Ethiopia. To this day the amazing complex of roads climbing what at first appear to be sheer cliff-sides remains a tribute to their short administration.

The long-term aim of Mussolini was to capture the Suez Canal, and so cut one of the Allies' most vital supply routes, and by the middle of 1940 his armies in East Africa had become extremely aggressive. In June they had captured Kassala and Gallabat, on the frontier between Abyssinia and Eastern Sudan, and they had marched deep into Kenya. In August they overran British Somaliland.

To counter this aggression, General Archibald Wavell, the Allied Commander-in-Chief Middle East, devised a plan whereby a huge pincer movement would be launched, from Khartoum in the north-west and Nairobi in the south, to drive eastwards and hound the enemy out of Abyssinia and Eritrea. The role of 5 Indian Division was to bolster the Allied forces in the northern sector, and the first destination of 21 Field Company was a point about 70 miles from Gallabat, which had been occupied by the Italians.

The Indians had little time to acclimatise. Within a couple of weeks 10 Brigade was in action, assaulting the fort on the hill at Gallabat, with the sappers of 21 Field Company in close support, and Prem playing a conspicuous part in the attack. One *naik* (corporal) recalled that 'Bhagat Sahib seemed to have a charmed life, because he went about his tasks with no apparent fear.'[18] Prem himself admitted in a letter to Mohini that he had been terrified, but was too modest to tell her that in his first experience of fighting he had shown outstanding courage.

When the attack on the hill fort was faltering under a heavy bombardment from the defenders, and some of the Indians looked as though they were about to turn back, the battalion commander, Lieutenant Colonel S. E. Taylor, climbed on to a prominent rock in full view of the enemy and urged his men on. Spurred by his magnificent example, Prem went up beside him and for several minutes stood there with him, until the attackers recovered their nerve and resumed their advance. 'I can tell you I was scared, standing on that exposed rock with death shrieking all around us,' Prem recounted later.

> I was tempted to jump down to safety but I stayed put, mainly because the Colonel stayed put. Then I noticed that the Colonel had begun to sway a bit, as if he was fighting back nausea or something. One of his arms hung loosely, and I was horrified to see blood flowing down from it. He had been hit by shrapnel, which had reduced his arm into a mass of mangled bone and gore. I reached out to help him but he snarled, 'Stay where you are. Don't let the men know I have been wounded.' And he kept standing somehow till the retreat had been averted. It was then and only then that he asked for medical aid. I was stunned. Never had I witnessed such cool bravery and dedication.[19]

In Prem's eyes, Taylor had shown true leadership, leading from the front by apparently fearless personal example. The Indians captured their objective and held it for a while, but then were forced to retreat by a vigorous counter-offensive. Once again Prem played a decisive role, vividly described in a commemorative issue of the *Bombay Sappers' Newsletter*:

> Temporary withdrawal is ordered, but the enemy is following up too closely. Sappers undertake road denial. A culvert becomes a vital bottleneck. Two derelict tanks are jammed on it and rigged with explosives. The charges are fired but only one tank blows up. The culvert cracks but does not crumble . . . The withdrawal threatens to become a rout.

> Suddenly in all this melée a young Indian officer dashes out from cover, sprints zig-zag to the unexploded tank and throws himself under it. He adjusts the charge, lights the fuse and runs back under a hail of death. Bullets kick up dust all around him as he dives into a depression in the ground.
>
> The tank explodes almost in the face of the enemy and the culvert collapses. The momentum of the pursuit has been broken, and a running battle is averted.[20]

For this desperate exploit Prem was recommended for a Military Cross. In the event he was not awarded one (although he did get a Mention in Despatches), but his initiation into battle changed his outlook sharply. His letters to Mohini became less facetious, more realistic. 'In actual battle,' he told her,

> One is heavily bombed from the air, there are mines in the ground and machine-gun bullets in the air . . . I have been in an area, mentioned on the wireless, where in forty minutes some fourteen aeroplanes just littered the place with bombs. I lay flat on the ground, and after the bombing was over I was covered with earth. Two bombs having dropped about five yards away.
>
> That was my first escape; the second from bombs was two days ago. They say a cat has nine lives . . . I do not know when my ninth will be over. They say I have been very brave for some small thing I did, but believe me I was the most scared person in the world.[21]

That was all he told her about his valiant actions – and throughout his life, modesty remained one of his most attractive characteristics.

Early in December 1940 the Allies won a tremendous victory at Sidi Barrani, far to the north in Egypt, on the Mediterranean coast, capturing some 38,000 enemy troops, as well as 400 guns and a number of tanks. In this triumph 4th Indian Division played a major role, but 5th Indian Division (of which Prem's unit was part) remained in the south, and had a relatively quiet month, still close to Gallabat. There he supervised the digging of fortifications and the laying of mines. According to one fellow officer, 'he was indefatigable, and drove his men hard. His leadership, charisma and concern for his men were transparently apparent.'[22]

In January 1941 a major Allied offensive returned the emperor of Ethiopia, Haile Selassie, to his country, and preparations went ahead for a confrontation with the Italian forces based on Asmara, in Eritrea. On 30 January the Italians, now under pressure from several directions, finally abandoned the frontier fort at Gallabat and began a general withdrawal.

At first light on 1 February the Allies sent out a small mobile column to probe along the road towards Gondar, some 100 miles to the east, and with it went a detachment of 21 Field Company, under Prem's command. A speedy advance was essential, for the aim was to overtake the enemy and engage them; but the Italians had booby-trapped the road with mines and other devices, among them steel traps which punctured tyres and locked the tracks of carrier vehicles. The mines – mostly buried an inch or so below the dirt surface – were of various types, and generally had to be defused by hand. The need for haste made clearance work all the more hazardous.

Mine-clearance requires a special type of courage and self-control, which seems to be endemic in sappers; its dangers can be compared to those inherent in bomb-disposal, with the additional hazard that it has to be carried out under enemy fire and frequently at night. It is not a pastime for those aspiring to a pension.

It was in these conditions that Prem led the advance, riding in a Bren-gun carrier (a lightly armoured, tracked vehicle with an open top, designed to mount a machine gun). To fire, the gunner had to expose himself, and the vehicle itself was crucially vulnerable to mines, due to its thin underbody armour. The carriers were quite fast, and of particular value in internal security operations, but of dubious and misleading value in terms of protection on a battlefield.

Prem knew the limitations of his transport all too well, yet he showed no sign of fear, spotting and defusing the mines himself. Inevitably one blew up under the vehicle. The driver took most of the blast and was killed, but Prem was thrown clear by the explosion.

His response was to commandeer another carrier and press on. Again he was blown up. This time two men were killed, but again he escaped undamaged, except by shock and concussion, and persevered.

Working from dawn to dusk, without breaks for food or sleep, he operated with such skill and tenacity that on the fourth day the column caught up with the fleeing Italians and ran into an ambush. Yet again Prem's carrier was blown up, and this time he was wounded, suffering a perforated eardrum. Yet even then, exhausted as he was by fatigue and nervous strain, he refused to stand down, claiming that he had discerned the pattern of the enemy's mine-laying technique so well that clearance would be quickest if he carried on. Eventually, after four days, 55 miles and fifteen minefields, he gave in, and was taken, with blood oozing from his ears, back to Gallabat and thence to the base hospital in Khartoum.

He himself did not think he had done anything out of the ordinary. Nevertheless, he was delighted to be in Khartoum, and his enforced rest gave him time to write Mohini an extra-long letter, as self-deprecating and understated as always:

> The last ten days have been a bit trying, especially as I have had three narrow escapes. Luckily the only damage done is that I have now got a deaf ear (right one). The doctor says the drum has gone. I wonder if that will make me permanently deaf in one ear. This has its advantages. I need not hear what I do not want to. I can also sing without knowing how badly I sing.
>
> The last ten days have been quite a revelation to me of war. Dead bodies lying on the road, some mangled and no one taking any notice of them. To think the very same body had life and enjoyed himself a few hours before is preposterous . . .
>
> The explosions were mines going off under my vehicle. A man standing next to me stopped the splinters. In fact I was saved by him. The man, needless to say, is not worrying about war any longer.[23]

He was still recovering in hospital when he heard he had been awarded a Victoria Cross: a colleague remembered him sitting up in bed surrounded by telegrams from well-wishers. Yet still he played down his achievement to Mohini and made no direct mention of the medal:

> I have been congratulated, for getting blown up twice, by the red hats. Though personally it does not make sense to me. After all, there were some people killed, and I was the lucky one to escape. They say a cat has nine lives. I have finished five. Still four to go. I must say the I'ties are not at all friendly, to put such gruesome objects in the ground.[24]

The citation for Prem's VC, published on 10 June 1941, described the action and concluded:

> His coolness over a period of ninety-six hours, and his persistence and gallantry not only in battle but throughout the long period during which the safety of the column and the speed at which it could advance were dependent on his personal efforts, were of the highest order.

The courage he displayed was clearly not of the flashpoint variety: on the contrary, he showed the most astonishing endurance. It is hard to imagine how he maintained his vigilance and concentration over such a long period, especially as, on the last day, he was often under fire. However he managed it, the example he set inspired his men.

After a spell of recuperation in Khartoum, he returned to 21 Field Company and took part in the final stages of the East African campaign, in which the Italian forces were ground down until, on 16 May, their Commander-in-Chief, the Duke of Aosta, formally surrendered. A captured Italian general complained, 'You have only defeated me because your Indian mechanised brigade came sixty miles to attack my rear over country which, I know from experience, is impossible for motor vehicles.'

In June the Allies held a victory parade in Asmara, where Wavell took the salute, and in a separate ceremony, held in the grounds of the palace, made presentations to two medal winners: Prem received the ribbon of his VC, and Second Lieutenant Cochrane, of a British battalion, the ribbon of a DSO.

Back in India on leave, Prem received a hero's welcome and instantly became a national figure. When he gave a broadcast on All India Radio, his talk was billed 'Our Hero', and his achievement was hailed with immense excitement, as it was taken to prove that, in the matter of courage, a native was at least the equal of anyone in the British Empire. In November he was presented with his medal by the Viceroy, Lord Linlithgow, in a fine ceremony staged in the forecourt of Viceregal Lodge in Delhi; and then, just as in England and America Churchill adopted Guy Gibson as a kind of mascot for propaganda purposes, so in India Prem was sent on tour to Maharashtra, the traditional recruiting area for Bombay Sappers:

> Everywhere he was eulogised as the 'the bravest of the brave' and idolised by the simple village folk as tales of his heroic exploits preceded him even to the remotest of villages. Had not this 'Bhagat Sahib' won the highest accolade for valour on the battlefield? Had not the British *Sarkar* [Governor] bestowed on him the Victoria Cross for acts of unparalleled bravery on the battlefield in the face of death? They flocked to see this man, this living legend, for themselves, to hear him speak. And enthusiastically they volunteered to join the ranks of the Bombay Sappers.[25]

On the domestic front things went equally well. Having proved himself in such spectacular fashion, Prem at last overcame the opposition of Mohini's father, who could no longer maintain that he would make an inadequate son-in-law, and the couple were married early in 1942. (Their son, officially named Rajendra, but known first as 'Bubkins' and then as 'Dubby', was born in May 1944, and their daughter Ashali, or 'Ashi', nine years later.)

Prem never returned to active operations: instead, he was ordered to raise a new unit, 448 Field Company, which was stationed near Nagpur, in the forested hills of the Central Provinces, training troops in jungle warfare, for operations against the

Japanese in Burma. After the war officers who trained under him remembered him as intelligent, cheerful and understanding, with an obvious love of his men.

The fact that he had an exceptional talent for spotting mines was strikingly confirmed by one of his platoon commanders, Captain Norman Elliott:

> Part of our training involved laying a minefield. The mines were primed but had safety-pins in them so that they were safe to walk over but certainly not safe to drive over. When my platoon had laid the minefield, mapped and camouflaged it, I reported the completion of the task to Bhagat.
>
> He said that it was not done too well, and he could see all the mines. I insisted he could not, at which he jumped into a jeep and drove right through the minefield. I spent a few terrifying moments and remember asking myself how I could possibly watch my OC blow himself up on my minefield.[26]

It took Prem many years to use up the four last lives which, he reckoned, remained to him after his near-escapes in Africa. He made several visits to England, the first in 1945, when, with the war still in progress, he attended a seven-month course at the Royal Military Academy, Sandhurst. He and a colleague, Major-General Danny Misra, based themselves in the Mayfair Hotel in London, where (Misra recorded) 'the rate was fantastically low because of Prem's decoration'.

In all, his army career lasted thirty-six years, and as a lieutenant general he rose to become the Army Commander of Central Command. In that capacity he took personal control of a crisis which threatened the city of Lucknow in the autumn of 1971, when the River Gomti burst its banks and created disastrous floods. Such was the drive with which he averted a catastrophe that the Government awarded him the Param Vishist Seva Medal, India's highest military decoration for service outside the battlefield.

He then took over Northern Command, and immediately set about bolstering defences along the frontier with Pakistan – a role in which he came to be known as 'The Grand Moghul', partly because of the flamboyant style in which he lived, and partly because he had such big ideas. He also represented the Chief of Army Staff at the Delineation Talks, designed to settle the border disputes which had led to the Indo-Pakistan war of 1971, and his diplomacy steered the meetings to a successful conclusion.

Colleagues assumed that he would become the next Chief of Army Staff, and were astounded when in 1974, without explanation, the prime minister, Indira Gandhi, sanctioned his early retirement from the army, and appointed him to take charge of the Damodar Valley Corporation – an immense organisation, modelled on the Tennessee Valley Authority in America, which had been formed twenty-five years earlier to develop the region along the banks of the River Damodar, which flows down out of Bihar to join the Hoogly some 30 miles south of Calcutta.

For a while DVC (as it was known) had flourished, but by the time Prem took over, in July 1974, the giant was sadly run down, and he threw himself into the huge task of revitalising it with characteristic energy. As usual, employees responded strongly to his warm, vigorous personality, and all seemed to be progressing well when he went down with a sudden fever and, after a short illness, died on 23 May 1975, aged fifty-seven.

He was mourned as a great soldier, a well-loved servant of his country. Fifteen years after his death his son Dubby described how one evening after dinner he had at last been persuaded to tell the story of his VC – the first time he had ever heard his father talk about it:

> Finally he unwound and told it like it was. How scared he was, and how tired. You got the stench of tiredness, the awful urge to give up, the fear of being blown up. And it was this extraordinary radiant quality of courage that made him see it through.
>
> His extraordinary reaction . . . was that it wasn't heroic, that it was not an epic deed . . . purely an incidental happening that took place because he had to do something. He felt it had to be done. So, what I suspect is that this courage that is much vaunted was an integral part of his nature. He insisted that he

> did nothing that was out of the ordinary. And he wasn't being shy or modest, or anything. He was just a very courageous person.[27]

Some of his friends noticed that after the war, Prem was markedly less wild and reckless than he had been as a youth. But in the words of his fellow officer Field Marshal Sam Manekshaw, he never allowed the medal, won so early in his life, to make him conceited, overbearing or obnoxious. 'He remained what he was, a thoroughly fun-loving, hard-working, dedicated officer, available to all – colleagues, subordinates and superiors – without any sign of show or superiority'.[28]

13

Canadian Aces

Canadian soldiers, sailors and airmen have always stood by Britain nobly at times of crisis, and the number of VCs they have won – ninety-five – reflects the great courage and patriotism of our transatlantic allies. Many stirring deeds are recorded in Canadian citations, but none is more poignant that that of a boy who was only eighteen when he was killed in France on 8 October 1916.

Private James Richardson, VC, 1898–1916

He was born and brought up in Scotland, but by 1914 his family had emigrated to British Columbia, where his father was chief of police in Chilliwack, and where he himself won several prizes for his playing on the bagpipes. When war broke out in Europe, Jimmy, like thousands of his contemporaries, rushed to join the Canadian military forces, enlisting in the 72nd Seaforth Highlanders at Vancouver, and he went to France with the first contingent of the Canadian Expeditionary Force.

A lively young fellow, he was always cheerful, always trying to help colleagues. He was also a natural writer, with a keen sense of humour, and sent home graphic accounts of the actions in which he immediately became involved – witness his description of a night when he got too far ahead of his comrades in following up a German retreat:

> Well, I may tell you I didn't get very far ahead, about forty yards, before I landed up at a farmhouse, and sure enough, the Fritzes were all clustered round it sheltering from the flying bullets. When I saw what I was up against, I didn't know what to do, but believe me, my brain worked like lightning. As it was dark save for the moonlight, I 'flopped', to see if I was spotted, and I really thought that while I was lying there they would hear my heart beating.
>
> Lying motionless, I saw an officer (judging by his voice and actions) coming towards me and waving his arms, as if to let his men know to follow on. My brain told me that I had two alternatives, namely to shoot the nearest man I saw (which was the officer) and make a dash for my pals, or give myself up as a prisoner. I risked the former and aimed as quick and true as I could at my man, who rolled over like a log. You talk about running – there isn't a man who could have covered the ground quicker than I did, and nobody could be more thankful than I was when I found myself amongst my own kith and kin.[1]

Jimmy's luck did not last long. On 8 October 1916, as part of the battle of the Somme, his company of the Canadian Scottish was scheduled to make an attack on the German trenches, and although he was not detailed to accompany the assault group, he obtained permission from his commanding officer to play them over the top. Forward they went, only to be held up by wire entanglements and caught in heavy fire. As casualties rapidly mounted, the men began to lose heart – whereupon Piper Richardson strode up and down in the open for fully ten minutes, playing his pipes with such verve and aplomb that he instantly restored morale. Galvanised by the braw, skirling notes, the men rushed the wire, broke through it and captured their objective.

It seems a miracle that Richardson escaped injury, for his deliberate perambulation must surely have attracted the enemy's attention. Soon afterwards he was detailed to bring in a wounded comrade and some prisoners, and he had almost accomplished the task when he realised that he had left his beloved pipes behind. He was strongly urged not to go looking for them, but he insisted – and was never seen again. The citation for his posthumous VC praised his 'most conspicuous bravery and devotion to duty' in setting the fearless example that spurred his company on at a critical moment. He was severely missed, for his cheerful acceptance of hazard and hardship had played an important part in keeping up his unit's morale.[2]

William Nelson Hall, VC, 1829–1904

Queen Victoria herself must have drawn satisfaction from the fact that the third VC awarded to a Canadian more than matched her stipulation that the medal should be open to all ranks, without class distinction. The son of a freed black slave resettled in Canada became the first Nova Scotian, the first Canadian sailor and the first black man to win the Cross. Such was Able Seaman William Nelson Hall, who saved the day on 16 November 1857 by helping breach the walls of the Shah Najaf compound in Lucknow and opening the way for the relief of the beleaguered garrison and families.

Hall's passage to India took many strange turns, and its origins lay in the inconclusive war of 1812 between Britain and the United States, which derived from Britain's oppressive maritime policy of forcing American and other vessels trading with France to call at British ports and pay duty. This high-handedness extended to stopping US ships on the high seas and impressing seamen alleged to be Royal Navy deserters. Since slavery was still part of the American way of life, particularly in the South, the Royal Navy extended its remit to arrest deserters to include the release of slaves found on American vessels.

It is not clear how William's father was set free, but on 13 May

1815 a black slave, 'Jacob', was sent to Halifax, in Nova Scotia, on board HMS *Ceylon*. Another released slave known as 'Lucy' seems to have arrived at the same time, and in due course the two were married.[3] As was the custom, a local family took them into employment and they adopted the family name. Certainly Jacob worked for a merchant, Peter Hall, and later for Abraham Cunard, father of the shipping magnate Samuel. He was employed as a rigger and caulker, and will have involved himself in the seagoing community, which became the background for the life of his youngest son William, in a family of three sons and four daughters.

Born at Minas Basin, Nova Scotia, on 25 April 1829,[4] William grew up into a powerfully built man with a kindly personality, but had minimal opportunities for education, and this showed through in his later life, possibly impairing his opportunities for promotion. However, it is probable that he attended an African School and that navigation was a subject taught, thus whetting his appetite for a seagoing life.[5]

The ocean called him in his mid-teens, when he shipped on board the *Kent*, carrying a load of timber to London. After two years tramping the world before the mast, at the age of eighteen he joined – surprisingly, in view of his family background – the United States Navy, serving in several ships including the US frigate *Savannah* in the Mexican War. He must have been financially aware, for after his discharge in 1849 he had a letter written to the Bureau of Pensions requesting a pension for his war service. This was rejected, as the Bureau judged that his time in Mexican waters was out of war, and did not qualify for the Mexican War Pension or Bounty Land Claim.[6]

All the same, his foray into a disciplined military environment suited him, and in 1852, after a further two years in the merchant service, he sailed out of Boston on the clipper *Tam O'Shanter* bound for England and enlistment into the Royal Navy, where he served for the next twenty years.

At this time the Royal Navy permitted the enlistment of foreigners 'provided that in every regiment, battalion or corps, the number shall not exceed the proportion of one to fifty of natural born subjects'.[7] Hall joined HMS *Rodney*, a vessel of ninety guns, and embarked on a dangerous and challenging career. An early commission took his ship to the Crimea, where the Royal Navy played a vital role in the Black Sea by shelling enemy shore positions, to assist with troop movements, and by reinforcing the army with 'naval brigades' ashore.

Numerically, these formations bore no relationship to army brigades, each of about 4000 men; but generous manning of ships enabled the Navy to deploy some seamen on land in an infantry or artillery role. The ship's guns were also landed, and at times the mother vessel, lacking sufficient crew to man her, became temporarily redundant – much to the dismay of the Lords of the Admiralty, who considered such emasculation by the generals to be taking joint-service cooperation a step too far.[8]

Hall gained his first experience of fighting on land when he volunteered to join a shore party landed from HMS *Rodney*. He is recorded as having served at the Battle of Inkerman on 5 November 1854, and it is quite possible that he supported that other VC winner, Private John Byrne of the 68th (chapter 4). Certainly he gained entitlement to the Crimean Medal, with bars for both Inkerman and Sevastopol.

Returning from the Crimea, he was discharged from *Rodney* to the holding ship HMS *Victory*, which lies at Portsmouth to this day. He is reported to have deserted from her and forfeited his previous time served in the Royal Navy, which no doubt could have diminished his pension.[9]

There is no record of his activities during his absence, which appears to be the only blemish in an otherwise faultless career. He next appears on the roll of HMS *Shannon*, commanded by Captain William Peel, the son of Sir Robert Peel, the British prime minister in the 1840s. (Captain Peel had already won the Victoria Cross leading a naval brigade in the Crimea.) The *Shannon* sailed for the China Station to provide reinforcement for a trade dispute with the recalcitrant emperor, which eventually led to the Second China War.

Despite his previous misdemeanours, Hall was appointed captain of the foretop, having demonstrated latent qualities of leadership and decisiveness. Ships at this time were still almost exclusively wooden and sail-driven, and where a steam capability had been fitted, it was more for giving an emergency boost during light winds, steam on its own being slower than sail. The men of the foretop manned the sails of the foremast and usually slung their hammocks at the forward end of the main deck. The senior sailor in charge of them was called the captain of the foretop, but he was not of commissioned rank.

HMS *Shannon* arrived in Singapore, where she anchored off, when news of the Indian Mutiny arrived on 11 June 1857; but she continued her journey to Hong Kong. Then Lord Canning, the governor general of India, sent a plea for assistance to Lord Elgin, a former governor general of Canada, who had gone to China with reinforcements to confront the Chinese emperor. He agreed that three of his ships, including *Shannon*, together with some marines, should be immediately dispatched to Calcutta.[10]

The reasons for the outbreak of the Indian Mutiny were complex, and went well beyond the immediate *casus belli* of the cartridges for the new rifle. These, it was rumoured, were lubricated with pork or cow grease, and they were forced upon the Hindu and Muslim sepoys against their religious beliefs. The British East India Company, and not the Crown, then ruled India, but the Company had lost touch with the people, and its officers had developed an aloof arrogance at a time when significant changes were being introduced to the life and traditions of the subcontinent.

In 1857 the seething discontent spilled over into organised rebellion, and British garrisons were overrun or put into a state of siege. Such was the fortune of the garrison at Lucknow when *Shannon* arrived in Calcutta, where Hall distinguished himself by playing a major role in rescuing a seaman from drowning in the Ganges. One of his contemporaries wrote of him, 'He was always a man remarkable for his steady good conduct and his athletic frame, at a foot race in camp he had distanced by far all competitors, and I have never seen his superior either as a swimmer or diver.'[11]

The Shannon Brigade of about four hundred men, together with six 68-pounders, eight 24-pounders, eight rockets and two howitzers, formed up to march up-country under the leadership of Captain Peel. The heavy artillery had to be left behind at Allahabad, but the naval guns were hauled in steamy heat and monsoon rain to join Sir Colin Campbell's force marching to the relief of the besieged garrison in Lucknow.[12]

The attack on Lucknow began on 14 November against the key enemy position of the Shah Najaf, a handsome, white-domed mosque set within a courtyard, behind whose massive outer walls the sepoys were entrenched and waiting in their thousands. Peel's guns and crews, including Hall, were placed in support of the 93rd Highlanders when at 1600 hours Sir Colin ordered the attack on the fortress mosque.

For three hours Peel manoeuvred his guns under fearsome crossfire, from which he suffered many casualties, as they tried in vain to blast a breach in the walls for the Highlanders. In a final attempt, and with his gun crews reduced to two, Peel took the desperate step of moving them to within a few yards of the walls. The continual blasting stirred up clouds of thick dust, providing some cover for the gunners, but despite this the casualties continued to mount. Eventually only one gun remained in action, and Hall volunteered to help man it. Presently the crew was reduced to two, Lieutenant Young and Hall, both of whom continued to work the gun, with Hall calmly sponging and loading without regard for his own life and safety. He was described later as a 'fine powerful man and as steady as a rock under fire'.[13] Just as Campbell looked to have lost the day, a breach was finally made, and the Highlanders overran the mosque to gain entry to the Residency beyond.

A contemporary report on the action was given by Lieutenant Colonel W. Gordon-Alexander, who served with the 93rd Highlanders in the battle. He wrote:

> I am, however perfectly certain that only one gun, one of Peel's 24-pounders, was dragged down, placed in position, and opened fire within a very few paces of the wall of the Shah Najaf, for I was close to it during the whole time it was in action . . .
>
> Peel's men having been so decimated that there were not enough now left to work the gun, in fact a fine fellow of a Negro AB was, I believe, the only man who had not been

> wounded, and latterly he had been doing duty for two or three of the regulation number of gunners. As in the Crimea, so here nothing could excel the splendidly cool courage and magnificent devotion to duty under fire of our unsurpassable Jack Tars, officers and men.[14]

Both Young and Hall were awarded the Cross, together with two other men from the naval brigade and seventeen men from other units over the period of 16, 17 and 18 November – a total of twenty-one Victoria Cross awards in a period of three days. The awards to Young and Hall were delayed, and were not gazetted until 1 February 1859, some fourteen months later. The hold-up was caused by the need for authentication of the reports, which required the support of their commanding officer, Captain Peel, who had stated his intention to recommend them but died of smallpox before formally doing so. It was only when Young (by then Commander) pointed out to the Admiralty that Peel had promised the Cross to him and Hall, and that the promise had been made in the presence of Lord Clyde, that the Admiralty backed his letter and the War Office agreed to forward the citations to the Queen.[15]

Hall continued service in India aboard HMS *Shannon* until she was paid off in the United Kingdom in 1859. His innate modesty and shyness led him to decline receiving his award from the Queen herself: rather, he preferred to have it presented by the commander-in-chief, Rear Admiral Charles Talbot, at a special ceremony in the presence of the entire crew of HMS *Donegal* in Queenstown Harbour, Ireland, on 28 October 1859. He was also entitled to wear the Indian Mutiny Medal, with clasps for Lucknow and the Relief of Lucknow.

Continuing to seek adventure, he shipped on the *Kangsoo* to serve on the Imperial Chinese Squadron for two years. He then returned to the Royal Navy and served in a number of ships, including the *Bellerophon*, on which he was appointed quartermaster. His last ship was the *Royal Adelaide*, on which he served for only a few months before being paid off and discharged with a certificate of good conduct on 4 July 1876 as a petty officer first class. He appears to have been offered a well-remunerated white-collar job in England, but declined it, preferring to return to his roots in Nova Scotia.

There he set himself up with a subsistence farm at Horton Bluff, which at the time was about four miles out of Hantsport, running a few cattle and poultry, together with one hectare of orchard, and living with two of his sisters, Mrs Rachel Hall Robinson and Mary Hall, who kept house for their bachelor brother. His hobby is recorded as shooting crows. He received a pension of £50 a year, which barely provided for them all, and when he died the sisters had to sell his medals, which now reside in the Nova Scotia Museum, to help pay off a $500 debt on the property.

Hall himself sought no publicity and gained none – although on one occasion a reporter, D. V. Warner, called on him and found an erect figure sharpening his scythe:

> 'It's rather late for haying isn't it?' he observed when I had taken the place of the small boy who was turning the stone. 'But I just want to get a little salt hay off the marsh.'
>
> 'By the way,' I said after a few turns of the grindstone, 'haven't you been in the British navy?'
>
> 'Yes, I served a good many years in the navy,' he replied. Then, lifting the scythe from the stone and carefully feeling the edge, 'I think she'll cut that grass all right now, thank you. It doesn't require a very sharp scythe.'
>
> He had to be coaxed to show the medal, but eventually he went into the cottage and took down a spool box, tipping the contents on the table. The blue ribbon on which it had originally hung was missing and Mr Hall had fastened his Victoria Cross to a heavy watch chain. He also kept his other medals in the same box.
>
> 'It's nothing to have a Cross now; they're as thick as peas,' the old man said. 'It isn't worth very much to a man after all, only ten pounds a year. If it wasn't for my regular navy pension of forty pounds a year besides, I don't know how we'd get along here. The farm is small, and my two sisters live with me, you know.'[16]

He died of paralysis at home on 27 August 1904, aged seventy-three. He received no military honours, but was buried at Stoney Baptist Church Cemetery and became labelled locally as 'The Forgotten Hero': he is no longer that, thanks to the Canadian Legion and the community of Hantsport. In 1945 his body was reburied in a place of honour in the town and a monument erected to him. At a memorial service in the church where he used to worship, the Reverend B. D. Knott said of him, 'He was a peaceable, God-fearing citizen. He was honoured and respected by all who knew him. He was ever humble.'

William Hall stands out as an upright, ordinary man, a Christian, who did his duty for his adopted nation. Coming from an obscure and disadvantaged family, he gave his working life for his country, and frequently put it on the line not only for his compatriots, but for fellow servicemen of Great Britain. I like to think that his life, and the Canadian people's unqualified acceptance of him, stand for all that is best in a young nation built on freedom and liberalism. His is a fine example of the courage and loyalty shown by so many Canadian servicemen over the years for Great Britain and their own country.

William Barker, VC, DSO and Bar, MC and two Bars, 1894–1930

When war broke out in Europe in August 1914, young Canadians rushed to enlist in the armed forces. Fired by loyalty to the Empire, and by the idea of serving overseas, they signed on in droves – and none was more eager to join the fray than William Barker, whom many compatriots came to regard as their country's greatest military hero.

The eldest son of George and Jane Barker, and the first of their ten children, he was born on 3 November 1894 at Dauphin, in north-western Manitoba, where his father worked for himself in a variety of roles: farmer, blacksmith, owner of a sawmill, a livery stable and a bakery. As a boy William did not shine intellectually, but he was intelligent and tenacious, and like his father good with his hands, with such a flair for handling and repairing machines that George often took him out of school to work on the farm or sawmill. He also became a deadly shot, particularly with a lever-action Winchester rifle, and once astonished his parents by knocking down a prairie chicken in mid-air, having fired from the hip as he rode beside the family wagon.

In 1912, at the age of eighteen, he enlisted as a trooper in the 32nd Light Horse Regiment of the Non-Permanent Active Militia – the equivalent of a Territorial unit in England. At occasional parades and two-week camps in the summer, he trained as a mounted rifleman, and then, in August 1914, while still at school, he became mustard-keen to join the regular army. With some difficulty his father persuaded him to complete the final year of his education – but once he had done that, there was no stopping him.

In November 1914 he volunteered for service with the Canadian Expeditionary Force, and enlisted in a new unit which had just been formed, the 1st Regiment, Canadian Mounted Rifles. He supposed he would go to war riding a horse and firing a carbine, but in the event the mounted regiments converted into infantry, fighting on their feet; Barker trained as a machine-gunner, and it was in that capacity that he sailed to England in June 1915 – a well-built man of about 5′ 10″, with penetrating brown eyes, a high forehead, hair combed straight back, and a habit of waving his hands about so freely when he talked that he was once derided for gesturing like a French chef. He was ambitious to do well, but likeable, and good company.

In September, after further training, he sailed from Southampton to Le Havre, and soon found himself backing up the British Expeditionary Force in Flanders. His letters home were seldom entirely literate, but they reflected his robust, cheerful outlook. 'Guns tore up Fritzes front line,' he told his mother one day,

> and I trained my gun so as to catch the German working parties when they as usual started to repair the damage done. I spent a lively night and fired two belts, five hundred shots, at this work during the night. Sometimes we almost sleep on our feet . . . Believe me it pays to play the soldier all the time . . .
>
> Howard [his uncle] & I went sniping yesterday morning we

> saw plainly two Germans in grey about 650 yards away. I took a strange rifle as No 1s [on machine guns] have none of their own. I fired carefully at one but missed him, however, he flopped, so I had some satisfaction. Better luck next time. I just got down from the parapet when smash, a sniper had spotted me & cut the very bag I was leaning on a second before. However, a miss is as good as a mile, but it makes a fellow think for a moment. They sure are dead shots & seldom miss.[17]

Barker revelled in the power of his machine gun; but he had long been fascinated by flying machines, and after six months of miserable trench existence he managed to get himself transferred to the Royal Flying Corps, joining 9 Squadron at an airfield near Amiens as a Corps Cooperation airman – that is, a gunner/observer whose role was to support the troops on the ground. At that stage of the war, with the RFC still in its infancy, even pilots received scant training: some were sent into action with fewer than twenty hours of flying behind them. Observers got no formal training at all, but had to learn as they went along. They were expected to perform many tasks, among them to reconnoitre enemy positions, carry out bombing raids, spot for the artillery, fly low-level patrols in support of infantry units, and drop spies behind the German lines.

At first Barker flew in BE2c two-seaters, huddled in the open cockpit in front of the pilot, spattered with engine oil and half-frozen, swaddled though he was in layers of silk, wool, flannel and leather. Notwithstanding the discomfort and the hazards, he much enjoyed the action. The little aircraft were relatively reliable, but their cruising speed was only about 70 mph, so that they could barely make headway into a strong wind, and sometimes, coming back westwards over the lines after a sortie, they had trouble reaching friendly territory. Their armament was a single Lewis .303 machine gun, which could only be fired at an angle away from the plane's heading, for fear of shattering the wooden propeller. Barker soon became adept at handling the weapon, yet he longed to be a pilot himself, and in particular to become a scout pilot – one of the men who flew the single-seat aircraft that went out to do battle with the Germans.

After only a few weeks as a probationary observer, he again applied for a transfer, and at the beginning of April 1916 his confidence and competence were rewarded. Not only was he taken on to the RFC's General List; he was also promoted temporary second lieutenant. All at once he was an officer, suddenly hoisted into a new branch of the service and into a new social dimension. 'Now, Father,' wrote the country boy from Manitoba, 'one thing I want to make plain is that the RFC is a class of (officers) Lords sons. Heirs & young men of rank and titles.'

After a week's leave in London, where he was kitted out with his new uniform, he was posted to 4 Squadron at Baizieux, a field close to the front lines. From there he continued to fly as an observer, and he survived numerous hazardous missions, as well as several crashes caused by engine failure. Still he longed to be a pilot himself – especially as he often found himself in the hands of beginners. 'I am a little uneasy,' he wrote home before an early-morning sortie,

> for the pilot is a brand new man just out & knows very little about flying & less about the country. I tell you I will be mighty glad when my term of observing is up & I learn to pilot myself. I certainly begrudge trusting my neck to some of the bloaks just over.

Even though temporarily frustrated, he was safer in the air than on the ground, where, on 2 June 1916, the 1st Battalion of the Canadian Mounted Rifles suffered dreadful casualties in their attempts to repel a huge German assault on the Ypres Salient. Of nearly seven hundred officers and men, only 135 survived the battle of Mount Sorrel, and the unit was effectively destroyed. In their twelve-day struggle to recapture the lost ground, the Canadian Corps suffered eight thousand casualties.

'I see where my Regiment CMRs have almost been wiped out,' William told his father:

> I always knew they would fight like tigers. I see where Colonel Shaw, who recommended me [for the RFC], gathered a

> company around him and fought to the end. When he was killed a junior officer took his place and died fighting. I do not know how Howard and Duncan are . . . I only wish I could have been with them on my old machine-gun with the Huns in sight.

Barker was shaken by the massacre on the ground. His letters became less bouncy, and he strongly advised his brother Percy, who had become a machine-gun instructor in Canada, not to volunteer for overseas service. Nevertheless, when he was transferred from 4 to 15 Squadron in July, he carried on with his habitual enthusiasm, acting as observer on long patrols, most of which were devoted to spotting for the artillery. He developed a penchant for aggressive low flying, claiming that such tactics produced the most accurate information, and escaped unhurt from numerous fights and crash landings. As he told his parents, he was 'very lucky', but inevitably the cumulative strain began to tell, and by the end of October he was in real need of a rest.

> Yesterday I was up doing [directing] a shoot with a 12 in Batty [battery] and when returning our engine failed & we crashed into a bank. Our machine was absolutely smashed to pieces. I was badly bruised but was able to fly today & have just had if anything a worse time. We were coming about 5 miles over when two shells burst right on us one on our tail & one just over us, putting in all 36 holes through us, stopping the engine, punctured the tank I sit on and shot away our lateral controls & the plane almost got out of control.
>
> However, we done pretty good but could not land so turned over in a field. I have just about had enough of it now & am soon going to apply for a sick leave if I don't soon go back to England.

Nervous exhaustion was a condition that senior RFC officers recognised, and on 8 November 1916 Barker's squadron commander, Major Brock, told him that he had been recommended for pilot training, which meant that he would be sent back to England before Christmas. In fact he had already become a competent pilot, taught unofficially by colleagues, and at least once he had taken over a dual-control plane when his pilot had been wounded.

Observers rarely won medals, but Barker received his first award – an MC – while still operating in that relatively humble capacity. Supporting the great attack that the Allies launched to recover the village of Beaumont Hamel, he flew over the enemy lines at only 200 or 300 feet, well within range of small-arms fire, and brought back priceless information about enemy positions. The citation for his MC, published in the *London Gazette* on 10 January 1917, praised his 'conspicuous gallantry in action', and recorded: 'On another occasion after driving off two hostile machines, he carried out an excellent photographic reconnaissance.'

Training in England, he made extraordinarily fast progress. His natural ability and determination were such that before the end of February 1917 he was back with 15 Squadron, a fully fledged pilot. His letters home were hardly modest – 'I went to Oxford & in 4 days I passed & graduated in all the written exams which as a rule take two months . . . I have broken all records in flying. It has taken me only 3 weeks to get my pilot's certificate' – but they accurately reflected his meteoric advance and natural ability as a pilot.

In France once again, he resumed his low-flying sorties. He was still on Corps Cooperation duties, but at least he was now in charge of his own aircraft, and often, as he returned from an intelligence-gathering mission, he landed to impart the information he had gained. If anyone challenged the accuracy of his reports, he had no qualms about going right to the top and telephoning a general, if necessary, to have artillery fire directed at the right spot. It was his moral as much as his physical courage that won him his second MC, 'for conspicuous gallantry and devotion to duty . . . under the most difficult and dangerous conditions'. The award was not gazetted until July 1917, but it recognised the outstanding work he had done in April and May.

Promoted temporary captain, he was given his own flight, and soon had new aircraft – the RE8s, which were replacing the old BE2s, and known in cockney rhyming slang as 'Harry Tates'. In spite of their top speed of 102 mph, and their endurance of 4½ hours, at first the up-to-date machines seemed unreliable, and several were lost in crashes, but Barker accepted them, and was glad to have a machine gun synchronised to fire through the arc of the propeller, as well as a Lewis gun for the observer. On the squadron he was popular, and in the words of his biographer Wayne Ralph,

> In the air Barker was not a cool-headed introvert who liked stalking and killing for its own sake, but rather an energetic extrovert who fought brilliantly, but emotionally, in the chaos around him . . . For a man who was so aggressive in the air, he was surprisingly amiable on the ground. He was quiet-spoken in conversation, but definitely had a presence, even in a crowded room.
>
> He never abandoned his Methodist upbringing, and throughout the war drank little alcohol. At a time when almost everyone smoked, he never did . . . He radiated boyish high spirits. Men who flew with Barker remembered him as tireless and likeable, but sometimes unpredictable, and sometimes truculent.[18]

Luck was still flying with him, and he survived the summer of 1917 intact, except for a wound over his left eye, inflicted by a splinter from an anti-aircraft shell that burst dangerously close. By the time he returned to England on 18 August, he had completed six months in France and, by his own account, had flown a total of 570 hours as observer and pilot.

Just as Albert Ball had been sent to Orfordness as an instructor in the autumn of 1916, to give him a rest from operations, so Barker was posted to 53 Training Squadron at Narborough, in Norfolk, to instruct *ab initio* pilots. But his whole being rebelled against the thought of vegetating in England while his compatriots were fighting for their lives across the Channel, and he behaved so disgracefully that he soon got himself sent back overseas. Apart from deliberately terrifying beginners who went up with him, he performed some unforgivable stunts, of which the most notorious was looping the loop in a borrowed Sopwith Pup low over Piccadilly Circus, in the heart of London.

Escaping any form of retribution, he joined 28 Squadron, which was re-equipping with the Sopwith Camel – an aircraft which was a pig to fly, but, in skilled hands, extremely agile, capable of very tight turns, and well armed with twin Vickers machine guns firing through the propeller. Barker was delighted to become the commander of C Flight. 'I have at last got what I wanted,' he told his mother. 'No more artillery observation no more wireless & contact patrol, just fighting Huns. Well mother I must close I am very keen on my work & hope to be able to send you news of victims soon.'

For the next twelve months he flew almost all his sorties in the same aircraft, Camel B 6313, and scored almost all his victories in it. Among the modifications which he had the fitters install was a V-shaped sight of his own design, welded between the guns, which exactly suited his instinctive aiming technique. He made his first kill on 20 October, when he shot down an Albatros, but a week later he almost came to grief when his attempt to raid a German airfield was broken up by an enemy formation. Having lost touch with his wingmen, both of whom were wounded (but limped back to base), he himself escaped the immediate threat by brilliant evasive flying, and then, in separate contacts, shot down two Albatroses.

Suddenly, to the amazement of himself and his colleagues, he was swept away into an entirely different theatre. In northern Italy, during the final week of October, enemy formations of German and Austro-Hungarian troops had launched a mass attack and broken through the Italian lines, driving the defenders back some 90 miles. In response to urgent appeals for support, the British Government dispatched a large force, including five RFC squadrons.

No long transit flight for the Camels: the aircraft were dismantled, packed into crates and sent off by sea, while the human element of the squadrons travelled by train. By the end of November 28 Squadron had established itself at Grossa airfield, north of Camisano on the Venetian plain, some twenty minutes' flying time from the front lines on the River Piave, to the east. The base lay in level, fertile ground, which was much beset by fog, but to the north the snow-capped peaks of the Italian Dolomites glittered on the horizon.

Soon Barker was once again at grips with the enemy, leading offensive patrols, escorting bombers, strafing enemy positions. In the words of his biographer, his 'style was relentless aggression at all times in the air, and . . . he believed in the adage, "Attack everything"'. He was not exactly squeamish – except that he greatly disliked shooting horses – but nevertheless felt disturbed when he brought another pilot down. 'It is a wonderful and terrible sight to see a machine go down burning like a torch,' he told his mother after one victory:

> At the time, I cheered as though I had won a game of something, but afterwards started to think of the fellow who was killed and of his family. This viewpoint fortunately wears off as one gets hardened to the idea.

His run of success quickly won him his third medal: a DSO, which was gazetted in February 1918. The citation recorded that he had destroyed enemy aircraft although twice attacked by superior forces. 'His splendid example of fearlessness and magnificent leadership have been of inestimable value to his squadron.' In March he was decorated yet again, with a second bar to his MC, 'for conspicuous gallantry and devotion to duty'. The citation told how he had once attacked eight enemy aircraft and shot down two, and how on another day he attacked seven and shot down one.

More than eighty years on, air historians still argue about the exact number of his victories. He was officially credited with forty-three victories in Italy – but did he really shoot down as many victims as he claimed? It hardly matters. More important was the fact that he had developed into an inspiring leader, teaching other pilots the arts of attack and evasion, and shepherding those who flew with him so efficiently that none of the aircraft he escorted was ever shot down.

In managing his emotions on the ground, he was less successful. When the commander of 28 Squadron was posted back to England, Barker felt that he had done enough to be allowed to take over; but another, relatively inexperienced officer was brought in, and Barker, in a fit of jealousy, demanded a transfer to another unit. So it was that on 10 April he took his own Camel and flew 15 miles low across country to join 66 Squadron at San Pietro in Gu.

Such high-handed action would not be tolerated by most senior officers, and the fact that Barker got away with it indicates the high esteem in which he was held. It also leaves open the question of why a man whose leadership and professional qualities were fully recognised was held back from a command appointment – unless his superiors were concerned at the increasing signs of battle fatigue.

Throughout April and May he flew incessantly, scoring more victories and earning the admiration of his new colleagues, and in July he was promoted temporary major – which will have given him the pay, if not the security, of becoming substantive major. Then, however, he met a severe rebuff. After only three months with 66, still seeking command of a squadron, he tried to get himself posted back to France, but instead, to his dismay, was ordered to take over the Z Flight of Bristol F2B fighters which had just been redesignated 139 Squadron, with the addition of a second flight, at Villaverla, only about twenty minutes' flying time to the north-west. What depressed him was the fact that he had been sent back to a formation flying two-seat aircraft. Perhaps as a sop, he was allowed to retain his beloved Camel, B 6313, for his own use, but he struck back by having it painted in gaudy colours, with a heart pierced by an arrow on the vertical tail fin: an audacious if not wise flaunting of the principles of camouflage, and perhaps another indication of battle fatigue.

The highlight of his time with 139 was one extraordinary mission organised by Captain William Wedgwood Benn, a British Member of Parliament, who had been given leave to join the RFC and had distinguished himself by crashing five aircraft during flying training.[19] His aim was to parachute a secret agent into enemy-held territory, and for the hazardous night flight he recruited the celebrated Canadian air ace, whom he greatly admired. To deliver the agent safely, Barker had to learn to fly a twin-engined SP4 bomber, which had space for an extra person in its bathtub-like fuselage, and he managed the task with aplomb, thereby earning himself a *Medaglio d'Argento*, or Silver Medal, for military valour.

In August Barker earned yet another award, a bar to his DSO, and the citation saluted him as 'a highly distinguished patrol leader whose courage, resource and determination has set a fine example to those around him'. By September, however, he had become seriously worn down: most scout pilots were sent home after six months in action, but Barker had lasted nearly a year, and he had logged nine hundred flying hours. His commanding officer, Lieutenant Colonel Philip Joubert,[20] was rightly worried about his state of health, and was determined to send him to England on leave – yet Barker's appetite for victories remained insatiable:

> I have been going to write for days past but I never seem to get time & if I do I feel too done in [he told his parents]. I think I have overdone it a bit as I have been feeling poorly lately.
>
> At last I am leaving this country. Orders have come through for me to proceed to England on the 15th October for a rest. I sure need it now but after it I am going to France & my ambition is to break all records. I have got thirty-seven Huns down & Major Richotfen[21] [*sic*] the German who is now dead claims eighty. I am going to try to break this record if only my health will hold out.
>
> After I have attained this I am coming home but not till I have done my best.

From Barker's own remarks it is clear that he was suffering from deep-seated exhaustion, and that he should never have returned to France. But somehow he talked the authorities into letting him go – and with a unique remit, granted purely because of his extraordinary achievement and reputation: he was allowed to take any aircraft he wanted from the depot at St Omer, and to attach himself for a period of ten days only to any squadron he chose. So it was that he flew a new Sopwith Snipe – a bigger and heavier aircraft than his beloved Camel – and joined 201 Squadron, whose commanding officer he knew. He was not by any means welcome in his temporary home: the other pilots regarded him as a jumped-up outsider who had boosted his tally of kills unfairly by taking on the weak Austro-Hungarians in a far-away theatre, while they had borne the brunt of the real air battle against the Germans.

Ignoring their hostility, Barker at once started flying offensive patrols, but a combination of bad luck and bad weather meant that his ten days almost ran out without him securing a victory. On 26 October 1918 he was ordered to return his Snipe to the supply depot next day, and that evening in the officers' mess he angrily announced that, on the way, he proposed to visit the front lines in search of one more fight.

That decision, made when his judgement was impaired by exhaustion, blighted the rest of his life. He got into a fight, all right, but it proved the most violent and disastrous that he had ever had.

Taking off alone around 0800, he climbed away to the east, searching for potential victims, until at 0825 he spotted an enemy two-seater at 21,000 feet, north-east of the forest of Mormal. The action that followed was tersely described in the official history of the RAF in the First World War, *The War in the Air*:

> Enemy aircraft climbed east and Major Barker following fired a short burst from underneath at point-blank range. Enemy aircraft broke up in the air and one of the occupants jumped with a parachute.
>
> He then observed a Fokker biplane 1,000 feet beneath below [*sic*], stalling and shooting at him, one of the bullets wounding him in the thigh. He fell into a spin from which he pulled out in the middle of a formation of about fifteen Fokkers, two of which he attacked indecisively, both aircraft spinning down. He turned, and getting on the tail of a third which was attacking him shot it down in flames from within ten yards' range.
>
> At this moment he was again wounded in the left thigh by others of the formation who were diving at him. He fainted and fell out of control again. On recovering, he pulled his machine out and was immediately attacked by another formation of twelve to fifteen enemy aircraft.
>
> He then noticed heavy smoke coming from his machine, and, under the impression he was on fire, tried to ram a Fokker just

> ahead of him. He opened fire on it from two to three yards' range and enemy aircraft fell in flames. He then dived to within a few thousand feet of the ground and began to fly towards our lines, but found his retreat was cut off by another formation of eight enemy aircraft who attacked him. He fired a few bursts at some of them and shaking them off dived down and returned to our lines a few feet above the ground, finally crashing close to one of our balloons.[22]

It was that amazing display of aggression and courage, carried through in spite of shocking wounds, that won Barker his VC. The citation was published on 30 November 1918, and after describing the action concluded that the combat had been 'a notable example of the exceptional bravery and disregard of danger which this very gallant officer has always displayed throughout his distinguished career'.

Yet the multiple encounters had almost cost him his life. If he had come down in no man's land, he would have died from loss of blood. As it was, he was saved by prompt attention from the crew of the observation balloon, who staunched the flow from an artery in his groin and got him to a field dressing station. He had been hit by three bullets – one in the left hip, which chipped the bone, one in the muscle of his right thigh, and one which shattered his left elbow. After numerous operations – as many as twenty – he regained most of his former mobility, but his left arm, with the elbow joint missing, never recovered, and hung limply by his side.

The psychological scars inflicted by prolonged stress and exposure to danger never healed. It was not the award of the VC that changed him: even though he was the most decorated Canadian of the First World War, and a nationally known hero, he remained modest about his medals. Rather, he was driven by ambition and the need to succeed. Just as during the conflict he had been desperate to surpass the record of the Red Baron, so in peacetime he became hell-bent on founding a civilian aviation business, and in 1919 he went into partnership with that other outstanding Canadian air ace, Billy Bishop, also a VC winner, forming Bishop-Barker Aeroplanes Ltd. He also went in for stunt-flying, and for air races, even though he had to fly with one hand. He began to drink far more than ever in the past, and together with Billy cut loose in bouts of antisocial behaviour, once crashing their car into the vehicle leading a funeral procession. Such was their fame that the police took no action against them.

It was symptomatic of how fighting had changed Barker's character that he was in no hurry to go home. At the start of the conflict he had been very close to his parents, writing to them repeatedly, but after the war, although he returned to Canada, he did not bother to see them for nearly six months – and when he did meet them again, the atmosphere was strained, because he had no intention of coming home to farm, as his father wanted. Nor did he ever revisit Dauphin, the town where he had grown up: the community was eager to give him a triumphal reception, but (according to which story you believe) he either refused the invitation or failed to show up on the day. After a while his parents stopped answering his occasional letters.

In 1920 he fell in love with Jean Kilbourn Smith, a 23-year-old cousin of Billy Bishop and, in social terms, a class above his own. When the couple were married in Toronto a year later, none of Barker's family attended the wedding, but for a while the couple were happy enough together, and in 1922 Jean gave birth to a daughter, known as Tony.

Earlier that year Bishop-Barker Aeroplanes Ltd had failed, and Barker, critically short of money, had felt obliged to join the Canadian Air Force, in which he was appointed a wing commander (the equivalent of a lieutenant colonel). He took command of the huge training airfield at Borden, fifty miles north of Toronto, and although he had strongly held views on the development of air power, and urged that Canada should create a strike force, his ideas found little favour; but men who worked close to him still found him inspiring.

In January 1924 he moved to Ottawa to become acting director of the air force, which, on 1 April, was officially designated the Royal Canadian Air Force. In the summer he moved to London, where he became the RCAF's liaison officer or representative in England. Early in 1925, seeking excitement, he went on a tour of

RAF stations in the Middle East, and later that year enrolled at the RAF Staff College at Andover. Among the many ideas which he floated there was one for the installation of multiple guns in the wings of fighter aircraft – a proposal which came to fruition in the Spitfire and Hurricane.

In June 1926 he and his family returned to Canada, but when he realised that he was never going to achieve the position he coveted – Director of the RCAF, which was held by his long-term rival Group Captain Jimmy Scott – he resigned from the service. Thereafter he went steeply downhill. He drank more heavily, partly to relieve the pain of his wounds, partly to blot out his disillusionment and feelings of failure. For a while he became president of a tobacco-growing firm, but his marriage was disintegrating, and in 1928 he was gaoled briefly for drunken driving.

His prospects seemed to improve in January 1930, when he was hired as sales manager by Fairchild, the successful aviation company which wanted to build aircraft for the RCAF; but then on 12 March he insisted on making a test flight in a small biplane, a Kr-21. There was nothing wrong with the aircraft, but through a combination of unfamiliarity with the machine and overconfidence, possibly exacerbated by the extreme weakness in his left hand, he went into a stall and crashed on to the ice of the frozen Ottawa River, killing himself instantly.

For a man who had fought like a demon, and fearlessly sought out enemies in countless sorties, it was a tame and miserable end. The news of his death sent shock waves right across Canada, and his funeral parade in Toronto was the largest the city had ever seen, bringing out some fifty thousand spectators, with a cortège of two thousand servicemen in uniform and aircraft flying in formation overhead.

Ever since, his countrymen have tended to forget the last eleven years of Barker's life, and to concentrate instead on his glorious fighting record, not wanting to recognise that even though it was the Great War which made his name immortal, it was also the Great War which destroyed him.

14

Reflections

There are no good and bad VCs. All signal a contribution of excellence that is beyond the norm in the field of courage. Perhaps some are more outstanding than others, but any such judgement must be subjective and open to question. The award of a Victoria Cross has always marked out a winner as someone special and elevated above his peers in terms of prowess on the field of battle. I held this view before starting this book, and I am reinforced in it now that I have finished.

From the moment on 21 June 1854 when Midshipman Charles Lucas leaped forward, when he could have run for safety, to throw overboard a live shell from the deck of HMS *Hecla* in the Baltic Sea, to the latest Cross, awarded to Sergeant Ian McKay of the Parachute Regiment during the Falklands war, every medal has rewarded an action of great gallantry, and all of them, with six exceptions, have been won in the face of the enemy.

Even though warfare has changed and developed over the century and a half, the core condition for winning a VC has altered not at all. In this respect it stands out from other British gallantry awards, most of which have been replaced, and all of which have changed radically. It remains open to women – though a woman has yet to win one – to all classes and ranks, and even to foreigners, such as the Danish Major Anders Lassen (chapter 11), serving with British forces.

It may be instructive to tabulate the outstanding characteristics, apart from courage, of this book's principal dramatis personae:

Albert Ball	Intense patriotism. Dogged determination.
William Barker	Ambition. Patriotism.
Prem Bhagat	Coolness in face of danger. Conviviality.
Roland Bradford	Outstanding leadership. Religious faith. Modesty.
John Byrne	Aggression. Streak of wildness.
Noel Chavasse	Compassion. Strong religious faith. Love of his men.
Guy Gibson	Patriotism. Hatred of Nazis. Love of flying.
William Hall	Loyalty. Physical strength. Service.
Albert Jacka	Independence. Resentment of authority. Single-mindedness.
Anders Lassen	Patriotism. Hatred of the enemy. Aggression. Liking for a fight.
Rambahadur Limbu	Selflessness. Focus. Service.
Charles Upham	Natural warrior. Hatred of Nazis. Humility.
David Wanklyn	Imperturbability. Outstanding leadership. Patriotism. Sense of duty.

It is not surprising that many winners have similar characteristics, of which courage is the common denominator. Thus courage is the theme running through this book. Selflessness is another predominant factor. Throughout the history of the medal, holders have put their lives on the line for other people and for their country – and no group more conspicuously than medical officers and padres. On the other hand, few winners have shown much religious faith –

although in my experience there is nothing like facing the risks of warfare or the deprivations of captivity to bring out any latent and previously unrevealed beliefs a serviceman may hold.

Selflessness shows through in many forms. For example, in the middle of the battle for Ruweisat Ridge, in the desert heat, Charles Upham offered the last of his water to wounded Germans when he himself was already wounded. Selflessness is a prerequisite of good leadership, and it is no surprise to find that the habit of placing the welfare of their men before themselves is endemic in officers and non-commissioned officers who win the Cross. Many winners could have taken a desk job or a base training commitment on the back of their distinction, yet most not only resisted such a posting, but positively fought against it. Lieutenant Commander David Wanklyn, pressured to take a rest and return to the United Kingdom after an outstanding tour in the Mediterranean, refused to do so. Arguably, he should have been ordered to rest – but so great was his loyalty to his men that he would not leave his submarine until the conclusion of her commission. When *Upholder* was lost, his reputation was such that a fourth hand in a sister submarine was heard to remark, 'If Wanks is gone, what hope is there for the rest of us?'[1]

Modesty is another common trait in nearly all winners. Roland Bradford of the Durham Light Infantry would never accept that his award was personal; he insisted that it reflected the achievements of his whole unit. To some extent this was true – but his battalion had responded to the outstanding and inspiring actions of one man, as did the King's Own Scottish Borderers when Bill Speakman led at least ten charges against attacking Chinese troops on 'United Hilltop' in Korea and enabled an orderly withdrawal to be conducted. In general, the citations make it clear that bravery for its own sake does not win VCs: to gain a Cross, it has nearly always been necessary to influence the battle in progress.

Two other common characteristics stand out: focus and luck. Without exception winners have been totally concentrated on the task in hand, to the exclusion of all else around them, including the preservation of their own lives. Those who won in a hot-blooded single action cast aside all personal consideration, while many of those who achieved a VC over a series of actions or a period of time were dedicated to fighting the enemy and exercising care and sacrifice for their fellow servicemen, and were possessed of almost fanatical patriotism. But hatred of the foe is not always a factor: doctors and padres especially regard enemies as fellow human beings, and as much deserving of their professional attention as their own compatriots.

Every VC is won with the backing of an element of luck – luck to stay alive long enough to do the deed where many fighting alongside die; luck to be noticed; luck to have the opportunity – although the lucky one must needs seize the chance. Luck provides the setting; the man does the deed.

There are no constant common factors in the family backgrounds of winners. Some come from well-to-do homes, others are poor as poor. The men are truly classless and rankless, exactly as Queen Victoria desired. Some are deeply religious, others never had a God. All had human emotions, and all had to conquer fear: even the toughest of them, who won their awards over a period of time, eventually showed signs of battle fatigue and stress. The record shows that the human spirit is amazingly flexible, and can stretch to extraordinary lengths in the matter of courage and endurance when put to the test of combat. Or, as Lord Moran pointed out, some people have an enormous bank balance of courage, such as shown by Noel Chavasse, the Reverend Theodore Hardy, Roland Bradford, Guy Gibson, Albert Ball, William Barker and Charles Upham – which enabled them to carry on their acutely stressful and dangerous jobs for an astonishing length of time.

Too many winners have been unable to cope with the consequences of the award and the high public profile into which they were projected. Many died paupers, while a tragic and disproportionate number committed suicide, indicating the high emotional cost of battlefield stress. The strain of war is all too apparent in veterans of heavy fighting, and VC holders are no exception.

The fortunes of winners in later life are well illustrated by the gallant rescue of Lieutenant Colonel Morris, who had led the 17th Lancers into the Valley of Death at Balaclava during the Crimean War, and was left lying severely wounded on an exposed hillside in full view of the Russians. Although the place was constantly swept by small-arms fire, Surgeon James Mouat and Sergeant Major Charles Wooden managed to reach him, dress his wounds and bring him to safety. Both were awarded the Victoria Cross.

After the war Mouat became Inspector-General of Hospitals, Honorary Surgeon to the Queen, and was appointed a Knight Commander of the Bath. He died peacefully at his home, aged eighty-three. Wooden, in contrast, served throughout the Crimean campaign and later in the Indian Mutiny. He was commissioned and subsequently stationed in Dover. Twenty-two years later the regimental surgeon was called to his room, to find him lying across his bed bleeding profusely from the nose and mouth. At the age of forty-seven he had shot himself, and the inquest recorded that he had suffered from depression.[2] VCs do not come cheap emotionally.

My selection of subjects had only two primary influencing factors. I wished all three services to be represented, and also as many countries of the Commonwealth as space allowed. I have also permitted myself the indulgence of giving emphasis to my own regiment, the Durham Light Infantry, which is typical of the best of the British infantry and which certainly influenced my whole army career.

The Army, which is always numerically the largest of the three services and by the nature of its operations the one most directly in contact with the enemy, can claim a majority of VC winners. It probably always will; but it is important to bear in mind that wars are not won by one service alone. Rather, a tri-service commander must ensure that he has the right balance of services and weapons, and that all blend together effectively to produce a coordinated impact on the enemy. So it is a good bet that in future VCs will continue to be shared between Army, Navy and Air Force.

The nature of warfare is always changing, in response to the pressures of international affairs. In recent years operations to fight international terrorism have brought a lower intensity of combat to the military, and lowered the likelihood of casualties. This has reduced the opportunities for achieving the level of gallantry required to win a Victoria Cross; and, assuming that the qualifications remain the same, awards will become even more rare in the future until methods of warfare change yet again – as they will.

I see no reason to expect the demise of international conflict, however desirable that may be. While there are enemies of the Queen at large, servicemen and women will put their lives on the line and have opportunities to win awards for bravery, including the Victoria Cross, and I am confident that the outstanding courage shown in previous conflicts will continue to manifest itself in future generations. It is reassuring to know that there is sufficient metal remaining from the Sevastopol cannon for a further eighty-five medals; but I sincerely hope that conflict will lessen, and that this lump of bronze, with all its implications for war casualties, will remain intact or be drawn on even less frequently than in the past.

With those few who have won the Cross of Bronze, Winston Churchill, soldier as well as politician, would surely share the tribute that his son Randolph paid to him:

> Your glory is enshrined forever on the unperishable plinth of your achievement; and can never be destroyed or tarnished. It will flow with the centuries.[3]

Afterword to the Paperback Edition: Private Johnson Beharry VC

1979–

Midshipman Charles Lucas became the first serviceman to win the Victoria Cross when on 2 June 1854 he saved his ship and his comrades by throwing a smouldering shell from the decks of HMS *Hecla* in the Baltic Sea. To the month, one hundred and fifty years later, Private Johnson Gideon Beharry, a soldier originally from the West Indian island of Grenada serving in the Princess of Wales's Royal Regiment (PWRR), fought with distinguished gallantry in two separate actions in the city of al-Amara in Iraq on 1 May and 11 June 2004. His story is an astonishing narrative of courage and leadership in adversity, bound together with selfless disregard for his personal safety. It comes at a time in British history when some suggest such qualities are in danger of being subsumed by a culture of self-interest.

Johnson Beharry had set out as a painter and decorator, following in the footsteps of his father, who worked in the building industry. At the age of twenty he left home in Grenada to join the British Army, leaving behind his parents, seven brothers and sisters and his decorating career; his uncle Raymond Beharry had already pioneered the family's presence in England, working as a local government official in south London. In August 2001 Johnson enlisted in the PWRR, a regiment with a history stretching back beyond the instigation of the Victoria Cross, and along with other recruits he undertook the standard ten-week infantry training course at Catterick, the training centre for all infantry soldiers. From there, and having in the meantime married his childhood sweetheart

Lynthia, he joined the 1st Battalion of the Princess of Wales's Royal Regiment in March 2002.

He settled in well to his new career in the British Army and became a popular member of his unit. According to his platoon officer, he possessed 'a terrible sense of humour. It's so bad he kept up his platoon's morale all the time.'

Early in 2004 he was posted with his battalion on a routine tour to carry out counter-insurgency and peace-keeping duties in Iraq. The situation in the al-Amara area in Southern Iraq was tense and dangerous, with Iraqi guerrilla forces constantly harassing the coalition troops. Beharry and his platoon were launched into the heart of the conflict.

The British had established their headquarters in the residence of the former Iraqi Provincial Governor, where the Iraqi dissidents subjected them to sporadic and frequent attacks using anti-tank grenades, mortars and other 'stand-off' weapons. The 1st Battalion engaged in continual patrolling designed to dominate the area, restore order and thus to enable the inhabitants to return to a normal, peaceful existence.

Beharry, as the driver of a Warrior armoured personnel carrier, lived his daily life in the thick of it. He drove the platoon commander's vehicle with a crew of the commander himself, gunner and driver, and up to seven foot-soldiers on board. It was his routine task to break through ambushes, escort soft-skinned vehicles and deliver his small section of men to the point where they would disembark and take the battle to the enemy in hand-to-hand fighting. As the driver of the command vehicle he held a special responsibility.

On 1 May 2004 his Warrior was the lead vehicle in an attempt to relieve an infantry patrol that had become isolated and was under fire. As they roared through the streets towards their objective, the alert platoon commander in Beharry's Warrior observed that the normally bustling street ahead lay quiet and deserted. His professional instinct told him that the guerrillas had probably cleared the public from the area, established an ambush and were waiting to spring it as the British passed through. He halted his rescue convoy only to find that the lead vehicles, including his own, with Beharry driving, were threatened.

Beharry's citation states that:

> [His] vehicle was then immediately hit by multiple rocket-propelled grenades.
>
> Eyewitnesses report that the vehicle was engulfed in a number of violent explosions, which physically rocked the 30-tonne Warrior.
>
> As a result of this ferocious initial volley of fire, both the platoon commander and the vehicle's gunner were incapacitated by concussion and other wounds, and a number of the soldiers in the rear of the vehicle were also wounded.

Beharry's radio was damaged, leaving him without guidance, and forcing him to assess the situation for himself. On his own initiative he chose to fight through the ambush for some 1500 metres. Under continual fire, and suffering from the acrid smoke caused by a fire in his vehicle, he opened the hatch, exposing himself as a target, to make a clearer assessment of the best course of action. He took a bullet to his helmet. Although shaken, he managed to break clear of the main ambush, and then, still under small-arms fire, and without thought for his personal safety, climbed onto the turret of his burning vehicle to rescue and drag clear his platoon commander, gunner and other injured crew-members. Only then did he take himself to the relative safety of another Warrior, where he collapsed from physical exhaustion and was evacuated for medical treatment.

Just weeks later, and as soon as he was fit, Beharry returned to duty; and on 11 June 2004 he engaged in a similar, quick-reaction patrol at night, when his vehicle was once again hit by ferocious enemy fire. His citation tells us that:

> During this initial heavy weight of enemy fire, a rocket-propelled grenade detonated on the vehicle's frontal armour, just six inches from Beharry's head, resulting in a serious head injury. Other rockets struck the turret and sides of the vehicle, incapacitating his commander and injuring several of the crew.
>
> With the blood from his head injury obscuring his vision, Beharry managed to continue to control his vehicle, and

> forcefully reversed the Warrior out of the ambush area. The vehicle continued to move until it struck the wall of a nearby building and came to rest. Beharry then lost consciousness as a result of his wounds. By moving the vehicle out of the enemy's chosen killing area he enabled other Warrior crews to be able to extract his crew from his vehicle, with a greatly reduced risk from incoming fire. Despite receiving a serious head injury, which later saw him being listed as very seriously injured and in a coma for some time, his level-headed actions in the face of heavy and accurate enemy fire at short range again almost certainly saved the lives of his crew and provided the conditions for their safe evacuation to medical treatment.

The final summary of his citation described his action as follows: 'Beharry displayed repeated extreme gallantry and unquestioned valour, despite intense direct attacks, personal injury and damage to his vehicle in the face of relentless enemy action.'

His actions over a sustained period are extraordinary enough in themselves, but become unique when his youthfulness and inexperience are taken into account. As General Sir Michael Jackson, Chief of General Staff at the time, commented: 'What he displayed was raw courage and determination . . . risking his life for his comrades and other members of his team.'

The counter-insurgency in Iraq poses great challenges, particularly to the soldier in the street. It requires the individual soldier on the one hand to mix and make friends with the local population, while always on the lookout for insurgents. It is a war that is fought and a peace that is maintained through the courage, judgement and initiative of the most junior ranks of the army. This is manifest in the many lesser awards for gallantry already made, including thirty-three to members of the battle-group in which Beharry himself served.

The intrinsic value of most medals is nominal, and while the gun-metal from which the Victoria Cross is made is practically worthless, the morale value of the award is of the greatest significance to the winner himself and to his unit. Gallantry awards are the only manifest recognition that a service person and his or her unit will receive for facing danger, death and injury.

Beharry's award exemplifies the impact of medals on military morale. At a time when the army had recently received damaging criticism for certain incidents and behaviour, both in Iraq and in the United Kingdom basic training system, his Victoria Cross came as a tonic to restore damaged confidence.

Among his Victoria Cross-winning peers, Beharry's citation places him in the top quartile for sustained courage. He demonstrated a level of decisiveness remarkable for a private soldier with his inexperience of the battlefield, when, despite his platoon commander being wounded and his radio knocked out, he saw clearly what he needed to do to make the best of a threatening situation – and then did it.

Inspiration and personal initiative stand out in his action. When events tempted him to look after himself and to escape from his blazing armoured vehicle, his concern was for his fellow servicemen and crew. He steadfastly fought for their safety, dragging them clear of the blazing vehicle while under enemy fire. His selflessness was in the very highest tradition of courage in the British Army.

True to another tradition among Victoria Cross winners, a thread of modesty runs strongly through his character. At his investiture he said: 'Having the medal is great. But when I did it, I didn't do it for a medal . . . I wasn't thinking about a medal. I didn't know what I was thinking, I just did it. And now looking back on it, if I hadn't done it, I wouldn't have been able to live with myself today, knowing that I could have helped other soldiers not to die.'

As I write this, Johnson Beharry's future is uncertain: he is recovering from his wounds, and his wish to continue his army career may be decided by his doctors. But it is certain his life is changed for ever: he will be faced with further challenges and will need the long-term support and guidance of his Regiment and the Army in handling the pressures of fame.

The Victoria Cross is the only gallantry award that requires the ultimate sanction of approval by the monarch of the day. I noted towards the beginning of this book that in 1856 Queen Victoria stipulated that the medal should go to 'Only those Officers and Men who have served Us in the presence of the enemy and shall then have performed some signal act of valour or devotion to their Country.'

Private Johnson Beharry did exactly that.

Postscript: Phoneys

One of the most attractive features of VC winners is their modesty – and no one can have been more self-effacing than Private Fred Hitch, who gained his medal in the Zulu war of 1879 and then became a popular London taxi-driver. When he died in 1913, the hundreds of fellow cabbies who turned out for his funeral were astonished to see the South Wales Borderers parading in full force – his mates having never had any inkling that he was a VC holder.

Almost all recipients have been delighted and proud to win the medal, and although some men brag about what they achieved, many – I would say most – have been extremely self-deprecating, maintaining that the award recognised the contribution of their unit, rather than that of any one person. This is particularly true after infantry actions in which a section, a platoon or even a whole company has been involved.

And yet, regrettably enough, there are men of entirely the opposite mindset, who crave fame and recognition so badly that they pretend to have won a VC when they have not, thereby causing acute embarrassment to their colleagues in the services, to others in their communities, and, in the end, to themselves.

One such was Sergeant Donald MacKechnie, who at the outbreak of war in 1914 was serving with the Instructional Corps in Melbourne. When he presented himself for service with the Australian Infantry Force, the recruiting officers were startled to see that first and foremost of the medal insignia on the breast of his tunic was the plain crimson ribbon of the Victoria Cross.

He was certainly a Scotsman, and he was then – by his own

account – thirty-six years old. He said he had served for twelve years with the Gordon Highlanders, and that as a private he had been a member of the Tirah expedition of 1897 in north-western Afghanistan. Then, as a sergeant in South Africa, he had fought in numerous actions against the Boers, before returning with his regiment to the North-West Frontier.

When he enlisted in the AIF, commanding officers competed to have him in their regiment: a battalion with a VC in its ranks would acquire instant celebrity. Restored to his original rank of sergeant, MacKechnie was allocated to the 7th Battalion, where he began knocking the brash colonial lads into shape. His methods were rough and old-fashioned: he shouted and cursed, and did not endear himself to his new colleagues, on duty or off: he was a heavy drinker, and when under the influence would bore his fellow warrant officers stiff with boastful tales of his past. And yet, because he had won a VC, they were prepared to tolerate him, believing that when they went to war, his qualities would stand them in good stead.

They went to war soon enough: after training in Egypt the 7th Battalion landed at Gallipoli on the night of 25 April 1915, as part of the Anzac force, at the start of a campaign that has gone down in history as one of the great military disasters (see chapter 6). When the 7th went ashore on a breathless night, they were confronted by terrain that bore no resemblance to the landscape described in their briefing: instead of the rolling plains they had been promised, they found sheer cliffs manned by Turkish riflemen, who opened fire as soon as they started to climb.

MacKechnie was one of the first casualties. Shot through the shoulder, he was evacuated to a hospital ship lying offshore, and then in May to the 2nd Australian General Hospital in Cairo. Once again, the presence of a VC holder caused something of a sensation – but his conduct was less than admirable: one night he slipped out of his ward, his absence was discovered, and when he lurched back through the hospital gates in the early hours, he was arrested by the Military Police. The result was that, in spite of his distinguished earlier record, he was reduced to the rank of private.

His wounds did not heal easily, for the bullet had shattered on impact, and not all the splinters could be removed. When arthritis set in, and then an eye infection, he was returned to Australia for special treatment, and, with his general health declining, he was discharged from the AIF on medical grounds.

A young clerk then started filling in forms so that MacKechnie could get a pension. Realising that all VC winners received a small gratuity, he assumed that this could be incorporated in the pension; but when he checked back, he could not find any record of the gratuity in MacKechnie's papers. Investigating further, he did indeed find a MacKechnie on the VC roll – but this man had won his award in 1854, and, if he were still alive, would be at least eighty years old. The clerk took his findings to the adjutant, who in turn took them to the commanding officer.

A cable to the headquarters of the Gordon Highlanders established that the regiment held no record of a Donald MacKechnie winning the VC. Later research has confirmed that the only winner of that surname before the First World War was Sergeant James McKechnie of the Scots Fusiliers Guards, who won his medal during the Crimean War at the battle of Alma in 1854. During the Tirah campaign no soldier called MacKechnie served with the Gordons, and during the Boer War only one man of that name, Private William McKechnie, served with the regiment.

Confronted with an official refutation, the impostor admitted that he was a fraud, and he was discharged from the army with ignominy. Nemesis soon caught up with him. His physical and mental health deteriorated, until in 1917 he was admitted to the Ballarat Hospital for the Insane, where he remained until his death three years later. At this distance in time it is impossible to determine what motivated him, but it seems likely that he was driven by some fundamental insecurity, which made him bluster and put on false airs. It is also probable that – as in many such cases – he began his fraud with a deliberate falsehood, but grew so accustomed to living with his lie that he became a fantasist – someone who has told the same story so often that he has come to believe it himself.

Few men carry dishonesty to such lengths – and in recent years the growth of the Internet has scotched many bogus claimants, because people can now check facts so easily. All the same, a steady stream of complaints and queries still flows into the office of the Victoria Cross & George Cross Association, where all the records are held, high above Horse Guards' Parade in the centre of London.

The person who bears the brunt of these inquiries is Mrs Didy Grahame, the Association's formidably knowledgeable Secretary, who cites as her own most difficult VC impostor Idi Amin, the crazed president of Uganda in the 1970s. Until 1963 her husband had been Amin's company commander in the Ugandan Rifles, and the two had kept in touch ever since. On her first visit to Uganda, in 1976, Mrs Grahame met the president and noticed a VC among his breastful of medals. During her ten-day stay in the country she was allowed to travel wherever she wanted, on condition that she spent twenty minutes with Amin every morning, to give him time to reminisce about his military feats.

During one of these sessions she said to him, 'You've really *got* to take that Victoria Cross off, because you don't deserve it.'

'Oh yes I do,' he answered.

Not many women would have stuck to their guns in front of such a monster – but she did.

'Quite frankly, I know you don't,' she told him. 'You're making yourself a laughing stock by wearing it.'

Crestfallen, he took it off.[1]

In London, most letters report the activities of impostors, and the Association's answers are always compassionate but firm: if a name given does not feature on the roll of honour, its advice is generally that the bogus VC claimant should be exposed – maybe in the local press. No further action is taken unless the person persists in trying to exploit his falsehoods.

Secrecy is often invoked as a form of camouflage, especially by con-men. One man who purported to be a VC holder said that he had been a member of the SAS, and that the operation for which he was decorated had been *so* secret that no one was allowed to see the records, as they would give away too much. He was wooing a rich young widow, but the woman's sister, sensing that something was wrong, rang up the Association for advice. The answer was that no VC holder with the suitor's name existed, and that whoever it was making the approaches to her sister must be up to no good. She left the letter lying around – and the man soon disappeared.

The anxieties caused by fraudulent claimants are all too apparent in the correspondence. 'I live in a small community, and no one will have anything to do with this person,' reported one letter, when a former submariner was telling obviously bogus stories about his VC. Another envelope enclosed a Victoria Cross that had been 'left behind in a box of soiled linen amongst my late father's effects . . . There does not appear to be any identification on the medal, so I cannot return it to the rightful owner.' There followed the ambiguous remark, 'The person last having the medal was a passing traveller.' In London, even a cursory examination showed that the bronze medal was a fake.

In the 1980s, a former serviceman began to appear at functions wearing what looked like a VC among a row of medals. When asked why he had not sported it before, he said that the decoration had just 'come through'; but he would not allow anyone to handle it or read the inscription on the back. Needless to say, the records showed that no one of his name had won the supreme award.

From County Cork, in southern Ireland, came a letter complaining that an American had put up a spurious citation, 'complete with spelling mistakes', in the bar of a local pub, and was conning drinks out of tourists on the strength of it. His story was that he had won a VC in Korea, when attached to the Royal Marines; but research in London immediately confirmed that the four Crosses awarded during the Korean War all went to British troops, and that in any case two of them were posthumous. The Association's advice was to expose the American as an impostor – and he did not last long. When a friend told him he was a fraud, he first assaulted his accuser, then complained to the Gardai (the police), who promptly arrested him for non-payment of traffic fines.

Exposure hurts – witness the pathetic plea sent in by an elderly man who had been wearing an unearned Cross, and had been rumbled. 'I want to offer my sincere and humble apologies,' he wrote. 'The said item was never meant to discredit any one of those gallant persons. So, as my time is running out, may I ask you . . . please don't expose me as this will surely put an end to me.'

A few people cannot resist the need simply to associate with medal-holders. In June 1920, when Sir Percival Marling went to Buckingham Palace to receive his VC from King George V, he was invited to lunch at Wellington Barracks before joining a procession of award-winners on the short route to the Palace. As he marched along Birdcage Walk, a man slipped out of the crowd and unobtrusively joined the section in front of him. Marling remarked to his neighbour that he didn't think the fellow had any right to be there:

> The man, however, walked along till we got to Buckingham Palace gates, and then went in with the procession. Directly we got inside the gates I called a policeman and told him our suspicions. The bobby went up to the man and found, as we thought, that he hadn't got a VC, and he was promptly turned out.[2]

In 1996 John Ainsworth-Davis, a former naval intelligence officer, claimed in his book *Op JB*, published under the pseudonym Christopher Creighton, that he had smuggled Hitler's deputy Martin Bormann out of the ruins of Berlin on the last night of the Second World War, 1/2 May 1945. He said that the successful exfiltration was achieved by means of Operation James Bond, a naval commando raid organised by Ian Fleming, who later assigned the name to his fictional hero. One of his most fantastical assertions was that the raiding party also brought Hitler out of the bunker with them, and that the Führer's head was blown off by a tank shell as they approached their canoes, secreted in the River Spree. Further, Ainsworth-Davis asserted that Bormann came to England and lived here incognito, first in London, then in Hampshire, until he was moved to South America in 1956.

The author also let it be known that he had been awarded a secret VC for other clandestine exploits during the war. In 1995 he even took a set of medals and displayed them to members of the Bormann family when he visited them near Munich in an attempt to vindicate his account.

When *Op JB* was published, the book was widely dismissed as unbelievable, but the author continued to maintain that it was true. The veteran intelligence officer and theatre critic Milton Shulman, who had helped prepare the text, offered a reward of £20,000 to anyone who could prove that the story was phoney – but no one came forward. Ainsworth-Davis himself smoothly brushed official denials aside by playing the secrecy card. People who have never been in deep-secret work, he explained patiently, simply do not understand. When challenged with the fact that no record of his VC exists, he would reply, 'Of course not,' because the operation for which he won it was allegedly *so* secret that it has never been officially admitted.

Notes

Chapter 1 The Medal

1 Quoted in M. J. Crook, *The Evolution of the Victoria Cross*, p. 34.
2 *The Times*, 27 June 1857.
3 Ibid.
4 Fifth provision of the Warrant instituting the Victoria Cross. Crook, op. cit., p. 280.
5 The pension in 2004 is £1300 per annum.
6 Crook, op. cit., p. 265.
7 Ibid., p. 46.
8 Ibid., p. 46.
9 Stephen, D. Shannon, *Beyond Praise*, p. 43.
10 Matthew Grant Little, *The Royal Marines and the Victoria Cross*, p. 3.
11 Crook, op. cit., p. 102.
12 Ibid., p. 82.
13 Colonel Sir Percy Marling, *Rifleman and Hussar*, pp. 110–11.
14 Crook, op. cit., pp. 168–9. The First World War offered him further opportunities for action, and again he excelled himself. While serving with 5 Field Ambulance at Ypres, he became one of only three people to win a bar to his VC.
15 Marling, op. cit., pp. 110–11.
16 Crook, op. cit., pp. 172–3, 292.
17 Ibid., p. 64.
18 Ibid., pp. 66–7.
19 David Harvey, *Monuments to Courage*, vol. 2.
20 John Winton, *Illustrated London News*, September 1979.
21 David Raw, *'It's Only Me'*, p. 21.

Chapter 2 On Courage

1 Field Marshal Sir William Slim, *Courage and Other Broadcasts*, p. 5.
2 Now Speakman-Pitt.
3 Lord Moran, *The Anatomy of Courage*, p. 69.
4 Ibid., p. 10.

5 M. R. D. Foot, *Six Faces of Courage*, p. 13.
6 John 15:13.
7 Bill Griffiths and Hugh Popham, *Blind to Misfortune,* foreword.
8 Ibid., p. 15.
9 Durham Light Infantry Museum archive.

Chapter 3 Captain Noel Chavasse

1 Unless otherwise specified, quotations from Noel's letters are taken from the collection of his correspondence in the Bodleian Library, Oxford.
2 Ann Clayton, *Chavasse Double VC*, p. 44.
3 In the course of transcription many small changes were made, sometimes (it seems) out of carelessness, and sometimes in misguided attempts to soften or improve the original text.
4 Jack Johnson, a huge man, became the first black heavyweight boxing world champion in 1908.
5 'Still going strong' is the motto of the whisky firm, founded by Johnnie Walker, a grocer, in 1820.
6 Clayton, op. cit., p. 126.
7 In *David Copperfield* Barkis the carrier courted Clara Peggotty by telling young David, when he went home to his nurse, to say, 'Barkis is willing.' Clara took the hint, and became Mrs Barkis.
8 Clayton, op. cit., pp. 161–2.
9 *Liverpool Daily Post & Mercury*, 27 October 1917.
10 The letter is preserved with the Chavasse papers in the Bodleian Collection.
11 Clayton, op. cit., p. 209.
12 Bodleian Collection; ibid., p. 210.
13 Ibid.
14 Ibid.
15 Selwyn Gummer, *The Chavasse Twins,* p. 64.

Chapter 4 Colour Sergeant John Byrne

1 Stephen Shannon, *Beyond Praise*, p. 6.
2 S. G. P. Ward, *The Faithful: the Story of the Durham Light Infantry*, p. 179.
3 Ibid., p. 184.

Chapter 5 Captain Albert Ball

1 Cecil Lewis, *Sagittarius Rising*, paperback edition, p. 174.
2 Chaz Bowyer, *Albert Ball, VC*, p. 81. Hill, a junior lieutenant in the RFC in 1916, became an air chief marshal and was knighted in 1944.
3 Unless otherwise specified, quotations from Albert's letters are taken from the collection of several hundred preserved in the Nottingham Public Archives.

4 E1 pilots were at first forbidden to cross the front lines, for fear that an aircraft would be shot down and the secret of the synchronised machine gun discovered.
5 The men who flew single-seat aircraft were known as 'scout pilots', and although their role was to do battle with the enemy, the term 'fighter pilot' had not yet been invented.
6 Sagittarius the Archer, the ninth sign of the Zodiac, governs weapons, voyages and all swift things.
7 Lewis, op. cit., p. 103.
8 W. M. Fry, *Air of Battle*, p. 82.
9 Noel Chavasse also communicated with families, but on the death of their loved ones – so far as he was able to keep up with the appallingly high casualty rate. The practice of units and their commanders keeping in touch with families remains an important aspect of command to this day, perhaps even more so than it used to be. Most units and ships operate a 'wives' club', where women are able to share the problems incurred by their husbands' long absences, and where they can support families who have suffered a death.
10 Trenchard, founder of the Royal Air Force, was knighted in 1919. He became Marshal of the RAF in 1927 and was created Baron Trenchard in 1930.
11 Maurice Baring, *RFC HQ, 1914–1918*. Wing Commander Maurice Baring, author and journalist and intelligence officer, became personal secretary to Trenchard at the beginning of 1918.
12 Lewis, op. cit., pp. 173–4.
13 Quoted in Bowyer, op. cit., p. 134.
14 Lewis, op. cit., pp. 174–5.
15 Ibid., pp. 176–7.
16 Ibid., pp. 178–9.
17 Personal letter. Translation held by the Army Museum.
18 Bowyer, op. cit., p. 168.

Chapter 6 Private Albert Jacka

1 Confusion of this kind is by no means uncommon in the chaos that is war. During my own time in the Middle East I was once responsible for deploying troops on to the coast of northern Oman. Surprise was to be achieved through a dawn assault by a combined force of SAS and Trucial Oman Scouts, to surprise and seize an Iraqi terrorist group. The force swept in from the sea, only to find that the objective, the village of Jumla, had been confused with a nearby village called Gumla, and it turned out that a cartographic error had transposed the names, so that the assault was directed on the wrong place.
2 The story of the Rechabites refusing wine is told in Jeremiah 35.
3 *Reveille*, 1 January 1939, reprinted in Ian Grant, *Jacka VC*, p. 171.
4 John North, *Gallipoli: The Fading Vision*, p. 209.

5 Grant, op. cit., p. 25.
6 *Pageant Magazine*, April/May 1993.
7 Martin Gilbert, *First World War*, p. 260.
8 C. W. Bean, *Official History of Australia in the War 1914–1918*, Vol. 3, p. 720.
9 Edgar John Rule, *Jacka's Mob*, p. 30.
10 After the war Peck recovered, to become Director of Supply and Transport to the Australian Army.
11 Grant, op. cit., p. 130.
12 *Reveille*, reprinted in ibid., p 123.
13 Grant, op. cit., p. 156.
14 Minute held in Australian War Museum, Canberra.
15 Letter held in Australian War Museum, Canberra.
16 Grant, op. cit., p. 161.
17 *Melbourne Herald*, 8 January 1932.

Chapter 7 Lieutenant Commander David Wanklyn

1 For much of the information in this chapter I am indebted to Jim Allaway's excellent book *Hero of the Upholder.*
2 Jim Allaway, *Hero of the Upholder*, p. 25.
3 Quotations from Wanklyn's personal correspondence are taken from photocopies of family letters preserved in the archive of the Submarine Museum in Portsmouth. Not all the letters are dated.
4 Copy in Submarine Museum.
5 In 2003 Captain Crawford, a vigorous octogenarian, contributed personal memories of Wanklyn in a most useful personal interview.
6 Allaway, op. cit., p. 81.
7 Wanklyn's key is preserved in the Submarine Museum.
8 Broadcast, printed in *The Listener*, 26 February 1942.
9 Another submariner privately recorded of an S boat in the Mediterranean during the 1950s: 'After 18 hours dived the reduction in oxygen levels and the increase in carbon monoxide made it impossible to light a match. Hands not on watch were encouraged to turn in, to save oxygen. After twenty-four hours it was impossible to breathe properly, and one was reduced to panting. When the conning tower hatch was opened after surfacing, the pressure in the boat forced out all the air, and it would be light brown.'
10 *Listener* broadcast, quoted above.
11 Report in the Submarine Museum archive.
12 Photocopy of journal in Submarine Museum archive.
13 Submarine Museum archive.
14 Public Record Office, ADM 236/48.
15 Allaway, op. cit., p. 135.
16 Personal communication with Wanklyn's son Ian, 2004.
17 Submarine Museum archive.
18 Ibid.

19 Ibid.
20 Ibid.

Chapter 8 Wing Commander Guy Gibson

1 Max Hastings, *Bomber Command*, p. 256.
2 Wing Commander Guy Gibson, *Enemy Coast Ahead* (2003 edition), p. 30.
3 Ibid., p. 28.
4 Ibid., p. 33.
5 Ibid., p. 27.
6 Ibid., p. 28.
7 Ibid., p. 35.
8 Ibid., p. 37.
9 Ibid., p. 152.
10 Ibid., p. 153.
11 Ibid., p. 108.
12 The kill numbers were substantially more modest than those achieved by pilots like Albert Ball and William Barker during the First World War. This reflects the greater sophistication of aerial warfare, rather than any lack of skill on the part of the pilots.
13 Richard Morris, *Guy Gibson*, p. 99.
14 Hastings, op. cit., p. 182.
15 Gibson, op. cit., p. 169.
16 Cochrane became an air chief marshal and Vice Chief of Air Staff. He was knighted in 1945.
17 Gibson, op. cit., p. 218.
18 Ibid., p. 228.
19 Ibid., p. 250.
20 Ibid., pp. 261–2.
21 Ibid., p. 264.
22 Ibid., p. 268.
23 Ibid., p. 269.
24 In his introduction to *Enemy Coast Ahead*, pp. 9–10.
25 Richard Morris, *Guy Gibson*, p. 307.
26 Gibson, op. cit., p. 9.

Chapter 9 Captain Charles Upham

1 *Citizen to Citizen* pamphlet by Captain Lindsay Amner in the Army Memorial Museum Exhibition at Waiouru, New Zealand, p. 18.
2 Ibid., p. 5.
3 Kenneth Sandford, *Mark of the Lion*, p. 31.
4 Later Major-General Kippenberger, one of New Zealand's greatest commanders.
5 His family had a struggle to furnish the statue with the details they wanted. Upham's son-in-law, Forbes MacKenzie, explains: 'The

statue shows him in the uniform they were wearing in Crete. We made him up as a captain, because he was always known as that, even though he was only a lieutenant at the time. He was not allowed to wear a Tommy gun on his back. We had a big job to be able to show hand grenades on his person. His revolver was OK, because it was out of sight. We had a huge battle to be allowed to put a helmet on his head. I pleaded that men did not go into battle bare-headed. Nevertheless, Mrs Upham had to insist before he got that helmet.'

6 Winston S. Churchill, *The Second World War*, vol. III, p. 246.
7 Jim Burrows, personal letter to Charles Upham, 1981.
8 Sandford, op. cit., p. 120.
9 Ibid., p. 145.
10 Unknown newspaper source, 1981. 40th Anniversary of Crete.
11 J. L. Scoullar, *Battle for Egypt* – Official New Zealand War History.
12 Sandford, op. cit., p. 17.
13 Ibid., p. 379.
14 *Citizen to Citizen*, op. cit., p. 17.
15 Conversation with the author.

Chapter 10 The Bradford Boys

1 None of the brothers married. They lived together in a kind of commune in Norfolk, looked after by their sister Mel, who survived to the age of almost 102.
2 For many of the details in this chapter I am indebted to Harry Moses, who generously allowed me to use extensive quotations from *The Fighting Bradfords*. Unless indicated otherwise, quotations in this chapter are from his book. Quotations from regimental records are taken from documents preserved in the Durham County Record Office and the Durham Light Infantry Museum. There is also much information on various websites, which can be found by searching for 'Bradford Brothers'.
3 A copy of this letter was sent to Roland's mother, after his death, by the publishers.
4 Quoted in *The Fighting Bradfords*, p. 100.
5 Some details of the action are taken from Captain Carpenter's own account, *The Blocking of Zeebrugge.*

Chapter 11 Major Anders Lassen

1 Mike Langley, *Anders Lassen, VC, MC, of the SAS*, p. 40.
2 Many details of Lassen's operations are taken from Mike Langley's biography.
3 Suzanne Lassen, *Anders Lassen, VC*, p. 38.
4 Langley, op. cit., pp. 89–90.
5 Lassen, op. cit., p. 54.

6 Interview with the author, 2003.
7 Langley, op. cit., pp. 147–8.
8 Ibid., pp. 189–90.
9 Ibid., p. 177.
10 Ibid., pp. 207–8.
11 *Operation Report 13*. Quoted in Langley, pp. 210–13.
12 Ibid.
13 Lassen, op. cit., p. 208.
14 Details of the operation are taken from Mike Langley's biography.
15 Langley, op. cit., pp. 243–4.
16 Personal interview, 2003.
17 Lassen, op. cit., p. 230.

Chapter 12 Eastern Allies: Gurkha and Indian VCs

1 Field Marshal Sir William Slim, *Defeat into Victory*, p. 336.
2 Ibid., p. 188.
3 Field Marshal Sir William Slim, *Courage and Other Broadcasts*, p. 8.
4 *Daily Telegraph*, 8 March 2004.
5 General Sir Walter Walker, *Fighting On*, p. 217.
6 Rambahadur Limbu, *My Life Story*.
7 Ibid.
8 Ibid.
9 Rambahadur gave this account to J. P. Cross and Buddhiman Gurung, editors of *Gurkhas at War*, pp. 250–2.
10 Lieutenant Colonel G. R. Stevens, *History of the 2nd King Edward VII's Own Goorkha Rifles*, vol. 3, pp. 75–6.
11 Ibid., pp. 253–4.
12 Walker, op. cit., p. 225, quoting Professor Sir Ralph Turner, MC.
13 Slim, *Courage and Other Broadcasts*, p. 96.
14 Ibid., p. 96.
15 Lieutenant General Matthew Thomas and Jasjit Mansingh, *Lt. Gen. P. S. Bhagat, PVSM, VC*, p 20.
16 Ibid., p. 50.
17 Ibid., pp. 51–2.
18 Ibid., p. 58.
19 Ibid., pp. 63–4.
20 Ibid., p. 62.
21 Ibid., pp. 60–1.
22 Ibid., pp. 68–9.
23 Ibid., p. 82.
24 Ibid., p. 84.
25 Ibid., pp. 99–100.
26 Ibid., p. 105.
27 Ibid., p. 480.
28 From the foreword to *Bhagat*.

Chapter 13 Canadian Aces

1 Canadian War Museum.
2 A set of bagpipes, which may have been Richardson's, was recovered from the Somme battlefield in 1917, and stored in the museum of a private school in Scotland.
3 Paper by David W. States, read before Royal Nova Scotia Historical Society, 25 February 1993. *Canadian Magazine of Politics, Science, Art and Literature*, Vol. XVIII, No. 2, June 1901, p. 113.
4 David Harvey, *Monuments to Courage*, vol. 1, p. 211.
5 States, op. cit.
6 Ibid.
7 Ibid.
8 The intervention role of the naval brigades contributed with dramatic effect to the impact of British Army forces fighting overseas. Naval units fought with great distinction in the Crimea, taking heavy casualties and providing undergunned British army formations with indispensable support. But today their role is filled by commando carrier ships and the fast-reaction capability of the Parachute Regiment. Above all, however, the third dimension of the Royal Air Force has dramatically altered the nature of intervention warfare, although the Royal Navy continues to provide air, missile and gunfire support from ship to shore.
9 PRO ADM 38/4910, Muster Book, HMS *Rodney*.
10 At a time when all communications travelled overland or by sea, flexibility, as well as speed of response and redeployment, was increased by much greater delegation of authority to overseas commanders than is allowed today. In modern warfare the politicians, under pressure from instant communications, require updating on a minute-by-minute basis, with the result that their involvement in operations can make heavy demands on commanders on the spot.
11 States, op. cit.; Robert Wilkinson-Lathen, *The Royal Navy, 1790–1970*, p. 35.
12 *The Dalhousie Review*, vol. 37, no. 3, autumn 1957, p. 253.
13 Ibid., p. 256.
14 Lieutenant Colonel W. Gordon-Alexander, *Recollections of a Highland Subaltern*, pp. 114ff.
15 M. J. Crook, *The Evolution of the Victoria Cross*, p. 218.
16 *The Dalhousie Review*, vol. 37, no. 3, autumn 1957 p. 257.
17 The quotations from William's letters home are taken from *Barker VC* by Wayne Ralph.
18 Wayne Ralph, *Barker VC*, p. 67.
19 Later Viscount Stansgate, father of Tony Benn, MP.
20 Later Air Chief Marshal, knighted in 1928.
21 The German ace Manfred von Richthofen, known as The Red Baron, had been killed in combat earlier that year.
22 Quoted in Ralph, op. cit., pp. 165–6.

Chapter 14 Reflections

1 Personal reminiscence via Ian Wanklyn, 2004.
2 *Illustrated London News*, September 1979, p. 51.
3 Martin Gilbert, *Churchill: a Life*, p. 959.

Postscript: Phoneys

1 Personal interview, 2003.
2 Colonel Sir Percival Marling, *Rifleman and Hussar*, pp. 370–1.

Glossary of Gallantry Medals Awarded for Military Action

(referred to in Supreme Courage*)*

VC (Victoria Cross)
The highest award for gallantry in battle.

GC (George Cross)
The highest award for civilians, and for the military when not in the face of the enemy.

DSO (Distinguished Service Order)
Originally established as an order. From 1917 it was frequently granted for gallantry and leadership in battle.

DSC (Distinguished Service Cross)
Normally awarded to officers up to the rank of lieutenant commander in the Royal Navy and Merchant Navy, and since 1940 to similar ranks in the Royal Air Force and Army officers serving afloat.

MC (Military Cross)
A gallantry award for issue to junior army officers and warrant officers.

DFC (Distinguished Flying Cross)
Recognises gallantry in the air during operations against the enemy. Available to all three services but more usually to the Royal Air Force.

DCM (Distinguished Conduct Medal)
Instituted by Royal Warrant in 1854 expressly for non-commissioned ranks in the Army. Apart from the Victoria Cross, it was the highest gallantry award available to them and is regarded as a particular distinction.

CGM (Conspicuous Gallantry Medal)
Awarded to non-commissioned ranks of Royal Navy and Royal Marines. Introduced as a counterpart for the DCM in 1855. It was reinstituted by an Order in Council in 1874 since when only 240 have been awarded.

MM (Military Medal)
Awarded to non-commissioned ranks in the Army for bravery.

MiD (Mention in Despatches)
Awarded to all ranks of all three services. Represented by a bronze oak leaf sewn on to the ribbon of campaign medal in which it is awarded. At one time only the Victoria Cross and MiD could be awarded posthumously for gallant, distinguished or meritorious service in operational conditions.

Bar
When one of the above awards is won more than once by the same person, he receives not a further medal, but a bar, which is fitted to the original medal ribbon.

Current Awards
There are other gallantry awards not mentioned in this book. A range of awards are available to both civilian and military when not in the face of the enemy, the highest of which is the George Cross, which ranks equally with the Victoria Cross. In 1993 the government of the day adopted changes to awards for gallantry while on military service against the enemy:

a. All awards available to all ranks of the three services, except the DSO.
b. DSM, DCM, MM, DFM, AFM, CGM to be discontinued.
c. Victoria Cross and George Cross recipients to receive an annuity, which in 2004 was £1300, and is reviewed every five years.
d. All awards to be available posthumously.
e. DSO, which is an Order and not available posthumously, ceases to be awarded for gallantry and is solely for outstanding and distinguished leadership, but remains an Order for commissioned officers only.
f. A new gallantry award has been introduced named the Conspicuous Gallantry Cross (CGC) to rank second in distinction to the Victoria Cross and to be available to all ranks of all services in action against the enemy.

Under this simplified system the current situation for purely military honours *available to all ranks* may be summarised:

Level of Award	Award
I	Victoria Cross
II	Conspicuous Gallantry Cross
III	Distinguished Service Cross
	Military Cross
	Distinguished Flying Cross
IV	Mention in Dispatches
	Queen's Commendation for Bravery
	Queen's Commendation for Bravery in the Air
	Queen's Commendation for Valuable Service

Bibliography

Allaway, Jim, *Hero of the Upholder* (Shrewsbury: Airlife, 1991).
Anonymous, *Brigadier-General R. B. Bradford, VC, MC, and his Brothers* (undated, printed in a limited edition of 300 copies for the Bradford family after the First World War).
Anonymous, *The Story of Gurkha VCs* (Winchester: Gurkha Museum, 1993).
Baring, Maurice, *R.F.C. H.Q.* (London: G. Bell, 1920).
Bean, C. W. *Official History of Australia in the War, 1914–18*, Vol. 3, *The A.I.F. in France* (Sydney: Angus & Robertson, 1942).
Bowyer, Chaz, *Albert Ball, VC* (Wrexham: Bridge Books, 1977 and 1994)
Brett-James, Anthony, *Ball of Fire* (Aldershot: Gale & Polden, 1951)
Burkett, B. G., and Whitley, Glenna, *Stolen Valor* (Dallas: Verity Press, 1998).
Capell, Richard, *Simiomata: A Greek Notebook* (London: MacDonald, 1946).
Carpenter, Captain A. F. B., *The Blocking of Zeebrugge* (London: H. Jenkins, 1922).
Churchill, Winston S., *The Second World War*, Vol. 3, *The Grand Alliance* (London: Cassell, 1950).
Clayton, Ann, *Chavasse Double VC* (London: Leo Cooper, 1992).
Crook, M. J., *The Evolution of the Victoria Cross* (Tunbridge Wells: Midas Books, in association with the Ogilby Trusts, 1975).
Cross, J. P., and Gurung, Buddhiman (eds.), *Gurkhas at War* (London: Greenhill Books, 2002).
Duckers, P., *British Gallantry Awards 1855–2000* (Princes Risborough: Shire Books, 2001)
Foot, M. R. D., *Six Faces of Courage* (London: Eyre Methuen, 1978).
Fry, W. M., *Air of Battle* (London: Kimber 1974).
Gibson, Wing Commander Guy, *Enemy Coast Ahead* (London: Michael Joseph, 1946) (an uncensored version was published by Crécy Books, Manchester, 2003).
Gilbert, Martin, *Churchill: A Life* (Reading: Cox & Wyman, 1992).
—— *First World War* (London: Weidenfeld & Nicolson, 1994).

Gordon-Alexander, Lieutenant Colonel W., *Recollections of a Highland Subaltern* (London: Edward Arnold, 1898).
Grant, Ian, *Jacka, VC* (South Melbourne: Macmillan Australia, 1989).
Griffiths, Bill, and Popham, Hugh, *Blind to Misfortune* (London: Leo Cooper, 1989).
Gummer, Selwyn, *The Chavasse Twins* (London: Hodder & Stoughton, 1963).
Hart, Sydney, *Submarine Upholder* (London: Oldbourne Book Co., 1960).
Harvey, David, *Monuments to Courage*, 2 vols. (privately published by the author, 1999).
Hastings, Max, *Bomber Command* (London: Michael Joseph, 1979).
Holland, James, *Fortress Malta* (London: Orion, 2003).
Jones, H. A., *The War in the Air*, 9 vols. (Oxford: Clarendon Press, 1928–37).
Kofod-Hansen, Mogens, *Andy* (Friends of the Copenhagen Museum, 1991).
Langley, Mike, *Anders Lassen, VC, MC, of the SAS* (London: Hodder & Stoughton, 1988).
Lassen, Suzanne, *Anders Lassen, VC* (London: Frederick Muller, 1965).
Lewis, Cecil, *Sagittarius Rising* (London: Peter Davies, 1936).
Limbu, Rambahadur, VC, *My Life Story* (London: Gurkha Welfare Trust, undated).
Little, Matthew Grant, *The Royal Marines and the Victoria Cross* (Southsea: Royal Marines Museum, 2002).
Marling, Colonel Sir Percival, *Rifleman and Hussar* (London: John Murray, 1931).
Marson, T. B., *Scarlet and Khaki* (London: Jonathan Cape, 1930).
Moran, Lord, *The Anatomy of Courage* (London: Constable, 1945).
Morris, Richard, *Guy Gibson* (London: Penguin, 1994).
Moses, Harry, *The Faithful Sixth: A History of the 6th Battalion Durham Light Infantry* (Durham: County Durham Books, 1995).
Moses, Harry, *The Gateshead Gurkhas: A History of the 9th Battalion Durham Light Infantry 1859–1967* (Durham: County Durham Books, 2001).
Moses, Harry, *The Fighting Bradfords* (Durham: County Durham Books, 2003).
North, John, *Gallipoli: The Fading Vision* (London: Faber Faber, 1936).
Padfield, Peter, *War Beneath the Sea* (London: John Murray, 1995).
Percival, John, *For Valour* (London: Methuen, 1985).
Ralph, Wayne, *Barker VC* (London: Grub Street, 1997).
Raw, David, *'It's Only Me'* (Gatebeck: Frank Peters Publishing, 1988).
Rule, Edgar John, *Jacka's Mob* (additional material compiled and edited by Carl Johnson and Andrew Barnes) (Prahran: Military Melbourne, 1999).
Sandford, Kenneth, *Mark of the Lion* (London: Hutchinson, 1962).
Scoullar, J. L., *Official History of New Zealand in the Second World War: The Battle for Egypt: The Summer of 1942* (Wellington: War History Branch, 1955)

Shannon, Stephen D., *Beyond Praise* (Durham: County Durham Books, 1998).

Simpson, Rear Admiral G. W. G, *Periscope View* (London: Macmillan, 1972).

Slim, Field Marshal Sir William, *Defeat into Victory* (London: Cassell, 1956).

—— *Courage and Other Broadcasts* (London: Cassell, 1957).

Stevens, Lieutenant Colonel G. R., *History of the 2nd King Edward VII's Own Goorkha Rifles (The Sirmoor Rifles)*, Vol. 3 (Aldershot: Gale & Polden, 1952).

Thomas, Lieutenant General Mathew, and Mansingh, Jasjit, *Lt. Gen. P. S. Bhagat, PVSM, VC* (New Delhi: Lancer International, 1994).

Walker, General Sir Walter, *Fighting On* (London: New Millennium, 1997).

Ward, S. G. P., *The Faithful: the Story of the Durham Light Infantry* (privately published by Thomas Nelson, 1962).

Wilkinson-Lathen, Robert, *The Royal Navy, 1790–1970* (London: Osprey, 1970).

Winton, John, *The Submariners*. (London: Constable, 1999).

Wilsey, John, *H. Jones VC* (London: Hutchinson, 2000).

Unpublished Sources

Army Museum, Waiouru, New Zealand
Kippenberger Library, New Zealand
Australian War Memorial Museum, Canberra
Bodleian Library, Oxford
Canadian War Museum, Ottawa
Durham Light Infantry Museum, Durham
Gurkha Museum, Winchester
Gurkha Welfare Trust, London
Imperial War Museum, London
National Army Museum, London
Nottingham Public Archives, Nottingham
Public Record Office, London
Royal Air Force Museum, Hendon
Royal Greenjackets Museum, Winchester
Submarine Museum, Portsmouth
Victoria Cross & George Cross Association

Index

The names of holders of the Victoria Cross are shown in the index in **bold type**